Python Algorithmic Trading Cookbook

All the recipes you need to implement your own algorithmic
trading strategies in Python

Pushpak Dagade

BIRMINGHAM - MUMBAI

Python Algorithmic Trading Cookbook

Copyright © 2020 Packt Publishing

Commissioning Editor: Sunith Shetty
Acquisition Editor: Ali Abidi
Content Development Editor: Athikho Sapuni Rishana
Senior Editor: Roshan Kumar
Technical Editor: Manikandan Kurup
Copy Editor: Safis Editing
Project Coordinator: Aishwarya Mohan
Proofreader: Safis Editing
Indexer: Manju Arasan
Production Designer: Vijay Kamble

First published: August 2020

Production reference: 1280820

Published by Packt Publishing Ltd.
Livery Place
35 Livery Street
Birmingham
B3 2PB, UK.

ISBN 978-1-83898-935-4

www.packt.com

Packt.com

Subscribe to our online digital library for full access to over 7,000 books and videos, as well as industry leading tools to help you plan your personal development and advance your career. For more information, please visit our website.

Why subscribe?

- Spend less time learning and more time coding with practical eBooks and Videos from over 4,000 industry professionals

- Improve your learning with Skill Plans built especially for you

- Get a free eBook or video every month

- Fully searchable for easy access to vital information

- Copy and paste, print, and bookmark content

Did you know that Packt offers eBook versions of every book published, with PDF and ePub files available? You can upgrade to the eBook version at www.packt.com and as a print book customer, you are entitled to a discount on the eBook copy. Get in touch with us at customercare@packtpub.com for more details.

At www.packt.com, you can also read a collection of free technical articles, sign up for a range of free newsletters, and receive exclusive discounts and offers on Packt books and eBooks.

Contributors

About the author

Pushpak Dagade has been working in the area of algorithmic trading for more than 3 years. He is the co-founder and CEO of AlgoBulls, an algorithmic trading platform. He is also a long-time Pythonista with more than a decade of Python experience. He is a graduate from the Indian Institute of Technology (Delhi) and holds engineering degrees in the fields of computer science, electronics, and physics.

About the reviewers

Ratanlal Mahanta is currently working as a quantitative analyst at bittQsrv, a global quantitative research company offering quant models for its investors. He has several years of experience in the modeling and simulation of quantitative trading. Ratanlal holds a master's degree in science in computational finance, and his research areas include quant trading, optimal execution, and high-frequency trading. He has over 9 years' experience in the finance industry and is gifted at solving difficult problems that lie at the intersection of markets, technology, research, and design.

Akhil Jain has a master's degree in computer science from the University of Mumbai. He started his IT career in 2007 in a multi-national company. He worked for 4 years as a Technology Analyst and finally decided to pursue his passion for teaching. He joined his UG alma mater as a lecturer in 2012 and has been teaching ever since. Akhil is using Python in his teachings which spans across the fields of data structures, artificial intelligence, cloud computing, and ethical hacking. He also uses Python extensively to perform stock market analysis and code algorithmic trading strategies. Akhil has also written a book titled *Protecting Your Email ID* in 2013.

Praxal Shah has a master's degree from IIT Delhi, one of the most reputable universities in India. He has been actively associated with trading derivatives in the Indian stock market for 4 years now and he has been developing a few of his own strategies for options trading, with the help of algo-trading, as a hobby. Praxal believes that this book is a good reference point for anyone who wants to start with algo-trading; this book can help you jump-start your learning as it covers most of the practical aspects of algo-trading.

Packt is searching for authors like you

If you're interested in becoming an author for Packt, please visit authors.packtpub.com and apply today. We have worked with thousands of developers and tech professionals, just like you, to help them share their insight with the global tech community. You can make a general application, apply for a specific hot topic that we are recruiting an author for, or submit your own idea.

Table of Contents

Preface

Python is a very popular language that is used to build and execute algorithmic trading strategies. If you want to find out how you can build a solid foundation in algorithmic trading using Python, this cookbook is here to help.

Starting by setting up the Python environment for trading and connectivity with brokers, you'll then learn the important aspects of financial markets. As you progress through this algorithmic trading book, you'll learn to fetch financial instruments, query and calculate various types of candles and historical data, and finally, compute and plot technical indicators. Next, you'll discover how to place various types of orders, such as regular, bracket, and cover orders, and understand their state transitions. You'll also uncover challenges faced while devising and executing powerful algorithmic trading strategies from scratch. Later chapters will take you through backtesting, paper trading, and finally real trading for the algorithmic strategies that you've created from the ground up. You'll even understand how to automate trading and find the right strategy for making effective decisions that would otherwise be impossible for human traders.

By the end of this book, you'll be able to use Python for algorithmic trading by implementing Python libraries to conduct key tasks in the algorithmic trading ecosystem.

Who this book is for

If you are a financial analyst, financial trader, data analyst, algorithmic trader, trading enthusiast or anyone who wants to learn algorithmic trading with Python and important techniques to address the challenges faced in the realm of finance, this book is for you. A basic working knowledge of the Python programming language is expected. Although some fundamental knowledge of trade-related terminology will be helpful, it is not mandatory.

What this book covers

Chapter 1, *Handling and Manipulating Date, Time, and Time Series Data*, explains everything about the Python DateTime module and pandas DataFrames that are required to handle time series data efficiently.

Chapter 2, *Stock Markets – Primer on Trading*, covers how to set up Python connectivity with a broker, fetch financial instruments, and get a quick hands-on at placing simple orders. You will also learn how to query margins and calculate brokerage and government taxes.

Chapter 3, *Fetching Financial Data*, covers financial instruments in-depth.

Chapter 4, *Computing Candlesticks and Historical Data*, explains how to fetch and understand historical data, and also how to fetch, compute, and plot various candlestick patterns, including Japanese (OHLC), Renko, Line Break, and Heikin-Ashi.

Chapter 5, *Computing and Plotting of Technical Indicators*, explains how to compute and plot 10 types of technical indicators, including trend indicators, momentum indicators, volatility indicators, and volume indicators.

Chapter 6, *Placing Regular Orders on the Exchange*, explains how to place 16 types of regular orders across two transaction types, two order codes, and four order varieties. You will learn how to query the order status in real time, while also learning about the possible order states supported by the broker and the order life cycle for regular orders.

Chapter 7, *Placing Bracket and Cover Orders on the Exchange*, explains how to place eight types of bracket orders and four types of cover orders across two transaction types and multiple order varieties and how to query the order status in real time. You will learn about target, stoploss, and trailing stoploss, along with the possible order states supported by the broker and the order life cycle for both bracket and cover orders.

Chapter 8, *Algorithmic Trading Strategies – Code Step by Step*, explains how to code your own algorithmic trading strategy from scratch using two strategy coding examples involving regular and bracket orders, respectively.

Chapter 9, *Algorithmic Trading – Backtesting*, covers how to backtest your own algorithmic trading strategy using two strategy coding examples involving regular and bracket orders, respectively. You will also learn how to fetch execution logs and various types of backtesting reports, including profit and loss reports, statistics reports, and order history logs for your strategy.

Chapter 10, *Algorithmic Trading – Paper Trading*, explains how to paper trade your own algorithmic trading strategy in live markets using two strategy coding examples involving regular and bracket orders, respectively. You will also learn how to fetch execution logs and various types of paper trading reports, including profit and loss reports, statistics reports, and order history logs, in real time for your strategy.

`Chapter 11`, *Algorithmic Trading – Real Trading,* explains how to real trade your own algorithmic trading strategy in live markets and real money using two strategy coding examples involving regular and bracket orders, respectively. You will also learn how to fetch execution logs and various types of real trading reports, including profit and loss reports and statistics reports, in real time for your strategy.

To get the most out of this book

This book is for anyone who is interested in the field of algorithmic trading. You are not expected to have any background in finance or algorithmic trading. You are expected to have a basic knowledge of the Python programming language. Each chapter introduces a new concept in algorithmic trading and takes you step by step, from zero to hero. This book can help you build a rock-solid foundation in algorithmic trading using Python.

You need to have the latest version of Python 3 installed on your computer. The recipes in this book were tested on Python 3.8.2 and they should work on any future release of Python as well.

You also need a broking account with Zerodha, a modern broker, to try out the recipes covered in most of the chapters. *Appendix I* provides detailed, step-by-step information on how to set up your Zerodha account in case you do not have one.

To execute trading strategies, you also need an account with AlgoBulls. *Appendix II* provides detailed, step-by-step information on how to set up your AlgoBulls account in case you do not have one.

Also, almost every chapter expects you to have additional Python packages installed, such as `pyalgotrading`. You can install these using `pip`. This is explained in the technical requirements section of every chapter.

All the recipes in this chapter are provided as Jupyter notebooks on our GitHub repository: `https://github.com/PacktPublishing/Python-Algorithmic-Trading-Cookbook`. You can install Jupyter Notebook as well if you would like to try out the recipes directly without typing any code. You can install this using `pip`: `pip install notebook`.

Software/hardware covered in the book	OS requirements
Python 3.7+ (`https://www.python.org/downloads/`)	Any OS that supports Python 3.7+; Linux, Windows, macOS X, and so on.

The requirements for each chapter are summarized in the following table:

Chapter number	Zerodha account	AlgoBulls account
1	No	No
2	Yes	No
3	Yes	No
4	Yes	No
5	Yes	No
6	Yes	No
7	Yes	No
8	No	Yes
9	No	Yes
10	No	Yes
11	No	Yes

If you are using the digital version of this book, we advise you to type the code yourself or access the code via the GitHub repository (link available in the next section). Doing so will help you avoid any potential errors related to the copying and pasting of code.

Download the example code files

You can download the example code files for this book from your account at `www.packt.com`. If you purchased this book elsewhere, you can visit `www.packtpub.com/support` and register to have the files emailed directly to you.

You can download the code files by following these steps:

1. Log in or register at `www.packt.com`.
2. Select the **Support** tab.
3. Click on **Code Downloads**.
4. Enter the name of the book in the **Search** box and follow the onscreen instructions.

Once the file is downloaded, please make sure that you unzip or extract the folder using the latest version of:

- WinRAR/7-Zip for Windows
- Zipeg/iZip/UnRarX for Mac
- 7-Zip/PeaZip for Linux

The code bundle for the book is also hosted on GitHub at `https://github.com/PacktPublishing/Python-Algorithmic-Trading-Cookbook`. In case there's an update to the code, it will be updated on the existing GitHub repository.

We also have other code bundles from our rich catalog of books and videos available at `https://github.com/PacktPublishing/`. Check them out!

Download the color images

We also provide a PDF file that has color images of the screenshots/diagrams used in this book. You can download it here: `https://static.packt-cdn.com/downloads/9781838989354_ColorImages.pdf`.

Conventions used

There are a number of text conventions used throughout this book.

`CodeInText`: Indicates code words in text, database table names, folder names, filenames, file extensions, pathnames, dummy URLs, user input, and Twitter handles. Here is an example: "The broker provides unique keys to each customer, typically as `api-key` and `api-secret` key pairs."

A block of code is set as follows:

```
>>> plot_candlestick_chart(historical_data,
                           PlotType.OHLC,
                           'Historical Data | '
                           'Japanese Candlesticks Pattern | '
                           'NSE:TATASTEEL | 1st Jan, 2020 | '
                           'Candle Interval: 1 Minute')
```

Any command-line input or output is written as follows:

```
$ pip install pyalgotrading
```

Bold: Indicates a new term, an important word, or words that you see on screen. For example, words in menus or dialog boxes appear in the text like this. Here is an example: "A Japanese candle is green in color if its **close** price is above its **open** price."

 Warnings or important notes appear like this.

 Tips and tricks appear like this.

Sections

In this book, you will find several headings that appear frequently (*Getting ready*, *How to do it...*, *How it works...*, *There's more...*, and *See also*).

To give clear instructions on how to complete a recipe, use these sections as follows:

Getting ready

This section tells you what to expect in the recipe and describes how to set up any software or any preliminary settings required for the recipe.

How to do it...

This section contains the steps required to follow the recipe.

How it works...

This section usually consists of a detailed explanation of what happened in the previous section.

There's more...

This section consists of additional information about the recipe in order to make you more knowledgeable about the recipe.

See also

This section provides helpful links to other useful information for the recipe.

Get in touch

Feedback from our readers is always welcome.

General feedback: If you have questions about any aspect of this book, mention the book title in the subject of your message and email us at customercare@packtpub.com.

Errata: Although we have taken every care to ensure the accuracy of our content, mistakes do happen. If you have found a mistake in this book, we would be grateful if you would report this to us. Please visit www.packtpub.com/support/errata, selecting your book, clicking on the Errata Submission Form link, and entering the details.

Piracy: If you come across any illegal copies of our works in any form on the internet, we would be grateful if you would provide us with the location address or website name. Please contact us at copyright@packt.com with a link to the material.

If you are interested in becoming an author: If there is a topic that you have expertise in, and you are interested in either writing or contributing to a book, please visit authors.packtpub.com.

Reviews

Please leave a review. Once you have read and used this book, why not leave a review on the site that you purchased it from? Potential readers can then see and use your unbiased opinion to make purchase decisions, we at Packt can understand what you think about our products, and our authors can see your feedback on their book. Thank you!

For more information about Packt, please visit packt.com.

1
Handling and Manipulating Date, Time, and Time Series Data

Time series data is ubiquitous when it comes to algorithmic trading. So, handling, managing, and manipulating time series data is essential to performing algorithmic trading successfully. This chapter has various recipes that demonstrate how algorithmic trading can be done using the Python standard library and pandas, which is a Python data analysis library.

For our context, time series data is a series of data consisting of equally spaced timestamps and multiple data points describing trading data in that particular time frame.

When handling time series data, the first thing you should know is how to read, modify, and create Python objects that understand date and time. The Python standard library includes the datetime module, which provides the datetime and timedelta objects, which can handle everything about the date and time. The first seven recipes in this chapter talk about this module. The remainder of this chapter talks about handling time series data using the pandas library, which is a very efficient library for data analysis. The pandas.DataFrame class will be used in our recipes.

The following is a list of the recipes in this chapter:

- Creating datetime objects
- Creating timedelta objects
- Operations on datetime objects
- Modifying datetime objects
- Converting a datetime to a string
- Creating a datetime object from a string
- The datetime object and time zones
- Creating a pandas.DataFrame object
- DataFrame manipulation—renaming, rearranging, reversing, and slicing
- DataFrame manipulation—applying, sorting, iterating, and concatenating
- Converting a DataFrame into other formats
- Creating a DataFrame from other formats

Technical requirements

You will need the following to successfully execute the recipes in this chapter:

- Python 3.7+
- Python package:
    - pandas (`$ pip install pandas`)

For all the recipes in this chapter, you will need the Jupyter notebook for this chapter, found at `https://github.com/PacktPublishing/Python-Algorithmic-Trading-Cookbook/tree/master/Chapter01`.

You can also open a new Jupyter notebook and try the hands-on exercises directly as they are shown in the recipes. Note that the output for some of these recipes might differ for you as they depend on the date, time, and time zone information provided at the time.

Creating datetime objects

The `datetime` module provides a `datetime` class, which can be used to accurately capture information relating to timestamps, dates, times, and time zones. In this recipe, you will create `datetime` objects in multiple ways and introspect their attributes.

How to do it...

Follow these steps to execute this recipe:

1. Import the necessary module from the Python standard library:

    ```
    >>> from datetime import datetime
    ```

2. Create a datetime object holding the current timestamp using the now()
    method and print it:

    ```
    >>> dt1 = datetime.now()
    >>> print(f'Approach #1: {dt1}')
    ```

    We get the following output. Your output will differ:

    ```
    Approach #1: 2020-08-12 20:55:39.680195
    ```

3. Print the attributes of dt1 related to date and time:

    ```
    >>> print(f'Year: {dt1.year}')
    >>> print(f'Month: {dt1.month}')
    >>> print(f'Day: {dt1.day}')
    >>> print(f'Hours: {dt1.hour}')
    >>> print(f'Minutes: {dt1.minute}')
    >>> print(f'Seconds: {dt1.second}')
    >>> print(f'Microseconds: {dt1.microsecond}')
    >>> print(f'Timezone: {dt1.tzinfo}')
    ```

    We get the following output. Your output would differ:

    ```
    Year: 2020
    Month: 8
    Day: 12
    Hours: 20
    Minutes: 55
    Seconds: 39
    Microseconds: 680195
    Timezone: None
    ```

4. Create a datetime object holding the timestamp for 1st January 2021::

    ```
    >>> dt2 = datetime(year=2021, month=1, day=1)
    >>> print(f'Approach #2: {dt2}')
    ```

    You will get the following output:

    ```
    Approach #2: 2021-01-01 00:00:00
    ```

5. Print the various attributes of `dt2` related to date and time:

```
>>> print(f'Year: {dt.year}')
>>> print(f'Month: {dt.month}')
>>> print(f'Day: {dt.day}')
>>> print(f'Hours: {dt.hour}')
>>> print(f'Minutes: {dt.minute}')
>>> print(f'Seconds: {dt.second}')
>>> print(f'Microseconds: {dt.microsecond}')
>>> print(f'Timezone: {dt2.tzinfo}')
```

You will get the following output:

```
Year: 2021
Month: 1
Day: 1
Hours: 0
Minutes: 0
Seconds: 0
Microseconds: 0
Timezone: None
```

How it works...

In *step 1*, you import the `datetime` class from the `datetime` module. In *step 2*, you create and print a `datetime` object using the `now()` method and assign it to `dt1`. This object holds the current timestamp information.

A `datetime` object has the following attributes related to date, time, and time zone information:

1	year	An integer between 0 and 23, both inclusive
2	month	An integer between 1 and 12, both inclusive
3	day	An integer between 1 and 31, both inclusive
4	hour	An integer between 0 and 23, both inclusive
5	minute	An integer between 0 and 59, both inclusive
6	second	An integer between 0 and 59, both inclusive
7	microsecond	An integer between 0 and 999999, both inclusive
8	tzinfo	An object of class `timezone`. (More information on time zones in *The datetime object and time zones* recipe).

In *step 3*, these attributes are printed for dt1. You can see that they hold the current timestamp information.

In *step 4*, you create and print another datetime object. This time you create a specific timestamp, which is 1st Jan 2021, midnight. You call the constructor itself with the parameters—year as 2021, month as 1, and day as 1. The other time related attributes default to 0 and time zone defaults to None. In *step 5*, you print the attributes of dt2. You can see that they hold exactly the same values as you had passed to the constructor in *step 4*.

There's more

You can use the date() and time() methods of the datetime objects to extract the date and time information, as instances of datetime.date and datetime.time classes respectively:

1. Use date() method to extract date from dt1. Note the type of the return value.

    ```
    >>> print(f"Date: {dt1.date()}")
    >>> print(f"Type: {type(dt1.date())}")
    ```

    You will get the following output. Your output may differ::

    ```
    Date: 2020-08-12
    Type: <class 'datetime.date'>
    ```

2. Use time() method to extract date from dt1. Note the type of the return value.

    ```
    >>> print(f"Time: {dt1.time()}")
    >>> print(f"Type: {type(dt1.time())}")
    ```

    We get the following output. Your output may differ:

    ```
    Time: 20:55:39.680195
    Type: <class 'datetime.time'>
    ```

3. Use date() method to extract date from dt2. Note the type of the return value.

    ```
    >>> print(f"Date: {dt2.date()}")
    >>> print(f"Type: {type(dt2.date())}")
    ```

    We get the following output:

    ```
    Date: 2021-01-01
    Type: <class 'datetime.date'>
    ```

4. Use `time()` method to extract date from `dt2`. Note the type of the return value.

```
>>> print(f"Time: {dt2.time()}")
>>> print(f"Type: {type(dt2.time())}")
```

We get the following output:

```
Time: 00:00:00
Type: <class 'datetime.time'>
```

Creating timedelta objects

The `datetime` module provides a `timedelta` class, which can be used to represent information related to date and time differences. In this recipe, you will create `timedelta` objects and perform operations on them.

How to do it...

Follow along with these steps to execute this recipe:

1. Import the necessary module from the Python standard library:

```
>>> from datetime import timedelta
```

2. Create a `timedelta` object with a duration of 5 days. Assign it to `td1` and print it:

```
>>> td1 = timedelta(days=5)
>>> print(f'Time difference: {td1}')
```

We get the following output:

```
Time difference: 5 days, 0:00:00
```

3. Create a `timedelta` object with a duration of 4 days. Assign it to `td2` and print it:

```
>>> td2 = timedelta(days=4)
>>> print(f'Time difference: {td2}')
```

We get the following output:

```
Time difference: 4 days, 0:00:00
```

4. Add `td1` and `td2` and print the output:

```
>>> print(f'Addition: {td1} + {td2} = {td1 + td2}')
```

We get the following output:

```
Addition: 5 days, 0:00:00 + 4 days, 0:00:00 = 9 days, 0:00:00
```

5. Subtract `td2` from `td1` and print the output:

```
>>> print(f'Subtraction: {td1} - {td2} = {td1 - td2}')
```

We will get the following output:

```
Subtraction: 5 days, 0:00:00 - 4 days, 0:00:00 = 1 day, 0:00:00
```

6. Multiply `td1` with a number (a `float`):

```
>>> print(f'Multiplication: {td1} * 2.5 = {td1 * 2.5}')
```

We get the following output:

```
Multiplication: 5 days, 0:00:00 * 2.5 = 12 days, 12:00:00
```

How it works...

In *step 1*, you import the `timedelta` class from the `datetime` module. In *step 2* you create a `timedelta` object that holds a time difference value of 5 days and assign it to `td1`. You call the constructor to create the object with a single attribute, `days`. You pass the value as 5 here. Similarly, in *step 3*, you create another `timedelta` object, which holds a time difference value of 4 days and assign it to `td2`.

In the next steps, you perform operations on the `timedelta` objects. In *step 4*, you add `td1` and `td2`. This returns another `timedelta` object which holds a time difference value of 9 days, which is the sum of the time difference values held by `td1` and `td2`. In *step 5*, you subtract `td2` from `td1`. This returns another `timedelta` object that holds a time difference value of 1 day, which is the difference of time difference values held by `td1` and `td2`. In *step 6*, you multiply `td1` with 2.5, a `float`. This again returns a `timedelta` object that holds a time difference value of twelve and a half days.

There's more

A `timedelta` object can be created using one or more optional arguments:

1	weeks	An integer. Default value is 0.
2	days	An integer. Default value is 0.
3	hours	An integer. Default value is 0.
4	minutes	An integer. Default value is 0.
5	seconds	An integer. Default value is 0.
6	milliseconds	An integer. Default value is 0.
7	microseconds	An integer. Default value is 0.

In *step 2* and *step 3*, we have used just the `days` argument. You can use other arguments as well. Also, these attributes are normalized upon creation. This normalization of `timedelta` objects is done to ensure that there is always a unique representation for every time difference value which can be held. The following code demonstrates this:

1. Create a `timedelta` object with hours as `23`, minutes as `59`, and seconds as `60`. Assign it to `td3` and print it. It will be normalized to a `timedelta` object with `days` as 1 (and other date and time-related attributes as 0):

```
>>> td3 = timedelta(hours=23, minutes=59, seconds=60)
>>> print(f'Time difference: {td3}')
```

We get the following output:

```
Time difference: 1 day, 0:00:00
```

The `timedelta` objects have a convenience method, `total_seconds()`. This method returns a `float` which represents the total seconds contained in the duration held by the `timedelta` object.

2. Call the `total_seconds()` method on `td3`. You get `86400.0` as the output:

```
>>> print(f'Total seconds in 1 day: {td3.total_seconds()}')
```

We get the following output:

```
Total seconds in 1 day: 86400.0
```

Operations on datetime objects

The datetime and timedelta classes support various mathematical operations to get dates in the future or the past. Using these operations returns another datetime object. . In this recipe, you would create datetime, date, time, and timedelta objects and perform mathematical operations on them.

How to do it...

Follow along with these steps to execute this recipe:

1. Import the necessary modules from the Python standard library:

```
>>> from datetime import datetime, timedelta
```

2. Fetch today's date. Assign it to date_today and print it:

```
>>> date_today = date.today()
>>> print(f"Today's Date: {date_today}")
```

We get the following output. Your output may differ:

```
Today's Date: 2020-08-12
```

3. Add 5 days to today's date using a timedelta object. Assign it to date_5days_later and print it:

```
>>> date_5days_later = date_today + timedelta(days=5)
>>> print(f"Date 5 days later: {date_5days_later}")
```

We get the following output. Your output may differ:

```
Date 5 days later: 2020-08-17
```

4. Subtract 5 days from today's date using a timedelta object. Assign it to date_5days_ago and print it:

```
>>> date_5days_ago = date_today - timedelta(days=5)
>>> print(f"Date 5 days ago: {date_5days_ago}")
```

We get the following output. Your output may differ:

```
Date 5 days ago: 2020-08-07
```

5. Compare `date_5days_later` with `date_5days_ago` using the > operator:

```
>>> date_5days_later > date_5days_ago
```

We get the following output:

```
True
```

6. Compare `date_5days_later` with `date_5days_ago` using the < operator:

```
>>> date_5days_later < date_5days_ago
```

We get the following output:

```
False
```

7. Compare `date_5days_later`, `date_today` and `date_5days_ago` together using the > operator:

```
>>> date_5days_later > date_today > date_5days_ago
```

We get the following output:

```
True
```

8. Fetch the current timestamp. Assign it to `current_timestamp`:

```
>>> current_timestamp = datetime.now()
```

9. Fetch the current time. Assign it to `time_now` and print it:

```
>>> time_now = current_timestamp.time()
>>> print(f"Time now: {time_now}")
```

We get the following output. Your output may differ:

```
Time now: 20:55:45.239177
```

10. Add 5 minutes to the current time using a `timedelta` object. Assign it to `time_5minutes_later` and print it:

```
>>> time_5minutes_later = (current_timestamp +
                            timedelta(minutes=5)).time()
>>> print(f"Time 5 minutes later: {time_5minutes_later}")
```

We get the following output. Your output may differ:

```
Time 5 minutes later: 21:00:45.239177
```

11. Subtract 5 minutes from the current time using a `timedelta` object. Assign it to `time_5minutes_ago` and print it:

```
>>> time_5minutes_ago = (current_timestamp -
                         timedelta(minutes=5)).time()
>>> print(f"Time 5 minutes ago: {time_5minutes_ago}")
```

We get the following output. Your output may differ:

```
Time 5 minutes ago: 20:50:45.239177
```

12. Compare `time_5minutes_later` with `time_5minutes_ago` using the < operator:

```
>>> time_5minutes_later < time_5minutes_ago
```

We get the following output. Your output may differ:

```
False
```

13. Compare `time_5minutes_later` with `time_5minutes_ago` using the > operator:

```
>>> time_5minutes_later > time_5minutes_ago
```

We get the following output. Your output may differ:

```
True
```

14. Compare `time_5minutes_later`, `time_now` and `time_5minutes_ago` together using the > operator:

```
>> time_5minutes_later > time_now > time_5minutes_ago
```

We get the following output. Your output may differ:

```
True
```

How it works...

In *step 1*, you import date, datetime, and timedelta classes from the datetime module. In *step 2*, you fetch today's date using the today() classmethod provided by the class date and assign it to a new attribute, date_today. (A classmethod allows you to call a method directly on a class without creating an instance.) The return object is of type datetime.date. In *step 3*, you create a date, 5 days ahead of today, by adding a timedelta object, holding a duration of 5 days, to date_today. You assign this to a new attribute, date_5days_later. Similarly, in *step 4*, you create a date, 5 days ago and assign it to a new attribute date_5days_ago.

In *step 5* and *step 6*, you compare date_5days_later and date_5days_ago using the > and < operators, respectively. The > operator returns True if the first operand holds a date ahead of that held by operand 2. Similarly, the < operator returns True if the second operand holds a date ahead of that held by operand 1. In *step 7*, you compare together all three date objects created so far. Note the outputs.

Step 8 to *step 14* perform the same operations as *step 2* to *step 7*, but this time on datetime.time objects—fetching current time, fetching a time 5 minutes ahead of the current time, fetching a time 5 minutes before the current time and comparing all the datetime.time objects which are created. The timedelta objects cannot be added to datetime.time objects directly to get time in the past or the future. To overcome this, you can add timedelta objects to datetime objects and then extract time from them using the time() method. You do this in *step 10* and *step 11*.

There's more

The operations shown in this recipe on date and time objects can similarly be performed on datetime objects. Besides +, –, < and >, you can also use the following operators on datetime, date, and time objects:

>=	Return True only if the first operand holds a datetime/date/time ahead or equal to that of the first operand
<=	Return True only if the first operand holds a datetime/date/time before or equal to that of the first operand
==	Return True only if the first operand holds a datetime/date/time equal to that of the first operand

This is not an exhaustive list of permissible operators. Refer to the official documentation on `datetime` module for more information: `https://docs.python.org/3.8/library/datetime.html`.

Modifying datetime objects

Often, you may want to modify existing `datetime` objects to represent a different date and time. This recipe includes code to demonstrate this.

How to do it...

Follow these steps to execute this recipe:

1. Import the necessary modules from the Python standard library:

```
>>> from datetime import datetime
```

2. Fetch the current timestamp. Assign it to `dt1` and print it:

```
>>> dt1 = datetime.now()
>>> print(dt1)
```

We get the following output. Your output would differ:

```
2020-08-12 20:55:46.753899
```

3. Create a new `datetime` object by replacing the `year`, `month`, and `day` attributes of `dt1`. Assign it to `dt2` and print it :

```
>>> dt2 = dt1.replace(year=2021, month=1, day=1)
>>> print(f'A timestamp from 1st January 2021: {dt2}')
```

We get the following output. Your output would differ:

```
A timestamp from 1st January 2021: 2021-01-01 20:55:46.753899
```

4. Create a new `datetime` object by specifying all the attributes directly. Assign it to `dt3` and print it:

```
>>> dt3 = datetime(year=2021,
                   month=1,
                   day=1,
                   hour=dt1.hour,
                   minute=dt1.minute,
                   second=dt1.second,
                   microsecond=dt1.microsecond,
                   tzinfo=dt1.tzinfo)
print(f'A timestamp from 1st January 2021: {dt3}')
```

We get the following output. Your output would differ:

```
A timestamp from 1st January 2021: 2021-01-01 20:55:46.753899
```

5. Compare `dt2` and `dt3`:

```
>>> dt2 == dt3
```

We get the following output.

```
True
```

How it works...

In *step 1*, you import the `datetime` class from the `datetime` module. In *step 2*, you fetch the current timestamp using the `now()` method of `datetime` and assign it to a new attribute, `dt1`. To get a modified timestamp from an existing `datetime` object, you can use the `replace()` method. In *step 3*, you create a new `datetime` object `dt2`, from `dt1`, by calling the `replace()` method. You specify the attributes to be modified, which are `year`, `month`, and `day`. The remaining attributes remain as it is, which are an `hour`, `minute`, `second`, `microsecond`, and `timezone`. You can confirm this by comparing the outputs of *step 2* and *step 3*. In *step 4*, you create another `datetime` object, `dt3`. This time you call the `datetime` constructor directly. You pass all the attributes to the constructor such that the timestamp created is the same as `dt2`. In *step 5*, you confirm that `dt2` and `dt3` hold exactly the same timestamp by using the `==` operator, which returns `True`.

Converting a datetime object to a string

This recipe demonstrates the conversion of the `datetime` objects into strings which finds application in printing and logging. Also, this is helpful while sending timestamps as JSON data over web APIs.

How to do it...

Execute the following steps for this recipe:

1. Import the necessary modules from the Python standard library:

   ```
   >>> from datetime import datetime
   ```

2. Fetch the current timestamp along with time zone information. Assign it to `now` and print it:

   ```
   >>> now = datetime.now().astimezone()
   ```

3. Cast `now` to a string and print it::

   ```
   >>> print(str(now))
   ```

   We get the following output. Your output may differ:

   ```
   2020-08-12 20:55:48.366130+05:30
   ```

4. Convert `now` to a string with a specific date-time format using `strftime()` and print it:

   ```
   >>> print(now.strftime("%d-%m-%Y %H:%M:%S %Z"))
   ```

   We get the following output. Your output may differ:

   ```
   12-08-2020 20:55:48 +0530
   ```

How it works...

In *step 1*, you import the datetime class from the datetime module. In *step 2*, you fetch the current timestamp with time zone and assign it to a new attribute, now. The now() method of datetime fetches the current timestamp, but without time zone information. Such objects are called time zone-native datetime objects. The astimezone() method adds time zone information from the system local time on this time zone-naive object, essentially converting it to a time zone-aware object. (More information in *The datetime object and time zones* recipe). In *step 3*, you cast now to a string object and print it. Observe that the output date format is fixed and may not be of your choice. The datetime module has a strftime() method which can convert the object to a string in a specific format as required. In *step 4*, you convert now to a string in the format DD-MM-YYYY HH:MM:SS +Z. The directives used in *step 4* are described as follows:

Directive	Meaning
%d	The day of the month as a zero-padded decimal number
%m	The month as a zero-padded decimal number
%Y	The year with the century as a decimal number
%H	The hour (24-hour clock) as a zero-padded decimal number
%M	The minute as a zero-padded decimal number
%S	The second as a zero-padded decimal number
%Z	The time zone name (empty string if the object is naive)

A complete list of the directives that can be given to .strptime() can be found at https:/
/docs.python.org/3.7/library/datetime.html#strftime-and-strptime-behavior.

Creating a datetime object from a string

This recipe demonstrates the conversion of well-formatted strings into datetime objects. This finds application in reading timestamps from a file. Also, this is helpful while receiving timestamps as JSON data over web APIs.

How to do it...

Execute the following steps for this recipe:

1. Import the necessary modules from the Python standard library:

    ```
    >>> from datetime import datetime
    ```

2. Create a string representation of timestamp with date, time, and time zone. Assign it to now_str:

    ```
    >>> now_str = '13-1-2021 15:53:39 +05:30'
    ```

3. Convert now_str to now, a datetime.datetime object. Print it:

    ```
    >>> now = datetime.strptime(now_str, "%d-%m-%Y %H:%M:%S %z")
    >>> print(now)
    ```

    We get the following output:

    ```
    2021-01-13 15:53:39+05:30
    ```

4. Confirm that now is of the datetime type:

    ```
    >>> print(type(now))
    ```

    We get the following output:

    ```
    <class 'datetime.datetime'>
    ```

How it works...

In *step 1*, you import the datetime class from the datetime module. In *step 2*, you create a string holding a valid timestamp and assign it to a new attribute, now_str. The datetime module has a strptime() method which can convert a string holding a valid timestamp in a specific format to a datetime object. In *step 3*, you convert now_str, a string in the format DD-MM-YYYY HH:MM:SS +Z, to now. In *step 4*, you confirm that now is indeed an object of the datetime type. The directives used in *step 3* are the same as those described in the *Converting a datetime object to a string* recipe.

There's more

When reading a string into a datetime object, the entire string should be consumed with appropriate directives. Consuming a string partially will throw an exception, as shown in the following code snippet. The error message shows what data was not converted and can be used to fix the directives provided to the strptime() method.

Try to convert now_str to a datetime object using strptime() method. Pass a string with directives for only the date part of the string. Note the error:

```
>>> now = datetime.strptime(now_str, "%d-%m-%Y")
```

The output is as follows:

```
# Note: It's expected to have an error below
------------------------------------------------------------------------
ValueError Traceback (most recent call last)
<ipython-input-96-dc92a0358ed8> in <module>
----> 1 now = datetime.strptime(now_str, "%d-%m-%Y")
      2 # Note: It's expected to get an error below

/usr/lib/python3.8/_strptime.py in _strptime_datetime(cls, data_string, format)
    566 """Return a class cls instance based on the input string and the
    567 format string."""
--> 568 tt, fraction, gmtoff_fraction = _strptime(data_string, format)
    569 tzname, gmtoff = tt[-2:]
    570 args = tt[:6] + (fraction,)

/usr/lib/python3.8/_strptime.py in _strptime(data_string, format)
    350 (data_string, format))
    351 if len(data_string) != found.end():
--> 352 raise ValueError("unconverted data remains: %s" %
    353 data_string[found.end():])
    354

ValueError: unconverted data remains: 15:53:39 +05:30
```

The datetime object and time zones

There are two types of datetime objects—time zone-naive and time zone-aware. Time zone-naive objects do not hold time zone information and timezone-aware objects hold time zone information. This recipe demonstrates multiple time zone related operations on datetime objects: creating time zone-naive and time zone-aware objects, adding time zone information to time zone-aware objects, removing time zone information from time zone-naive objects, and comparing time zone-aware and time zone-naive objects.

How to do it...

Execute the following steps for this recipe:

1. Import the necessary modules from the Python standard library:

   ```
   >>> from datetime import datetime
   ```

2. Create a time zone-naive datetime object. Assign it to now_tz_naive and print it:

   ```
   >>> now_tz_unaware = datetime.now()
   >>> print(now_tz_unaware)
   ```

   We get the following output. Your output may differ:

   ```
   2020-08-12 20:55:50.598800
   ```

3. Print the time zone information of now_tz_naive. Note the output:

   ```
   >>> print(now_tz_unaware.tzinfo)
   ```

   We get the following output:

   ```
   None
   ```

4. Create a time zone-aware datetime object. Assign it to now_tz_aware and print it:

   ```
   >>> now_tz_aware = datetime.now().astimezone()
   >>> print(now_tz_aware)
   ```

   We get the following output. Your output may differ:

   ```
   2020-08-12 20:55:51.004671+05:30
   ```

5. Print the time zone information of `now_tz_aware`. Note the output:

```
>>> print(now_tz_aware.tzinfo)
```

We get the following output. Your output may differ:

```
IST
```

6. Create a new timestamp by adding time zone information to `now_tz_naive` from `now_tz_aware`. Assign it to `new_tz_aware` and print it:

```
>>> new_tz_aware = now_tz_naive.replace(tzinfo=now_tz_aware.tzinfo)
>>> print(new_tz_aware)
```

The output is as follows. Your output may differ:

```
2020-08-12 20:55:50.598800+05:30
```

7. Print the timezone information of `new_tz_aware` using the `tzinfo` attribute. Note the output:

```
>>> print(new_tz_aware.tzinfo)
```

The output is as follows. Your output may differ:

```
IST
```

8. Create a new timestamp by removing timezone information from `new_tz_aware`. Assign it to `new_tz_naive` and print it:

```
>>> new_tz_naive = new_tz_aware.replace(tzinfo=None)
>>> print(new_tz_naive)
```

The output is as follows. Your output may differ:

```
2020-08-12 20:55:50.598800
```

9. Print the timezone information of `new_tz_naive` using the `tzinfo` attribute. Note the output:

```
>>> print(new_tz_naive.tzinfo)
```

The output is as follows:

```
None
```

How it works...

In *step 1*, you import the `datetime` class from the `datetime` module. In *step 2*, you create a time zone-naive `datetime` object using the `now()` method and assign it to a new attribute `now_tz_naive`. In *step 3*, you print the time zone information held by `now_tz_naive` using the `tzinfo` attribute. Observe that the output is `None` as this is a time zone-naive object.

In *step 4*, you create a time zone-aware `datetime` object using the `now()` and `astimezone()` methods and assign it to a new attribute `now_tz_aware`. In *step 5*, you print the time zone information held by `now_tz_aware` using the `tzinfo` attribute. Observe that the output is `IST` and not `None`; as this is a time zone-aware object.

In `step 6`, you create a new `datetime` object by adding time zone information to `now_tz_naive`. The time zone information is taken from `now_tz_aware`. You do this using the `replace()` method (Refer to *Modifying datetime objects* recipe for more information). You assign this to a new variable, `new_tz_aware`. In *step 7*, you print the time zone information held by `new_tz_aware`. Observe it is the same output as in *step 5* as you have taken time zone information from `now_tz_aware`. Similarly, in *step 8* and *step 9*, you create a new `datetime` object, `new_tz_naive`, but this time you remove the time zone information.

There's more

You can use comparison operators only between time zone-naive or time zone-aware `datetime` objects. You cannot compare a time zone-naive `datetime` object with a time zone-aware `datetime` object. Doing so will throw an exception. This is demonstrated in the following steps:

1. Compare 2 timezone-naive objects, `new_tz_naive` and `now_tz_naive`. Note the output:

   ```
   >>> new_tz_naive <= now_tz_naive
   ```

2. Compare 2-time zone-aware objects, `new_tz_aware`, and `now_tz_aware`. Note the output:

   ```
   >>> new_tz_aware <= now_tz_aware
   ```

   We get the following output:

   ```
   True
   ```

3. Compare a time zone-aware object and a time zone-naive object, `new_tz_aware`, and `now_tz_naive`. Note the error:

```
>>> new_tz_aware > now_tz_naive
```

We get the following output:

```
---------------------------------------------------------------
            TypeError Traceback (most recent call last)
<ipython-input-167-a9433bb51293> in <module>
----> 1 new_tz_aware > now_tz_naive
      2 # Note: It's expected to get an error below

TypeError: can't compare offset-naive and offset-aware datetimes
```

Creating a pandas.DataFrame object

Now that we are done with handling date and time, let's move on to handling time series data. The `pandas` library has a `pandas.DataFrame` class, which is useful for handling and manipulating such data. This recipe starts by creating these objects.

How to do it...

Execute the following steps for this recipe:

1. Import the necessary modules from the Python standard library:

```
>>> from datetime import datetime
>>> import pandas
```

2. Create a sample time-series data as a list of dictionary objects. Assign it to `time_series` data:

```
>>> time_series_data = \
[{'date': datetime.datetime(2019, 11, 13, 9, 0),
  'open': 71.8075, 'high': 71.845, 'low': 71.7775,
  'close': 71.7925, 'volume': 219512},
 {'date': datetime.datetime(2019, 11, 13, 9, 15),
  'open': 71.7925, 'high': 71.8,   'low': 71.78,
  'close': 71.7925, 'volume': 59252},
 {'date': datetime.datetime(2019, 11, 13, 9, 30),
  'open': 71.7925, 'high': 71.8125, 'low': 71.76,
  'close': 71.7625, 'volume': 57187},
 {'date': datetime.datetime(2019, 11, 13, 9, 45),
```

```
    'open': 71.76,    'high': 71.765,   'low': 71.735,
    'close': 71.7425, 'volume': 43048},
  {'date': datetime.datetime(2019, 11, 13, 10, 0),
    'open': 71.7425, 'high': 71.78,     'low': 71.7425,
    'close': 71.7775, 'volume': 45863},
  {'date': datetime.datetime(2019, 11, 13, 10, 15),
    'open': 71.775,  'high': 71.8225, 'low': 71.77,
    'close': 71.815,  'volume': 42460},
  {'date': datetime.datetime(2019, 11, 13, 10, 30),
    'open': 71.815,  'high': 71.83,     'low': 71.7775,
    'close': 71.78,    'volume': 62403},
  {'date': datetime.datetime(2019, 11, 13, 10, 45),
    'open': 71.775,  'high': 71.7875, 'low': 71.7475,
    'close': 71.7525, 'volume': 34090},
  {'date': datetime.datetime(2019, 11, 13, 11, 0),
    'open': 71.7525, 'high': 71.7825, 'low': 71.7475,
    'close': 71.7625, 'volume': 39320},
  {'date': datetime.datetime(2019, 11, 13, 11, 15),
    'open': 71.7625, 'high': 71.7925, 'low': 71.76,
    'close': 71.7875, 'volume': 20190}]
```

3. Create a new `DataFrame` from `time_series_data`. Assign it to `df` and print it:

```
>>> df = pandas.DataFrame(time_series_data)
>>> df
```

We get the following output:

```
                  date    open    high     low   close volume
0 2019-11-13 09:00:00 71.8075 71.8450 71.7775 71.7925 219512
1 2019-11-13 09:15:00 71.7925 71.8000 71.7800 71.7925  59252
2 2019-11-13 09:30:00 71.7925 71.8125 71.7600 71.7625  57187
3 2019-11-13 09:45:00 71.7600 71.7650 71.7350 71.7425  43048
4 2019-11-13 10:00:00 71.7425 71.7800 71.7425 71.7775  45863
5 2019-11-13 10:15:00 71.7750 71.8225 71.7700 71.8150  42460
6 2019-11-13 10:30:00 71.8150 71.8300 71.7775 71.7800  62403
7 2019-11-13 10:45:00 71.7750 71.7875 71.7475 71.7525  34090
8 2019-11-13 11:00:00 71.7525 71.7825 71.7475 71.7625  39320
9 2019-11-13 11:15:00 71.7625 71.7925 71.7600 71.7875  20190
```

4. Get the list of columns in `df`:

```
>>> df.columns.tolist()
```

We get the following output:

```
['date', 'open', 'high', 'low', 'close', 'volume']
```

5. Create a `DataFrame` object again using the `time_series_data`. This time, specify the columns in the order you want:

```
>>> pandas.DataFrame(time_series_data,
        columns=['close','date', 'open', 'high', 'low', 'volume'])
```

We get the following output:

```
      close                 date      open     high      low volume
0  71.7925  2019-11-13 09:00:00  71.8075  71.8450  71.7775 219512
1  71.7925  2019-11-13 09:15:00  71.7925  71.8000  71.7800  59252
2  71.7625  2019-11-13 09:30:00  71.7925  71.8125  71.7600  57187
3  71.7425  2019-11-13 09:45:00  71.7600  71.7650  71.7350  43048
4  71.7775  2019-11-13 10:00:00  71.7425  71.7800  71.7425  45863
5  71.8150  2019-11-13 10:15:00  71.7750  71.8225  71.7700  42460
6  71.7800  2019-11-13 10:30:00  71.8150  71.8300  71.7775  62403
7  71.7525  2019-11-13 10:45:00  71.7750  71.7875  71.7475  34090
8  71.7625  2019-11-13 11:00:00  71.7525  71.7825  71.7475  39320
9  71.7875  2019-11-13 11:15:00  71.7625  71.7925  71.7600  20190
```

How it works...

In *step 1*, you import the `datetime` class from the `datetime` module and the `pandas` package. In *step 2*, you create a time-series data, which is typically returned by 3rd party APIs for historical data. This data is a list of dictionaries, and each dictionary has the same set of keys—`date`, `open`, `high`, `low`, `close`, and `volume`. Observe that the value for the `date` key is a `datetime` object and for the other keys are `float` objects.

In *step 3*, you create a pandas `DataFrame` object by directly calling the constructor with `time_series_data` as an argument and assign the return data to `df`. The keys of the dictionaries become the column names of `df` and values become the data. In *step 4*, you fetch the columns of `df` as a list using the `columns` attribute and the `tolist()` method. You can verify that the column names are the same as the keys of the dictionaries in `time_series_data`.

In *step 5*, you create a `DataFrame` with the columns in a specific order by passing a `columns` argument to the constructor with the required order as a list of strings.

There's more

When a `DataFrame` object is created, an index is assigned to it automatically, which is an address for all the rows. The leftmost column in the preceding example is the index column. By default, the index starts from 0. A custom index can be set by passing an `index` argument to the `DataFrame` constructor with the required indices as an iterator. This is shown as follows:

1. Create a new DataFrame object from `time_series_data`, with a custom index:

```
>>> pandas.DataFrame(time_series_data, index=range(10, 20))
```

We get the following output:

```
                   date     open     high      low    close  volume
10  2019-11-13 09:00:00  71.8075  71.8450  71.7775  71.7925  219512
11  2019-11-13 09:15:00  71.7925  71.8000  71.7800  71.7925   59252
12  2019-11-13 09:30:00  71.7925  71.8125  71.7600  71.7625   57187
13  2019-11-13 09:45:00  71.7600  71.7650  71.7350  71.7425   43048
14  2019-11-13 10:00:00  71.7425  71.7800  71.7425  71.7775   45863
15  2019-11-13 10:15:00  71.7750  71.8225  71.7700  71.8150   42460
16  2019-11-13 10:30:00  71.8150  71.8300  71.7775  71.7800   62403
17  2019-11-13 10:45:00  71.7750  71.7875  71.7475  71.7525   34090
18  2019-11-13 11:00:00  71.7525  71.7825  71.7475  71.7625   39320
19  2019-11-13 11:15:00  71.7625  71.7925  71.7600  71.7875   20190
```

Note the index in the output starts from 10 and goes up to 19. The default index values would have ranged from 0 to 9.

DataFrame manipulation—renaming, rearranging, reversing, and slicing

After creating a `DataFrame` object, you can perform various operations on it. This recipe covers the following operations on `DataFrame` objects. Renaming a column, rearranging columns, reversing the `DataFrame`, and slicing the `DataFrame` to extract a row, column, and a subset of data.

Getting ready

Make sure the `df` object is available in your Python namespace. Refer to *Creating a pandas.DataFrame object* recipe of this chapter to set up this object.

How to do it...

Execute the following steps for this recipe:

1. Rename the `date` column to `timestamp` for `df`. Print it:

```
>>> df.rename(columns={'date':'timestamp'}, inplace=True)
>>> df
```

We get the following output:

```
                timestamp    open    high     low    close volume
0 2019-11-13 09:00:00 71.8075 71.8450 71.7775 71.7925 219512
1 2019-11-13 09:15:00 71.7925 71.8000 71.7800 71.7925  59252
2 2019-11-13 09:30:00 71.7925 71.8125 71.7600 71.7625  57187
3 2019-11-13 09:45:00 71.7600 71.7650 71.7350 71.7425  43048
4 2019-11-13 10:00:00 71.7425 71.7800 71.7425 71.7775  45863
5 2019-11-13 10:15:00 71.7750 71.8225 71.7700 71.8150  42460
6 2019-11-13 10:30:00 71.8150 71.8300 71.7775 71.7800  62403
7 2019-11-13 10:45:00 71.7750 71.7875 71.7475 71.7525  34090
8 2019-11-13 11:00:00 71.7525 71.7825 71.7475 71.7625  39320
9 2019-11-13 11:15:00 71.7625 71.7925 71.7600 71.7875  20190
```

2. Create a new `DataFrame` object by rearranging the columns in `df`:

```
>>> df.reindex(columns=[
            'volume',
            'close',
            'timestamp',
            'high',
            'open',
            'low'
        ])
```

We get the following output:

```
    volume    close            timestamp    high    open     low
0 219512 71.7925 2019-11-13 09:00:00 71.8450 71.8075 71.7775
1  59252 71.7925 2019-11-13 09:15:00 71.8000 71.7925 71.7800
2  57187 71.7625 2019-11-13 09:30:00 71.8125 71.7925 71.7600
3  43048 71.7425 2019-11-13 09:45:00 71.7650 71.7600 71.7350
4  45863 71.7775 2019-11-13 10:00:00 71.7800 71.7425 71.7425
5  42460 71.8150 2019-11-13 10:15:00 71.8225 71.7750 71.7700
6  62403 71.7800 2019-11-13 10:30:00 71.8300 71.8150 71.7775
7  34090 71.7525 2019-11-13 10:45:00 71.7875 71.7750 71.7475
8  39320 71.7625 2019-11-13 11:00:00 71.7825 71.7525 71.7475
9  20190 71.7875 2019-11-13 11:15:00 71.7925 71.7625 71.7600
```

3. Create a new `DataFrame` object by reversing the rows in `df`:

```
>>> df[::-1]
```

We get the following output:

```
                timestamp     open     high      low    close  volume
9  2019-11-13 11:15:00  71.7625  71.7925  71.7600  71.7875   20190
8  2019-11-13 11:00:00  71.7525  71.7825  71.7475  71.7625   39320
7  2019-11-13 10:45:00  71.7750  71.7875  71.7475  71.7525   34090
6  2019-11-13 10:30:00  71.8150  71.8300  71.7775  71.7800   62403
5  2019-11-13 10:15:00  71.7750  71.8225  71.7700  71.8150   42460
4  2019-11-13 10:00:00  71.7425  71.7800  71.7425  71.7775   45863
3  2019-11-13 09:45:00  71.7600  71.7650  71.7350  71.7425   43048
2  2019-11-13 09:30:00  71.7925  71.8125  71.7600  71.7625   57187
1  2019-11-13 09:15:00  71.7925  71.8000  71.7800  71.7925   59252
0  2019-11-13 09:00:00  71.8075  71.8450  71.7775  71.7925  219512
```

4. Extract the `close` column from `df`:

```
>>> df['close']
```

We get the following output:

```
0    71.7925
1    71.7925
2    71.7625
3    71.7425
4    71.7775
5    71.8150
6    71.7800
7    71.7525
8    71.7625
9    71.7875
Name: close, dtype: float64
```

5. Extract the first row from `df`:

```
>>> df.iloc[0]
```

We get the following output:

```
timestamp    2019-11-13 09:00:00
open                     71.8075
high                      71.845
low                      71.7775
close                    71.7925
volume                    219512
Name: 10, dtype: object
```

6. Extract a 2 × 2 matrix with the first two rows and first two columns only:

```
>>> df.iloc[:2, :2]
```

We get the following output:

```
            timestamp      open
0 2019-11-13 09:00:00  71.8075
1 2019-11-13 09:15:00  71.7925
```

How it works...

Renaming: In *step 1*, you rename the date column to timestamp using the rename() method of pandas DataFrame. You pass the columns argument as a dictionary with the existing names to be replaced as keys and their new names as the corresponding values. You also pass the inplace argument as True so that df is modified directly. If it is not passed, the default value is False, meaning a new DataFrame would be created instead of modifying df.

Rearranging: In *step 2*, you use the reindex() method to create a new DataFrame from df by rearranging its columns. You pass the columns argument with a list of column names as strings in the required order.

Revering: In *step 3*, you create a new DataFrame from df with its rows reversed by using the indexing operator in a special way – [::-1]. This is similar to the way we reverse regular Python lists.

Slicing: In *step 4*, you extract the column close by using the indexing operator on df. You pass the column name, close, as the index here. The return data is a pandas.Series object. You can use the iloc property on DataFrame objects to extract a row, a column, or a subset DataFrame object. In *step 5*, you extract the first-row using iloc with 0 as the index. The return data is a pandas.Series object In *step 6*, you extract a 2x2 subset from df using iloc with (:2, :2) as the index. This implies all data in rows until index 2 (which are 0 and 1) and columns until index 2 (which again are 0 and 1) would be extracted. The return data is a pandas.DataFrame object.

 For all the operations shown in this recipe where a new DataFrame object is returned, the original DataFrame object remains unchanged.

There's more

The `.iloc()` property can also be used to extract a column from a `DataFrame`. This is shown in the following code.

Extract the 4th column from `df`. Observe the output:

```
>>> df.iloc[:, 4]
```

We get the following output:

```
0      71.7925
1      71.7925
2      71.7625
3      71.7425
4      71.7775
5      71.8150
6      71.7800
7      71.7525
8      71.7625
9      71.7875
Name: close, dtype: float64
```

Note that this output and the output of *step 4* are identical.

DataFrame manipulation—applying, sorting, iterating, and concatenating

Adding to the previous recipe, this recipe demonstrates more operations that can be performed on `DataFrame` objects: applying a function to all elements in a column, sorting based on a column, iterating over the rows, and concatenating multiple `DataFrame` objects vertically and horizontally.

Getting ready

Make sure you have followed the previous recipe before trying out this recipe. Ensure you have `df` in your Python namespace from the previous recipe.

How to do it...

Execute the following steps for this recipe:

1. Import the necessary modules

   ```
   >>> import random
   >>> import pandas
   ```

2. Modify the values in the timestamp column of `df` with a different date and time format `DD-MM-YYYY HH:MM:SS`:

   ```
   >>> df['timestamp'] = df['timestamp'].apply(
                       lambda x: x.strftime("%d-%m-%Y %H:%M:%S"))
   >>> df
   ```

   We get the following output:

   ```
              timestamp    open     high     low    close  volume
   0  13-11-2019 09:00:00  71.8075  71.8450  71.7775  71.7925  219512
   1  13-11-2019 09:15:00  71.7925  71.8000  71.7800  71.7925   59252
   2  13-11-2019 09:30:00  71.7925  71.8125  71.7600  71.7625   57187
   3  13-11-2019 09:45:00  71.7600  71.7650  71.7350  71.7425   43048
   4  13-11-2019 10:00:00  71.7425  71.7800  71.7425  71.7775   45863
   5  13-11-2019 10:15:00  71.7750  71.8225  71.7700  71.8150   42460
   6  13-11-2019 10:30:00  71.8150  71.8300  71.7775  71.7800   62403
   7  13-11-2019 10:45:00  71.7750  71.7875  71.7475  71.7525   34090
   8  13-11-2019 11:00:00  71.7525  71.7825  71.7475  71.7625   39320
   9  13-11-2019 11:15:00  71.7625  71.7925  71.7600  71.7875   20190
   ```

3. Create a new `DataFrame` object by sorting the `close` column in ascending order:

   ```
   >>> df.sort_values(by='close', ascending=True)
   ```

   We get the following output:

   ```
              timestamp    open     high     low    close  volume
   3  13-11-2019 09:45:00  71.7600  71.7650  71.7350  71.7425   43048
   7  13-11-2019 10:45:00  71.7750  71.7875  71.7475  71.7525   34090
   2  13-11-2019 09:30:00  71.7925  71.8125  71.7600  71.7625   57187
   8  13-11-2019 11:00:00  71.7525  71.7825  71.7475  71.7625   39320
   4  13-11-2019 10:00:00  71.7425  71.7800  71.7425  71.7775   45863
   6  13-11-2019 10:30:00  71.8150  71.8300  71.7775  71.7800   62403
   9  13-11-2019 11:15:00  71.7625  71.7925  71.7600  71.7875   20190
   0  13-11-2019 09:00:00  71.8075  71.8450  71.7775  71.7925  219512
   1  13-11-2019 09:15:00  71.7925  71.8000  71.7800  71.7925   59252
   5  13-11-2019 10:15:00  71.7750  71.8225  71.7700  71.8150   42460
   ```

4. Create a new `DataFrame` object by sorting the `open` column in descending order:

```
>>> df.sort_values(by='open', ascending=False)
```

We get the following output:

```
              timestamp      open      high       low     close  volume
6  13-11-2019 10:30:00  71.8150  71.8300  71.7775  71.7800   62403
0  13-11-2019 09:00:00  71.8075  71.8450  71.7775  71.7925  219512
2  13-11-2019 09:30:00  71.7925  71.8125  71.7600  71.7625   57187
1  13-11-2019 09:15:00  71.7925  71.8000  71.7800  71.7925   59252
7  13-11-2019 10:45:00  71.7750  71.7875  71.7475  71.7525   34090
5  13-11-2019 10:15:00  71.7750  71.8225  71.7700  71.8150   42460
9  13-11-2019 11:15:00  71.7625  71.7925  71.7600  71.7875   20190
3  13-11-2019 09:45:00  71.7600  71.7650  71.7350  71.7425   43048
8  13-11-2019 11:00:00  71.7525  71.7825  71.7475  71.7625   39320
4  13-11-2019 10:00:00  71.7425  71.7800  71.7425  71.7775   45863
```

5. Iterate over `df` to find the average of `open`, `close`, `high`, and `low` values for each row:

```
>>> for _, row in df.iterrows():
        avg = (row['open'] + row['close'] + row['high'] +
            row['low'])/4
        print(f"Index: {_} | Average: {avg}")
```

We get the following output:

```
Index: 0 | Average: 71.805625
Index: 1 | Average: 71.79124999999999
Index: 2 | Average: 71.781875
Index: 3 | Average: 71.750625
Index: 4 | Average: 71.760625
Index: 5 | Average: 71.795625
Index: 6 | Average: 71.800625
Index: 7 | Average: 71.765625
Index: 8 | Average: 71.76124999999999
Index: 9 | Average: 71.775625
```

6. Iterate column-wise over all the values of the first row of `df`:

```
>>> for value in df.iloc[0]:
        print(value)
```

We get the following output:

```
13-11-2019 09:00:00
71.8075
71.845
71.7775
71.7925
219512
```

7. Create a sample time-series data as a list of dictionary objects. Assign it to `df_new`:

```
>>> df_new = pandas. DataFrame([
    {'timestamp': datetime.datetime(2019, 11, 13, 11, 30),
     'open': 71.7875,
     'high': 71.8075,
     'low': 71.77,
     'close': 71.7925,
     'volume': 18655},
    {'timestamp': datetime.datetime(2019, 11, 13, 11, 45),
     'open': 71.7925,
     'high': 71.805,
     'low': 71.7625,
     'close': 71.7625,
     'volume': 25648},
    {'timestamp': datetime.datetime(2019, 11, 13, 12, 0),
     'open': 71.7625,
     'high': 71.805,
     'low': 71.75,
     'close': 71.785,
     'volume': 37300},
    {'timestamp': datetime.datetime(2019, 11, 13, 12, 15),
     'open': 71.785,
     'high': 71.7925,
     'low': 71.7575,
     'close': 71.7775,
     'volume': 15431},
    {'timestamp': datetime.datetime(2019, 11, 13, 12, 30),
     'open': 71.7775,
     'high': 71.795,
     'low': 71.7725,
     'close': 71.79,
     'volume': 5178}])
>>> df_new
```

We get the following output:

```
           timestamp     open     high      low    close  volume
0  2019-11-13 11:30:00  71.7875  71.8075  71.7700  71.7925   18655
1  2019-11-13 11:45:00  71.7925  71.8050  71.7625  71.7625   25648
2  2019-11-13 12:00:00  71.7625  71.8050  71.7500  71.7850   37300
3  2019-11-13 12:15:00  71.7850  71.7925  71.7575  71.7775   15431
4  2019-11-13 12:30:00  71.7775  71.7950  71.7725  71.7900    5178
```

8. Create a new DataFrame by concatenating `df` and `df_new` vertically:

```
>>> pandas.concat([df, df_new]).reset_index(drop=True)
```

We get the following output:

```
            timestamp      open     high      low    close  volume
0   13-11-2019 09:00:00  71.8075  71.8450  71.7775  71.7925  219512
1   13-11-2019 09:15:00  71.7925  71.8000  71.7800  71.7925   59252
2   13-11-2019 09:30:00  71.7925  71.8125  71.7600  71.7625   57187
3   13-11-2019 09:45:00  71.7600  71.7650  71.7350  71.7425   43048
4   13-11-2019 10:00:00  71.7425  71.7800  71.7425  71.7775   45863
5   13-11-2019 10:15:00  71.7750  71.8225  71.7700  71.8150   42460
6   13-11-2019 10:30:00  71.8150  71.8300  71.7775  71.7800   62403
7   13-11-2019 10:45:00  71.7750  71.7875  71.7475  71.7525   34090
8   13-11-2019 11:00:00  71.7525  71.7825  71.7475  71.7625   39320
9   13-11-2019 11:15:00  71.7625  71.7925  71.7600  71.7875   20190
10  2019-11-13 11:30:00  71.7875  71.8075  71.7700  71.7925   18655
11  2019-11-13 11:45:00  71.7925  71.8050  71.7625  71.7625   25648
12  2019-11-13 12:00:00  71.7625  71.8050  71.7500  71.7850   37300
13  2019-11-13 12:15:00  71.7850  71.7925  71.7575  71.7775   15431
14  2019-11-13 12:30:00  71.7775  71.7950  71.7725  71.7900    5178
```

How it works...

In *step 1*, you import the `pandas` package.

Applying: In *step 2*, you modify all the values in the `timestamp` column of `df` by using the `apply` method. This method takes a function as an input to be applied. You pass a lambda function here which expects a `datetime` object as a single input, and converts it to a string in the required format using `strftime()`. (Refer to *Converting a datetime object to a string* recipe for more details on `strftime()`). The `apply` method is called on the `timestamp` column of `df`, which is a `pandas.Series` object. The lambda function is applied to each value in the column. This call returns a new `pandas.Series` object, which you assign back to the `timestamp` column of `df`. Note, after this, the `timestamp` column of `df` holds timestamps as string objects, and not `datetime` objects as earlier.

Sorting: In *step 3*, you create a new `DataFrame` object by sorting the `close` column of `df` in ascending order. You use the `sort_values()` method to perform the sorting. Similarly, in *step 4*, you create a new `DataFrame` object by sorting the `open` column of `df` in descending order.

Iterating: In *step 5*, you iterate over df using the `iterrows()` method to find and print the average of `open`, `close`, `high`, and `low` values for each row. The `iterrows()` method iterates over each row as an `(index, pandas.Series)` pair. In *step 6*, you iterate over all the values of the first row of `df` using `df.iloc[0]`. You get the `timestamp`, `open`, `high`, `low`, `close`, and `volume` column values for the first row as the output.

Concatenation: In *step 6*, you create a new `DataFrame` similar to the one created in *step 2* of *Creating a pandas.DataFrame object* recipe, and assign it to `df_new`. You use the `pandas.concat()` function to create a new `DataFrame` by vertically concatenating `dt` and `df_new`. This implies that a new `DataFrame` would be created with the rows of `df_new` appended below the rows of `df`. You pass a list containing `df` and `df_new` as an argument to the `pandas.concat()` function. Also, to create a fresh index starting from 0, you use the `reset_index()` method with the argument drop passed as `True`. If you don't use `reset_index()`, the indices of the concatenated `DataFrame` would look something like this—0, 1, 2, 3, 4, 5, 6, 7, 8, 9, 0, 1, 2, 3, 4. (Refer to *Creating a pandas.DataFrame object* recipe to know more about the `DataFrame` index.)

There's more

You can also use the `pandas.concat()` function to concatenate two `DataFrame` objects together horizontally, which is column-wise by, passing the `axis` argument a value of `1` to the `pandas.concat()` method. This is shown in the following steps:

1. Import `random` module from the Python standard library:

   ```
   >>> import random
   ```

2. Create a DataFrame object with a single column, `open`, and random values. Assign it to `df1` and print it:

   ```
   >>> df1 = pandas.DataFrame([random.randint(1,100) for i in
                               range(10)], columns=['open'])
   >>> df1
   ```

We get the following output. Your output may differ:

```
   open
0    99
1    73
2    16
3    53
4    47
5    74
6    21
7    22
8     2
9    30
```

3. Create another `DataFrame` object with a single column, `close`, and random values. Assign it to `df2` and print it:

```
>>> df2 = pandas.DataFrame([random.randint(1,100) for i in
                            range(10)], columns=['close'])
>>> df2
```

We get the following output:

```
   close
0     63
1     84
2     44
3     56
4     25
5      1
6     41
7     55
8     93
9     82
```

4. Create a new `DataFrame` by concatenating `df1` and `df2` horizontally

```
>>> pandas.concat([df1, df2], axis=1)
```

We get the following output. Your output may differ:

```
     open  close
0      99     93
1      73     42
2      16     57
3      53     56
4      47     25
5      74      1
6      21     41
7      22     55
8       2     93
9      30     82
```

Converting a DataFrame into other formats

This recipe demonstrates the conversion of DataFrame objects into other formats, such as .csv files, json objects, and pickle objects. Conversion into a .csv file makes it easier to further work on the data using a spreadsheet application. The json format is useful for transmitting DataFrame objects over web APIs. The pickle format is useful for transmitting DataFrame objects created in one Python session to another Python session over sockets without having to recreate them.

Getting ready

Make sure the object df is available in your Python namespace. Refer to *Creating a pandas.DataFrame object* recipe of this chapter to set up this object.

How to do it...

Execute the following steps for this recipe:

1. Convert and save df as a CSV file:

   ```
   >>> df.to_csv('dataframe.csv', index=False)
   ```

2. Convert df to a JSON string:

   ```
   >>> df.to_json()
   ```

We get the following output:

```
'{
    "timestamp":{
        "0":"13-11-2019 09:00:00","1":"13-11-2019 09:15:00",
        "2":"13-11-2019 09:30:00","3":"13-11-2019 09:45:00",
        "4":"13-11-2019 10:00:00","5":"13-11-2019 10:15:00",
        "6":"13-11-2019 10:30:00","7":"13-11-2019 10:45:00",
        "8":"13-11-2019 11:00:00","9":"13-11-2019 11:15:00"},
    "open":{
        "0":71.8075,"1":71.7925,"2":71.7925, "3":71.76,
        "4":71.7425,"5":71.775,"6":71.815, "7":71.775,
        "8":71.7525,"9":71.7625},
    "high"{
        "0":71.845,"1":71.8,"2":71.8125,"3":71.765,
        "4":71.78,"5":71.8225,"6":71.83,"7":71.7875,
        "8":71.7825,"9":71.7925},
    "low":{
        "0":71.7775,"1":71.78,"2":71.76,"3":71.735,
        "4":71.7425,"5":71.77,"6":71.7775,"7":71.7475,
        "8":71.7475,"9":71.76},
    "close":{
        "0":71.7925,"1":71.7925,"2":71.7625,"3":71.7425,
        "4":71.7775,"5":71.815,"6":71.78,"7":71.7525,
        "8":71.7625,"9":71.7875},
    "volume":{
        "0":219512,"1":59252,"2":57187,"3":43048,
        "4":45863,"5":42460,"6":62403,"7":34090,
        "8":39320,"9":20190}}'
```

3. Pickle `df` to a file:

```
>>> df.to_pickle('df.pickle')
```

How it works...

In *step 1,* you use the `to_csv()` method to save `df` as a `.csv` file. You pass `dataframe.csv`, a file path where the `.csv` file should be generated, as the first argument and index as `False` as the second argument. Passing index as `False` prevents the index from being dumped to the `.csv` file. If you want to save the `DataFrame` along with its index, you can pass the index as `True` to the `to_csv()` method.

In *step 2,* you use the `to_json()` method to convert `df` into a JSON string. You do not pass any additional arguments to the `to_json()` method.

In *step 3*, you use the `to_pickle()` method to pickle (serialize) the object. Again you do not pass any additional arguments to the `to_pickle()` method.

> The methods `to_csv()`, `to_json()`, and `to_pickle()` can take more optional arguments than the ones shown in this recipe. Refer to the official docs for complete information on these methods:
>
> - `to_csv()`: https://pandas.pydata.org/pandas-docs/stable/reference/api/pandas.DataFrame.to_csv.html
> - `to_json()`: https://pandas.pydata.org/pandas-docs/stable/reference/api/pandas.DataFrame.to_json.html
> - `to_pickle()`: https://pandas.pydata.org/pandas-docs/stable/reference/api/pandas.DataFrame.to_pickle.html

Creating a DataFrame from other formats

In this recipe, you will create `DataFrame` objects from other formats, such as `.csv` files, `.json` strings, and `pickle` files. A `.csv` file created using a spreadsheet application, valid JSON data received over web APIs, or valid pickle objects received over sockets can all be processed further using Python by converting them to `DataFrame` objects.

> Loading pickled data received from untrusted sources can be unsafe. Please use `read_pickle()` with caution. You can find more details here: https://docs.python.org/3/library/pickle.html. If you are using this function on the pickle file created in the previous recipe, it is perfectly safe to use `read_pickle()`.

Getting ready

Make sure you have followed the previous recipe before starting this recipe.

How to do it...

Execute the following steps for this recipe:

1. Create a DataFrame object by reading a CSV file:

```
>>> pandas.read_csv('dataframe.csv')
```

We get the following output:

```
            timestamp     open    high     low   close  volume
0  2019-11-13 09:00:00  71.8075  71.8450  71.7775  71.7925  219512
1  2019-11-13 09:15:00  71.7925  71.8000  71.7800  71.7925   59252
2  2019-11-13 09:30:00  71.7925  71.8125  71.7600  71.7625   57187
3  2019-11-13 09:45:00  71.7600  71.7650  71.7350  71.7425   43048
4  2019-11-13 10:00:00  71.7425  71.7800  71.7425  71.7775   45863
5  2019-11-13 10:15:00  71.7750  71.8225  71.7700  71.8150   42460
6  2019-11-13 10:30:00  71.8150  71.8300  71.7775  71.7800   62403
7  2019-11-13 10:45:00  71.7750  71.7875  71.7475  71.7525   34090
8  2019-11-13 11:00:00  71.7525  71.7825  71.7475  71.7625   39320
9  2019-11-13 11:15:00  71.7625  71.7925  71.7600  71.7875   20190
```

2. Create a DataFrame object by reading a JSON string:

```
>>> pandas.read_json("""{
    "timestamp": {
        "0":"13-11-2019 09:00:00", "1":"13-11-2019 09:15:00",
        "2":"13-11-2019 09:30:00","3":"13-11-2019 09:45:00",
        "4":"13-11-2019 10:00:00","5":"13-11-2019 10:15:00",
        "6":"13-11-2019 10:30:00","7":"13-11-2019 10:45:00",
        "8":"13-11-2019 11:00:00","9":"13-11-2019 11:15:00"},

    "open":{
        "0":71.8075,"1":71.7925,"2":71.7925,"3":71.76,
        "4":71.7425,"5":71.775,"6":71.815,"7":71.775,
        "8":71.7525,"9":71.7625},

    "high":{
        "0":71.845,"1":71.8,"2":71.8125,"3":71.765,"4":71.78,
        "5":71.8225,"6":71.83,"7":71.7875,"8":71.7825,
        "9":71.7925},

    "low":{
        "0":71.7775,"1":71.78,"2":71.76,"3":71.735,"4":71.7425,
        "5":71.77,"6":71.7775,"7":71.7475,"8":71.7475,
        "9":71.76},

    "close":{
        "0":71.7925,"1":71.7925,"2":71.7625,"3":71.7425,
        "4":71.7775,"5":71.815,"6":71.78,"7":71.7525,
        "8":71.7625,"9":71.7875},

    "volume":{
        "0":219512,"1":59252,"2":57187,"3":43048,"4":45863,
        "5":42460,"6":62403,"7":34090,"8":39320,"9":20190}}
        """)
```

We get the following output:

```
            timestamp    open    high     low   close volume
0 2019-11-13 09:00:00 71.8075 71.8450 71.7775 71.7925 219512
1 2019-11-13 09:15:00 71.7925 71.8000 71.7800 71.7925  59252
2 2019-11-13 09:30:00 71.7925 71.8125 71.7600 71.7625  57187
3 2019-11-13 09:45:00 71.7600 71.7650 71.7350 71.7425  43048
4 2019-11-13 10:00:00 71.7425 71.7800 71.7425 71.7775  45863
5 2019-11-13 10:15:00 71.7750 71.8225 71.7700 71.8150  42460
6 2019-11-13 10:30:00 71.8150 71.8300 71.7775 71.7800  62403
7 2019-11-13 10:45:00 71.7750 71.7875 71.7475 71.7525  34090
8 2019-11-13 11:00:00 71.7525 71.7825 71.7475 71.7625  39320
9 2019-11-13 11:15:00 71.7625 71.7925 71.7600 71.7875  20190
```

3. Create a `DataFrame` object by unpickling the `df.pickle` file:

```
>>> pandas.read_pickle('df.pickle')
```

We get the following output:

```
            timestamp    open    high     low   close volume
0 2019-11-13 09:00:00 71.8075 71.8450 71.7775 71.7925 219512
1 2019-11-13 09:15:00 71.7925 71.8000 71.7800 71.7925  59252
2 2019-11-13 09:30:00 71.7925 71.8125 71.7600 71.7625  57187
3 2019-11-13 09:45:00 71.7600 71.7650 71.7350 71.7425  43048
4 2019-11-13 10:00:00 71.7425 71.7800 71.7425 71.7775  45863
5 2019-11-13 10:15:00 71.7750 71.8225 71.7700 71.8150  42460
6 2019-11-13 10:30:00 71.8150 71.8300 71.7775 71.7800  62403
7 2019-11-13 10:45:00 71.7750 71.7875 71.7475 71.7525  34090
8 2019-11-13 11:00:00 71.7525 71.7825 71.7475 71.7625  39320
9 2019-11-13 11:15:00 71.7625 71.7925 71.7600 71.7875  20190
```

How it works...

In *step 1*, you use the `pandas.read_csv()` function to create a DataFrame object from a `.csv` file. You pass `dataframe.csv`, the file path from where the `.csv` file should be read, as an argument. Recall, you have created `dataframe.csv` in *step 1* of the previous recipe.

In *step 2*, you use the `pandas.read_json()` function to create a `DataFrame` object from a valid JSON string. You pass the JSON string from the output of *step 2* in the previous recipe as an argument to this function.

In *step 3*, you use the `pandas.read_pickle()` method to create a `DataFrame` object from a `pickle` file. You pass `df.pickle`, the file path from where the pickle file should be read, as an argument to this function. Recall, what you created `df.pickle` in *step 3* of the previous recipe.

If you have followed the previous recipe, the outputs for all the three steps would all be the same `DataFrame` object. And this would be identical to `df` from the previous recipe.

> The methods `read_csv()`, `read_json()`, and `read_pickle()` can take more optional arguments than the ones shown in this recipe. Refer to the official docs for complete information on these methods.
>
> - `read_csv()`: https://pandas.pydata.org/pandas-docs/ stable/reference/api/pandas.read_csv.html#pandas.read_ csv
> - `read_json()`: https://pandas.pydata.org/pandas-docs/ stable/reference/api/pandas.read_json.html#pandas.read_ json
> - `read_pickle()`: https://pandas.pydata.org/pandas-docs/ stable/reference/api/pandas.read_pickle.html#pandas. read_pickle

Stock Markets – Primer on Trading 2

When building algorithmic trading systems, it is essential to have an account open with a modern broker that provides APIs for placing and querying trades programmatically. This allows us to control the broking account, which is conventionally operated manually using the broker's website, using our Python script, which would be part of our larger algorithmic trading system. This chapter demonstrates various essential recipes that introduce the essential broker API calls needed for developing a complete algorithmic trading system.

This chapter covers the following recipes:

- Setting up Python connectivity with the broker
- Querying a list of instruments
- Fetching an instrument
- Querying a list of exchanges
- Querying a list of segments
- Knowing other attributes supported by the broker
- Placing a simple REGULAR order
- Placing a simple BRACKET order
- Placing a simple DELIVERY order
- Placing a simple INTRADAY order
- Querying margins and funds
- Calculating the brokerage charged
- Calculating the government taxes charged

Let's get started!

Technical requirements

You will need the following to successfully execute the recipes in this chapter:

- Python 3.7+
- The Python `pyalgotrading` package (`$ pip install pyalgotrading`)

The latest Jupyter Notebook for this chapter can be found on GitHub at `https://github.com/PacktPublishing/Python-Algorithmic-Trading-Cookbook/tree/master/Chapter02`.

This chapter demonstrates the APIs of a modern broker, `ZERODHA`, which is supported by `pyalgotrading`. You may wish to choose other brokers supported by `pyalgotrading` as well. The recipes in this chapter should be more or less the same for any other broker. The `pyalgotrading` package abstracts broker APIs behind a unified interface, so you don't need to worry about the underlying broker API calls.

To set up a broking account with `ZERODHA`, please refer to the detailed steps provided in *Appendix I*.

Setting up Python connectivity with the broker

The first thing you need to set up connectivity with the broker is API keys. The broker provides unique keys to each customer, typically as an `api-key` and `api-secret` key pair. These API keys are chargeable, usually on a monthly subscription basis. You need to get your copies of `api-key` and `api-secret` from the broker's website before you start this recipe. Please refer to *Appendix I* for more details.

How to do it...

We execute the following steps to complete this recipe:

1. Import the necessary modules:

   ```
   >>> from pyalgotrading.broker.broker_connection_zerodha import
   BrokerConnectionZerodha
   ```

2. Get the `api_key` and `api_secret` keys from the broker. These are unique to you and will be used by the broker to identify your Demat account:

```
>>> api_key = "<your-api-key>"
>>> api_secret = "<your-api-secret>"
>>> broker_connection = BrokerConnectionZerodha(api_key,
api_secret)
```

You will get the following result:

```
Installing package kiteconnect via pip...
Please login to this link to generate your request token:
https://kite.trade/connect/login?api_key=<your-api-key>&v=3
```

3. Get the request token from the preceding URL:

```
>>> request_token = "<your-request-token>"
>>> broker_connection.set_access_token(request_token)
```

How it works...

In *step 1*, you import the `BrokerConnectionZerodha` class from `pyalgotrading`. The `BrokerConnectionZerodha` class provides an abstraction around the broker-specific APIs. For *step 2*, you need your API key and API secret from the broker. If you do not have them, please refer to *Appendix I* for detailed instructions with screenshots on getting this keys. In *step 2*, you assign your API key and API secret to the new `api_key` and `api_secret` variables and use them to create `broker_connection`, an instance of the `BrokerConnectionZerodha` class. If you are running this for the first time and `kiteconnect` is not installed, `pyalgotrading` will automatically install it for you. (`kiteconnect` is the official Python package that talks to the Zerodha backend; `BrokerConnectionZerodha` is a wrapper on top of `kiteconnect`.) *Step 2* generates a login URL. Here, you need to click on the link and log in with your Zerodha credentials. If the authentication process is successful, you will see a link in your browser's address bar that looks similar to the following:

```
https://127.0.0.1/?request_token=&action=login&status=success
```

For example, the full link would be as follows:

```
https://127.0.0.1/?request_token=H06I6Ydv95y23D2Dp7NbigFjKweGwRP7&action=lo
gin&status=success
```

Copy the alphanumeric-token, `H06I6Ydv95y23D2Dp7NbigFjKweGwRP7`, and paste it into `request_token` as part of *step 3*. The `broker_connection` instance is now ready to perform API calls.

Querying a list of instruments

Once the `broker_connection` handle is ready, it can be used to query the list containing all the financial instruments provided by the broker.

Getting ready

Make sure the `broker_connection` object is available in your Python namespace. Refer to the previous recipe in this chapter to set up this object.

How to do it...

We execute the following steps to complete this recipe:

1. Display all the instruments:

    ```
    >>> instruments = broker_connection.get_all_instruments()
    >>> instruments
    ```

    You will get an output similar to the following. The exact output may differ for you:

    ```
        instrument_token exchange_token tradingsymbol name last_price
    expiry strike tick_size lot_size instrument_type segment exchange
    0 267556358 1045142 EURINR20AUGFUT EURINR 0.0 2020-08-27 0.0 0.0025
    1 FUT BCD-FUT BCD
    1 268660998 1049457 EURINR20DECFUT EURINR 0.0 2020-12-29 0.0 0.0025
    1 FUT BCD-FUT BCD
    2 266440966 1040785 EURINR20JULFUT EURINR 0.0 2020-07-29 0.0 0.0025
    1 FUT BCD-FUT BCD
    3 266073606 1039350 EURINR20JUNFUT EURINR 0.0 2020-06-26 0.0 0.0025
    1 FUT BCD-FUT BCD
    4 265780742 1038206 EURINR20MAYFUT EURINR 0.0 2020-05-27 0.0 0.0025
    1 FUT BCD-FUT BCD

    ... ... ... ... ... ... ... ... ... ... ... ... ...
    64738 978945 3824 ZODJRDMKJ ZODIAC JRD-MKJ 0.0 0.0 0.0500 1 EQ NSE
    NSE
    ```

```
64739 2916865 11394 ZOTA ZOTA HEALTH CARE 0.0 0.0 0.0500 1 EQ NSE
NSE
64740 7437825 29054 ZUARI-BE ZUARI AGRO CHEMICALS 0.0 0.0 0.0500 1
EQ NSE NSE
64741 979713 3827 ZUARIGLOB ZUARI GLOBAL 0.0 0.0 0.0500 1 EQ NSE
NSE
64742 4514561 17635 ZYDUSWELL ZYDUS WELLNESS 0.0 0.0 0.0500 1 EQ
NSE NSE

64743 rows × 12 columns
```

2. Print the total number of instruments:

```
>>> print(f'Total instruments: {len(instruments)}')
```

We get the following output (your output may differ):

```
Total instruments: 64743
```

How it works...

The first step fetches all the available financial instruments using the `get_all_instruments()` method of `broker_connection`. This method returns a `pandas.DataFrame` object. This object is assigned to a new variable, `instruments`, which is shown in the output of *step 1*. This output may differ for you as new financial instruments are frequently added and existing ones expire regularly. The final step shows the total number of instruments provided by the broker.

 An explanation of the data that was returned by the preceding API call will be discussed in depth in `Chapter 3`, *Analyzing Financial Data*. For this recipe, it suffices to know the method for fetching the list of instruments.

Fetching an instrument

Instruments, also known as **financial instruments** or **securities**, are assets that can be traded in an exchange. In an exchange, there can easily be tens of thousands of instruments. This recipe demonstrates how to fetch an instrument based on its **exchange** and **trading symbol**.

Getting ready

Make sure the `broker_connection` object is available in your Python namespace. Refer to the first recipe in this chapter to set up this object.

How to do it...

Fetch an instrument for a specific trading symbol and exchange:

```
>>> broker_connection.get_instrument(segment='NSE',
tradingsymbol='TATASTEEL')
```

You'll get the following output:

```
segment: NSE
exchange: NSE
tradingsymbol: TATASTEEL
broker_token: 895745
tick_size: 0.05
lot_size: 1
expiry:
strike_price: 0.0
```

How it works...

The `broker_connection` object provides a handy method, `get_instrument`, for fetching any financial instrument. It takes `segment` and `tradingsymbol` as attributes before returning an instrument. The return object is an instance of the `Instrument` class.

Querying a list of exchanges

An **exchange** is a marketplace where instruments are traded. Exchanges ensure that the trading process is fair and happens in an orderly fashion at all times. Usually, a broker supports multiple exchanges. This recipe demonstrates how to find the list of exchanges supported by the broker.

Getting ready

Make sure the `instruments` object is available in your Python namespace. Refer to the second recipe of this chapter to learn how to set up this object.

How to do it...

Display the exchanges supported by the broker:

```
>>> exchanges = instruments.exchange.unique()
>>> print(exchanges)
```

You will get the following output:

```
['BCD' 'BSE' 'NSE' 'CDS' 'MCX' 'NFO']
```

How it works...

`instruments.exchange` returns a `pandas.Series` object. Its `unique()` method returns a `numpy.ndarray` object consisting of unique exchanges supported by the broker.

Querying a list of segments

A segment is essentially a categorization of instruments based on their types. The various types of segments that are commonly found at exchanges include cash/equities, futures, options, commodities, and currency. Each segment may have a different operating time. Usually, a broker supports multiple segments within multiple exchanges. This recipe demonstrates how to find the list of segments supported by the broker.

Getting ready

Make sure the `instruments` object is available in your Python namespace. Refer to the second recipe of this chapter to learn how to set up this object.

How to do it...

Display the segments supported by the broker:

```
>>> segments = instruments.segment.unique()
>>> print(segments)
```

You will get the following output:

```
['BCD-FUT' 'BCD' 'BCD-OPT' 'BSE' 'INDICES' 'CDS-FUT' 'CDS-OPT' 'MCX-FUT'
'MCX-OPT' 'NFO-OPT' 'NFO-FUT' 'NSE']
```

How it works...

`instruments.segment` returns a `pandas.Series` object. Its unique method returns a `numpy.ndarray` object consisting of unique segments supported by the broker.

Knowing other attributes supported by the broker

For placing an order, the following attributes are needed: order transaction type, order variety, order type, and order code. Different brokers may support different types of order attributes. For example, some brokers may support just regular orders, while others may support regular and bracket orders. The value for each of the attributes supported by the broker can be queried using the broker specific constants provided by the `pyalgotrading` package.

How to do it...

We execute the following steps to complete this recipe:

1. Import the necessary class from the `pyalgotrading` module:

```
>>> from pyalgotrading.broker.broker_connection_zerodha import
BrokerConnectionZerodha
```

2. List the order transaction types:

```
>>> list(BrokerConnectionZerodha.ORDER_TRANSACTION_TYPE_MAP.keys())
```

We'll get the following output:

```
[<BrokerOrderTransactionTypeConstants.BUY: 'BUY'>,
 <BrokerOrderTransactionTypeConstants.SELL: 'SELL'>]
```

3. List the order varieties:

```
>>> list(BrokerConnectionZerodha.ORDER_VARIETY_MAP.keys())
```

We'll get the following output:

```
[<BrokerOrderVarietyConstants.MARKET: 'ORDER_VARIETY_MARKET'>,
 <BrokerOrderVarietyConstants.LIMIT: 'ORDER_VARIETY_LIMIT'>,
 <BrokerOrderVarietyConstants.STOPLOSS_LIMIT:
 'ORDER_VARIETY_STOPLOSS_LIMIT'>,
 <BrokerOrderVarietyConstants.STOPLOSS_MARKET:
 'ORDER_VARIETY_STOPLOSS_MARKET'>]
```

4. List the order types:

```
>>> list(BrokerConnectionZerodha.ORDER_TYPE_MAP.keys())
```

We'll get the following output:

```
[<BrokerOrderTypeConstants.REGULAR: 'ORDER_TYPE_REGULAR'>,
 <BrokerOrderTypeConstants.BRACKET: 'ORDER_TYPE_BRACKET'>,
 <BrokerOrderTypeConstants.COVER: 'ORDER_TYPE_COVER'>,
 <BrokerOrderTypeConstants.AMO: 'ORDER_TYPE_AFTER_MARKET_ORDER'>]
```

5. List the order codes:

```
>>> list(BrokerConnectionZerodha.ORDER_CODE_MAP.keys())
```

We'll get the following output:

```
[<BrokerOrderCodeConstants.INTRADAY: 'ORDER_CODE_INTRADAY'>,
 <BrokerOrderCodeConstants.DELIVERY: 'ORDER_CODE_DELIVERY_T0'>]
```

How it works...

In *step 1*, we import the `BrokerConnectionZerodha` class from `pyalgotrading`. This class holds the order attributes mapping between `pyalgotrading` and broker specific constants as dictionary objects. The next steps fetch and print these mappings. Step 2 shows that your broker supports both BUY and SELL order transaction types.

Step 3 shows that your broker supports MARKET, LIMIT, STOPLOSS_LIMIT, and STOPLOSS_MARKET order varieties. *Step 4* shows that your broker supports REGULAR, BRACKET, COVER, and AFTER_MARKET order types. *Step 5* shows that your broker supports INTRADAY and DELIVERY order codes.

The outputs may differ from broker to broker, so consult your broker documentation if you are using a different broker. A detailed explanation of all these types of parameters will be covered in Chapter 6, *Placing Trading Orders on the Exchange*. This recipe is to just give an overview of the parameters, as they are needed in the subsequent recipes of this chapter.

Placing a simple REGULAR order

This recipe demonstrates how to place a REGULAR order on the exchange via the broker. REGULAR orders are the simplest types of orders. After trying out this recipe, check your broking account by logging into the broker's website; you will find that an order has been placed there. You can match the order ID with the one that's returned in the last code snippet shown in this recipe.

Getting ready

Make sure the broker_connection object is available in your Python namespace. Refer to the first recipe of this chapter to learn how to set up this object.

How to do it...

We execute the following steps to complete this recipe:

1. Import the necessary constants from pyalgotrading:

   ```
   >>> from pyalgotrading.constants import *
   ```

2. Fetch an instrument for a specific trading symbol and exchange:

   ```
   >>> instrument = broker_connection.get_instrument(segment='NSE',
                                            tradingsymbol='TATASTEEL')
   ```

3. Place a simple regular order – a BUY, REGULAR, INTRADAY, MARKET order:

```
>>> order_id = broker_connection.place_order(
                instrument=instrument,
                order_transaction_type= \
                    BrokerOrderTransactionTypeConstants.BUY,
                order_type=BrokerOrderTypeConstants.REGULAR,
                order_code=BrokerOrderCodeConstants.INTRADAY,
                order_variety= \
                    BrokerOrderVarietyConstants.MARKET,
                quantity=1)
>>> order_id
```

We'll get the following output:

```
191209000001676
```

How it works...

In *step 1*, you import constants from `pyalgotrading`. In *step 2*, you fetch the financial instrument with `segment = 'NSE'` and `tradingsymbol = 'TATASTEEL'` using the `get_instrument()` method of `broker_connection`. In *step 3*, you place a REGULAR order using the `place_order()` method of `broker_connection`. The descriptions of the parameters accepted by the `place_order()` method are as follows:

- `instrument`: The financial instrument for which the order must be placed. Should an instance of the `Instrument` class. You pass `instrument` here.
- `order_transaction_type`: The order transaction type. Should be an enum of type `BrokerOrderTransactionTypeConstants`. You pass `BrokerOrderTransactionTypeConstants.BUY` here.
- `order_type`: The order type. Should be an enum of type `BrokerOrderTypeConstants`. You pass `BrokerOrderTypeConstants.REGULAR` here.
- `order_code`: The order code. Should be an enum of type `BrokerOrderCodeConstants`. You pass `BrokerOrderCodeConstants.INTRADAY` here.
- `order_variety`: The order variety. Should be an enum of type `BrokerOrderVarietyConstants`. You pass `BrokerOrderVarietyConstants.MARKET` here.
- `quantity`: The number of shares to be traded for the given instrument. Should be a positive integer. We pass 1 here.

If the order placement is successful, the method returns an order ID which you can use at any point in time later on for querying the status of the order.

 A detailed explanation of the different types of parameters will be covered in Chapter 6, *Placing Trading Orders on the Exchange*. This recipe is intended to give you an idea of how to place a REGULAR order, one of the various types of possible orders.

Placing a simple BRACKET order

This recipe demonstrates how to place a BRACKET order on the exchange via the broker. BRACKET orders are two-legged orders. Once the first order is executed, the broker automatically places two new orders – a STOPLOSS order and a TARGET order. Only one of them is executed at any time; the other is canceled when the first order is completed. After trying out this recipe, check your broking account by logging into the broker's website; you will find that an order has been placed there. You can match the order ID with the one that's returned in the last code snippet shown in this recipe.

Getting ready

Make sure the broker_connection object is available in your Python namespace. Refer to the first recipe of this chapter to learn how to set up this object.

How to do it...

We execute the following steps to complete this recipe:

1. Import the necessary modules:

```
>>> from pyalgotrading.constants import *
```

2. Fetch an instrument for a specific trading symbol and exchange:

```
>>> instrument = broker_connection.get_instrument(segment='NSE',
                                    tradingsymbol='ICICIBANK')
```

3. Fetch the last traded price of the instrument:

```
>>> ltp = broker_connection.get_ltp(instrument)
```

4. Place a simple BRACKET order – a BUY, BRACKET, INTRADAY, LIMIT order:

```
>>> order_id = broker_connection.place_order(
                instrument=instrument,
                order_transaction_type= \
                    BrokerOrderTransactionTypeConstants.BUY,
                order_type=BrokerOrderTypeConstants.BRACKET,
                order_code=BrokerOrderCodeConstants.INTRADAY,
                order_variety=BrokerOrderVarietyConstants.LIMIT,
                quantity=1, price=ltp-1,
                stoploss=2, target=2)
>>> order_id
```

We'll get the following output:

```
191212001268839
```

If you get the following error while executing this code, it would mean that Bracket orders are blocked by the broker due to high volatility in the markets:

```
InputException: Due to expected higher volatility in the
markets, Bracket orders are blocked temporarily.
```

You should try the recipe later when the broker starts allowing Bracket orders. You can check for updates on the Broker site from time to time to know when Bracket orders would be allowed.

How it works...

In *step 1*, you import the constants from `pyalgotrading`. In *step 2*, you fetch the financial instrument with `segment = 'NSE'` and `tradingsymbol = 'ICICBANK'` using the `get_instrument()` method of `broker_connection`. In *step 3*, you fetch the **last traded price** or **LTP** of the instrument. (LTP will be explained in more detail in the *Last traded price of a financial instrument* recipe of `Chapter 3`, *Analyzing Financial Data*.) In *step 4*, you place a `BRACKET` order using the `place_order()` method of `broker_connection`. The descriptions of the parameters accepted by the `place_order()` method are as follows:

- `instrument`: The financial instrument for which the order must be placed. Should be an instance of the `Instrument` class. You pass `instrument` here.
- `order_transaction_type`: The order transaction type. Should be an enum of type `BrokerOrderTransactionTypeConstants`. You pass `BrokerOrderTransactionTypeConstants.BUY` here.
- `order_type`: The order type. Should be an enum of type `BrokerOrderTypeConstants`. You pass `BrokerOrderTypeConstants.BRACKET` here.
- `order_code`: The order code. Should be an enum of type `BrokerOrderCodeConstants`. You pass `BrokerOrderCodeConstants.INTRADAY` here.
- `order_variety`: The order variety. Should be an enum of type `BrokerOrderVarietyConstants`. You pass `BrokerOrderVarietyConstants.LIMIT` here.
- `quantity`: The number of shares to be traded for the given instrument. Should be a positive integer. You pass `1` here.
- `price`: The limit price at which the order should be placed. You pass `ltp-1` here, which means 1 unit price below the `ltp` value.
- `stoploss`: The price difference from the initial order price, at which the stoploss order should be placed. Should be a positive integer or float value. You pass `2` here.
- `target`: The price difference from the initial price, at which the target order should be placed. Should be a positive integer or float value. You pass `2` here.

If the order placement is successful, the method returns an order ID which you can use at any point in time later on for querying the status of the order.

 A detailed explanation of the different types of parameters will be covered in `Chapter 6`, *Placing Trading Orders on the Exchange*. This recipe is intended to give you an idea of how to place a BRACKET order, one of the various types of possible orders.

Placing a simple DELIVERY order

This recipe demonstrates how to place a DELIVERY order on the exchange via the broker. A DELIVERY order is delivered to the user's Demat account and exists until it is explicitly squared-off by the user. Positions created by delivery orders at the end of a trading session are carried forwarded to the next trading session. They are not explicitly squared-off by the broker. After trying out this recipe, check your broking account by logging into the broker's website; you will find that an order has been placed there. You can match the order ID with the one that's returned in the last code snippet shown in this recipe.

Getting ready

Make sure the `broker_connection` object is available in your Python namespace. Refer to the first recipe of this chapter to learn how to set up this object.

How to do it...

We execute the following steps to complete this recipe:

1. Import the necessary modules:

    ```
    >>> from pyalgotrading.constants import *
    ```

2. Fetch an instrument for a specific trading symbol and exchange:

    ```
    >>> instrument = broker_connection.get_instrument(segment='NSE',
                                        tradingsymbol='AXISBANK')
    ```

3. Place a simple DELIVERY order – a SELL, REGULAR, DELIVERY, MARKET order:

    ```
    >>> order_id = broker_connection.place_order(
                        instrument=instrument,
    ```

```
                    order_transaction_type= \
                        BrokerOrderTransactionTypeConstants.SELL,
                    order_type=BrokerOrderTypeConstants.REGULAR,
                    order_code=BrokerOrderCodeConstants.DELIVERY,
                    order_variety= \
                        BrokerOrderVarietyConstants.MARKET,
                     quantity=1)
>>> order_id
```

We'll get the following output:

```
191212001268956
```

How it works...

In *step 1,* you import the constants from `pyalgotrading`. In *step 2,* you fetch the financial instrument with `segment = 'NSE'` and `tradingsymbol = 'AXISBANK'` using the `get_instrument()` method of `broker_connection`. In *step 3,* you place a `DELIVERY` order using the `place_order()` method of `broker_connection`. This method accepts the following arguments:

- `instrument`: The financial instrument for which the order must be placed. Should be an instance of the `Instrument` class. You pass `instrument` here.
- `order_transaction_type`: The order transaction type. Should be an enum of type `BrokerOrderTransactionTypeConstants`. You pass `BrokerOrderTransactionTypeConstants.SELL` here.
- `order_type`: The order type. Should be an enum of type `BrokerOrderTypeConstants`. You pass `BrokerOrderTypeConstants.REGULAR` here.
- `order_code`: The order code. Should be an enum of type `BrokerOrderCodeConstants`. You pass `BrokerOrderCodeConstants.DELIVERY` here.
- `order_variety`: The order variety. Should be an enum of type `BrokerOrderVarietyConstants`. You pass `BrokerOrderVarietyConstants.MARKET` here.
- `quantity`: The number of shares to be traded for the given instrument. Should be a positive integer. We pass `1` here.

If the order placement is successful, the method returns an order ID which you can use at any point in time later on for querying the status of the order.

A detailed explanation of the different types of parameters will be covered in Chapter 6, *Placing Trading Orders on the Exchange.* This recipe is intended to give you an idea of how to place a DELIVERY order, one of the various types of possible orders.

Placing a simple INTRADAY order

This recipe demonstrates how to place an INTRADAY order via the broker API. An INTRADAY order is not delivered to the user's Demat account. Positions created by intraday orders have a lifetime of a single day. The positions are explicitly squared off by the broker at the end of a trading session and are not carried forward to the next trading session. After trying out this recipe, check your broking account by logging into the broker's website; you will find that an order has been placed there. You can match the order ID with the one that's returned in the last code snippet shown in this recipe.

Getting ready

Make sure the broker_connection object is available in your Python namespace. Refer to the first recipe of this chapter to learn how to set up this object.

How to do it...

We execute the following steps to complete this recipe:

1. Import the necessary modules:

   ```
   >>> from pyalgotrading.constants import *
   ```

2. Fetch an instrument for a specific trading symbol and exchange:

   ```
   >>> instrument = broker_connection.get_instrument(segment='NSE',
                                          tradingsymbol='HDFCBANK')
   ```

3. Fetch the last traded price of the instrument:

   ```
   >>> ltp = broker_connection.get_ltp(instrument)
   ```

4. Place a simple INTRADAY order – a SELL, BRACKET, INTRADAY, LIMIT order:

```
>>> order_id = broker_connection.place_order(
                instrument=instrument,
                order_transaction_type= \
                    BrokerOrderTransactionTypeConstants.SELL,
                order_type=BrokerOrderTypeConstants.BRACKET,
                order_code=BrokerOrderCodeConstants.INTRADAY,
                order_variety=BrokerOrderVarietyConstants.LIMIT,
                quantity=1, price=ltp+1, stoploss=2, target=2)
>>> order_id
```

We'll get the following output:

```
191212001269042
```

If you get the following error while executing this code, it would mean that Bracket orders are blocked by the broker due to high volatility in the markets:

```
InputException: Due to expected higher volatility in the
markets, Bracket orders are blocked temporarily.
```

You should try the recipe later when the broker starts allowing Bracket orders. You can check for updates on the Broker site from time to time to know when Bracket orders would be allowed.

How it works...

In *step 1*, you import the constants from `pyalgotrading`. In *step 2*, you fetch the financial instrument with `segment` = `'NSE'` and `tradingsymbol` = `'HDFCBANK'` using the `get_instrument()` method of `broker_connection`. In *step 3*, you fetch the LTP of the instrument. (LTP will be explained in detail in the *Last traded price of a financial instrument* recipe of `Chapter 3`, *Analyzing Financial Data*.) In *step 4*, you place a BRACKET order using the `place_order()` method of the `broker_connection`. The descriptions of the parameters accepted by the `place_order()` method are as follows:

- `instrument`: The financial instrument for which the order must be placed. Should be an instance of the `Instrument` class. You pass `instrument` here.
- `order_transaction_type`: The order transaction type. Should be an enum of type `BrokerOrderTransactionTypeConstants`. You pass `BrokerOrderTransactionTypeConstants.SELL` here.

- `order_type`: The order type. Should be an enum of type `BrokerOrderTypeConstants`. You pass `BrokerOrderTypeConstants.BRACKET` here.
- `order_code`: The order code. Should be an enum of type `BrokerOrderCodeConstants`. You pass `BrokerOrderCodeConstants.INTRADAY` here.
- `order_variety`: The order variety. Should be an enum of type `BrokerOrderVarietyConstants`. You pass `BrokerOrderVarietyConstants.LIMIT` here.
- `quantity`: The number of shares to be traded for the given instrument. Should be a positive integer. You pass `1` here.

- `price`: The limit price at which the order should be placed. You pass `ltp+1` here, which means 1 unit price above the `ltp` value.
- `stoploss`: The price difference from the initial order price, at which the stoploss order should be placed. Should be a positive integer or float value. You pass `2` here.
- `target`: The price difference from the initial order price, at which the target order should be placed. Should be a positive integer or float value. You pass `2` here.

If the order placement is successful, the method returns an order ID which you can use at any point in time later on for querying the status of the order.

A detailed explanation of the different types of parameters will be covered in `Chapter 6`, *Placing Trading Orders on the Exchange*. This recipe is intended to give you an idea of how to place an `INTRADAY` order, one of the various types of possible orders.

Querying margins and funds

Before placing orders, it is important to ensure that you have enough margins and funds available in your broking account to place the orders successfully. A lack of sufficient funds would result in the rejection of any orders placed by the broker, which means the others would never get placed on the exchange. This recipe shows you how to find the available margins and funds in your broking account at any point in time.

Getting ready

Make sure the `broker_connection` object is available in your Python namespace. Refer to the first recipe of this chapter to learn how to set it up.

How to do it...

We execute the following steps to complete this recipe:

1. Display the equity margins:

    ```
    >>> equity_margins = broker_connection.get_margins('equity')
    >>> equity_margins
    ```

    We'll get the following output (your output may differ):

    ```
    {'enabled': True,
     'net': 1623.67,
     'available': {'adhoc_margin': 0,
      'cash': 1623.67,
      'opening_balance': 1623.67,
      'live_balance': 1623.67,
      'collateral': 0,
      'intraday_payin': 0},
     'utilised': {'debits': 0,
      'exposure': 0,
      'm2m_realised': 0,
      'm2m_unrealised': 0,
      'option_premium': 0,
      'payout': 0,
      'span': 0,
      'holding_sales': 0,
      'turnover': 0,
      'liquid_collateral': 0,
      'stock_collateral': 0}}
    ```

2. Display the equity funds:

    ```
    >>> equity_funds = broker_connection.get_funds('equity')
    >>> equity_funds
    ```

    We'll get the following output (your output may differ):

    ```
    1623.67
    ```

3. Display the commodity margins:

```
>>> commodity_margins = get_margins(commodity')
>>> commodity_margins
```

We'll get the following output (your output may differ):

```
{'enabled': True,
 'net': 16215.26,
 'available': {'adhoc_margin': 0,
  'cash': 16215.26,
  'opening_balance': 16215.26,
  'live_balance': 16215.26,
  'collateral': 0,
  'intraday_payin': 0},
 'utilised': {'debits': 0,
  'exposure': 0,
  'm2m_realised': 0,
  'm2m_unrealised': 0,
  'option_premium': 0,
  'payout': 0,
  'span': 0,
  'holding_sales': 0,
  'turnover': 0,
  'liquid_collateral': 0,
  'stock_collateral': 0}}
```

4. Display the commodity funds:

```
>>> commodity_funds = broker_connection.get_funds('commodity')
>>> commodity_funds
```

We'll get the following output (your output may differ):

```
0
```

How it works...

The `broker_connection` object provides methods for fetching the available margins and funds for your broking account:

- `get_margins()`
- `get_funds()`

The broker Zerodha keeps track of margins and funds separately for `equity` and `commodity` products. If you are using a different broker supported by `pyalgotrading`, it may or may not track the funds and margins separately for `equity` and `commodity`.

Step 1 shows how margins can be queried for the `equity` product using the `get_margins()` method of the `broker_connection` object, with `equity` as an argument. *Step 2* shows how funds can be queried for the `equity` product using the `get_funds()` method of the `broker_connection` object, with the `equity` string as an argument.

Steps 3 and *4* show how margins and funds can be queried for the `commodity` product in a similar way with the `commodity` string as an argument.

Calculating the brokerage charged

For every order completed successfully, the broker may charge a certain fee, which is usually a small fraction of the price at which the instrument was bought or sold. While the amount may seem small, it is important to keep track of the brokerage as it may end up eating a significant chunk of your profit at the end of the day.

The brokerage that's charged varies from broker to broker and also from segment to segment. For the purpose of this recipe, we will consider a brokerage of 0.01%.

How to do it...

We execute the following steps to complete this recipe:

1. Calculate the brokerage that's charged per trade:

```
>>> entry_price = 1245
>>> brokerage = (0.01 * 1245)/100
>>> print(f'Brokerage charged per trade: {brokerage:.4f}')
```

We'll get the following output:

```
Brokerage charged per trade: 0.1245
```

2. Calculate the total brokerage that's charged for 10 trades:

```
>>> total_brokerage = 10 * (0.01 * 1245) / 100
>>> print(f'Total Brokerage charged for 10 trades: \
            {total_brokerage:.4f}')
```

We'll get the following output:

```
Total Brokerage charged for 10 trades: 1.2450
```

How it works...

In *step 1*, we start with the price at which a trade was bought or sold, `entry_price`. For this recipe, we have used `1245`. Next, we calculate 0.01% of the price, which comes to `0.1245`. Then, we calculate the total brokerage for 10 such trades, which comes out as `10 * 0.1245 = 1.245`.

 For every order, the brokerage is charged twice. The first time is when the order has entered a position, while the second time is when it has exited the position. To get the exact details of the brokerage that's been charged for your trades, please refer to the list of charges offered by your broker.

Calculating the government taxes charged

For every order that's completed successfully, the government may charge a certain fee, which is a fraction of the price at which the instrument was bought or sold. While the amount may seem small, it is important to keep track of government taxes as they may end up eating a significant chunk of your profit at the end of the day.

The government charge depends on the location of the exchange, and varies from segment to segment. For the purpose of this recipe, we will consider government taxes at a rate of 0.1%.

How to do it...

We execute the following steps to complete this recipe:

1. Calculate the government taxes that are charged per trade:

```
>>> entry_price = 1245
>>> brokerage = (0.1 * 1245)/100
>>> print(f'Government taxes charged per trade: {brokerage:.4f}')
```

We'll get the following output:

```
Government taxes charged per trade: 1.2450
```

2. Calculate the total government taxes that are charged for 10 trades:

```
>>> total_brokerage = 10 * (0.1 * 1245) / 100
>>> print(f'Total Government taxes charged for 10 trades: \
            {total_brokerage:.4f}')
```

We'll get the following output:

```
Total Government taxes charged for 10 trades: 12.4500
```

How it works...

In *step 1*, we start with the price at which a trade was bought or sold, `entry_price`. For this recipe, we have used `1245`. Next, we calculate 0.1% of the price, which comes to `1.245`. Then, we calculate the total brokerage for 10 such trades, which comes out as `10 * 1.245 = 12.245`.

For every order, government taxes are charged twice. The first time is when the order has entered a position, while the second time is when it has exited the position. To get the exact details of the government taxes that are charged for your trades, please refer to the list of government taxes provided by your exchange.

Fetching Financial Data

3

Having financial data handy is essential for carrying out algorithmic trading. Financial data can be both static and dynamic in nature. Static financial data is data that doesn't change during trading hours. Static data consists of lists of financial instruments, the attributes of financial instruments, the circuit limits of financial instruments, and the recorded close price of the last trading day. Dynamic financial data is data that may change continuously during trading hours. Dynamic data consists of market depth, the last traded prices, the time and quantity of financial instruments, and the recorded high and low prices of the day. This chapter includes recipes on fetching various types of financial data.

The following is a list of the recipes in this chapter:

- Fetching the list of financial instruments
- Attributes of a financial instrument
- Expiry of financial instruments
- Circuit limits of a financial instrument
- The market depth of a financial instrument
- The total pending buy quantity of a financial instrument
- The total pending sell quantity of a financial instrument
- The total volume traded for the day of a financial instrument
- The last traded price of a financial instrument
- The last traded time of a financial instrument
- The last traded quantity of a financial instrument
- The recorded open price of the day of a financial instrument
- The recorded highest price of the day of a financial instrument
- The recorded lowest price of the day of a financial instrument
- The recorded close price of the last traded day of a financial instrument

Technical requirements

You will need the following to successfully execute the recipes in this chapter:

- Python 3.7+
- The `pyalgotrading` Python package (`$ pip install pyalgotrading`)

The latest Jupyter notebook for this chapter can be found on GitHub at `https://github.com/PacktPublishing/Python-Algorithmic-Trading-Cookbook`.

The following code will help you set up the broker connection with Zerodha, which will be used in all the recipes in this chapter. Please make sure you have followed these steps before trying out any recipes.

The first thing needed for setting up connectivity with the broker is getting the API keys. The broker would provide unique keys to each customer, typically as an `api-key` and `api-secret` key pair. These API keys are chargeable, usually on a monthly subscription basis. You need to get your copy of `api-key` and `api-secret` from the broker website before starting this. You can refer to *Appendix I* for more details.

Execute the following steps:

1. Import the necessary modules:

   ```
   >>> from pyalgotrading.broker.broker_connection_zerodha import
   BrokerConnectionZerodha
   ```

2. Get the `api_key` and `api_secret` keys from the broker. These are unique to you and will be used by the broker to identify your Demat account:

   ```
   >>> api_key = "<your-api-key>"
   >>> api_secret = "<your-api-secret>"
   >>> broker_connection = BrokerConnectionZerodha(api_key, \
                                                   api_secret)
   ```

   You will get the following output:

   ```
   Installing package kiteconnect via pip...
   Please login to this link to generate your request token:
   https://kite.trade/connect/login?api_key=<your-api-key>&v=3
   ```

If you are running this for the first time and `kiteconnect` is not installed, `pyalgotrading` will automatically install it for you. The final output of *step 2* will be a link. Click on the link and log in with your Zerodha credentials. If the authentication is successful, you will see a link in your browser's address bar similar to this:

```
https://127.0.0.1/?request_token=<alphanumeric-token>&action=lo
gin&status=success.
```

The following is an example:

```
https://127.0.0.1/?request_token=H06I6Ydv95y23D2Dp7NbigFjKweGwRP7&a
ction=login&status=success
```

3. Copy the alphanumeric-token and paste it in `request_token`:

```
>>> request_token = "<your-request-token>"
>>> broker_connection.set_access_token(request_token)
```

The `broker_connection` instance is now ready to perform API calls.

> The `pyalgotrading` package supports multiple brokers and provides a connection object class per broker, with the same methods. It abstracts broker APIs behind a unified interface, so you need not worry about the underlying broker API calls and you can use all the recipes in this chapter as is. Only the procedure to set up the broker connection will vary from broker to broker. You can refer to the pyalgotrading documentation for setting up the broker connection if you are not using Zerodha as your broker. For Zerodha users, the previous steps will suffice.

Fetching the list of financial instruments

Financial instruments, also known as **securities**, are assets that can be traded in an exchange. In an exchange, there can be tens of thousands of financial instruments. The list of financial instruments is static in nature, as it doesn't change during the live trading hours. Financial instruments may change from time to time, but never within the same day. Having this data handy is the first step for algorithmic trading. This recipe shows how to fetch the list of financial instruments.

Getting ready

Make sure the `broker_connection` object is available in your Python namespace. Refer to the *Technical requirements* section of this chapter to set it up.

How to do it…

Fetch and display all the available financial instruments using `broker_connection`:

```
>>> instruments = broker_connection.get_all_instruments()
>>> instruments
```

We get the following output (your output may differ):

	instrument_token	exchange_token	tradingsymbol	name	last_price	expiry	strike	tick_size	lot_size	instrument_type	segment	exchange
0	544844550	2128299	EURINR20AUG79.2500CE	EURINR	0.0	2020-08-27	79.25	0.0025	1	CE	BCD-OPT	BCD
1	544836918	2128277	EURINR20AUG79.2500PE	EURINR	0.0	2020-08-27	79.25	0.0025	1	PE	BCD-OPT	BCD
2	544788742	2128081	EURINR20AUG79.5000CE	EURINR	0.0	2020-08-27	79.50	0.0025	1	CE	BCD-OPT	BCD
3	544782342	2128056	EURINR20AUG79.5000PE	EURINR	0.0	2020-08-27	79.50	0.0025	1	PE	BCD-OPT	BCD
4	544739078	2127887	EURINR20AUG79.7500CE	EURINR	0.0	2020-08-27	79.75	0.0025	1	CE	BCD-OPT	BCD
...	...	...	...	...	...	...	...	...	...	...	...	...
65292	1945089	7598	ZODJRDMKJ-BE	ZODIAC JRD MKJ-	0.0		0.00	0.0500	1	EQ	NSE	NSE
65293	2916865	11394	ZOTA	ZOTA HEALTH CARE	0.0		0.00	0.0500	1	EQ	NSE	NSE
65294	7436801	29050	ZUARI	ZUARI AGRO CHEMICALS	0.0		0.00	0.0500	1	EQ	NSE	NSE
65295	979713	3827	ZUARIGLOB	ZUARI GLOBAL	0.0		0.00	0.0500	1	EQ	NSE	NSE
65296	4514561	17635	ZYDUSWELL	ZYDUS WELLNESS	0.0		0.00	0.0500	1	EQ	NSE	NSE

65297 rows × 12 columns

How it works…

This recipe fetches all the available financial instruments using the `get_all_instruments()` method of `broker_connection`, which returns a `pandas.DataFrame` object. This object is assigned to a new attribute, `instruments`, which is displayed in the output. This output may differ for you as new financial instruments are frequently added and existing ones expire regularly.

Attributes of a financial instrument

Financial instruments have various attributes that give more insight into the instrument, such as the trading symbol, exchange, segment, tick size, and so on. Some of these attributes are also needed while placing orders. This recipe lists and explains all the attributes supported by the broker. All the attributes are static, meaning they don't change during the live trading hours.

Getting ready

Make sure the `instruments` object is available in your Python namespace. Refer to the *Fetching the list of financial instruments* recipe of this chapter to set it up.

How to do it...

List all the attributes of a financial instrument provided by the broker:

```
>>> list(instruments.columns)
```

We get the following output:

```
['instrument_token',
 'exchange_token',
 trading-symbol,
 'name',
 'last_price',
 'expiry',
 'strike',
 'tick_size',
 'lot_size',
 'instrument_type',
 'segment',
 exchange]
```

How it works...

The *Fetching a list of financial instruments* recipe fetches all the instruments as a `pandas.DataFrame` object. Calling its `columns` attribute returns all the columns available. Each column is an attribute for every financial instrument. You can find more details at `https://kite.trade/docs/connect/v3/market-quotes/#csv-response-columns`.

Expiry of financial instruments

Financial instruments may or may not have a fixed expiry date. If they do, they are last available for trading on their expiry date. Typically, instruments from a cash segment do not expire, whereas derivative instruments (those from the futures and options segment) have a short validity period, and expire on the given date. This recipe shows both types of instruments and how their expiry date can be fetched. An expiry date is static data, meaning it doesn't change during the live market hours.

Getting ready

Make sure the `broker_connection` and `instruments` objects are available in your Python namespace. Refer to the *Technical requirements* section of this chapter to set up `broker_connection`. Refer to the first recipe of this chapter to set up `instruments`.

How to do it...

We execute the following steps for this recipe:

1. Get an instrument object using `broker_connection`:

   ```
   >>> instrument1 = broker_connection.get_instrument('NSE',
                                                       'TATASTEEL')
   ```

2. Check and print whether `instrument1` will expire:

   ```
   >>> print(f'Instrument expires: {instrument1.will_expire()}')
   ```

   We get the following output:

   ```
   Instrument expires: False
   ```

3. Get another instrument object using `broker_connection`:

   ```
   >>> instrument2 = broker_connection.get_instrument('NFO-FUT',
                                                       TATASTEEL20AUGFUT)
   ```

   You shouldn't get any output here. This implies you have successfully fetched the instrument.

Please note that if you get the following output for this step, even after typing it correctly, please try this step with the latest available NFO-FUT segment script by referring to the table from the output in the *Fetching the list of financial instruments* recipe of this chapter:

```
ERROR: Instrument not found. Either it is expired and hence not
available, or you have misspelled the "segment" and "tradingsymbol"
parameters.
```

This can happen because the instrument, with tradingsymbol TATASTEEL20AUGFUT, was available at the time of writing this book, but has since expired and so isn't available anymore.

4. Check and print whether instrument2 will expire:

```
>>> print(f'Instrument expires: {instrument2.will_expire()}')
```

We get the following output:

```
Instrument expires: True
```

5. Print the expiry date of instrument2:

```
>>> print(f'Expiry date: {instrument2.expiry}')
```

We get the following output (your output may differ):

```
Expiry date: 2020-08-27
```

How it works...

Step 1 uses the get_instrument() method of the BrokerConnectionZerodha class to fetch an instrument and assign it to a new attribute, instrument1. This object is an instance of the Instrument class. The two parameters needed to call get_instrument are the exchange (NSE) and the trading symbol (TATASTEEL). In *step 2*, we check whether the instrument will expire using the will_expire() method. The output of this step is False. We repeat the same procedure in *steps 3* and *4*, this time for a different instrument, assigned to a new attribute, instrument2, which gives an output of True for the will_expire() method. This is shown in the output of *step 4*. Finally, in *step 5*, we fetch the expiry date of instrument2 using the expiry attribute.

Circuit limits of a financial instrument

Each financial instrument has a well-defined price band. The instrument price is expected to be within this price band for the day. During the market hours, if the instrument price breaches the band on the upper or lower side, trading may be halted for the instrument by the exchange for a certain time or the entire day. This is done to prevent the sudden rise or fall in an instrument's price within a single day. The upper edge of the price band is known as the **upper circuit limit** and the lower edge of the price band is known as the **lower circuit limit**. This data is static, meaning it doesn't change during the day. However, it can significantly change from one day to another. This recipe helps find the circuit limits for a financial instrument.

Getting ready

Make sure the `broker_connection` and `instrument1` objects are available in your Python namespace. Refer to the *Technical requirements* section of this chapter to set up `broker_connection`. Refer to the *Attributes of a financial instrument* recipe of this chapter to set up `instrument1`.

How to do it...

Fetch and print the lower and upper circuit limits of `instrument1`:

```
>>> lower_circuit_limit, upper_circuit_limit = \
                    broker_connection.get_circuit_limits(instrument1)
>>> print(f'Lower circuit limit: {lower_circuit_limit}')
>>> print(f'Upper circuit limit: {upper_circuit_limit}')
```

We get the following output (your output may differ):

```
Lower circuit limit: 315.9
Upper circuit limit: 386
```

How it works...

The `get_circuit_limits()` method of the `BrokerConnectionZerodha` class fetches the lower and upper circuit limits as a tuple for the given financial instrument. This method takes an object of the `Instrument` type as a parameter. We use `instrument1` as the parameter here.

The market depth of a financial instrument

The market depth of a financial instrument is a chronological list of data on buyers and sellers in the market. The buyers list is a list of prices and their respective quantities at which the buyers are willing to buy the instrument for. Similarly, the sellers list is a list of prices and their respective quantities at which the sellers are willing to sell the instrument for. If you are new to the concept of **market depth**, the explanation in the *How it works...* section of this recipe will give you more clarity.

Market depth helps in predicting where the price of an instrument is heading. It also helps to understand whether an order with a large quantity can change the price significantly or not. Market depth is dynamic in nature, meaning it changes constantly during the live trading hours. This recipe helps find out the market depth of a financial instrument in real time.

Getting ready

Make sure the `broker_connection` and `instrument1` objects are available in your Python namespace. Refer to the *Technical requirements* section of this chapter to set up `broker_connection`. Refer to the *Attributes of a financial instrument* recipe of this chapter to set up `instrument1`.

How to do it...

Fetch and print the buy market depth and sell market depth of `instrument1`:

```
>>> buy_market_depth, sell_market_depth = \
                    broker_connection.get_market_depth(instrument1)
>>> print(f'Buy Market Depth:\n{buy_market_depth}')
>>> print(f'Sell Market Depth:\n{sell_market_depth}')
```

We get the following output (your output may differ):

```
Buy Market Depth:
   orders  price quantity
0       1 350.05        1
1      16 350.00    43294
2       5 349.95     1250
3       8 349.90     3134
4       5 349.85     1078

Sell Market Depth:
```

```
     orders  price quantity
0         1 350.10       25
1         7 350.15     1367
2        13 350.20     4654
3        13 350.25     2977
4        21 350.30     5798
```

How it works...

The `get_market_depth()` method of the `BrokerConnectionZerodha` class fetches the market depth for the given financial instrument. This method takes an object of the `Instrument` type as a parameter. We use `instrument1` as the parameter here. The market depths are shown in separate tables for the **buy side** and the **sell side**.

The **buy market depth** is a table of five entries or bids, in descending order of price. Each entry indicates an available buyer in the market at that point in time, with the price being offered and the quantity available at that price.

The **sell market depth** is a table of five entries or bids, in ascending order of price. Each entry indicates an existing seller in the market at that point in time, with the price being offered and the quantity available at that price.

When a buyer and seller match, the order is executed at the exchange and the entries are removed from the buy- and sell-side tables.

The total pending buy quantity of a financial instrument

The total pending buy quantity for a financial instrument is the sum total of the quantity of all the pending buy orders available at an instant. This data is dynamic in nature and may change at any moment during the live trading hours.

Getting ready

Make sure the `broker_connection` and `instrument1` objects are available in your Python namespace. Refer to the *Technical requirements* section of this chapter to set up `broker_connection`. Refer to the *Attributes of a financial instrument* recipe of this chapter to set up `instrument1`.

How to do it...

Fetch and print the total pending buy quantity of `instrument1`:

```
>>> total_pending_buy_quantity = \
        broker_connection.get_total_pending_buy_quantity(instrument1)
>>> print(f'Total pending BUY quantity: {total_pending_buy_quantity}')
```

We get the following output (your output may differ):

```
Total pending BUY quantity: 1319590
```

How it works...

The `get_total_pending_buy_quantity()` method of the `BrokerConnectionZerodha` class fetches the total buy quantity for the given financial instrument at any given moment. This method takes an object of the `Instrument` type as a parameter. We use `instrument1` as the parameter here.

The total pending sell quantity of a financial instrument

The total pending sell quantity for a financial instrument is the sum total of the quantity of all pending sell orders available at an instant. This data is dynamic in nature and may change at any moment during the live trading hours.

Getting ready

Make sure the `broker_connection` and `instrument1` objects are available in your Python namespace. Refer to the *Technical requirements* section of this chapter to set up `broker_connection`. Refer to the *Attributes of a financial instrument* recipe of this chapter to set up `instrument1`.

How to do it...

Fetch and print the total pending sell quantity of `instrument1`:

```
>>> total_pending_sell_quantity = \
        broker_connection.get_total_pending_sell_quantity(instrument1)
>>> print(f'Total pending SELL quantity: {total_pending_sell_quantity}')
```

We get the following output (your output may differ):

```
Total pending SELL quantity: 968602
```

How it works...

The `get_total_pending_sell_quantity()` method of the `BrokerConnectionZerodha` class fetches the total sell quantity of the given financial instrument at any given moment. This method takes an object of the `Instrument` type as a parameter. We use `instrument1` as the parameter here.

The total volume traded for the day of a financial instrument

The total volume traded for a financial instrument is the sum total of all quantities that were traded (bought and sold, but counted once) in the day. For example, if *trader A* buys 10 quantities of stock *X* from *trader B*, while *trader C* sells 20 quantities of the same stock *X* to *trader D*, the total volume traded for *X* would be 10 + 20 = 30. It won't be 10 + 10 + 20 + 20 = 60 because the contribution of the trade to the total volume is considered only once. This data is dynamic in nature and may increase at any moment during the live trading hours.

Getting ready

Make sure the `broker_connection` and `instrument1` objects are available in your Python namespace. Refer to the *Technical requirements* section of this chapter to set up `broker_connection`. Refer to the *Attributes of a financial instruments* recipe of this chapter to set up `instrument1`.

How to do it...

Fetch and print the total traded volume for the day of an instrument:

```
>>> total_volume_day = broker_connection.get_total_volume_day(instrument1)
>>> print(f'Total Volume for the day so far: {total_volume_day}')
```

We get the following output (your output may differ):

```
Total Volume for the day so far: 24416975
```

How it works...

The `get_total_volume_day()` method of the `BrokerConnectionZerodha` class fetches the total traded volume of the given financial instrument at any given moment since the beginning of the day. This method takes an object of the `Instrument` type as a parameter. We use `instrument1` as the parameter here.

The last traded price of a financial instrument

The **last traded price** (**LTP**) of a financial instrument is the latest price at which an order was executed for that instrument. It is essentially an indicator of the current price at which the instrument can be bought or sold (assuming the liquidity is good). As the description suggests, this data is dynamic in nature and it may change continuously during the live trading hours. This recipe shows how to fetch the LTP of a financial instrument.

Getting ready

Make sure the `broker_connection` and `instrument1` objects are available in your Python namespace. Refer to the *Technical requirements* section of this chapter to set up `broker_connection`. Refer to the *Attributes of a financial instrument* recipe of this chapter to set up `instrument1`.

How to do it...

Fetch and print the LTP of `instrument1`:

```
>>> ltp = broker_connection.get_ltp(instrument1)
>>> print(f'Last traded price: {ltp}')
```

We get the following output (your output may differ):

```
Last traded price: 350.95
```

How it works...

The `get_ltp()` method of the `BrokerConnectionZerodha` class fetches the LTP of the given financial instrument at any given moment. This method takes an object of the `Instrument` type as a parameter. We use `instrument1` as the parameter here. The fetched data is of the `float` type.

The last traded time of a financial instrument

The **last traded time** (**LTT**) of a financial instrument is the latest time at which an order was executed for that instrument. This data is dynamic in nature as it may change continuously during the live trading hours. This recipe helps fetch the LTT of a financial instrument.

Getting ready

Make sure the `broker_connection` and `instrument1` objects are available in your Python namespace. Refer to the *Technical requirements* section of this chapter to set up `broker_connection`. Refer to the *Attributes of a financial instrument* recipe of this chapter to set up `instrument1`.

How to do it...

Fetch and print the LTT of `instrument1`:

```
>>> ltt = broker_connection.get_ltt(instrument1)
>>> print(f'Last traded time: {ltt}')
```

We get the following output (your output may differ):

```
Last traded time: 2020-07-17 14:42:54
```

How it works...

The `get_ltt()` method of the `BrokerConnectionZerodha` class fetches the LTT of the given financial instrument at any given moment. This method takes an object of the `Instrument` type as a parameter. We use `instrument1` as the parameter here. The fetched data is an instance of the `datetime.datetime` class.

The last traded quantity of a financial instrument

The **last traded quantity (LTQ)** of a financial instrument is the quantity that was traded the last time an order was executed for that instrument. This data is dynamic in nature as it may change continuously during the live trading hours. This recipe demonstrates how to fetch the LTQ of a financial instrument.

Getting ready

Make sure the `broker_connection` and `instrument1` objects are available in your Python namespace. Refer to the *Technical requirements* section of this chapter to set up `broker_connection`. Refer to the *Attributes of a financial instrument* recipe of this chapter to set up `instrument1`.

How to do it...

Fetch and print the LTQ of `instrument1`:

```
>>> ltq = broker_connection.get_ltq(instrument1)
>>> print(f'Last traded quantity: {ltq}')
```

We get the following output (your output may differ):

```
Last traded quantity: 19
```

How it works...

The `get_ltq()` method of the `BrokerConnectionZerodha` class fetches the LTQ of the given financial instrument at any given moment. This method takes an object of the `Instrument` type as a parameter. We use `instrument1` as the parameter here. The fetched data is of the `int` type.

The recorded open price of the day of a financial instrument

Often, trading strategies use the current day opening price of a financial instrument as one of the first qualifying conditions before making decisions to place new trades. Comparing the current day's opening price with the previous day's close price may give a hint as to whether the market price is bound to rise or fall for the current day for an instrument. If the open price is significantly higher than the previous day's close price, the price may continue to rise for the day. Similarly, if the open price is significantly lower than the previous day's close price, the price may continue to fall for the day. The recorded open price data is static in nature, meaning it does not change during the live trading hours. This recipe shows how to fetch the current day's opening price of a financial instrument.

Getting ready

Make sure the `broker_connection` and `instrument1` objects are available in your Python namespace. Refer to the *Technical requirements* section of this chapter to set up `broker_connection`. Refer to the *Attributes of a financial instrument* recipe of this chapter to set up `instrument1`.

How to do it...

Fetch and print the open price of the day of `instrument1`:

```
>>> open_price_day = broker_connection.get_open_price_day(instrument1)
>>> print(f'Open price today: {open_price_day}')
```

We get the following output (your output may differ):

```
Open price today: 346
```

How it works...

The `get_open_price_day()` method of the `BrokerConnectionZerodha` class fetches the open price of the day for the given financial instrument. This method takes an object of the `Instrument` type as a parameter. We use `instrument1` as the parameter here. The fetched data is of the `float` type.

The recorded highest price of the day of a financial instrument

Often, trading strategies use the current day's highest price of a financial instrument as one of the qualifying conditions before making decisions to place new trades. This data is dynamic in nature as it may change continuously during the live trading hours. This recipe shows how to fetch the current day's highest recorded price of a financial instrument.

Getting ready

Make sure the `broker_connection` and `instrument1` objects are available in your Python namespace. Refer to the *Technical requirements* section of this chapter to set up `broker_connection`. Refer to the *Attributes of a financial instrument* recipe of this chapter to set up `instrument1`.

How to do it...

Fetch and print the recorded highest price of the day of `instrument1`:

```
>>> high_price_day = broker_connection.get_high_price_day(instrument1)
>>> print(f'Highest price today: {high_price_day}')
```

We get the following output. Your output may differ:

```
Highest price today: 356.8
```

How it works...

The `get_high_price_day()` method of the `BrokerConnectionZerodha` class fetches the highest recorded price of the day for the given financial instrument. This method takes an object of the `Instrument` type as a parameter. We use `instrument1` as the parameter here. The fetched data is of the `float` type.

The recorded lowest price of the day of a financial instrument

Often, trading strategies use the current day's lowest price of a financial instrument as one of the qualifying conditions before making decisions to place new trades. This data is dynamic in nature as it may change continuously during the live trading hours. This recipe demonstrates how to fetch the current day's lowest recorded price of a financial instrument.

Getting ready

Make sure the `broker_connection` and `instrument1` objects are available in your Python namespace. Refer to the *Technical requirements* section of this chapter to set up `broker_connection`. Refer to the *Attributes of a financial instrument* recipe of this chapter to set up `instrument1`.

How to do it...

Fetch and print the recorded lowest price of the day of `instrument1`:

```
>>> low_price_day = broker_connection.get_low_price_day(instrument1)
>>> print(f'Lowest price today: {low_price_day}')
```

We get the following output (your output may differ):

```
Lowest price today: 345.15
```

How it works...

The `get_low_price_day()` method of the `BrokerConnectionZerodha` class fetches the lowest recorded price of the day for the given financial instrument. This method takes an object of the `Instrument` type as a parameter. We use `instrument1` as the parameter here. The fetched data is of the `float` type.

The recorded close price of the last traded day of a financial instrument

Often, trading strategies use the previous day's closing price of a financial instrument as one of the first qualifying conditions before making decisions to place trades. Comparing the current day's opening price with the previous day's close price may give a hint as to whether the market price is bound to rise or fall for the current day for an instrument. If the open price is significantly higher than the previous day's close price, the price may continue to rise for the day. Similarly, if the open price is significantly lower than the previous day's close price, the price may continue to fall for the day. The recorded close price data is static in nature, meaning it does not change during the live trading hours. This recipe shows how to fetch the previous day's close price of a financial instrument.

Getting ready

Make sure the `broker_connection` and `instrument1` objects are available in your Python namespace. Refer to the *Technical requirements* section of this chapter to set up `broker_connection`. Refer to the *Attributes of a financial instrument* recipe of this chapter to set up `instrument1`.

How to do it...

Fetch and print the recorded close price of the last trading day of `instrument1`:

```
>>> close_price_last_day = \
            broker_connection.get_close_price_last_day(instrument1)
>>> print(f'Close price of last trading day: {close_price_last_day}')
```

We get the following output (your output may differ):

```
Close price of last trading day: 341.65
```

How it works...

The `get_close_price_day()` method of the `BrokerConnectionZerodha` class fetches the close price of the previous trading day for the given financial instrument. This method takes an object of the `Instrument` type as a parameter. We use `instrument1` as the parameter here. The fetched data is of the `float` type.

4
Computing Candlesticks and Historical Data

The historical data of a financial instrument is data about all the past prices at which a financial instrument was brought or sold. An algorithmic trading strategy is always vpot_candlestickirtually executed on historical data to evaluate its past performance before it's deployed with real money. This process is called **backtesting**. Historical data is quintessential for backtesting (covered in detail in Chapter 8, *Backtesting Strategies*). Also, historical data is needed for computing technical indicators (covered in detail in Chapter 5, *Computing and Plotting Technical Indicators*), which help in making buy-or-sell decisions in real-time. Candlestick patterns are widely used tools for stock analysis. Various types of candlestick patterns are commonly used by analysts. This chapter provides recipes that show you how to fetch historical data using broker APIs, how to fetch and compute multiple candlestick patterns – Japanese (**open-high-low-close (OHLC)**), Line Break, Renko, and Heikin-Ashi – and how to fetch historical data using a third-party tool.

In this chapter, we will cover the following recipes:

- Fetching historical data using the broker API
- Fetching historical data with the Japanese (OHLC) candlestick pattern
- Fetching the Japanese candlestick pattern with variations in candle intervals
- Fetching historical data with the Line Break candlestick pattern
- Fetching historical data with the Renko candlestick pattern
- Fetching historical data with the Heikin-Ashi candlestick pattern
- Fetching historical data using Quandl

Let's get started!

Technical requirements

You will need the following to successfully execute the recipes in this chapter:

- Python 3.7+
- Python packages:
  - pyalgotrading ($ pip install pyalgotrading)
  - quandl ($pip install quandl) this is optional and only needed for the last recipe

The latest Jupyter Notebook for this chapter can be found on GitHub at https://github.com/PacktPublishing/Python-Algorithmic-Trading-Cookbook/tree/master/Chapter04.

The following code will help you set up the broker connection with Zerodha, which will be used by all the recipes in this chapter. Please make sure you have followed these steps before trying out any of the recipes provided.

The first thing you need to do to set connectivity with the broker is to gather the required API keys. The broker provides unique keys to each customer, typically as api-key and api-secret key pairs. These API keys are chargeable, usually on a monthly subscription basis. You need to get your copies of api-key and api-secret from the broker website before you start this chapter. You can refer to *Appendix I* for more details.

Execute the following steps:

1. Import the necessary modules:

```
>>> from pyalgotrading.broker.broker_connection_zerodha import
BrokerConnectionZerodha
```

2. Get the api_key and api_secret keys from the broker. These are unique to you and will be used by the broker to identify your Demat account:

```
>>> api_key = "<your-api-key>"
>>> api_secret = "<your-api-secret>"
>>> broker_connection = BrokerConnectionZerodha(api_key,
                                                api_secret)
```

   You will get the following URL:

```
Installing package kiteconnect via pip...
Please login to this link to generate your request token:
https://kite.trade/connect/login?api_key=<your-api-key>&v=3
```

If you are running this for the first time and `kiteconnect` is not installed, `pyalgotrading` will automatically install it for you. The final output of *step 2* will be a link. Click on the link and log in with your Zerodha credentials. If the authentication is successful, you will see a link in your browser's address bar similar
to `https://127.0.0.1/?request_token=&action=login&status=success`.

For example:

```
https://127.0.0.1/?request_token=H06I6Ydv95y23D2Dp7NbigFjKweGwRP7&a
ction=login&status=success
```

3. Copy the alphanumeric token and paste it into `request_token`:

```
>>> request_token = "<your-request-token>"
>>> broker_connection.set_access_token(request_token)
```

The `broker_connection` instance is now ready for performing API calls.

The `pyalgotrading` package supports multiple brokers and provides a connection object class per broker, with the same methods. It abstracts broker APIs behind a unified interface so that users don't need to worry about the underlying broker API calls and use all the recipes in this chapter as-is.

Only the procedure of setting up the broker connection will vary from broker to broker. You can refer to the pyalgotrading documentation to learn how to set up the broker connection if you are not using Zerodha as your broker. For Zerodha users, the aforementioned steps will suffice.

Fetching historical data using the broker API

The historical data of a financial instrument is time-series data for the timestamps in the past. It can be fetched using the Broker API for a given duration. This recipe demonstrates how to set up a broker connection and how to fetch historical data for a financial instrument for the duration of a single day.

Getting ready

Make sure the `broker_connection` object is available in your Python namespace. Refer to the *Technical requirements* section of this chapter to learn how to set it up.

How to do it...

Execute the following steps to complete this recipe:

1. Fetch the historical data for an instrument:

```
>>> instrument = broker_connection.get_instrument('NSE',
                                                  'TATASTEEL')
>>> historical_data = broker_connection.get_historical_data(
                      instrument=instrument,
                      candle_interval='minute',
                      start_date='2020-01-01',
                      end_date='2020-01-01')
>>> historical_data
```

You will get the following output:

	timestamp	open	high	low	close	volume
0	2020-01-01 09:15:00+05:30	473.00	474.45	472.75	473.90	97244
1	2020-01-01 09:16:00+05:30	473.90	474.25	472.85	473.15	104766
2	2020-01-01 09:17:00+05:30	473.20	474.05	473.20	473.50	37920
3	2020-01-01 09:18:00+05:30	473.55	473.80	473.20	473.80	51424
4	2020-01-01 09:19:00+05:30	473.80	474.40	473.70	474.30	45331
...	...	...	...	...	...	...
370	2020-01-01 15:25:00+05:30	467.80	468.00	467.60	467.85	25907
371	2020-01-01 15:26:00+05:30	467.85	468.00	467.70	467.80	19267
372	2020-01-01 15:27:00+05:30	467.80	467.95	467.55	467.70	30234
373	2020-01-01 15:28:00+05:30	467.70	467.80	467.65	467.65	32464
374	2020-01-01 15:29:00+05:30	467.65	467.75	467.45	467.55	37885

375 rows × 6 columns

2. Print the available columns of the `historical_data` DataFrame:

```
>>> historical_data.columns
```

You will get the following output:

```
>>> Index(['timestamp', 'open', 'high', 'low', 'close', 'volume'],
         dtype='object')
```

How it works...

In *step 1*, you use the `get_instrument()` method of `broker_connection` to fetch an instrument and assign it to a new attribute, `instrument`. This object is an instance of the `Instrument` class. The two parameters needed to call `get_instrument()` are the exchange (`'NSE'`) and the trading symbol (`'TATASTEEL'`). Next, you fetch the historical data for `instrument` using the `get_historical_data()` method. This method takes four arguments, which are described as follows:

- `instrument`: The financial instrument for which the historical data must be placed. Should be an instance of the `Instrument` class. You pass `instrument` here.
- `candle_interval`: A valid string that denotes the duration of each candlestick in the historical data. You pass `minute` here. (Possible values can be `minute`, `3minute`, `5minute`, `10minute`, `30minute`, `60minute`, and `day`.)
- `start_date`: The date from which the historical data must be fetched. Should be a string in the `YYYY-MM-DD` format. You pass `2020-01-01` here.
- `end_date`: The date until which the historical data must be fetched, inclusive of this date. Should be a string in the `YYYY-MM-DD` format. You pass `2020-01-01` here.

In *step 2*, you fetch and print the available columns of `historical_data`. You get the columns as `timestamp`, `open`, `high`, `low`, `close`, and `volume`.

> More information on candlesticks will be covered in the next recipe, *Fetching historical data using the Japanese (OHLC) candlestick pattern*, and the third recipe in this chapter, *Fetching the Japanese candlestick pattern with variations in candle intervals*.

Fetching historical data using the Japanese (OHLC) candlestick pattern

The historical data of a financial instrument is an array of candlesticks. Each entry in the historical data is a single candlestick. There are various types of candlestick patterns.

This recipe demonstrates the most commonly used candlestick pattern – the Japanese candlestick pattern. It is a type of candlestick pattern where each candlestick holds a duration and indicates all the prices the instrument would have taken on during that duration. This data is represented using four parameters – Open, High, Low, and Close. These can be described as follows:

- **Open**: The price of the financial instrument at the beginning of the candle's duration
- **High**: The highest recorded price of the financial instrument during the entire duration of the candle
- **Low**: The lowest recorded price of the financial instrument during the entire duration of the candle
- **Close**: The price of the financial instrument at the end of the candle's duration

The Japanese candlestick pattern is also known as the **OHLC candlestick pattern** based on these parameters. All the timestamps in a Japanese candlestick pattern are equally spaced (within market hours). For example, the timestamps on a trading day would look like 9:15 a.m., 9:16 a.m., 9:17 a.m., 9:18 a.m., and so on for a 1-minute candle interval, where each timestamp is equally spaced at intervals of 1 minute.

Getting ready

Make sure the `broker_connection` and `historical_data` objects are available in your Python namespace. Refer to the *Technical requirements* section of this chapter to set up `broker_connection`. Refer to the previous recipe to set up `historical_data`.

How to do it...

We execute the following steps to for this recipe:

1. Import the necessary modules:

```
>>> from pyalgotrading.utils.func import plot_candlestick_chart,
PlotType
```

2. Create a green candle from one of the rows of `historical_data`:

```
>>> candle_green = historical_data.iloc[:1,:]
# Only 1st ROW of historical data
>>> plot_candlestick_chart(candle_green,
                           PlotType.JAPANESE,
                           "A 'Green' Japanese Candle")
```

You will get the following output:

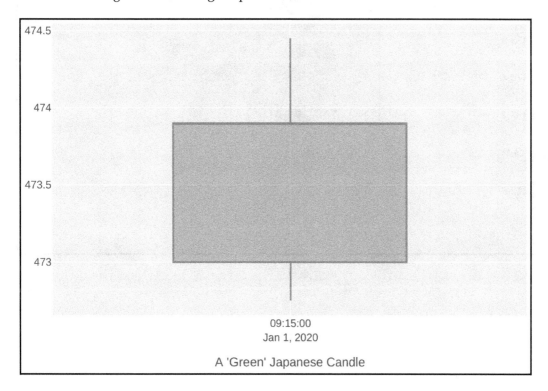

3. Create a red candle from one of the rows of `historical_data`:

```
# A 'Red' Japanese Candle
>>> candle_red = historical_data.iloc[1:2,:]
# Only 2nd ROW of historical data
>>> plot_candlestick_chart(candle_red,
                            PlotType.OHLC,
                            "A 'Red' Japanese Candle")
```

This will give you the following output:

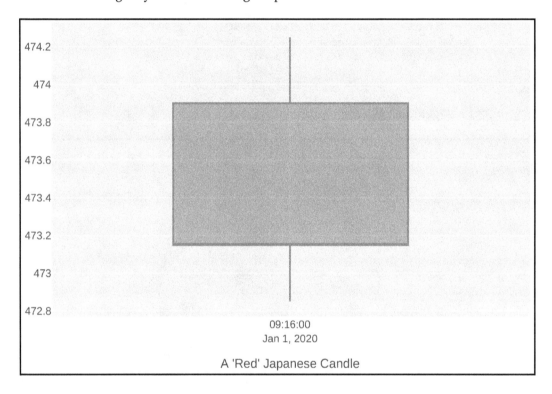

4. Plot a chart for the historical data of an instrument:

```
>>> plot_candlestick_chart(historical_data,
                           PlotType.OHLC,
                           'Historical Data | '
                           'Japanese Candlesticks Pattern | '
                           'NSE:TATASTEEL | 1st Jan, 2020 | '
                           'Candle Interval: 1 Minute')
```

This will give you the following output:

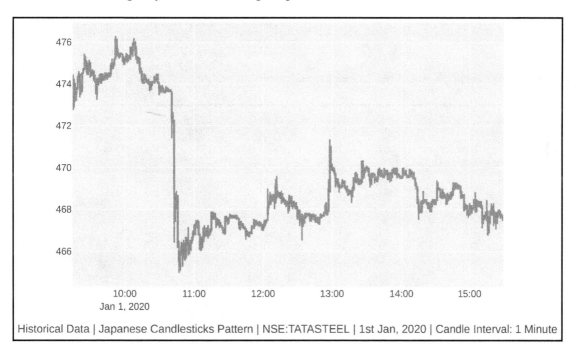

Historical Data | Japanese Candlesticks Pattern | NSE:TATASTEEL | 1st Jan, 2020 | Candle Interval: 1 Minute

5. Plot a chart for the historical data of another instrument:

```
>>> instrument2 = broker_connection.get_instrument('NSE', 'INFY')
>>> historical_data = \
        broker_connection.get_historical_data(instrument2,
                                               'minute',
                                               '2020-01-01',
                                               '2020-01-01')
>>> plot_candlestick_chart(historical_data,
                           PlotType.OHLC,
                           'Historical Data | '
                           'Japanese Candlesticks Pattern | '
                           'NSE:INFY | 1st Jan, 2020 | '
                           'Candle Interval: 1 Minute')
```

This will give you the following output:

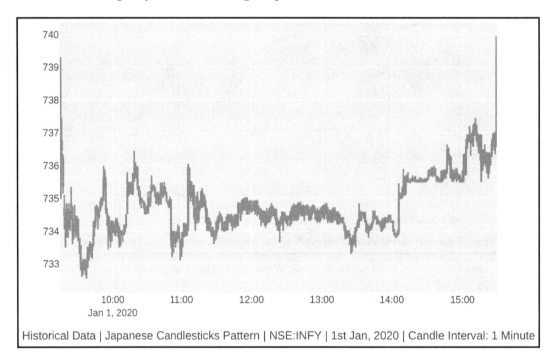

Historical Data | Japanese Candlesticks Pattern | NSE:INFY | 1st Jan, 2020 | Candle Interval: 1 Minute

6. Plot a chart for the historical data of yet another instrument:

```
>>> instrument3 = broker_connection.get_instrument('NSE',
                                                  'ICICIBANK')
>>> historical_data =
            broker_connection.get_historical_data(instrument3,
                                                'minute',
                                                '2020-01-01',
                                                '2020-01-01')
>>> plot_candlestick_chart(historical_data, PlotType.OHLC,
                        'Historical Data | '
                        'Japanese Candlesticks Pattern | '
                        'NSE:ICICIBANK | 1st Jan, 2020 | '
                        'Candle Size: 1 Minute')
```

This will give you the following output:

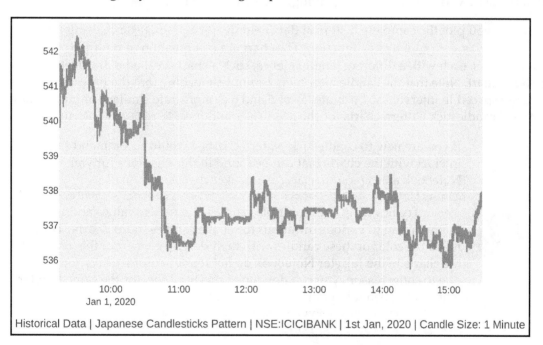

How it works...

In *step 1*, you import `plot_candlestick_chart`, a quick utility function for plotting candlestick pattern charts, and `PlotType`, an enum for various types of candlestick patterns. The next two steps introduce two types of candlesticks, or simply **candles** – a green candle and a red candle. As we mentioned earlier, each entry in historical data is a candle. These two steps selectively extract a green and red candle from the data. (Please note that the indices that are passed to `historical_data.iloc` will be different if you choose a different duration for `historical_data`, as in the *Fetching historical data using the broker API* recipe). A Japanese candle is green in color if its **close** price is above its **open** price. A green candle is also called a **bullish** candle as it is indicative that the price was bullish, meaning rising, during that duration. A Japanese candle is red in color if its **close** price is below its **open** price. A red candle is also called a **bearish** candle as it is indicative that the price was bearish, meaning falling, during that duration.

In *step 4*, you plot the complete historical data held by `historical_data` using the `plot_candlestick_chart()` function. The chart is a combination of multiple candlesticks, each with a different length. Hence, such a chart is called a **candlestick pattern chart**. Note that the candle interval is 1 minute, meaning that the timestamps are equally spaced in intervals of 1 minute. *Steps 5* and *6* demonstrate similar 1-minute candle interval candlestick pattern charts for the `NSE:INFY` and `NSE:ICICIBANK` instruments.

 If you are new to candlestick pattern charts, I would recommend that you interact with the charts that can be found in this chapter's Jupyter Notebook at `https://github.com/PacktPublishing/Python-Algorithmic-Trading-Cookbook/blob/master/Chapter04/CHAPTER%204.ipynb`. Try hovering over multiple candles to see their values and zoom in/out or pan to various durations to see the candles more clearly. Try to relate the color of these candles with their descriptions from this recipe. If the charts in the Jupyter Notebook do not render automatically for you due to some reason, you can download this html file, for the same Jupyter Notebook, open it in your browser and interact with it: `https://github.com/PacktPublishing/Python-Algorithmic-Trading-Cookbook/blob/master/Chapter04/CHAPTER%204.ipynb`.

Fetching the Japanese candlestick pattern with variations in candle intervals

The historical data of a financial instrument can be analyzed in the form of Japanese candlesticks pattern with varying candle intervals. Brokers typically support candle intervals of 1 minute, 3 minutes, 5 minutes, 10 minutes, 15 minutes, 30 minutes, 1 hour, 1 day, and so on. A shorter candle interval hints at a localized price movement trend, while a larger candle interval indicates an overall price movement trend. Depending on the algorithmic trading strategy, you may need a shorter candle interval or a larger one. A candle interval of 1 minute is often the smallest available candle interval. This recipe demonstrates the historical data of a financial instrument for a duration of a day in various candle intervals.

Getting ready

Make sure the `broker_connection` object is available in your Python namespace. Refer to the *Technical requirements* section of this chapter to learn how to set up `broker_connection`.

How to do it...

We execute the following steps for this recipe:

1. Import the necessary modules:

   ```
   >>> from pyalgotrading.utils.func import plot_candlestick_chart,
   PlotType
   ```

2. Fetch an instrument:

   ```
   >>> instrument = broker_connection.get_instrument('NSE',
                                                      'TATASTEEL')
   ```

3. Plot a chart for the historical data of the instrument with a 1-minute candle interval:

   ```
   >>> historical_data_1minute = \
           broker_connection.get_historical_data(instrument,
                                                  'minute',
                                                  '2020-01-01',
                                                  '2020-01-01')
   ```

```
>>> plot_candlestick_chart(historical_data_1minute,
                           PlotType.OHLC,
                           'Historical Data | '
                           'Japanese Candlesticks Pattern | '
                           'NSE:TATASTEEL | '
                           '1st Jan, 2020 | '
                           'Candle Interval: 1 Minute')
```

You will get the following output:

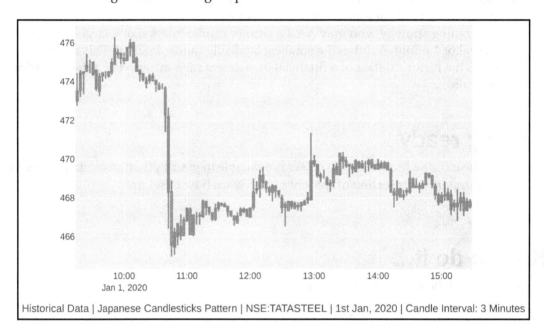

Historical Data | Japanese Candlesticks Pattern | NSE:TATASTEEL | 1st Jan, 2020 | Candle Interval: 3 Minutes

4. Plot a chart for the historical data of the instrument with a 3-minute candle interval:

```
>>> historical_data_3minutes = \
        broker_connection.get_historical_data(instrument,
                                              '3minute',
                                              '2020-01-01',
                                              '2020-01-01')
>>> plot_candlestick_chart(historical_data_3minutes,
                           PlotType.OHLC,
                           'Historical Data | '
                           'Japanese Candlesticks Pattern | '
                           'NSE:TATASTEEL | '
                           '1st Jan, 2020 | '
                           'Candle Interval: 3 Minutes')
```

You will get the following output:

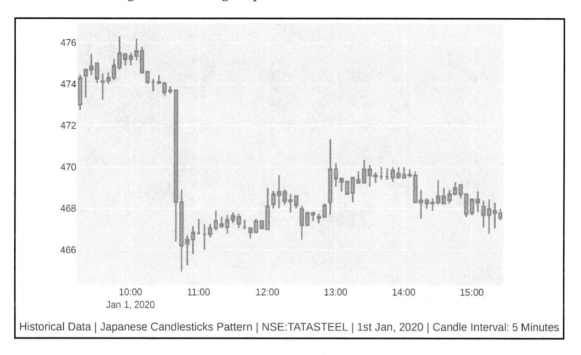

Historical Data | Japanese Candlesticks Pattern | NSE:TATASTEEL | 1st Jan, 2020 | Candle Interval: 5 Minutes

5. Plot a chart for the historical data of the instrument with a 5-minute candle interval:

```
>>> historical_data_5minutes = \
          broker_connection.get_historical_data(instrument,
                                          '5minute',
                                          '2020-01-01',
                                          '2020-01-01')
>>> plot_candlestick_chart(historical_data_5minutes,
                      PlotType.OHLC,
                      'Historical Data | '
                      'Japanese Candlesticks Pattern | '
                      'NSE:TATASTEEL | '
                      '1st Jan, 2020 | '
                      'Candle Interval: 5 Minutes')
```

You will get the following output:

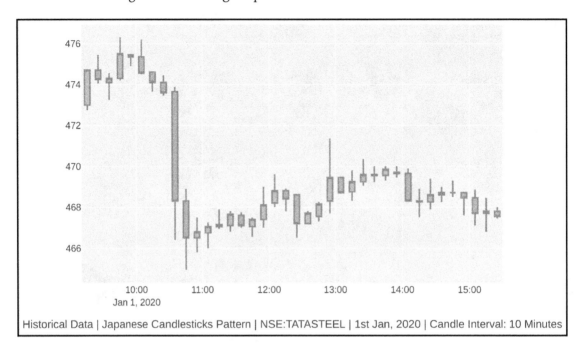

Historical Data | Japanese Candlesticks Pattern | NSE:TATASTEEL | 1st Jan, 2020 | Candle Interval: 10 Minutes

6. Plot a chart for the historical data of the instrument with a 10-minute candle interval:

```
>>> historical_data_10minutes = \
        broker_connection.get_historical_data(instrument,
                                              '10minute',
                                              '2020-01-01',
                                              '2020-01-01')
>>> plot_candlestick_chart(historical_data_10minutes,
                PlotType.OHLC,
                'Historical Data | '
                'Japanese Candlesticks Pattern | '
                'NSE:TATASTEEL | '
                '1st Jan, 2020 | '
                'Candle Interval: 10 Minutes')
```

You will get the following output:

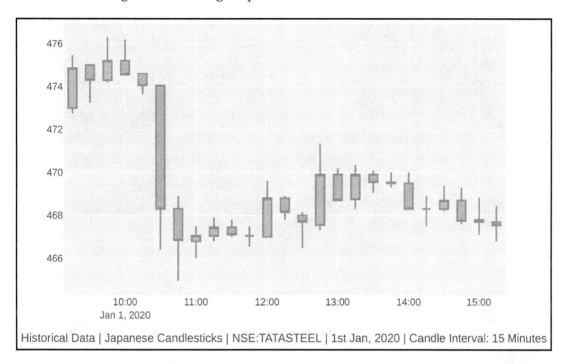

Historical Data | Japanese Candlesticks | NSE:TATASTEEL | 1st Jan, 2020 | Candle Interval: 15 Minutes

7. Plot a chart for the historical data of the instrument with a 15-minute candle interval:

```
>>> historical_data_15minutes = \
            broker_connection.get_historical_data(instrument,
                                        '15minute',
                                        '2020-01-01',
                                        '2020-01-01')
>>> plot_candlestick_chart(historical_data_15minutes,
                    PlotType.OHLC,
                    'Historical Data | '
                    'Japanese Candlesticks Pattern | '
                    'NSE:TATASTEEL | '
                    '1st Jan, 2020 | '
                    'Candle Interval: 15 Minutes')
```

You will get the following output:

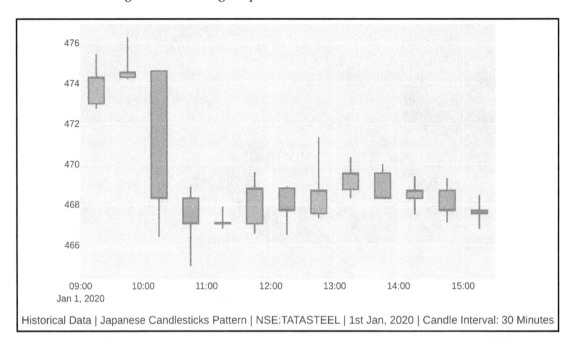

Historical Data | Japanese Candlesticks Pattern | NSE:TATASTEEL | 1st Jan, 2020 | Candle Interval: 30 Minutes

8. Plot a chart for the historical data of the instrument with a 30-minute candle interval:

```
>>> historical_data_30minutes = \
        broker_connection.get_historical_data(instrument,
                                               '30minute',
                                               '2020-01-01',
                                               '2020-01-01')
>>> plot_candlestick_chart(historical_data_30minutes,
                           PlotType.OHLC,
                           'Historical Data | '
                           'Japanese Candlesticks Pattern | '
                           'NSE:TATASTEEL | '
                           '1st Jan, 2020 | '
                           'Candle Interval: 30 Minutes')
```

You will get the following output:

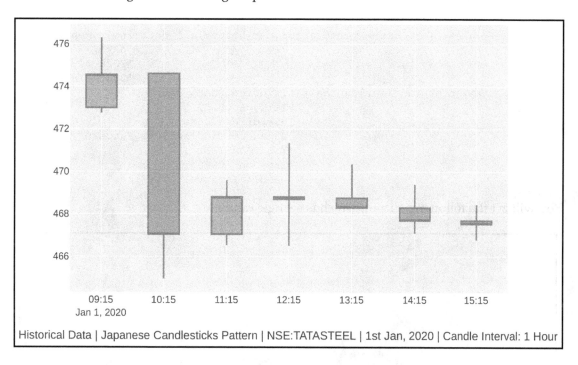

Historical Data | Japanese Candlesticks Pattern | NSE:TATASTEEL | 1st Jan, 2020 | Candle Interval: 1 Hour

9. Plot a chart for the historical data of the instrument with a 1-hour candle interval:

```
>>> historical_data_1hour = \
        broker_connection.get_historical_data(instrument,
                                              'hour',
                                              '2020-01-01',
                                              '2020-01-01')
>>> plot_candlestick_chart(historical_data_1hour,
                           PlotType.OHLC,
                           'Historical Data | '
                           'Japanese Candlesticks Pattern | '
                           'NSE:TATASTEEL | '
                           '1st Jan, 2020 | '
                           'Candle Interval: 1 Hour')
```

10. Plot a chart for the historical data of the instrument with a 1-day candle interval:

```
>>> historical_data_day = \
            broker_connection.get_historical_data(instrument,
                                                  'day',
                                                  '2020-01-01',
                                                  '2020-01-01')
>>> plot_candlestick_chart(historical_data_day,
                           PlotType.OHLC,
                           'Historical Data | '
                           'Japanese Candlesticks Pattern | '
                           'NSE:TATASTEEL | '
                           '1st Jan, 2020 | '
                           'Candle Interval: Day')
```

You will get the following output, which is a single candle:

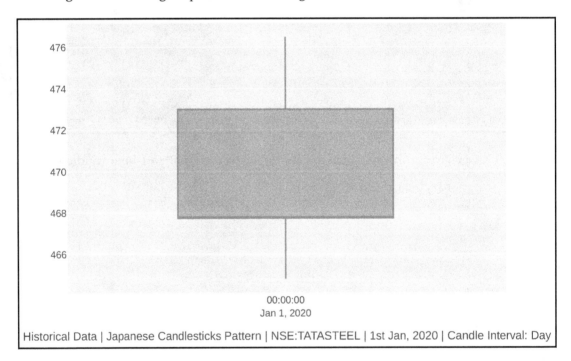

Historical Data | Japanese Candlesticks Pattern | NSE:TATASTEEL | 1st Jan, 2020 | Candle Interval: Day

How it works...

In *step 1*, you import `plot_candlestick_chart`, a quick utility function for plotting candlestick pattern charts, and `PlotType`, an enum for various types of candlestick patterns. In *step 2*, the `get_instrument()` method of `broker_connection` to fetch an instrument and assign it to a new attribute, `instrument`. This object is an instance of the `Instrument` class. The two parameters needed to call `get_instrument()` are the exchange (`'NSE'`) and the trading symbol (`'TATASTEEL'`). *Steps 3* and *4* fetch and plot the historical data for the candle intervals; that is, 1 minute, 3 minutes, 5 minutes, 10 minutes, 15 minutes, 30 minutes, 1 hour, and 1 day. You use the `get_historical_data()` method to fetch historical data for the same instruments and the same start and end dates, with only a different candle interval. You use the `plot_candlestick_chart()` function to plot Japanese candlestick pattern charts. You can observe the following differences between the charts as the candle interval increases:

- The total number of candlesticks decreases.
- The spikes in the charts due to sudden price movement are minimized. Smaller candle interval charts have more spikes as they focus on local trends, while larger candle interval charts have fewer spikes and are smoother.
- A long-term trend in the stock price becomes visible.
- Decision-making may become slower because you have to wait longer to get new candle data. Slower decisions may or may not be desirable, depending on the strategy. For example, for confirming trends, using a combination of data with a smaller candle interval, say 3 minutes, and data with a larger candle interval, say 15 minutes, would be desirable. On the other hand, for grabbing opportunities in intraday trading, data with larger candle intervals, such as 1 hour or 1 day, would not be desirable.
- The price range (y-axis spread) of adjacent candles may or may not overlap.
- All the timestamps are equally spaced in time (within market hours).

Fetching historical data using the Line Break candlestick pattern

The historical data of a financial instrument can be analyzed in the form of the Line Break candlestick pattern, a candlestick pattern that focuses on price movement. This differs from the Japanese candlestick pattern, which focuses on the time movement. Brokers typically do not provide historical data for the Line Break candlestick pattern via APIs. Brokers usually provide historical data using the Japanese candlestick pattern that needs to be converted into the Line Break candlestick pattern. A shorter candle interval hints at a localized price movement trend, while a larger candle interval indicates an overall price movement trend. Depending on your algorithmic trading strategy, you may need the candle interval to be small or large. A candle interval of 1 minute is often the smallest available candle interval.

The Line Break candlestick pattern works as follows:

1. Each candle has only `open` and `close` attributes.
2. The user defines a `Number of Lines` (*n*) setting, which is usually taken as 3.
3. At the end of each candle interval, a green candle is formed if the stock price goes higher than the highest of the previous *n* Line Break candles.
4. At the end of each candle interval, a red candle is formed if the stock price goes lower than the lowest of the previous *n* Line Break candles.
5. At the end of each candle interval, if neither point 3 nor point 4 are satisfied, no candle is formed. Hence, the timestamps don't need to be equally spaced.

This recipe shows how we can fetch historical data using the Japanese candlestick pattern using the broker API, convert the historical data into a Line Break candlestick pattern, and plot it. This is done for multiple candle intervals.

Getting ready

Make sure the `broker_connection` object is available in your Python namespace. Refer to the *Technical requirements* section of this chapter to learn how to set up `broker_connection`.

How to do it...

We execute the following steps for this recipe:

1. Import the necessary modules:

```
>>> from pyalgotrading.utils.func import plot_candlestick_chart,
PlotType
>>> from pyalgotrading.utils.candlesticks.linebreak import
Linebreak
```

2. Fetch the historical data for an instrument and convert it into Line Break data:

```
>>> instrument = broker_connection.get_instrument('NSE',
                                                  'TATASTEEL')
>>> historical_data_1minute = \
            broker_connection.get_historical_data(instrument,
                                                  'minute',
                                                  '2019-12-01',
                                                  '2019-12-31')
>>> historical_data_1minute_linebreak = \
                                Linebreak(historical_data_1minute)
>>> historical_data_1minute_linebreak
```

You will get the following output:

```
          close       open                   timestamp
0         424.00      424.95   2019-12-02 09:15:00+05:30
1         424.50      424.00   2019-12-02 09:16:00+05:30
2         425.75      424.80   2019-12-02 09:17:00+05:30
3         423.75      424.80   2019-12-02 09:19:00+05:30
4         421.70      423.75   2019-12-02 09:20:00+05:30
           ...         ...                    ....
1058      474.90      474.55   2019-12-31 10:44:00+05:30
1059      471.60      474.55   2019-12-31 11:19:00+05:30
1060      471.50      471.60   2019-12-31 14:19:00+05:30
1061      471.35      471.50   2019-12-31 15:00:00+05:30
1062      471.00      471.35   2019-12-31 15:29:00+05:30
```

3. Create a green Line Break candle from one of the rows of `historical_data`:

```
>>> candle_green_linebreak =
historical_data_1minute_linebreak.iloc[1:2,:]
# Only 2nd ROW of historical data
>>> plot_candlestick_chart(candle_green_linebreak,
                    PlotType.LINEBREAK,
                    "A 'Green' Line Break Candle")
```

You will get the following output:

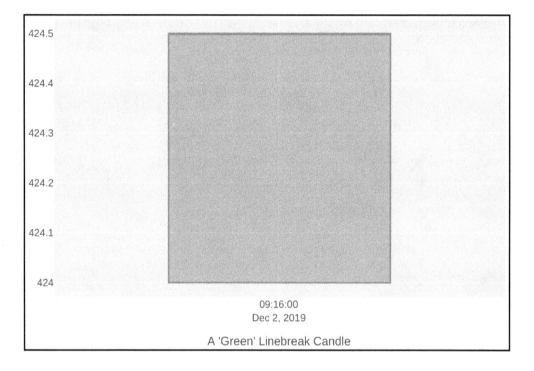

4. Create a red Line Break candle from one of the rows of `historical_data`:

```
>>> candle_red_linebreak =
historical_data_1minute_linebreak.iloc[:1,:]
# Only 1st ROW of historical data
>>> plot_candlestick_chart(candle_red_linebreak,
                           PlotType.LINEBREAK,
                           "A 'Red' Line Break Candle")
```

You will get the following output:

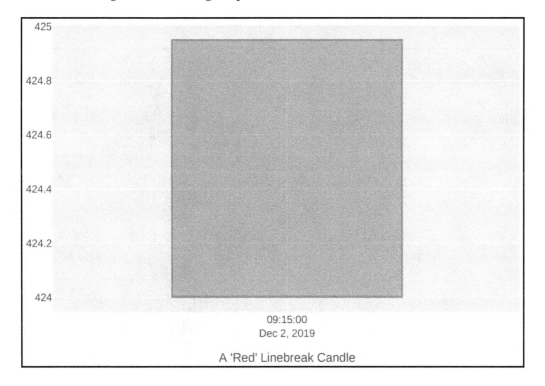

A 'Red' Linebreak Candle

5. Plot a chart for the historical data of the instrument with a 1-minute candle interval:

```
>>> plot_candlestick_chart(historical_data_1minute_linebreak,
                           PlotType.LINEBREAK,
                           'Historical Data | '
                           'Line Break Candlesticks Pattern | '
                           'NSE:TATASTEEL | '
                           'Dec, 2019 | '
                           'Candle Interval: 1 Minute', True)
```

You will get the following output:

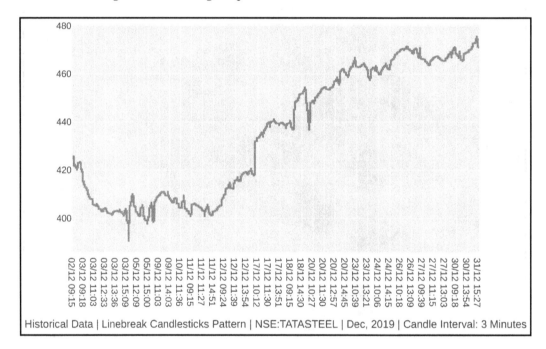

Historical Data | Linebreak Candlesticks Pattern | NSE:TATASTEEL | Dec, 2019 | Candle Interval: 3 Minutes

6. Plot a chart for the historical data of the instrument with a 3-minute candle interval:

```
>>> historical_data_3minutes = \
            broker_connection.get_historical_data(instrument,
                                                  '3minute',
                                                  '2019-12-01',
                                                  '2019-12-31')
>>> historical_data_3minutes_linebreak = \
                Linebreak(historical_data_3minutes)
>>> plot_candlestick_chart(historical_data_3minutes_linebreak,
                    PlotType.LINEBREAK,
                    'Historical Data | '
                    'Line Break Candlesticks Pattern | '
                    'NSE:TATASTEEL | '
                    'Dec, 2019 | '
                    'Candle Interval: 3 Minutes', True)
```

You will get the following output:

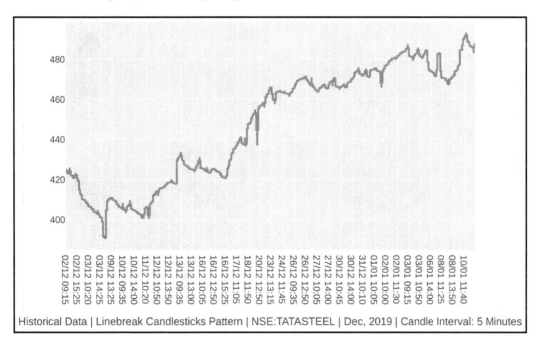

7. Plot a chart for the historical data of the instrument with a 5-minute candle interval:

```
>>> historical_data_5minutes = \
        broker_connection.get_historical_data(instrument,
                                              '5minute',
                                              '2019-12-01',
                                              '2020-01-10')
>>> historical_data_5minutes_linebreak = \
                        Linebreak(historical_data_5minutes)
>>> plot_candlestick_chart(historical_data_5minutes_linebreak,
                        PlotType.LINEBREAK,
                        'Historical Data | '
                        'Line Break Candlesticks Pattern | '
                        'NSE:TATASTEEL | '
                        'Dec, 2019 | '
                        'Candle Interval: 5 Minutes', True)
```

You will get the following output:

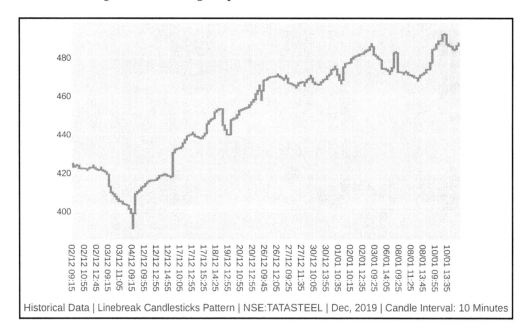

Historical Data | Linebreak Candlesticks Pattern | NSE:TATASTEEL | Dec, 2019 | Candle Interval: 10 Minutes

8. Plot a chart for the historical data of the instrument with a 10-minute candle interval:

```
>>> historical_data_10minutes = \
            broker_connection.get_historical_data(instrument,
                                                '10minute',
                                                '2019-12-01',
                                                '2020-01-10')
>>> historical_data_10minutes_linebreak = \
                            Linebreak(historical_data_10minutes)
>>> plot_candlestick_chart(historical_data_10minutes_linebreak,
                            PlotType.LINEBREAK,
                            'Historical Data | '
                            'Line Break Candlesticks Pattern | '
                            'NSE:TATASTEEL | '
                            'Dec, 2019 | '
                            'Candle Interval: 10 Minutes', True)
```

You will get the following output:

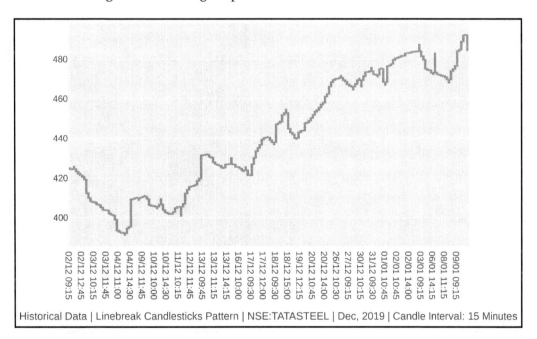

Historical Data | Linebreak Candlesticks Pattern | NSE:TATASTEEL | Dec, 2019 | Candle Interval: 15 Minutes

9. Plot a chart for the historical data of the instrument with a 15-minute candle interval:

```
>>> historical_data_15minutes = \
          broker_connection.get_historical_data(instrument,
                                          '15minute',
                                          '2019-12-01',
                                          '2020-01-10')
>>> historical_data_15minutes_linebreak = \
                          Linebreak(historical_data_15minutes)
>>> plot_candlestick_chart(historical_data_15minutes_linebreak,
                          PlotType.LINEBREAK,
                          'Historical Data | '
                          'Line Break Candlesticks Pattern | '
                          'NSE:TATASTEEL | '
                          'Dec, 2019 | '
                          'Candle Interval: 15 Minutes', True)
```

You will get the following output:

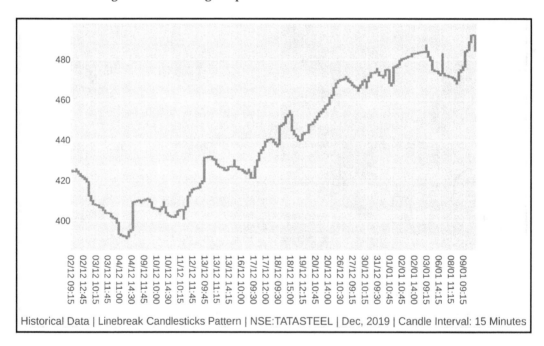

Historical Data | Linebreak Candlesticks Pattern | NSE:TATASTEEL | Dec, 2019 | Candle Interval: 15 Minutes

10. Plot a chart for the historical data of the instrument with a 30-minute candle interval:

```
>>> historical_data_30minutes = \
          broker_connection.get_historical_data(instrument,
                                                '30minute',
                                                '2019-12-01',
                                                '2020-01-10')
>>> historical_data_30minutes_linebreak = \
                        Linebreak(historical_data_30minutes)
>>> plot_candlestick_chart(historical_data_30minutes_linebreak,
                        PlotType.LINEBREAK,
                        'Historical Data | '
                        'Line Break Candlesticks Pattern | '
                        'NSE:TATASTEEL | '
                        'Dec, 2019 | '
                        'Candle Interval: 30 Minutes', True)
```

You will get the following output:

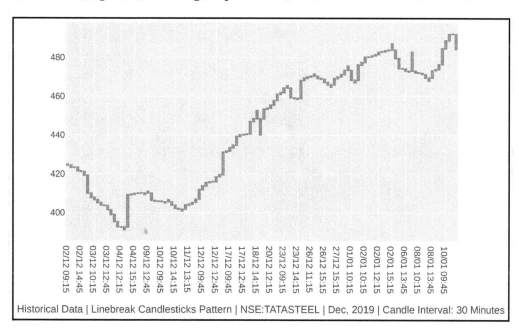

Historical Data | Linebreak Candlesticks Pattern | NSE:TATASTEEL | Dec, 2019 | Candle Interval: 30 Minutes

11. Plot a chart for the historical data of the instrument with a 1-hour candle interval:

```
>>> historical_data_1hour = \
            broker_connection.get_historical_data(instrument,
                                                  'hour',
                                                  '2019-12-01',
                                                  '2020-01-10')
>>> historical_data_1hour_linebreak = \
                              Linebreak(historical_data_1hour)
>>> plot_candlestick_chart(historical_data_1hour_linebreak,
                           PlotType.LINEBREAK,
                           'Historical Data | '
                           'Line Break Candlesticks Pattern | '
                           'NSE:TATASTEEL | '
                           'Dec, 2019 | '
                           'Candle Interval: 1 Hour', True)
```

You will get the following output:

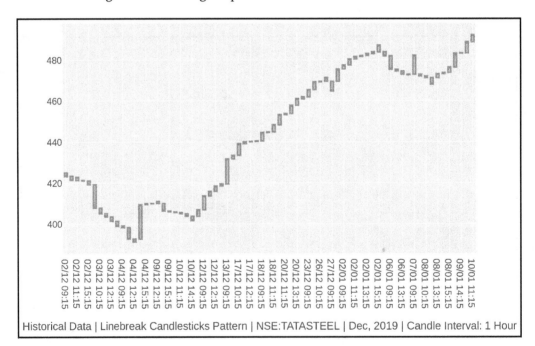

Historical Data | Linebreak Candlesticks Pattern | NSE:TATASTEEL | Dec, 2019 | Candle Interval: 1 Hour

12. Plot a chart for the historical data of the instrument with a 1-day candle interval:

```
>>> historical_data_day = \
            broker_connection.get_historical_data(instrument,
                                                  'day',
                                                  '2019-12-01',
                                                  '2020-01-10')
>>> historical_data_day_linebreak = \
                            Linebreak(historical_data_day)
>>> plot_candlestick_chart(historical_data_day_linebreak,
                           PlotType.LINEBREAK,
                           'Historical Data | '
                           'Line Break Candlesticks Pattern | '
                           'NSE:TATASTEEL | '
                           'Dec, 2019 | '
                           'Candle Interval: 1 Day', True)
```

You will get the following output:

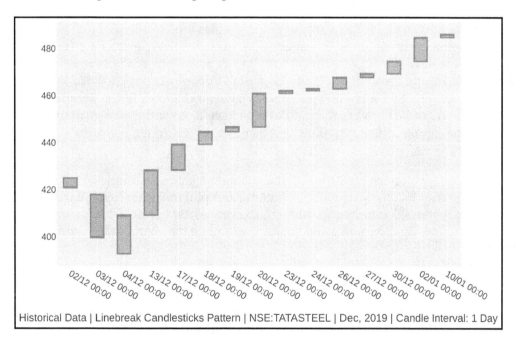

Historical Data | Linebreak Candlesticks Pattern | NSE:TATASTEEL | Dec, 2019 | Candle Interval: 1 Day

How it works...

In *step 1*, you import `plot_candlestick_chart`, a quick utility function for plotting candlestick pattern charts, `PlotType`, an enum for various types of candlestick patterns, and the `Linebreak` function, which can convert historical data from the Japanese candlestick pattern in the Line Break candlestick pattern. In *step 2*, you use the `get_instrument()` method of `broker_connection` to fetch an instrument and assign it to a new attribute, `instrument`. This object is an instance of the `Instrument` class. The two parameters needed to call get_instrument() are the exchange (`'NSE'`) and the trading symbol (`'TATASTEEL'`). Next, you use the `get_historical_data()` method of the `broker_connection` object to fetch the historical data for the instrument for the duration of December 2019, with a candle interval of 1 minute. The time-series data returned is in the form of the Japanese candlestick pattern. The `Linebreak()` function converts this data into a Line Break candlestick pattern, another `pandas.DataFrame` object. You assign it to `historical_data_1minute_linebreak`. Observe that `historical_data_1minute_linebreak` has only `timestamp`, `open`, and `close` columns. Also, observe that the timestamps are not equidistant as the Line Break candles are based on price movement and not time. In *steps 3* and *4*, you selectively extract a green and a red candle from the data. (Please note, the indices passed to `historical_data.iloc` would be different if you choose a different duration for `historical_data` fetched in the first recipe of this chapter.) Observe that the candles have no shadows (lines extending on either side of the main candle body) as the candles only have `open` and `close` attributes. In *steps 5*, you plot the complete historical data held by `historical_data` using the `plot_candlestick_chart()` function.

In *steps 6* until *12*, you fetch the historical data using the Japanese candlestick pattern, convert it into the Line Break candlestick pattern, and plot the converted data for candle intervals of 3 minutes, 5 minutes, 10 minutes, 15 minutes, 30 minutes, 1 hour, and 1 day. Observe the following differences and similarities among the charts as the candle interval increases:

- The total number of candlesticks decreases.
- The spikes in the charts due to sudden price movement are minimized. Smaller candle interval charts have more spikes as they focus on local trends, while larger candle interval charts have fewer spikes and are smoother.
- A long-term trend in the stock price becomes visible.

- Decision-making may become slower because you have to wait longer to get new candle data. Slower decisions may or may not be desirable, depending on the strategy. For example, to confirm trends, using a combination of data with a smaller candle interval, say 3 minutes, and data with a larger candle interval, say 15 minutes, would be desirable. On the other hand, to grab opportunities in intraday trading, data with larger candle intervals, say 1 hour or 1 day, would not be desirable.

- The price ranges (y-axis spread) of two adjacent candles don't overlap with each other. Adjacent candles always share one of their ends.

- None of the timestamps need to be equally spaced in time (unlike the Japanese candlestick pattern) as candles are formed based on price movement and not time movement.

 If you are interested in finding out about the Math and implementation of Line Break candles, please refer to its source code in the `pyalgotrading` package at `https://github.com/algobulls/pyalgotrading/blob/master/pyalgotrading/utils/candlesticks/linebreak.py`.

Fetching historical data using the Renko candlestick pattern

The historical data of a financial instrument can be analyzed in the form of the Renko candlestick pattern, a candlestick pattern that focuses on price movement. This differs from the Japanese candlestick pattern, which focuses on time movement. Brokers typically do not provide historical data as the Renko candlestick pattern via APIs. Brokers usually provide historical data by using the Japanese candlestick pattern, which needs to be converted into the Renko candlestick pattern. A shorter candle interval hints at a localized price movement trend, while a larger candle interval indicates an overall price movement trend. Depending on your algorithmic trading strategy, you may need the candle interval to be small or large. A candle interval of 1 minute is often the smallest available candle interval.

The Renko candlestick pattern works as follows:

1. Each candle only has `open` and `close` attributes.
2. You define a **Brick Count** (b) setting, which is usually set to 2.
3. Each candle is always fixed and is equal to `Brick Count`. Hence, a candle is also called a **brick** here.

4. At the end of every candle interval, a green brick is formed if the stock price goes b points higher than the highest of the previous brick. If the price goes much higher than b points in a single candle interval, as many Renko bricks are formed to account for the price change.

   For example, say the price goes 21 points higher than the high of the previous brick. If the brick size is 2, 10 Renko bricks would be formed with the same timestamp to account for the 20-point change. For the remaining 1-point change (21-20), no brick would be formed until the price goes at least 1 point higher.

5. At the end of every candle interval, a red candle is formed if the stock price goes b points lower than the lowest of the previous Renko candle. If the price goes much lower than b points in a single candle interval, as many Renko bricks are formed to account for the price change.

   For example, say the price goes 21 points lower than the highest previous brick. If the brick size is 2, 10 Renko bricks would be formed with the same timestamp to account for the 20-point change. For the remaining 1-point change (21-20), no brick would be formed until the price goes at least 1 point lower.

6. No two adjacent candles overlap with each other. Adjacent candles always share one of their ends.

7. None of the timestamps need to be equally spaced (unlike the Japanese candlestick pattern) as candles are formed based on price movement and not time movement. Also, unlike other patterns, there may be multiple candles with the same timestamp.

This recipe shows how you can fetch historical data as the Japanese candlestick pattern using the broker API, as well as how to convert and plot the historical data using the Renko candlestick pattern for various candle intervals.

Getting ready

Make sure the `broker_connection` object is available in your Python namespace. Refer to the *Technical requirements* section of this chapter to learn how to set up `broker_connection`.

How to do it...

We execute the following steps for this recipe:

1. Import the necessary modules:

```
>>> from pyalgotrading.utils.func import plot_candlestick_chart,
PlotType
>>> from pyalgotrading.utils.candlesticks.renko import Renko
```

2. Fetch the historical data for an instrument and convert it into Renko data:

```
>>> instrument = broker_connection.get_instrument('NSE',
                                                  'TATASTEEL')
>>> historical_data_1minute = \
        broker_connection.get_historical_data(instrument,
                                              'minute',
                                              '2019-12-01',
                                              '2020-01-10')
>>> historical_data_1minute_renko = Renko(historical_data_1minute)
>>> historical_data_1minute_renko
```

You will get the following output:

```
       close    open                    timestamp
0      424.0    424.95      2019-12-02 09:15:00+05:30
1      422.0    424.00      2019-12-02 09:20:00+05:30
2      426.0    424.00      2019-12-02 10:00:00+05:30
3      422.0    424.00      2019-12-02 10:12:00+05:30
4      420.0    422.00      2019-12-02 15:28:00+05:30
        ...      ...            ...          ...
186    490.0    488.00      2020-01-10 10:09:00+05:30
187    492.0    490.00      2020-01-10 11:41:00+05:30
188    488.0    490.00      2020-01-10 13:31:00+05:30
189    486.0    488.00      2020-01-10 13:36:00+05:30
190    484.0    486.00      2020-01-10 14:09:00+05:30
```

3. Create a green Renko candle from one of the rows of `historical_data`:

```
>>> candle_green_renko = historical_data_1minute_renko.iloc[2:3,:]
# Only 3rd ROW of historical data
>>> plot_candlestick_chart(candle_green_renko,
                           PlotType.RENKO,
                           "A Green 'Renko' Candle")
```

You will get the following output:

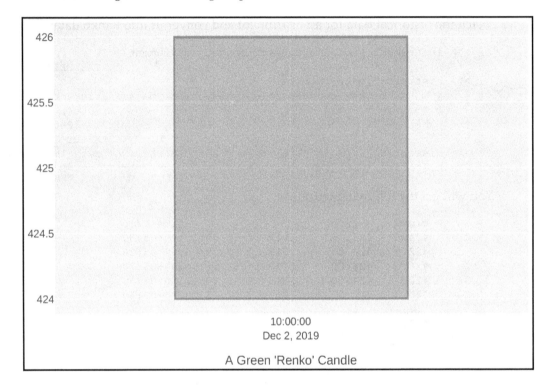

4. Create a red Renko candle from one of the rows of `historical_data`:

```
>>> plot_candlestick_chart(historical_data_1minute_renko,
                           PlotType.RENKO,
                           'Historical Data | '
                           'Renko Candlesticks Pattern | '
                           'NSE:TATASTEEL | '
                           'Dec, 2019 | '
                           'Candle Interval: 1 Minute', True)
```

You will get the following output:

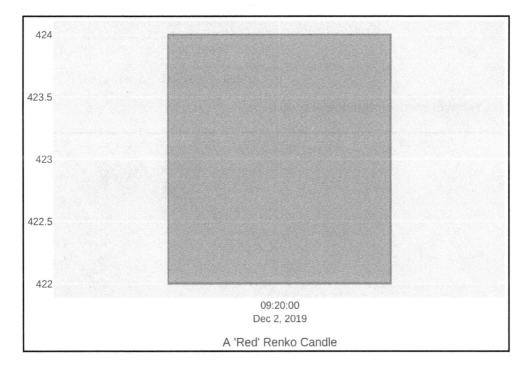

5. Plot a chart for the historical data of the instrument with a 1-minute candle interval:

```
>>> historical_data_3minutes = \
            broker_connection.get_historical_data(instrument,
                                                  '3minute',
                                                  '2019-12-01',
                                                  '2019-12-31')
>>> historical_data_3minutes_renko = \
                            Renko(historical_data_3minutes)
>>> plot_candlestick_chart(historical_data_3minutes_renko,
                    PlotType.RENKO,
                    'Historical Data | '
                    'Renko Candlesticks Pattern | '
                    'NSE:TATASTEEL | '
                    'Dec, 2019 | '
                    'Candle Interval: 3 Minutes', True)
```

You will get the following output:

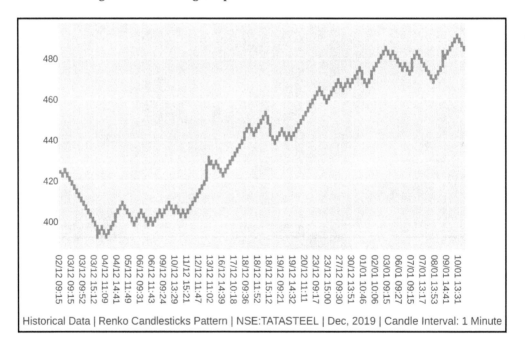

6. Plot a chart for the historical data of the instrument with a 3-minute candle interval:

```
>>> historical_data_5minutes = \
            broker_connection.get_historical_data(instrument,
                                            '5minute',
                                            '2019-12-01',
                                            '2019-12-31')
>>> historical_data_5minutes_renko = \
                            Renko(historical_data_5minutes)
>>> plot_candlestick_chart(historical_data_5minutes_renko,
                        PlotType.RENKO,
                        'Historical Data | '
                        'Renko Candlesticks Pattern | '
                        'NSE:TATASTEEL | '
                        'Dec, 2019 | '
                        'Candle Interval: 5 Minutes', True)
```

You will get the following output:

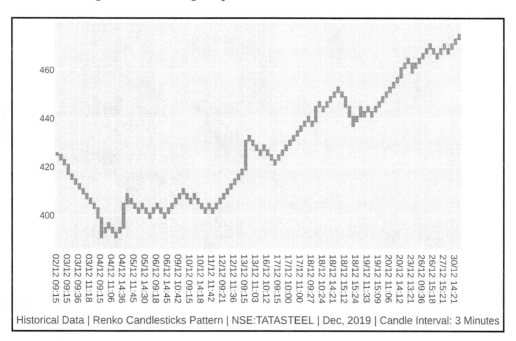

Historical Data | Renko Candlesticks Pattern | NSE:TATASTEEL | Dec, 2019 | Candle Interval: 3 Minutes

7. Plot a chart for the historical data of the instrument with a 5-minute candle interval:

```
>>> historical_data_10minutes = \
            broker_connection.get_historical_data(instrument,
                                                  '10minute',
                                                  '2019-12-01',
                                                  '2019-12-31')
>>> historical_data_10minutes_renko = \
                              Renko(historical_data_10minutes)
>>> plot_candlestick_chart(historical_data_10minutes_renko,
                           PlotType.RENKO,
                           'Historical Data | '
                           'Renko Candlesticks Pattern | '
                           'NSE:TATASTEEL | '
                           'Dec, 2019 | '
                           'Candle Interval: 10 Minutes', True)
```

You will get the following output:

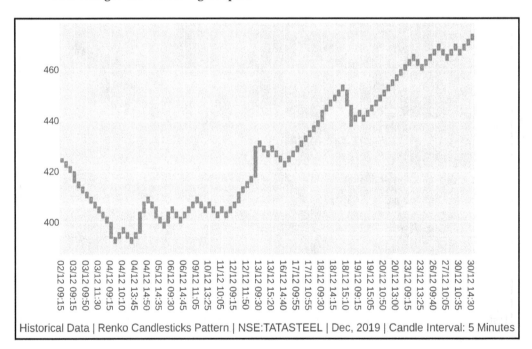

Historical Data | Renko Candlesticks Pattern | NSE:TATASTEEL | Dec, 2019 | Candle Interval: 5 Minutes

8. Plot a chart for the historical data of the instrument with a 10-minute candle interval:

```
>>> historical_data_15minutes = \
        broker_connection.get_historical_data(instrument,
                                              '15minute',
                                              '2019-12-01',
                                              '2019-12-31')
>>> historical_data_15minutes_renko = \
                    Renko(historical_data_15minutes)
>>> plot_candlestick_chart(historical_data_15minutes_renko,
                    PlotType.RENKO,
                    'Historical Data | '
                    'Renko Candlesticks Pattern | '
                    'NSE:TATASTEEL | '
                    'Dec, 2019 | '
                    'Candle Interval: 15 Minutes', True)
```

You will get the following output:

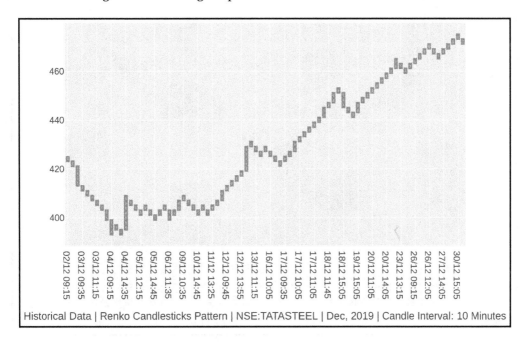

Historical Data | Renko Candlesticks Pattern | NSE:TATASTEEL | Dec, 2019 | Candle Interval: 10 Minutes

9. Plot a chart for the historical data of the instrument with a 15-minute candle interval:

```
>>> historical_data_15minutes = \
           broker_connection.get_historical_data(instrument,
                                                 '15minute',
                                                 '2019-12-01',
                                                 '2019-12-31')
>>> historical_data_15minutes_renko = \
                         Renko(historical_data_15minutes)
>>> plot_candlestick_chart(historical_data_15minutes_renko,
                      PlotType.RENKO,
                      'Historical Data | '
                      'Renko Candlesticks Pattern | '
                      'NSE:TATASTEEL | '
                      'Dec, 2019 | '
                      'Candle Interval: 15 Minutes', True)
```

You will get the following output:

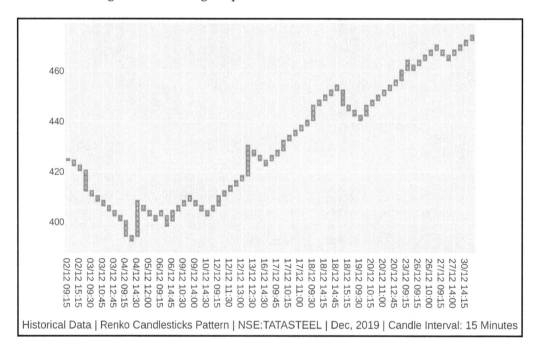

Historical Data | Renko Candlesticks Pattern | NSE:TATASTEEL | Dec, 2019 | Candle Interval: 15 Minutes

10. Plot a chart for the historical data of the instrument with a 30-minute candle interval:

```
>>> historical_data_30minutes = \
        broker_connection.get_historical_data(instrument,
                                               '30minute',
                                               '2019-12-01',
                                               '2019-12-31')
>>> historical_data_30minutes_renko = \
                        Renko(historical_data_30minutes)
>>> plot_candlestick_chart(historical_data_30minutes_renko,
                           PlotType.RENKO,
                           'Historical Data | '
                           'Renko Candlesticks Pattern | '
                           'NSE:TATASTEEL | '
                           'Dec, 2019 | '
                           'Candle Interval: 30 Minutes', True)
```

You will get the following output:

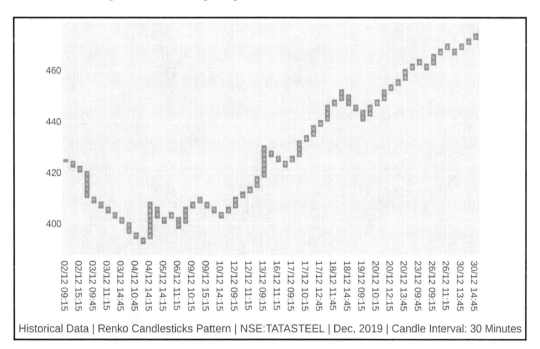

Historical Data | Renko Candlesticks Pattern | NSE:TATASTEEL | Dec, 2019 | Candle Interval: 30 Minutes

11. Plot a chart for the historical data of the instrument with a 1-hour candle interval:

```
>>> historical_data_1hour = \
        broker_connection.get_historical_data(instrument,
                                              'hour',
                                              '2019-12-01',
                                              '2019-12-31')
>>> historical_data_1hour_renko = Renko(historical_data_1hour)
>>> plot_candlestick_chart(historical_data_1hour_renko,
                           PlotType.RENKO,
                           'Historical Data | '
                           'Renko Candlesticks Pattern | '
                           'NSE:TATASTEEL | '
                           'Dec, 2019 | '
                           'Candle Interval: 1 Hour', True)
```

You will get the following output:

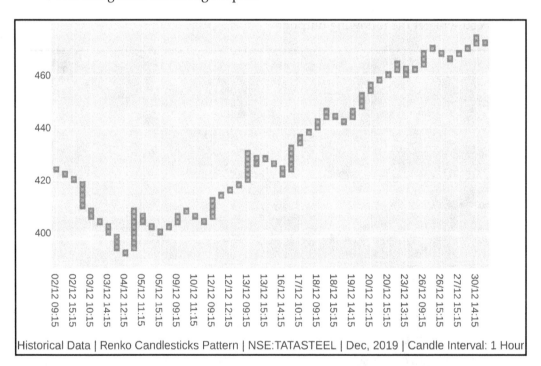

Historical Data | Renko Candlesticks Pattern | NSE:TATASTEEL | Dec, 2019 | Candle Interval: 1 Hour

12. Plot a chart for the historical data of the instrument with a 1-day candle interval:

```
>>> historical_data_day = \
            broker_connection.get_historical_data(instrument,
                                                    'day',
                                                    '2019-12-01',
                                                    '2019-12-31')
>>> historical_data_day_renko = Renko(historical_data_day)
>>> plot_candlestick_chart(historical_data_day_renko,
                            PlotType.RENKO,
                            'Historical Data | '
                            'Renko Candlesticks Pattern | '
                            'NSE:TATASTEEL | '
                            'Dec, 2019 | '
                            'Candle Interval: Day', True)
```

You will get the following output:

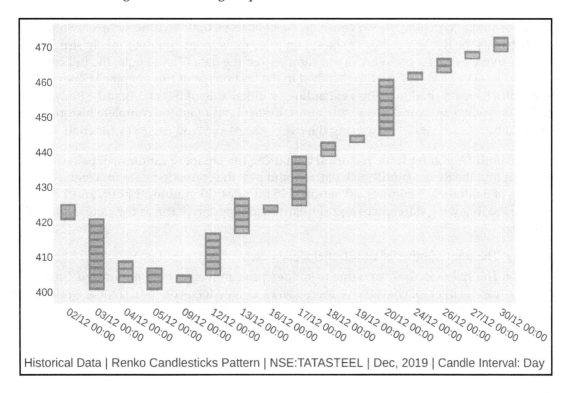

Historical Data | Renko Candlesticks Pattern | NSE:TATASTEEL | Dec, 2019 | Candle Interval: Day

How it works...

In *step 1*, you import `plot_candlestick_chart`, a quick utility function for plotting candlestick pattern charts, `PlotType`, an enum for various types of candlestick patterns, and the `Renko` function, which can convert historical data from the Japanese candlestick pattern into the Renko candlestick pattern. In *step 2*, you use the `get_instrument()` method of `broker_connection` to fetch an instrument and assign it to a new attribute, `instrument`. This object is an instance of the `Instrument` class. The two parameters needed to call get_instrument() are the exchange (`'NSE'`) and the trading symbol (`'TATASTEEL'`). Next, you use the `get_historical_data()` method of the `broker_connection` object to fetch the historical data for the duration of December 2019, with a candle interval of 1 minute. The time-series data returned is in the form of Japanese candlestick pattern. The `Renko()` function converts this data into a Renko candlestick pattern, another `pandas.DataFrame` object. You assign it to `historical_data_1minute_renko`. Observe that `historical_data_1minute_renko` has `timestamp`, `open`, and `close` columns. Also, observe that the timestamps are not equidistant as the Renko candles are based on price movement and not time. In *step 3 and 4*, you selectively extract a green and a red candle from the data (Please note, the indices passed to `historical_data.iloc` fetched in the first recipe of this chapter.) Observe that the candles have no shadows (lines extending on either side of the main candle body) as the candles only have `open` and `close` attributes. In *step 5*, you plot the complete historical data held by `historical_data` using the `plot_candlestick_chart()` function.

In *steps 6* until *12*, you fetch the historical data using the Japanese candlestick pattern, convert it into the Renko candlestick pattern, and plot the converted data for candle intervals of 3 minutes, 5 minutes, 10 minutes, 15 minutes, 30 minutes, 1 hour, and 1 day. Observe the following differences and similarities among the charts as the candle interval increases:

- The total number of candlesticks decreases.
- The spikes in the charts due to sudden price movement are minimized. Smaller candle interval charts have more spikes as they focus on local trends, while larger candle interval charts have fewer spikes and are smoother.
- A long-term trend in the stock price becomes visible.

- Decision-making may become slower because you have to wait longer to get new candle data. Slower decisions may or may not be desirable, depending on the strategy. For example, to confirm trends, using a combination of data with a smaller candle interval, say 3 minutes, and data with a larger candle interval, say 15 minutes, would be desirable. On the other hand, to grab opportunities in intraday trading, data with larger candle intervals, say 1 hour or 1 day, would not be desirable.
- The price ranges (y-axis spread) of two adjacent candles don't overlap with each other. Adjacent candles always share one of their ends.
- None of the timestamps need to be equally spaced in time (unlike in the Japanese candlestick pattern) as candles are formed based on price movement and not time movement.

 If you are interested in finding out about the Math and implementation of Renko candles, please refer to its source code in the `pyalgotrading` package at `https://github.com/algobulls/pyalgotrading/blob/master/pyalgotrading/utils/candlesticks/renko.py`.

Fetching historical data using the Heikin-Ashi candlestick pattern

The historical data of a financial instrument can be analyzed in the form of the Heikin-Ashi candlestick pattern. Brokers typically do not provide historical data using the Heikin-Ashi candlestick pattern via APIs. Brokers usually provide historical data using the Japanese candlestick pattern, which needs to be converted to the Heikin-Ashi candlestick pattern. A shorter candle interval hints at a localized price movement trend, while a larger candle interval indicates an overall price movement trend. Based on your algorithmic trading strategy, you may need the candle interval to be small or large. A candle interval of 1 minute is often the smallest available candle interval.

The Heikin-Ashi candlestick pattern works as follows:

- Each candle has `Close`, `Open`, `High`, and `Low` attributes. For each candle, the following occurs:
  - `Close` is calculated as the average of the `Open`, `High`, `Low`, and `Close` attributes of the current Japanese candle.
  - `Open` is the average of the `Open` and `Close` attributes of the previous Heikin-Ashi candle.

- `High` is max of:
  - `Open` of current Heikin-Ashi candle
  - `Close` of current Heikin-Ashi candle
  - `High` of current Japanese candle
- `Low` is the min of:
  - `Open` of current Heikin-Ashi candle
  - `Close` of current Heikin-Ashi candle
  - `Low` of current Japanese Candle
- A green candle is formed when `Close` is higher than `Open`. (This is the same as the green candle in the Japanese candlestick pattern.)
- A red candle is formed when `Close` is lower than `Open`. (This is the same as the red candle in the Japanese candlestick pattern.)
- All the timestamps are equally spaced (within market hours).

This recipe shows you how to fetch historical data using Japanese candlestick pattern when using the broker API, as well as how to convert and plot the historical data using the Heikin-Ashi candlestick pattern for various candle intervals.

Getting ready

Make sure the `broker_connection` object is available in your Python namespace. Refer to the *Technical requirements* section of this chapter to learn how to set up `broker_connection`.

How to do it...

We execute the following steps for this recipe:

1. Import the necessary modules:

```
>>> from pyalgotrading.utils.func import plot_candlestick_chart,
PlotType
>>> from pyalgotrading.utils.candlesticks.heikinashi import
HeikinAshi
```

2. Fetch the historical data for an instrument and convert it into Heikin-Ashi data:

```
>>> instrument = broker_connection.get_instrument('NSE',
                                                  'TATASTEEL')
>>> historical_data_1minute = \
        broker_connection.get_historical_data(instrument,
                                              'minute',
                                              '2019-12-01',
                                              '2019-12-31')
>>> historical_data_1minute_heikinashi = \
                        HeikinAshi(historical_data_1minute)
>>> historical_data_1minute_heikinashi
```

You will get the following output:

	timestamp	open	high	low	close
0	2019-12-02 09:15:00+05:30	424.475000	424.950000	422.550000	424.1125
1	2019-12-02 09:16:00+05:30	424.293750	424.900000	423.400000	424.2000
2	2019-12-02 09:17:00+05:30	424.246875	426.000000	424.246875	425.2375
3	2019-12-02 09:18:00+05:30	424.742188	425.700000	424.500000	425.1250
4	2019-12-02 09:19:00+05:30	424.933594	425.200000	423.100000	424.2125
...	...	...	...	...	...
7870	2019-12-31 15:25:00+05:30	472.098314	472.200000	471.800000	471.9875
7871	2019-12-31 15:26:00+05:30	472.042907	472.042907	471.600000	471.7250
7872	2019-12-31 15:27:00+05:30	471.883954	471.950000	471.600000	471.7750
7873	2019-12-31 15:28:00+05:30	471.829477	471.950000	471.450000	471.7750
7874	2019-12-31 15:29:00+05:30	471.802238	471.802238	470.650000	471.3125

7875 rows × 5 columns

3. Create a green Heikin-Ashi candle for one row of data:

```
>>> candle_green_heikinashi = \
            historical_data_1minute_heikinashi.iloc[2:3,:]
# Only 3rd ROW of historical data
>>> plot_candlestick_chart(candle_green_heikinashi,
                        PlotType.HEIKINASHI,
                        "A 'Green' HeikinAshi Candle")
```

You will get the following output:

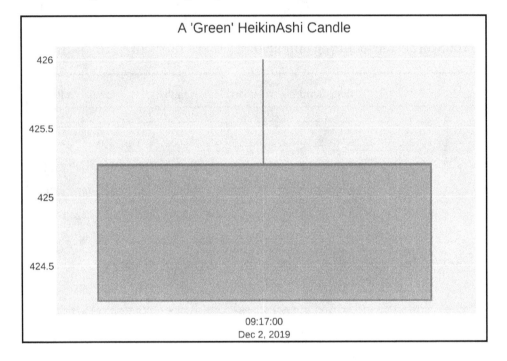

4. Create a red Heikin-Ashi candle for one row of data:

```
# A 'Red' HeikinAshi Candle
>>> candle_red_heikinashi = \
        historical_data_1minute_heikinashi.iloc[4:5,:]
# Only 1st ROW of historical data
>>> plot_candlestick_chart(candle_red_heikinashi,
                      PlotType.HEIKINASHI,
                      "A 'Red' HeikinAshi Candle")
```

You will get the following output:

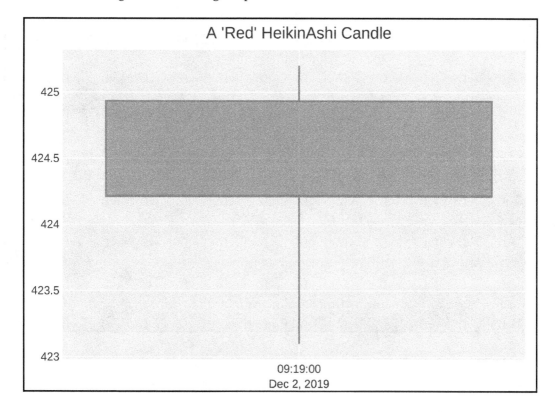

5. Plot a chart for the historical data of the instrument with a 1-minute candle interval:

```
>>> plot_candlestick_chart(historical_data_1minute_heikinashi,
                           PlotType.HEIKINASHI,
                           'Historical Data | '
                           'Heikin-Ashi Candlesticks Pattern | '
                           'NSE:TATASTEEL | '
                           'Dec, 2019 | '
                           'Candle Interval: 1 minute', True)
```

You will get the following output:

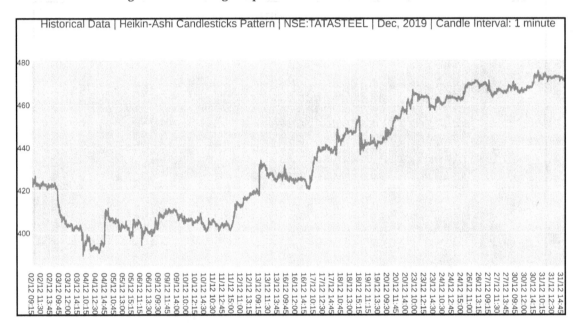

6. Plot a chart for the historical data of the instrument with a 3-minute candle interval:

```
>>> historical_data_3minutes = \
            broker_connection.get_historical_data(instrument,
                                                  '3minute',
                                                  '2019-12-01',
                                                  '2019-12-31')
>>> historical_data_3minutes_heikinashi = \
                            HeikinAshi(historical_data_3minutes)
>>> plot_candlestick_chart(historical_data_3minutes_heikinashi,
                            PlotType.HEIKINASHI,
                            'Historical Data | '
                            'Heikin-Ashi Candlesticks Pattern | '
                            'NSE:TATASTEEL | '
                            'Dec, 2019 | '
                            'Candle Interval: 3 minutes', True)
```

You will get the following output:

7. Plot a chart for the historical data of the instrument with a 5-minute candle interval:

```
>>> historical_data_5minutes = \
        broker_connection.get_historical_data(instrument,
                                              '5minute',
                                              '2019-12-01',
                                              '2019-12-31')
>>> historical_data_5minutes_heikinashi = \
                        HeikinAshi(historical_data_5minutes)
>>> plot_candlestick_chart(historical_data_5minutes_heikinashi,
                    PlotType.HEIKINASHI,
                    'Historical Data | '
                    'Heikin-Ashi Candlesticks Pattern | '
                    'NSE:TATASTEEL | '
                    'Dec, 2019 | '
                    'Candle Interval: 5 minutes', True)
```

You will get the following output:

8. Plot a chart for the historical data of the instrument with a 10-minute candle interval:

```
>>> historical_data_10minutes = \
          broker_connection.get_historical_data(instrument,
                                                '10minute',
                                                '2019-12-01',
                                                '2019-12-31')
>>> historical_data_10minutes_heikinashi = \
                    HeikinAshi(historical_data_10minutes)
>>> plot_candlestick_chart(historical_data_10minutes_heikinashi,
                    PlotType.HEIKINASHI,
                    'Historical Data | '
                    'Heikin-Ashi Candlesticks Pattern | '
                    'NSE:TATASTEEL | '
                    'Dec, 2019 | '
                    'Candle Interval: 10 minutes', True)
```

You will get the following output:

9. Plot a chart for the historical data of the instrument with a 15-minute candle interval:

```
>>> historical_data_15minutes = \
            broker_connection.get_historical_data(instrument,
                                                   '15minute',
                                                   '2019-12-01',
                                                   '2019-12-31')
>>> historical_data_15minutes_heikinashi = \
                        HeikinAshi(historical_data_15minutes)
>>> plot_candlestick_chart(historical_data_15minutes_heikinashi,
                        PlotType.HEIKINASHI,
                        'Historical Data | '
                        'Heikin-Ashi Candlesticks Pattern | '
                        'NSE:TATASTEEL | '
                        'Dec, 2019 | '
                        'Candle Interval: 15 minutes', True)
```

You will get the following output:

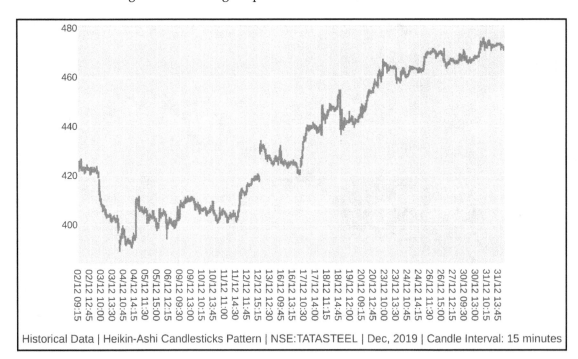

Historical Data | Heikin-Ashi Candlesticks Pattern | NSE:TATASTEEL | Dec, 2019 | Candle Interval: 15 minutes

10. Plot a chart for the historical data of the instrument with a 30-minute candle interval:

```
>>> historical_data_30minutes = \
            broker_connection.get_historical_data(instrument,
                                            '30minute',
                                            '2019-12-01',
                                            '2019-12-31')
>>> historical_data_30minutes_heikinashi = \
                        HeikinAshi(historical_data_30minutes)
>>> plot_candlestick_chart(historical_data_30minutes_heikinashi,
                        PlotType.HEIKINASHI,
                        'Historical Data | '
                        'Heikin-Ashi Candlesticks Pattern | '
                        'NSE:TATASTEEL | '
                        'Dec, 2019 | '
                        'Candle Interval: 30 minutes', True)
```

You will get the following output:

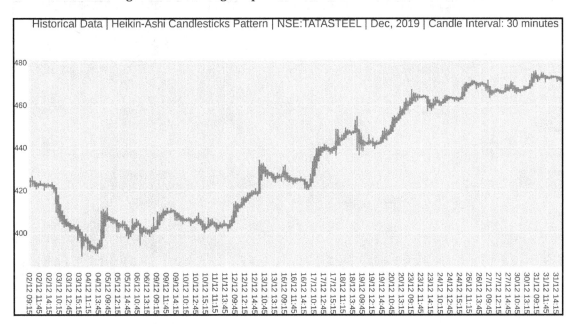

11. Plot a chart for the historical data of the instrument with a 1-hour candle interval:

```
>>> historical_data_1hour =
        broker_connection.get_historical_data(instrument,
                                              'hour',
                                              '2019-12-01',
                                              '2019-12-31')
>>> historical_data_1hour_heikinashi = \
                        HeikinAshi(historical_data_1hour)
>>> plot_candlestick_chart(historical_data_1hour_heikinashi,
                        PlotType.HEIKINASHI,
                        'Historical Data | '
                        'Heikin-Ashi Candlesticks Pattern | '
                        'NSE:TATASTEEL | '
                        'Dec, 2019 | '
                        'Candle Interval: 1 Hour', True)
```

You will get the following output:

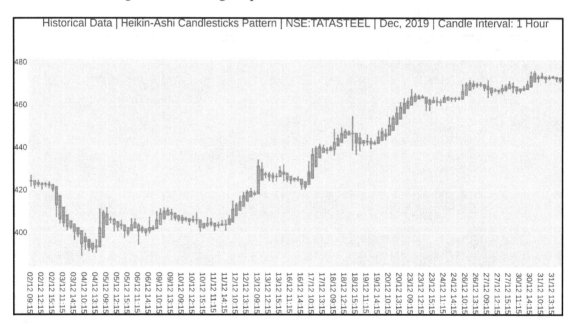

12. Plot a chart for the historical data of the instrument with a 1-day candle interval:

```
>>> historical_data_day = \
            broker_connection.get_historical_data(instrument,
                                            'day',
                                            '2019-12-01',
                                            '2019-12-31')
>>> historical_data_day_heikinashi = \
                                HeikinAshi(historical_data_day)
>>> plot_candlestick_chart(historical_data_day_heikinashi,
                        PlotType.HEIKINASHI,
                        'Historical Data | '
                        'Heikin-Ashi Candlesticks Pattern | '
                        'NSE:TATASTEEL | '
                        'Dec, 2019 | '
                        'Candle Interval: Day', True)
```

You will get the following output:

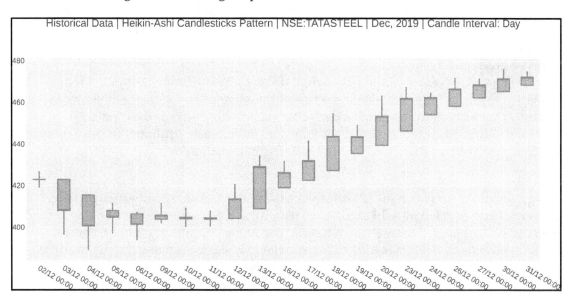

How it works...

In *step 1*, you import `plot_candlestick_chart`, a quick utility function for plotting candlestick pattern charts, `PlotType`, an enum for various types of candlestick patterns, and the `HeikinAshi` function, which can convert historical data from the Japanese candlestick pattern into data that's applicable to the Heikin-Ashi candlestick pattern. In *step 2*, you use the `get_instrument()` method of `broker_connection` to fetch an instrument and assign it to a new attribute, `instrument`. This object is an instance of the `Instrument` class. The two parameters needed to call `get_instrument()` are the exchange (`'NSE'`) and the trading symbol (`'TATASTEEL'`). Next, you use the `get_historical_data()` method of the `broker_connection` object to fetch the historical data for the duration of December 2019, with a candle interval of 1 minute. The time-series data returned is in the form of Japanese candlestick pattern. The `HeikinAshi()` function converts this data to Heikin-Ashi candlestick pattern, another `pandas.DataFrame` object. You assign it to `historical_data_1minute_heikinashi`. Observe that `historical_data_1minute_heikinashi` has `timestamp`, `close`, `open`, `high`, and `low` columns. Also, observe that the timestamps are equidistant as the Heikin-Ashi candles are based on the average values of the Japanese candles. In *steps 3* and *4*, you selectively extract a green and a red candle from the data. (Please note, this indices passed to `historical_data.iloc` would be different if you choose a different duration for `historical_data` fetched in the first recipe of this chapter.) Observe that the candles have shadows (lines extending on either side of the main candle body) as the candle have `high` and `low` attributes, along with the `open` and `close` attributes. In *step 5*, you plot the complete historical data held by `historical_data` using the `plot_candlstick_charts()` function.

In *steps 6* until *12*, you fetch the historical data using the Japanese candlestick pattern, converts it into the Heikin-Ashi candlestick pattern, and plots the converted data for candle intervals of 3 minutes, 5 minutes, 10 minutes, 15 minutes, 30 minutes, 1 hour, and 1 day, respectively. Observe the following differences and similarities among the charts as the candle interval increases:

- The total number of candlesticks decreases.
- The spikes in the charts due to sudden price movement are minimized. Smaller candle interval charts have more spikes as they focus on local trends, while larger candle interval charts have fewer spikes and are smoother.
- A long-term trend in the stock price becomes visible.

- Decision-making may become slower because you have to wait longer to get new candle data. Slower decisions may or may not be desirable, depending on the strategy. For example, to confirm trends, using a combination of data with a smaller candle interval, say 3 minutes, and data with a larger candle interval, say 15 minutes, would be desirable. On the other hand, to grab opportunities in intraday trading, data with larger candle intervals, say 1 hour or 1 day, would not be desirable.
- The price ranges (y-axis spread) of adjacent candles may or may not overlap.
- All the timestamps are equally spaced in time (within market hours).

If you are interested in finding out about the Math and implementation of Heikin-Ashi candles, please refer to the source code in the `pyalgotrading` **package** at https://github.com/algobulls/pyalgotrading/blob/master/pyalgotrading/utils/candlesticks/heikinashi.py.

Fetching historical data using Quandl

So far, in all the recipes in this chapter, you have used the broker connection to fetch historical data. In this recipe, you will fetch historical data using a third-party tool, Quandl (https://www.quandl.com/tools/python). It has a free to use Python version which can be easily installed using `pip`. This recipe demonstrates the use of `quandl` to fetch historical data of **FAAMG** stock prices (Facebook, Amazon, Apple, Microsoft, and Google).

Getting ready

Make sure you have installed the Python `quandl` package. If you haven't, you can install it using the following `pip` command:

```
$ pip install quandl
```

How to do it...

We execute the following steps for this recipe:

1. Import the necessary modules:

```
>>> from pyalgotrading.utils.func import plot_candlestick_chart,
PlotType
>>> import quandl
```

2. Plot a chart for the historical data of Facebook with a 1-day candle interval:

```
>>> facebook = quandl.get('WIKI/FB',
                          start_date='2015-1-1',
                          end_date='2015-3-31')
>>> plot_candlestick_chart(facebook,
                           PlotType.QUANDL_OHLC,
                           'Historical Data | '
                           'Japanese Candlesticks Pattern | '
                           'FACEBOOK | '
                           'Jan-March 2015 | '
                           'Candle Interval: Day', True)
```

You will get the following output:

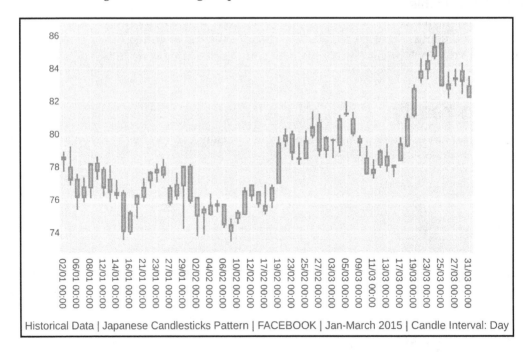

Historical Data | Japanese Candlesticks Pattern | FACEBOOK | Jan-March 2015 | Candle Interval: Day

3. Plot a chart for the historical data of Amazon with a 1-day candle interval:

```
>>> amazon = quandl.get('WIKI/AMZN',
                        start_date='2015-1-1',
                        end_date='2015-3-31')
>>> plot_candlestick_chart(amazon,
                           PlotType.QUANDL_OHLC,
                           'Historical Data | '
                           'Japanese Candlesticks Pattern | '
                           'AMAZON | '
                           'Jan-March 2015 | '
                           'Candle Interval: Day', True)
```

You will get the following output:

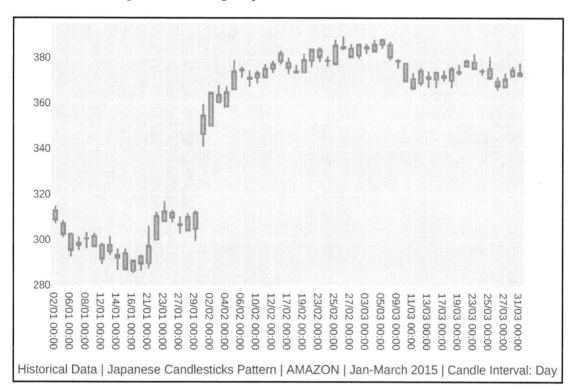

4. Plot a chart for the historical data of Apple with a 1-day candle interval:

```
>>> apple = quandl.get('WIKI/AAPL',
                       start_date='2015-1-1',
                       end_date='2015-3-31')
>>> plot_candlestick_chart(apple,
                 PlotType.QUANDL_OHLC,
                 'Historical Data | '
                 'Japanese Candlesticks Pattern | '
                 'APPLE | '
                 'Jan-March 2015 | '
                 'Candle Interval: Day', True)
```

You will get the following output:

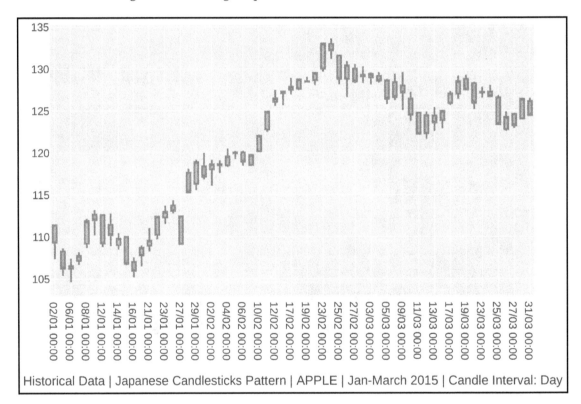

5. Plot a chart for the historical data of Microsoft with a 1-day candle interval:

```
>>> microsoft = quandl.get('WIKI/MSFT',
                            start_date='2015-1-1',
                            end_date='2015-3-31')
>>> plot_candlestick_chart(microsoft,
                            PlotType.QUANDL_OHLC,
                            'Historical Data | '
                            'Japanese Candlesticks Pattern | '
                            'MICROSOFT | '
                            'Jan-March 2015 | '
                            'Candle Interval: Day', True)
```

You will get the following output:

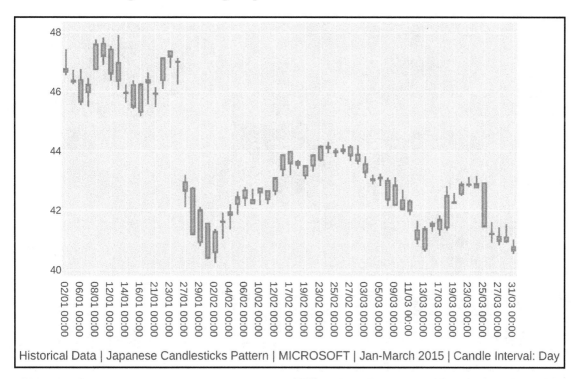

Historical Data | Japanese Candlesticks Pattern | MICROSOFT | Jan-March 2015 | Candle Interval: Day

6. Plot a chart for the historical data of Google with a 1-day candle interval:

```
>>> google = quandl.get('WIKI/GOOGL',
                        start_date='2015-1-1',
                        end_date='2015-3-31')
>>> plot_candlestick_chart(google,
                        PlotType.QUANDL_OHLC,
                        'Historical Data | '
                        'Japanese Candlesticks Pattern | '
                        'GOOGLE | '
                        'Jan-March 2015 | '
                        'Candle Interval: Day', True)
```

You will get the following output:

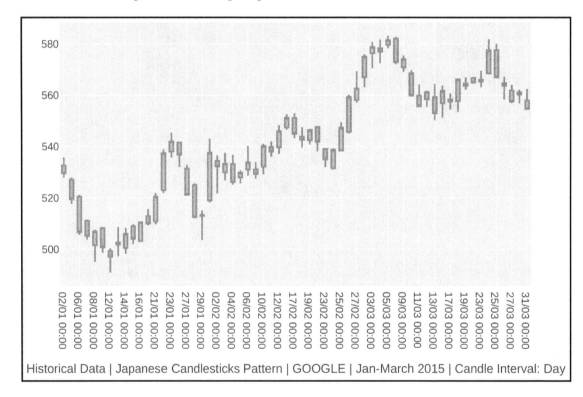

How it works...

In *step 1*, you import `plot_candlestick_chart`, a quick utility function for plotting candlestick pattern charts, `PlotType`, an enum for various types of candlestick patterns, and the `quandl` module. In the remaining steps, historical data for the Facebook, Amazon, Apple, Microsoft, and Google stocks are fetched using `quandl.get()` and plotted using the `plot_candlestick_chart()` method. The data that's returned by the `quandl` is in the OHLC (open, high, low, close) format.

The upside of such third-party modules is that they are free and you don't need to set up a broker connection to fetch the historical data. The downside is that this data from the free package has its limitations. For example, the data cannot be fetched in real-time and the data cannot be fetched for intraday trading (1-minute candle, 3-minute candle, and so on).

So, whether you want to use this data depends on your requirements. It may be good for testing or flow flushing the existing code base, but not good enough for providing live data feeds, which are needed during real trading sessions.

5
Computing and Plotting Technical Indicators

Technical analysis is a discipline in trading that employs mathematical functions, called **technical indicators**, to predict and find profitable opportunities in stock markets. Technical indicators analyze data based on past and current prices and volumes of a financial instrument and give out statistical information. This helps in predicting where the future prices of a financial instrument may go (either up or down). With this knowledge, you as a trader can make informed decisions when trading and hence increase your odds of success.

Technical indicators do not take into account any of the fundamental aspects of the business of the underlying financial instrument, such as revenue, earnings, profit, and so on. However, they do take past and current prices and volumes into account, which helps in predicting short-term price movements.

Most brokers provide technical indicator charts, superimposed on historical data plots, in real time. This helps in visually predicting trends in price movements. However, there are a few limitations to only doing visual analysis:

- You can view and analyze only a handful of charts at a time, while there could potentially be thousands of charts you may want to analyze to help search for a profitable opportunity.
- Analyzing multiple charts visually is tedious and subject to delay and human error. Delays and errors are not viable when we want to instantly and accurately grab a good trading opportunity.

Hence, it is best to let a computer analyze historical data for a large number of financial instruments in real time. For this reason, it is important to learn to compute technical indicators for a given financial instrument using its historical data. This chapter has recipes that introduce code for computing various technical indicators using Python.

There may be scenarios where you would want to plot complex charts. However, it may not be possible to do so with the tools provided by most brokers. For example, you may want to plot a **simple moving average** (**SMA**) on the **relative strength index** (**RSI**) of the close of historical data (mathematically, this is *SMA(RSI(close, timeperiod=10), timeperiod=5)*) and analyze it over a period of, say, 3 months, to aid in the development of your trading strategy. On these occasions, it would help to know how to plot technical indicators for a given financial instrument. The recipes of this chapter also include code to plot technical indicators using Python.

Every technical indicator belongs to one of the following two mentioned categories:

- **Leading**: This category of indicators gives trade signals when the trend is about to start or a reversal is about to happen. In other words, they *lead* the trend. So, these indicators are helpful in predicting the upcoming trend. (The trend can be **bullish** if the prices are going up, or **bearish** if they are going down.)
- **Lagging**: This category of indicators gives trade signals after a trend has started or after a reversal has happened. So, these indicators are helpful in finding out the current trend.

Technical indicators can also be broadly classified into four types, based on the insight they give:

- **Trend indicators or oscillators**: These indicators indicate the trend in the market, if there is a trend. These indicators are also called **oscillators** as they often oscillate between high and low values with time, like an oscillating wave. Such indicators are usually *lagging*, but can sometimes be *leading* as well.
- **Momentum indicators**: These indicators tell us how strong the current trend is and also if a reversal in the current trend is likely to occur. These indicators are usually *leading* indicators.
- **Volatility indicators**: These indicators measure the rate of change of price movement, irrespective of the direction (that is, **bearish** or **bullish**). These indicators help us understand how fast or slow prices are changing. A very volatile market might not be good for your trading strategy, as by the time you query the market and place an order at a particular price, the price might have moved significantly away from the specified price. These indicators are usually *lagging* indicators.
- **Volume indicators**: These are indicators that indicate how fast or slow the volume is changing with time. The higher the volume, the stronger the current trend would be, so these indicators help in finding the strength of the current trend. These indicators can be both *leading* and *lagging*.

This chapter discusses 10 technical indicators across all the previously mentioned categories and types. Each recipe does the following:

1. Introduces a new technical indicator
2. Shows how it can be computed on given historical data using Python
3. Shows how it can be plotted on a Japanese candlestick pattern chart using Python
4. Explains the insight provided by the indicator from the plot

In this chapter, we will cover the following recipes:

- Trend indicators – simple moving average
- Trend indicators – exponential moving average
- Trend indicators – moving average convergence divergence
- Trend indicators – parabolic stop and reverse
- Momentum indicators – relative strength index
- Momentum indicators – stochastic oscillator
- Volatility indicators – Bollinger Bands
- Volatility indicators – average true range
- Volume indicators – on balance volume
- Volume indicators – volume-weighted average price

The main focus of this chapter is to demonstrate how the most commonly used technical indicators can be computed and plotted. Although each technical indicator is introduced at the beginning of every recipe, understanding them in depth is beyond the scope of this book. If you are interested in this, please refer to the work of renowned personalities, such as Jack Schwager, Martin Pring, John Murphy, Steve Nison, and Thomas Bulkowski, to name a few. You can also use widely accepted web resources, such as `https://www.investopedia.com/`.

Technical requirements

You will need the following to successfully execute the recipes in this chapter:

- Python 3.7+
- The following Python packages:
  - pyalgotrading ($ pip install pyalgotrading)
  - TA-Lib ($ pip install TA-Lib)

If you face errors while installing TA-Lib, it will mostly be due to missing dependencies. You can follow these instructions to fix the issue:

- **For Mac OS X, use the following**:

  ```
  $ brew install ta-lib
  ```

- **For Windows, use the following instructions**:

  You can install the latest TA-Lib binary from https://www.lfd.uci.edu/~gohlke/pythonlibs/#ta-lib based on your Windows build (32 bit/64 bit) and Python version. So, for example, this link on the site TA_Lib-0.4.18-cp38-cp38-win_amd64.whl, is for TA-Lib version 0.4.18 (TA_Lib-0.4.18) and Python version 3.8 (cp38) and is Windows 64-bit-compatible (win_amd64).

- **For Linux, take the following steps**:

  Download the gzip file from http://prdownloads.sourceforge.net/ta-lib/ta-lib-0.4.0-src.tar.gz and run the following commands from your Linux Terminal:

  1. Extract the downloaded gzip file containing the source code for TA-Lib:

     ```
     $ tar -xzf ta-lib-0.4.0-src.tar.gz
     ```

  2. Change your current working directory to the extracted folder:

     ```
     $ cd ta-lib/
     ```

  3. Run the configure command to configure TA-Lib for your machine:

     ```
     $ ./configure --prefix=/usr
     ```

4. Run the `make` command to build `TA-Lib` from the downloaded source code:

   ```
   $ make
   ```

5. Run the `install` command to install built executables and libraries to specific directories on your machine:

   ```
   $ sudo make install
   ```

If this doesn't help and you still get errors, please refer to the official `TA-Lib` GitHub page at `https://github.com/mrjbq7/ta-lib#dependencies`.

The latest Jupyter notebook for this chapter can be found on GitHub at `https://github.com/PacktPublishing/Python-Algorithmic-Trading-Cookbook/tree/master/Chapter05`.

It is recommended that you try out the recipes of this chapter in a Jupyter notebook. All of the recipes have a plot as an output. You can interact with those plots conveniently in Jupyter Notebook using its features such as select, pan, zoom, and so on.

The first thing needed for setting connectivity with the broker is getting the API keys. The broker will provide unique keys to each customer, typically as an `api-key` and `api-secret` key pair. These API keys are chargeable, usually on a monthly subscription basis. You need to get your copy of `api-key` and `api-secret` from the broker website before starting this. You can refer to *Appendix I* for more details.

The following steps will help you import the necessary modules, set up the broker connection with Zerodha, and fetch and keep some historical data handy, which will be used by all the recipes in this chapter. Please make sure you have followed these steps before trying out any of the recipes:

1. Import the necessary modules:

   ```
   >>> import pandas as pd
   >>> import talib
   >>> from pyalgotrading.broker.broker_connection_zerodha import
   BrokerConnectionZerodha
   >>> from pyalgotrading.utils.func import plot_candlesticks_chart,
   PlotType
   ```

   These modules will be needed throughout this chapter.

The `plot_candlesticks_chart` function is used in every recipe. It takes the following arguments:

- `data`: The historical data to be plotted, which should be a `pandas.DataFrame` object with `timestamp`, `open`, `high`, `low`, and `close` columns.
- `plot_type`: An instance of the `pyalgotrading.plot_type` enum class specifying the type of candlesticks pattern chart.
- `indicators` (optional): A list of dictionaries, specifying the indicator that should also be plotted along with the candlesticks pattern chart. Each `dict` should have the following key-value pairs:
  - `name`: The name of the plot for the legend
  - `data`: The `pandas.Series` object representing the indicator data to be plotted
  - `extra` (optional): The `dict` of attributes, which will be passed to the `plotly.graph_objects.Scatter` constructor (more information on this class can be found at `https://plot.ly/python-api-reference/generated/plotly.graph_objects.Scatter.html`)
- `plot_indicators_separately` (optional): If `False`, indicators will be plotted on the same plot as the historical data. If `True`, indicators will be plotted separately. The default value is `False`.
- `caption` (optional): Add a string caption to the plot.

2. Get the `api_key` and `api_secret` keys from the broker. These are unique to you and will be used by the broker to identify your Demat account:

```
>>> api_key = "<your-api-key>"
>>> api_secret = "<your-api-secret>"
>>> broker_connection = BrokerConnectionZerodha(api_key,
                                                api_secret)
```

We get the following output:

```
Installing package kiteconnect via pip. This may take a while...
Please login to this link to generate your request token:
https://kite.trade/connect/login?api_key=<your-api-key>&v=3
```

If you are running this for the first time and `kiteconnect` is not installed, `pyalgotrading` will automatically install it for you. The final output of *step 2* will be a link. Click on the link and log in with your Zerodha credentials. If the authentication is successful, you will see a link in your browser's address bar similar
to `https://127.0.0.1/?request_token=<aplphanumeric-token>&action =login&status=success`—for
example, `https://127.0.0.1/?request_token=H06I6Ydv95y23D2Dp7NbigF jKweGwRP7&action=login&status=success`.

3. Copy the alphanumeric token and paste it in `request_token`:

```
>>> request_token = "<your-request-token>"
>>> broker_connection.set_access_token(request_token)
```

4. Fetch and print the historical data for an instrument and assign it to `historical_data`:

```
>>> instrument = broker_connection.get_instrument('NSE',
                                                   'TATASTEEL')
>>> historical_data = \
        broker_connection.get_historical_data(
                        instrument=instrument,
                        candle_interval='minute',
                        start_date='2020-01-01 12:00:00',
                        end_date='2020-01-01 14:00:00')
>>> historical_data
```

We get the following output:

```
                      timestamp   open    high     low   close  volume
  0 2020-01-01 12:00:00+05:30   467.00  467.30  467.00  467.15    5694
  1 2020-01-01 12:01:00+05:30   467.15  467.50  467.10  467.35   10852
  2 2020-01-01 12:02:00+05:30   467.35  467.45  467.20  467.45    4171
  3 2020-01-01 12:03:00+05:30   467.50  467.50  467.35  467.45    2897
...                       ...      ...     ...     ...     ...     ...
117 2020-01-01 13:57:00+05:30   469.70  469.70  469.55  469.60    9442
118 2020-01-01 13:58:00+05:30   469.60  469.70  469.50  469.60    7609
119 2020-01-01 13:59:00+05:30   469.60  469.60  469.50  469.50    8155
120 2020-01-01 14:00:00+05:30   469.50  469.60  469.45  469.60    6973
```

This step uses the `get_instrument()` method of the `BrokerConnectionZerodha` class to fetch an instrument and assign it to a new attribute, `instrument`. This object is an instance of the `Instrument` class. The two parameters needed to call `get_instrument` are the exchange (`'NSE'`) and the trading-symbol (`'TATASTEEL'`). Next, historical data is fetched and printed for `instrument` using the `get_historical_data()` method. This method takes four arguments, described as follows:

- `instrument` (`Instrument`): The object returned by the `get_instrument()` method of `broker_connection`.
- `candle_interval` (`str`): A valid string that denotes the duration of each candlestick in the historical data. Possible values can be `'minute'`, `'3minute'`, `'5minute'`, `'10minute'`, `'15minute'`, `'30minute'`, `'60minute'`, and `'day'`. We pass `'minute'` to this argument in *step 4*.
- `start_date` (`str`): Historical data will be fetched starting from this timestamp. We pass `'2020-01-01 12:00:00'` to this argument in *step 4*.
- `end_date` (`str`): Historical data will be fetched up to this timestamp. We pass `'2020-01-01 14:00:00'` to this argument in *step 4*.

The `historical_data` object will be needed throughout this chapter.

The `pyalgotrading` package supports multiple brokers and provides a connection object class per broker, with the same methods. It abstracts broker APIs behind a unified interface, so you need not worry about the underlying broker API calls and can use all the recipes in this chapter as it is. Only the procedure to set up the broker connection will vary from broker to broker. You can refer to the `pyalgotrading` documentation for information on setting up the broker connection if you are not using Zerodha as your broker. For Zerodha users, the steps mentioned in the preceding section will suffice.

Trend indicators – simple moving average

SMA is a **lagging trend indicator**. It is used to smooth the price data by eliminating noise and thus identifying trends.

SMA is the simplest form of a moving average. Each output value is the average of the previous *n* values of the historical data. You can define the value of *n*, which is also called the **time period**. In SMA, each value in the time period carries the same weight, and values outside the time period are not included. This makes it less responsive to recent changes compared to previous changes in the data, and is thus useful for smoothing out the prices' data. A consecutive rise in SMA indicates a clear bullish trend, while a consecutive fall indicates a **bearish** trend. Thus, it is a **trend indicator**. Also, since it indicates the trend after it has started, it is a **lagging indicator**.

SMA is widely used in technical analysis. It is also used for calculating other technical indicators, either in combination with itself or other indicators, with the same or different time periods.

The formula for calculating SMA is as follows:

$$SMA = \sum_{i=1}^{n} price_i$$

(*n* >= 1), and here, *n* is the time period and has to be defined by the user.

Although it is a good idea to know the mathematics behind how this works, this recipe does not require you to understand or remember the given formula. We use a third-party Python package, `talib`, which provides a ready function for calculating SMA.

Getting started

Make sure your Python namespace has the following objects:

1. `talib` (package)
2. `plot_candlesticks_chart` (function)
3. `PlotType` (enum)
4. `historical_data` (a pandas DataFrame)

Refer to the *Technical requirements* section of this chapter to set up these objects.

How to do it...

We will execute the following steps for this recipe:

1. Calculate the SMA on `historical_data`. Assign it to `sma_9` and print it:

```
>>> sma_9 = talib.SMA(historical_data['close'],
                            timeperiod=9)
>>> sma_9
```

We get the following output:

```
0                NaN
1                NaN
2                NaN
3                NaN
4                NaN
5                NaN
6                NaN
7                NaN
8          467.927778
9          468.100000
10         468.211111
11         468.400000
             ...
117        469.738889
118        469.744444
119        469.716667
120        469.716667
```

2. Plot `sma_9` on `historical_data`:

```
>>> indicators = [
    {
        'name': 'SMA 9',
        'data': sma_9,
        'extra': {
            'mode': 'lines',
            'line': {
                'color': 'gray'
            }
        }
    }
]
>>> plot_candlesticks_chart(data=historical_data,
                                plot_type=PlotType.JAPANESE,
```

```
indicators=indicators,
caption='Trend Indicator: '
'Simple Moving Average | '
'NSE:TATASTEEL | '
'1st Jan, 2020 | '
'Candle Interval: 1 Minute')
```

We get the following output:

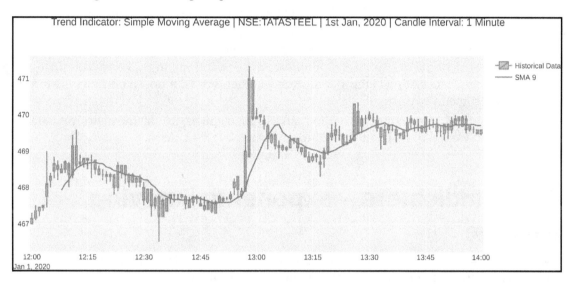

The `plotly` Python package (https://github.com/plotly/plotly.py) is required for plotting charts. The `plot_candlesticks_chart` function will install it for you if you don't have it installed already.

How it works...

The `talib` package provides a ready-to-use `talib.SMA` function. We use this in *step 1* to compute SMA on `historical_data` and assign it to a new attribute, `sma_9`. Along with the close series of `historical_data`, this function takes `timeperiod` as a parameter, which should be an `int` value. We use 9 as the parameter here. The `sma_9` object is a `pandas.Series` object. This is printed in *step 1*. We plot `sma_9` on `historical_data` in *step 2* using the `plot_candlesticks_chart` function.

Observe the following points regarding the SMA indicator values and chart:

- The SMA plot is missing for the first eight timestamp values as the output values are NaN (the index starts from 0, so indices 0 to 7 are the first eight values). This is because the `talib.SMA` function requires at least a time period number of entries to compute the SMA, which is 9 in our case. From the ninth row onward, we can see the computed values of the **Simple moving average (SMA)** and the corresponding timestamp of the `historical_data` object.
- The SMA increases as the prices go up and decreases as the prices go down, though not immediately in the next timestamp.
- The rise or fall of the SMA plot follows the rise and fall in the corresponding prices. Hence, it's a lagging indicator. In other words, it doesn't predict the trend outcome in advance.
- The SMA plot is smooth, without any sudden spikes, unlike the historical data plot. Hence, SMA is often used to smoothen out the prices.

Trend indicators – exponential moving average

EMA is a lagging trend indicator. It is used to smooth the price data by eliminating noise and thus identifying trends, with more weightage to recent values.

The EMA technical indicator calculation is cumulative and includes all the data with decreasing weights. Past values have a lower contribution to the average, while recent values have a greater contribution. The further away the value, the smaller the contribution. Thus, EMA is a moving average that is more responsive to recent changes in the data.

The EMA technical indicator is not like the SMA technical indicator, where each value in the time period carries equal weight and values outside of the time period are not included in the calculation.

EMA is widely used in technical analysis. It is also used for calculating other technical indicators, either in combination with itself or other indicators, with the same or different time periods.

A recursive formula for calculating EMA is as follows:

$$K = \frac{2}{n+1}$$
$$EMA_n = K \times input + (1 - K) \times EMA_{n-1}$$

$(n >= 1)$, and here, *n* is the **time period** and has to be defined by the user. *K* is sometimes called the **smoothing** or **weighting factor**.

Although it is a good idea to know the mathematics of how this works, this recipe does not require you to understand or remember the given formula. We use a third-party Python package, `talib`, which provides a ready function for calculating EMA.

Getting started

Make sure your Python namespace has the following objects:

1. `talib` (package)
2. `plot_candlesticks_chart` (function)
3. `PlotType` (enum)
4. `historical_data` (a pandas DataFrame)

Refer to the *Technical requirements* section of this chapter to set up these objects.

How to do it...

We will execute the following steps for this recipe:

1. Calculate the EMA on `historical_data`. Assign it to `ema_9` and print it:

```
>>> ema_9 = talib.EMA(historical_data['close'],
                      timeperiod=9)
>>> ema_9
```

We get the following output:

```
0            NaN
1            NaN
2            NaN
3            NaN
4            NaN
5            NaN
6            NaN
7            NaN
8       467.927778
9       468.082222
10      468.135778
11      468.338622
        . . .
```

```
117     469.728790
118     469.703032
119     469.662426
120     469.649941
```

2. Plot `ema_9` on `historical_data`:

```
>>> indicators = [
    {
        'name': 'EMA 9',
        'data': ema_9,
        'extra': {
            'mode': 'lines',
            'line': {
                'color': 'gray'
            }
        }
    }
]
>>> plot_candlesticks_chart(data=historical_data,
                            plot_type=PlotType.JAPANESE,
                            indicators=indicators,
                            caption='Trend Indicator: '
                            'Exponential Moving Average | '
                            'NSE:TATASTEEL | '
                            '1st Jan, 2020 | '
                            'Candle Interval: 1 Minute')
```

We get the following output:

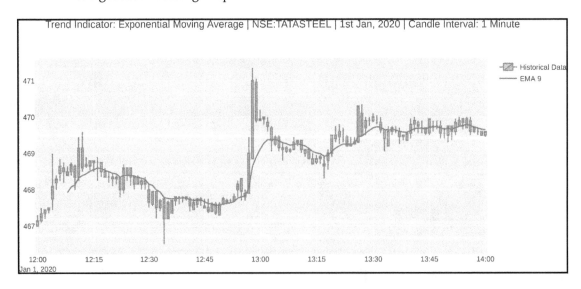

How it works...

The `talib` package provides a ready-to-use `talib.EMA` function. We use this in *step 1* to compute the EMA on `historical_data` and assign it to a new attribute, `ema_9`. Along with the close series of `historical_data`, this function takes `timeperiod` as a parameter, which should be an `int` value. We use `9` as the parameter here. The `ema_9` object is a `pandas.Series` object. This is printed in *step 1*. We plot `ema_9` on `historical_data` in *step 2* using the `plot_candlesticks_chart` function.

Observe the following points regarding the EMA indicator values and chart:

- The EMA plot is missing for the first eight timestamp values as the output values are `NaN` (the index starts from `0`, so indices `0` to `7` are first eight values). This is because the `talib.EMA` function requires at least a time period number of entries to compute EMA, which is `9` in our case. From the ninth row onward, we can see the EMA computed, each entry being the EMA for the corresponding timestamp of the `historical_data` object.

- The EMA increases as the prices go up and decreases as the prices go down, closely following the prices. Hence, it's a trend indicator.

- The rise or fall of the EMA plot follows the rise and fall in the corresponding prices. Hence, it's a lagging indicator. In other words, it doesn't predict the trend outcome in advance.

- The EMA plot is smooth, without any sudden spikes, unlike the historical data plot. Hence, EMA is used to smooth out the prices.

- The EMA plot, when compared to the SMA plot from the *Plotting trend indicator – simple moving average* recipe, shows that the EMA plot follows the price trend more closely than the SMA plot. That is because EMA gives more weightage to recent values, unlike SMA, where each bit of data used for computation has equal weightage.

 For more information on the usage of the `plot_candlesticks_chart` function, please refer to the *How it works...* section of the *Plotting trend indicator – simple moving average* recipe of this chapter.

Trend indicators – moving average convergence divergence

Moving average convergence divergence (**MACD**) is a lagging trend indicator. MACD has three components: the MACD line, MACD signal, and MACD histogram. The MACD line helps in identifying trend changes as it signals the start of a new trend direction. Large positive values of the MACD line indicate that the shorter EMA is much larger than the longer EMA. This suggests that there is an *overbought* condition in the market, which means prices will be going up. Similarly, large negative values of the MACD line indicate that the shorter EMA is much smaller than the longer EMA. This suggests that there is an *oversold* condition in the market, which means the prices will be going down. When the MACD line crosses above the MACD signal and is positive, a **buy** signal is generated; and the MACD line crosses below the MACD signal and becomes negative, a **sell** signal is generated.

The formulae for computing the three components of MACD are given as follows:

- The MACD line is the difference between two different time period EMAs—the EMA of a shorter time period, m, and the EMA of a longer time period, n:

$$MACD\ line = EMA_m - EMA_n$$
$$where\ m < n(m, n)\epsilon\ Integers$$

- The MACD signal is the EMA of the MACD line, with time period p:

$$MACD\ signal = EMA(MACD\ line)_p$$

- The MACD histogram is the difference between the MACD line and the MACD signal:

$$MACD\ histogram = MACD\ line - MACD\ signal$$

The time periods for the MACD line are often given as 12 (m) and 26 (n) and the time period for the MACD signal is often given as 9 (p).

Although it is a good idea to know the mathematics of how this works, this recipe does not require you to understand or remember the given formula. We use a third-party Python package, `talib`, which provides a ready function for calculating MACD.

Getting started

Make sure your Python namespace has the following objects:

1. `talib` (package)
2. `pd` (module)
3. `plot_candlesticks_chart` (function)
4. `PlotType` (enum)
5. `historical_data` (a pandas DataFrame)

Refer to the *Technical requirements* section of this chapter to set up these objects.

How to do it...

We will execute the following steps for this recipe:

1. Calculate MACD on `historical_data`. Assign it to `macd_line`, `macd_signal`, and `macd_historgram`. Also, print it:

```
>>> macd_line, macd_signal, macd_histogram = \
                    talib.MACD(historical_data['close'],
                               fastperiod=12,
                               slowperiod=26,
                               signalperiod=9)
>>> pd.DataFrame({
    'Line': macd_line,
    'Signal': macd_signal,
    'Histogram': macd_histogram
})
```

We get the following output:

```
        Line    Signal Histogram
0        NaN       NaN       NaN
1        NaN       NaN       NaN
2        NaN       NaN       NaN
3        NaN       NaN       NaN
4        NaN       NaN       NaN
...      ...       ...       ...
116 0.075136 0.087038 -0.011901
117 0.057580 0.081146 -0.023566
118 0.043170 0.073551 -0.030381
119 0.023410 0.063523 -0.040113
120 0.015639 0.053946 -0.038307
```

2. Plot `macd_line`, `macd_signal`, and `macd_histogram`, along with `historical_data`:

```
>>> indicators = [
    {
        'name': 'MACD Line',
        'data': macd_line,
        'extra': {
            'mode': 'lines',
            'line': {
                'width': 1
            }
        }
    },
    {
        'name': 'MACD Signal',
        'data': macd_signal,
        'extra': {
            'mode': 'lines',
            'line': {
                'width': 1
            }
        }
    },
    {
        'name': 'MACD Histogram',
        'data': macd_histogram,
        'extra': {
            'mode': 'lines',
            'line': {
                'dash': 'dot',
                'width': 2
            }
        }
    }
]

>>> plot_candlesticks_chart(data=historical_data,
                            plot_type=PlotType.JAPANESE,
                            indicators=indicators,
                            plot_indicators_separately=True,
                            caption='Trend Indicator: Moving '
                            'Average Convergence/Divergence | '
                            'NSE:TATASTEEL | '
                            '1st Jan, 2020 | '
                            'Candle Interval: 1 Minute',
                            plot_height=700)
```

We get the following output:

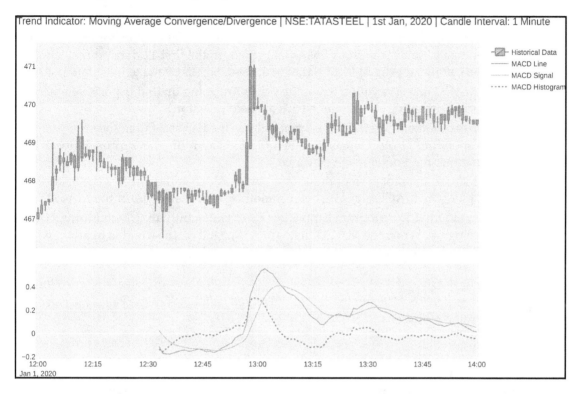

How it works...

The `talib` package provides a ready-to-use `talib.MACD` function. We use this in *step 1* to compute MACD on `historical_data`. Along with the close series of `historical_data`, this function takes `fastperiod`, `slowperiod`, and `signalperiod` as parameters, all of which should be objects of the `int` type. We use `26`, `12`, and `9` as the respective parameters here. The `talib.MACD` function returns three `pandas.Series` objects, which we assign to new attributes: `macd_line`, `macd_signal`, and `macd_histogram`. These three objects are concatenated into a `pandas.DataFrame` object and printed in *step 1*. We plot `macd_line`, `macd_signal`, and `macd_histogram` along with `historical_data` in *step 2* using the `plot_candlesticks_chart` function.

Observe the following points regarding the MACD indicator values and chart:

- The MACD plot is missing for the first 34 timestamp values and starts appearing only at the 35th timestamp. This is because it takes 26 data points for the first long EMA data to come (the short EMA data comes in the first 12 data points), and 9 of these points for the MACD signal to appear. So, 26 + 9 make it 35 data points.
- The MACD line is negative when the prices are going up and is positive when the prices are going down. Hence, it's a trend indicator.
- The rise or fall of the MACD line plot follows the rise and fall in the corresponding prices. Hence, it's a lagging indicator. In other words, it doesn't predict the trend outcome in advance.
- The MACD line plot is smooth, without any sudden spikes, unlike the historical data plot. The MACD signal is even smoother, as it is an EMA of the MACD line.
- When the MACD histogram is positive, the trend is **bullish**, which means prices are going up. When the MACD histogram is negative, the trend is **bearish**, which means the prices are going down.

> For usage of the `plot_candlesticks_chart` function, please refer to the *How it works...* section of the *Plotting trend indicator – simple moving average* recipe of this chapter.

Trend indicators – parabolic stop and reverse

Parabolic **stop and reverse** (**SAR**) is a leading trend indicator.

The parabolic SAR computes a trailing stop loss for every data point. As the data points are stop-loss points, they are away from the prices when there is a trend and cross the price line during a trend reversal. The parabolic SAR takes two parameters as input: the `acceleration factor` and the `maximum` point.

The formula for computing the parabolic SAR is not straightforward and is hence not mentioned here. If you are interested in the underlying math, please refer to the official documentation of `TA-Lib` on parabolic SAR at `http://www.tadoc.org/indicator/SAR.htm`. Although it is a good idea to know the mathematics of how this works, this recipe does not require you to understand or remember the given formula. We use a third-party Python package, `talib`, which provides a ready function for calculating the parabolic SAR.

Getting started

Make sure your Python namespace has the following objects:

1. `talib` (package)
2. `plot_candlesticks_chart` (function)
3. `PlotType` (enum)
4. `historical_data` (a `pandas` DataFrame)

Refer to the *Technical requirements* section of this chapter to set up these objects.

How to do it...

We will execute the following steps for this recipe:

1. Calculate the parabolic SAR on `historical_data`. Assign it to `psar` and print it:

```
>>> psar = talib.SAR(historical_data['high'],
                     historical_data['low'],
                     acceleration=0.02,
                     maximum=0.2)
>>> psar
```

We get the following output:

```
0              NaN
1       467.000000
2       467.010000
3       467.019800
4       467.029404
           ...
116     469.175426
117     469.208409
118     469.240073
119     469.270470
120     469.299651
```

2. Plot `psar` on `historical_data`:

```
>>> indicators = [
    {
        'name': 'PSAR',
        'data': psar,
        'extra': {
            'mode': 'lines',
            'line': {
                'dash': 'dot',
                'width': 2,
                'color': 'purple'
            }
        }
    }
]

>>> plot_candlesticks_chart(data=historical_data,
                            plot_type=PlotType.JAPANESE,
                            indicators=indicators,
                            caption='Trend Indicator: '
                            'Parabolic Stop and Reverse | '
                            'NSE:TATASTEEL | '
                            '1st Jan, 2020 | '
                            'Candle Interval: 1 Minute')
```

We get the following output:

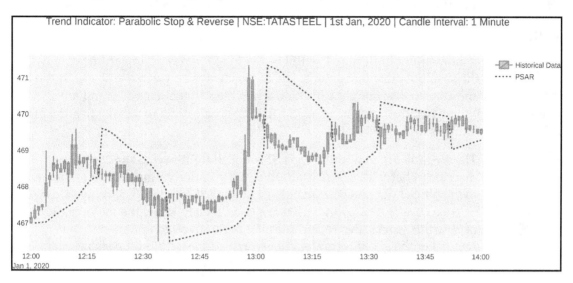

How it works...

The `talib` package provides a ready-to-use `talib.SAR` function. We use this in *step 1* to compute the parabolic SAR on `historical_data` and assign it to a new attribute, `psar`. Along with the high and low series of `historical_data`, this function takes `acceleration` and `maximum` as parameters, both of which should be objects of the `float` type. We use `0.02` and `0.2` as the respective parameters here. The `psar` object is a `pandas.Series` object. This is printed in *step 1*. We plot `psar`, along with `historical_data`, in *step 2* using the `plot_candlesticks_chart` function.

Observe the following points regarding the parabolic SAR indicator values and chart:

- The parabolic SAR is plotted as discrete points, as each point represents the stop loss. The stop loss point changes every time. So, it is a *trailing* stop loss.
- When the parabolic SAR plot is below the OHLC plot, the trend is **bullish**, and when it is above the OHLC plot, the trend is **bearish**. Hence, it's a trend indicator.

For more information on the usage of the `plot_candlesticks_chart` function, please refer to the *How it works...* section of the *Plotting trend indicator – simple moving average* recipe of this chapter.

Momentum indicators – relative strength index

RSI is a leading momentum indicator. The RSI is a ratio of the recent upward price movement to the absolute price movement. The RSI is always between 0 and 100. It can be interpreted to indicate an overbought condition when the value is above 70 and an oversold condition when the value is below 30. The RSI indicates a reversal when the prices are making new highs or new lows.

 The formula for computing the RSI is not straightforward and is hence not mentioned here. If you are interested in the underlying math, please refer to the official documentation of TA-Lib on RSI at http://www.tadoc.org/indicator/RSI.htm. Although it is a good idea to know the mathematics of how this works, this recipe does not require you to understand or remember the given formula. We use a third-party Python package, talib, which provides a ready function for calculating the RSI.

Getting started

Make sure your Python namespace has the following objects:

1. talib (package)
2. plot_candlesticks_chart (function)
3. PlotType (enum)
4. historical_data (a pandas DataFrame)

Refer to the *Technical requirements* section of this chapter to set up these objects.

How to do it...

We will execute the following steps for this recipe:

1. Calculate the RSI on historical_data. Assign it to rsi_14 and print it:

```
>>> rsi_14 = talib.RSI(historical_data['close'],
                       timeperiod=14)
>>> rsi_14
```

We get the following output:

```
0            NaN
1            NaN
2            NaN
3            NaN
         ...
12           NaN
13           NaN
14      70.886076
15      69.932757
16      69.932757
17      64.873530
18      61.976413
         ...
116     48.449209
117     48.449209
118     48.449209
119     45.997672
120     48.788323
```

2. Plot `rsi_14` along with `historical_data`:

```
>>> indicators = [
    {
        'name': 'RSI (14)',
        'data': rsi_14,
        'extra': {
            'mode': 'lines',
            'line': {
                'width': 2,
                'color': 'purple'
            }
        }
    }
]

>>> plot_candlesticks_chart(data=historical_data,
                            plot_type=PlotType.JAPANESE,
                            indicators=indicators,
                            plot_indicators_separately=True,
                            caption='Momentum Indicator: '
                            'Relative Strength Index | '
                            'NSE:TATASTEEL | '
                            '1st Jan, 2020 | '
                            'Candle Interval: 1 Minute')
```

We get the following output:

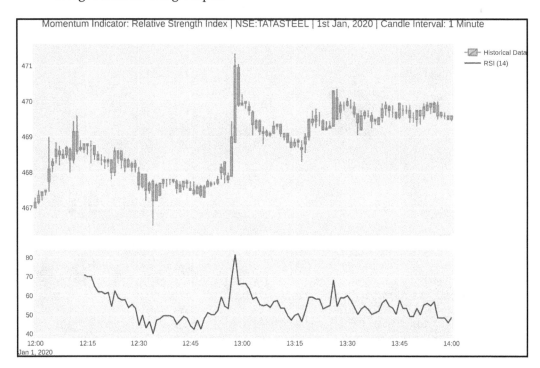

How it works...

The `talib` package provides a ready-to-use `talib.RSI` function. We use this in *step 1* to compute the RSI on `historical_data` and assign it to a new attribute, `rsi_14`. Along with the close series of `historical_data`, this function takes `timeperiod` as a parameter, which should be an `int` value. We use `14` as the parameter here. The `rsi_14` object is a `pandas.Series` object. This is printed in *step 1*. We plot `rsi_14` on `historical_data` in *step 2* using the `plot_candlesticks_chart` function.

Observe the following points regarding the RSI indicator values and chart:

- The first 13 values in the output are `NaN` (the index starts from `0`, so indices `0` to `12` are the first 13 values) because the function requires at least a time period number of entries to compute the RSI, which is `14` in our case. From the 14th row onward, we can see the RSI computed, each entry being the RSI for the corresponding timestamp of the `historical_data` object.

- The RSI is always between 0 and 100.
- For the given plot, the price peaks suddenly between 12:45 P.M. to 1:00 P.M., and the RSI moves above 70. Thus, it correctly indicates an *overbought* condition. Also, since it indicates the strength of the price movement, it is a momentum indicator.

 For more information on the usage of the `plot_candlesticks_chart` function, please refer to the *How it works...* section of the *Plotting trend indicator – simple moving average* recipe of this chapter.

Momentum indicators – stochastic oscillator

The stochastic oscillator is a leading momentum indicator. It is also called **STOCH** for short. STOCH compares the latest close with the recent trading range. *Fast K* is a ratio and has a value between 0 and 100. *Fast K* can have haphazard movement, and hence it is smoothed using a moving average, which is the *slow K*. *Slow K* is further smoothed using another moving average, which is the *slow D*. Values of *slow K* over 75 indicate an overbought condition, while values below 25 indicate an oversold condition. When *slow K* crosses above *slow D*, it is considered a **buy** signal. Similarly, when *slow K* crosses below *slow D*, it is considered a **sell** signal.

The formula for computing STOCH is as follows:

$$Fast\ K = 100 \times \frac{close - Min_{last\ n\ time\ periods}}{Max_{last\ n\ time\ periods} - Min_{last\ n\ time\ periods}}$$
$$Slow\ K = MA(Fast\ K)$$
$$Slow\ D = MA(Slow\ K)$$

MA stands for **moving average**, and can be either SMA or EMA. For this recipe, we have used SMA. This formula needs three time periods: one of them is *n* and the other two are the time periods of the MAs. The range over which we analyze data is defined by *n*.

Although it is a good idea to know the mathematics of how this works, this recipe does not require you to understand or remember the given formula. We use a third-party Python package, `talib`, which provides a ready function for calculating STOCH.

Getting started

Make sure your Python namespace has the following objects:

1. `talib` (package)
2. `pd` (module)
3. `plot_candlesticks_chart` (function)
4. `PlotType` (enum)
5. `historical_data` (a pandas DataFrame)

Refer to the *Technical requirements* section of this chapter to set up these objects.

How to do it...

We will execute the following steps for this recipe:

1. Calculate the stochastic oscillator on `historical_data`. Assign it to `slowk` and `slowd`. Also, print it:

```
>>> slowk, slowd = talib.STOCH(historical_data['high'],
                               historical_data['low'],
                               historical_data['close'],
                               fastk_period=5,
                               slowk_period=3,
                               slowk_matype=0,
                               slowd_period=3,
                               slowd_matype=0)
>>> pd.DataFrame({
        'Slow K': slowk,
        'Slow D': slowd
    })
```

We get the following output:

```
     Slow K     Slow D
0       NaN        NaN
1       NaN        NaN
2       NaN        NaN
3       NaN        NaN
4       NaN        NaN
5       NaN        NaN
6       NaN        NaN
7       NaN        NaN
8 70.514283  69.296302
```

```
  9  71.113411  70.921500
 10  61.606578  67.744757
 11  67.613252  66.777747
 12  52.662272  60.627367
...        ...         ...
116  63.626374  77.374847
117  44.102564  64.420024
118  20.000000  42.576313
119  13.333333  25.811966
120  15.757576  16.363636
```

2. Plot `slowk` **and** `slowd`, **along with** `historical_data`:

```
>>> indicators = [
    {
        'name': 'Slow K',
        'data': slowk,
        'extra': {
            'mode':'lines',
            'line': {
                'width': 2
            }
        }
    },
    {
        'name': 'Slow D',
        'data': slowd,
        'extra': {
            'mode': 'lines',
            'line': {
                'width': 2
            }
        }
    }
]

>>> plot_candlesticks_chart(data=historical_data,
                            plot_type=PlotType.JAPANESE,
                            indicators=indicators,
                            plot_indicators_separately=True,
                            caption='Trend Indicator: '
                            'Stochastic Oscillator (Slow) | '
                            'NSE:TATASTEEL | '
                            '1st Jan, 2020 | '
                            'Candle Interval: 1 Minute',
                            plot_height=700)
```

We get the following output:

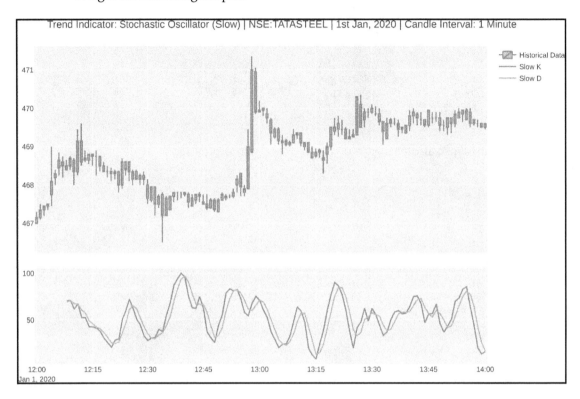

How it works...

The `talib` package provides a ready-to-use `talib.STOCH` function. We use this in *step 1* to compute the stochastic oscillator on `historical_data`. Along with the high, low, and close series of `historical_data`, this function takes the following parameters:

- `fastk_period` (`int`): The range over which we analyze the data. Here, we took the value as `5`.

- `slowk_period` (`int`): The time period for calculating the moving average on *fast K*. Here, we took the value as `3`.

- `slowk_matype` (`int`): The moving average type. A value of `0` implies SMA and `1` implies EMA. Here, we took the value as `0`.

- `slowd_period` (`int`): The time period for calculating the moving average on *slow K*. Here, we took the value as `3`.

- `slowd_matype` (`int`): The moving average type. A value of `0` implies SMA and `1` implies EMA. Here, we took the value as `0`.

The `talib.STOCH` function returns two `pandas.Series` objects, which we assign to new attributes: `slowk` and `slowd`. These two objects are concatenated into a `pandas.DataFrame` object and printed in *step 1*. We plot `slowk` and `slowd`, along with `historical_data`, in *step 2* using the `plot_candlesticks_chart` function.

Observe the following points regarding the STOCH indicator values and chart:

- The first eight values in the output are `NaN` (the index starts from `0`, so indices `0` to `7` are the first 8 values). That's because it takes the first five values to get a *fast K*, three *fast K*s to get a *slow K*, and three *slow K*s to get a *slow D*. So, that's 5 + (3 - 1) + (2 - 1) = 9. (We subtract `1` twice as the last value for previous computation is the first value for the next computation, so that's already counted once.) From the ninth row onward, we can see the computed values of *slow K* and *slow D* and the corresponding timestamp of the `historical_data` object.
- The *slow K* and *slow D* values are always between `0` and `100`.

- The rise or fall of the *slow K* and *slow D* plot is followed by the rise and fall in the corresponding prices for most of the time, particularly evident in the plot after 12:45 P.M. Hence, it's a leading indicator. In other words, it predicts the trend outcome in advance.
- Since it's a leading indicator, it reacts to prices quickly. This often results in false signals, as can be seen in the plot between 12:30 P.M. to 12:45P.M. (To safeguard yourself from these scenarios, you can use more indicators in your strategy to get additional confirmation of trends or reversals.)

Volatility indicators – Bollinger Bands

Bollinger Bands are a lagging volatility indicator. Bollinger Bands consist of three lines, or bands—the **middle band**, the **lower band**, and the **upper band**. The gap between the bands widens when the price volatility is high and reduces when the price volatility is low.

Bollinger Bands are an indicator of overbought or oversold conditions. When the price is near the upper band or the lower band, this indicator predicts that a reversal will happen soon. The middle band acts as a support or resistance level.

The upper band and lower band can also be interpreted as price targets. When the price bounces off of the upper band and crosses the middle band, the lower band becomes the price target, and vice versa.

The formulae for computing the Bollinger Bands are as follows.

Bollinger Bands define the **typical price** (**TP**) as the average of the high, low, and close of a candle. The TP is used for computing the middle band, lower band, and upper band:

$$TP = \frac{high + low + close}{3}$$

The middle band is the SMA of the TP:

$$Midband = SMA(TP)$$

The upper band and lower band are an integer (*F*) number of the standard deviation above and below the middle band. The typical value of *F* is 2:

$$Upperband = Midband + F \times \sigma(TP)$$
$$Lowerband = Midband - F \times \sigma(TP)$$

Although it is a good idea to know the mathematics of how this works, this recipe does not require you to understand or remember the given formula. We use a third-party Python package, `talib`, which provides a ready function for calculating the Bollinger Bands.

Getting started

Make sure your Python namespace has the following objects:

1. `talib` (package)
2. `pd` (module)
3. `plot_candlesticks_chart` (function)
4. `PlotType` (enum)
5. `historical_data` (a `pandas` DataFrame)

Refer to the *Technical requirements* section of this chapter to set up these objects.

How to do it...

We execute the following steps for this recipe:

1. Calculate the Bollinger Bands on `historical_data`. Assign it to `upperband`, `middleband`, and `lowerband`. Also, print it:

```
>>> upperband, middleband, lowerband = talib.BBANDS(
                                        historical_data['close'],
                                        timeperiod=5,
                                        nbdevup=2,
                                        nbdevdn=2,
                                        matype=0)
>>> pd.DataFrame({
    'Upperband': upperband,
    'Middleband': middleband,
    'Lowerband': lowerband
})
```

We get the following output:

	Upperband	Middleband	Lowerband
0	NaN	NaN	NaN
1	NaN	NaN	NaN
2	NaN	NaN	NaN
3	NaN	NaN	NaN
4	468.138749	467.50	466.861251
...	...	...	...
116	470.071661	469.83	469.588339
117	470.080666	469.78	469.479334
118	470.020666	469.72	469.419334
119	469.959839	469.65	469.340161
120	469.660000	469.58	469.500000

2. **Plot** `upperband`, `middleband`, **and** `lowerband` **on** `historical_data`:

```
>>> indicators = [
    {
        'name': 'Upperband',
        'data': upperband,
        'extra': {
            'mode': 'lines',
            'line': {
                'width': 1
            }
        }
    },
    {
        'name': 'Middleband',
        'data': middleband,
        'extra': {
            'mode':'lines',
            'line': {
                'width': 1
            }
        }
    },
    {
        'name': 'Lowerband',
        'data': lowerband,
        'extra': {
            'mode': 'lines',
            'line': {
                'width': 1
            }
        }
    }
]

>>> plot_candlesticks_chart(data=historical_data,
                            plot_type=PlotType.JAPANESE,
                            indicators=indicators,
                            caption='Volatility Indicator: '
                            'Bollinger Bands | '
                            'NSE:TATASTEEL | '
                            '1st Jan, 2020 | '
                            'Candle Interval: 1 Minute')
```

We get the following output:

How it works...

The `talib` package provides a ready-to-use `talib.BBANDS` function. We use this in *step 1* to compute the Bollinger Bands on `historical_data`. Along with the close series of `historical_data`, this function takes the following parameters:

- `timeperiod` (int): The time period for calculating the SMA on the TP. The TP is the average of the high, low, and close prices. Here, we took the value as 5.

- `nbdevup` (int): The number of unbiased standard deviations from the mean for the upper band. Here, we took the value as 2.

- `nbdevdn` (int): The number of unbiased standard deviations from the mean for the lower band. Here, we took the value as 2.

- `matype` (int): The moving average type. A value of 0 implies SMA and 1 implies EMA. Here, we took the value as 0.

The `talib.BBANDS` function returns three `pandas.Series` objects, which we assign to new attributes: `upperband`, `middleband`, and `lowerband`. These three objects are concatenated into a `pandas.DataFrame` object and printed in *step 1*. We plot `upperband`, `middleband`, and `lowerband` on `historical_data` in *step 2* using the `plot_candlesticks_chart` function.

Observe the following points regarding the Bollinger Bands indicator values and chart:

- The first four values in the output are NaN (the index starts from 0, so indices 0 to 3 are the first four values) because the talib.BBANDS function requires at least a time period number of entries to compute the Bollinger Bands, which is 5 in our case. From the fifth row onward, we can see all the computed values of all three bands and the corresponding timestamp of the historical_data object.

- The rise or fall of the bands follow the rise and fall in the corresponding prices. Hence, Bollinger Bands are a lagging indicator. In other words, they don't predict the trend outcome in advance.

- Around 12:45 P.M. in the plot, we see that the bands have become narrow. This is because of low volatility (slow rate of price change) around that time.

- Just before 1 P.M. in the plot, we see that the gap between the bands has widened drastically. This is because of high volatility (rapid rate of price change) around that time.

- Most of the time, when the price touches the upper band, it starts moving downward (the opposite direction). You can use these instances as **sell** signals for your strategy.

- Most of the time, when the price touches the lower band, it starts moving upward (the opposite direction). You can use these instances as **buy** signals for your strategy.

Volatility indicators – average true range

Average true range (**ATR**) is a lagging volatility indicator. ATR is a measure of volatility. High ATR values indicate high volatility, and low values indicate low volatility.

The formula for computing ATR is not straightforward and is hence not mentioned here. If you are interested in the underlying math, please refer to the official documentation of TA-Lib on ATR at http://www.tadoc.org/indicator/ATR.htm. Although it is a good idea to know the mathematics of how this works, this recipe does not require you to understand or remember the given formula. We use a third-party Python package, talib, which provides a ready function for calculating ATR.

Getting started

Make sure your Python namespace has the following objects:

1. `talib` (package)
2. `pd` (module)
3. `plot_candlesticks_chart` (function)
4. `PlotType` (enum)
5. `historical_data` (a pandas DataFrame)

Refer to the *Technical requirements* section of this chapter to set up these objects.

How to do it...

We will execute the following steps for this recipe:

1. Calculate the ATR on `historical_data`. Assign it to `atr_14` and print it:

```
>>> atr_14 = talib.ATR(historical_data['high'],
                       historical_data['low'],
                       historical_data['close'],
                       timeperiod=14)
>>> atr_14
```

We get the following output:

```
0           NaN
1           NaN
2           NaN
3           NaN
4           NaN
5           NaN
6           NaN
7           NaN
8           NaN
9           NaN
10          NaN
11          NaN
12          NaN
13          NaN
14     0.575000
15     0.555357
16     0.562117
17     0.550538
```

```
18      0.529071
          ...
116     0.375902
117     0.359766
118     0.348354
119     0.330614
120     0.317713
```

2. Plot `atr_14`, along with `historical_data`:

```
>>> indicators = [
    {
        'name': 'ATR (14)',
        'data': atr_14,
        'extra': {
            'mode': 'lines',
            'line': {
                'width': 2,
                'color': 'purple'
            }
        }
    }
]

>>> plot_candlesticks_chart(data=historical_data,
                            plot_type=PlotType.JAPANESE,
                            indicators=indicators,
                            plot_indicators_separately=True,
                            caption='Volatility Indicator: '
                            'Average True Range | '
                            'NSE:TATASTEEL | '
                            '1st Jan, 2020 | '
                            'Candle Interval: 1 Minute',
                            plot_height=700)
```

We get the following output:

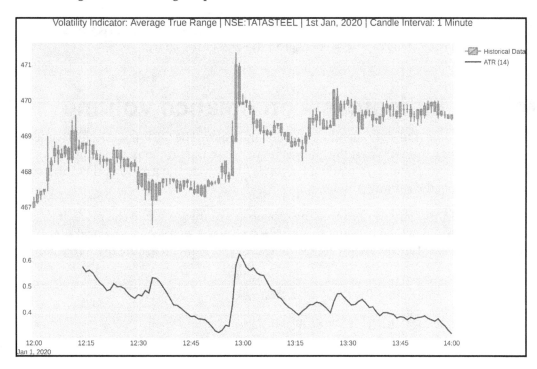

How it works...

The `talib` package provides a ready-to-use `talib.ATR` function. We use this in *step 1* to compute the ATR on `historical_data` and assign it to a new attribute, `atr_14`. Along with the high, low, and close series of `historical_data`, this function takes `timeperiod` as a parameter, which should be an `int` value. We use `14` as the parameter here. The `rsi_14` object is a `pandas.Series` object. This is printed in *step 1*. We plot `atr_14` on `historical_data` in *step 2* using the `plot_candlesticks_chart` function.

Observe the following points regarding the ATR indicator values and chart:

- The first 14 values in the output are `NaN` (the index starts from `0`, so indices `0` to `13` are the first 14 values) because the `talib.ATR` function requires at least one more than the time period number of entries to compute the ATR, which is `14` in our case. From the 15th row onward, we can see all the computed values of the ATR and the corresponding timestamp of the `historical_data` object.

- When there is high volatility (rapid rate of price change), the ATR starts increasing. This can be seen in the chart around 1 P.M.
- When there is low volatility (slow rate of price change), the ATR starts decreasing. This can be seen around the end of the chart.

Volume indicators – on balance volume

On balance volume (OBV) is a leading volume indicator. The OBV is a cumulative total of the up and down volume. When the close is higher than the previous close, the volume is added to the running total, and when the close is lower than the previous close, the volume is subtracted from the running total.

To interpret the OBV, you can observe the movement of the OBV and the price. If the price moves before the OBV, then it is a non-confirmed move. A series of rising peaks, or falling troughs, in the OBV indicates a strong trend. If the OBV is flat, then the market is not trending.

The formulae for computing the OBV are as follows:

- If $close > close_{-1}$, then $OBV = OBV_{-1} + volume$
- If $close < close_{-1}$, then $OBV = OBV_{-1} - volume$
- If $close = close_{-1}$, then $OBV = OBV_{-1}$

Although it is a good idea to know the mathematics of how this works, this recipe does not require you to understand or remember the given formula. We use a third-party Python package, `talib`, which provides a ready function for calculating the OBV.

Getting started

Make sure your Python namespace has the following objects:

1. `talib` (package)
2. `pd` (module)
3. `plot_candlesticks_chart` (function)
4. `PlotType` (enum)
5. `historical_data` (a `pandas` DataFrame)

Refer to the *Technical requirements* section of this chapter to set up these objects.

How to do it...

We will execute the following steps for this recipe:

1. Calculate the OBV on `historical_data`. Assign it to `obv` and print it:

```
>>> obv = talib.OBV(historical_data['close'],
                    historical_data['volume'])
>>> obv
```

We get the following output:

```
0            5694.0
1           16546.0
2           20717.0
3           20717.0
4          211302.0
           ...
116        406508.0
117        406508.0
118        406508.0
119        398353.0
120        405326.0
```

2. Plot `obv`, along with `historical_data`:

```
>>> indicators = [
    {
        'name': 'On Balance Volume',
        'data': obv,
        'extra': {
            'mode': 'lines',
            'line': {
                'width': 2,
                'color': 'purple'
            }
        }
    }
]

>>> plot_candlesticks_chart(data=historical_data,
                plot_type=PlotType.JAPANESE,
                indicators=indicators,
                plot_indicators_separately=True,
                caption='Volume Indicator: '
                'On Balance Volume | '
                'NSE:TATASTEEL | '
                '1st Jan, 2020 | '
```

```
                                'Candle Interval: 1 Minute',
                                plot_height=700)
```

We get the following output:

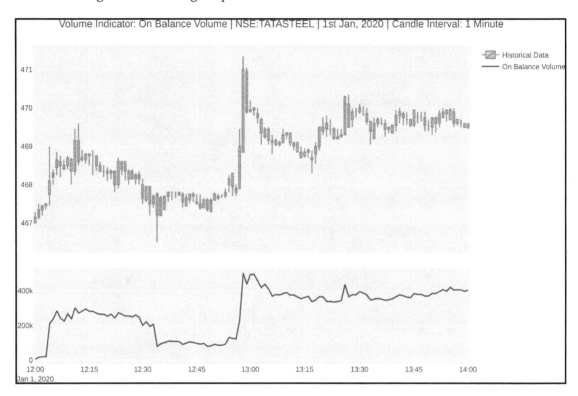

How it works...

The `talib` package provides a ready-to-use `talib.OBV` function. We use this in *step 1* to compute the OBV on `historical_data` and assign it to a new attribute, `obv`. This function takes the close and volume series of `historical_data` as parameters. The `obv` object is a `pandas.Series` object. This is printed in *step 1*. We plot `obv`, along with `historical_data`, in *step 2* using the `plot_candlesticks_chart` function.

Observe the following points regarding the OBV indicator values and chart:

- There are no `NaN` outputs in the table. From the first row itself, we can see all the computed values of the OBV and the corresponding timestamp of the `historical_data` object. One single data point is sufficient to calculate the OBV.
- The values are always positive.
- The rise or fall of the OBV plot is closely followed by the rise and fall of the corresponding prices for most of the time. Hence, it's a leading indicator. In other words, it predicts the trend outcome in advance. (Since it's a leading indicator, it reacts to prices quickly. This often results in false signals. To safeguard yourself from these scenarios, you can use more indicators in your strategy to get additional confirmation of trends or reversals.)

Volume indicators – volume-weighted average price

Volume-weighted average price (**VWAP**) is a lagging volume indicator. The VWAP is a weighted moving average that uses the volume as the weighting factor so that higher volume days have more weight. It is a non-cumulative moving average, so only data within the time period is used in the calculation.

Although this function is available in `talib`, we will show you how to compute an indicator manually here by creating its formula. This will help you create your own indicators at times when you may use customer technical indicators or not-so-popular indicators that are missing from `talib`.

The formula for calculating VWAP is as follows:

$$VWAP = \frac{\sum_1^n (price \times volume)}{\sum_1^n volume}$$

Here, *n* is the *time period* and has to be defined by the user.

Getting started

Make sure your Python namespace has the following objects:

1. `pd` (module)
2. `plot_candlesticks_chart` (function)
3. `PlotType` (enum)
4. `historical_data` (a pandas DataFrame)

Refer to the *Technical requirements* section of this chapter to set up these objects.

How to do it...

We will execute the following steps for this recipe:

1. Define a function for computing VWAP:

```
>>> def VWAP(hist_data_df):
        """
        Returns VWAP computed over the given historical data
        hist_data_df: A pandas DataFrame of historical data with
                        columns
        'timestamp', 'high', 'low', 'close' and 'volume'
        """
        hist_data_df['date'] = \
                hist_data_df['timestamp'].apply(lambda x: x.date())
        unique_dates = sorted(set(hist_data_df['date']))
        vwap = []

        """
        Compute vwap for each day's data and append it to vwap
        variable
        """
        for i, date in enumerate(unique_dates):
            day_df = hist_data_df.loc[hist_data_df['date'] == date]
            typical_price_day_df = (day_df.high + day_df.low +
                                    day_df.close)/3
            vwap_day = list(((typical_price_day_df *
                            day_df.volume).cumsum()) /
                            day_df.volume.cumsum())
            vwap += vwap_day

        return pd.Series(vwap)
```

2. Calculate `VWAP` on `historical_data`. **Assign** it to `vwap` **and print it:**

```
>>> vwap = VWAP(historical_data)
>>> vwap
```

We get the following output:

```
0        467.150000
1        467.259311
2        467.280925
3        467.299623
4        468.085910
             . . .
116      468.965162
117      468.967599
118      468.969499
119      468.971309
120      468.972893
```

3. Plot `vwap` along with `historical_data`:

```
>>> indicators = [
    {
        'name': 'VWAP',
        'data': vwap,
        'extra': {
            'mode': 'lines',
            'line': {
                'width': 2,
                'color': 'purple'
            }
        }
    }
]

>>> plot_candlesticks_chart(data=historical_data,
                            plot_type=PlotType.JAPANESE,
                            indicators=indicators,
                            plot_indicators_separately=True,
                            caption='Volume Indicator: '
                            'Volume Weighted Average Price | '
                            'NSE:TATASTEEL | '
                            '1st Jan, 2020 | '
                            'Candle Interval: 1 Minute',
                            plot_height=700)
```

We get the following output:

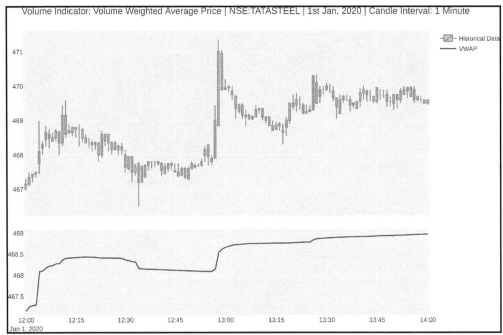

How it works...

We define a function that calculates VWAP in *step 1* for the given historical data as a `pandas.DataFrame` object. It works as follows:

1. Finds all the unique dates in the historical data
2. Iterates over all the unique dates:

   - Extracts `day_df`, a `pandas.DataFrame` object with entries from `historical_data` that fall on the unique date
   - Calculates `typical_price_day_df`, the typical price, which is the average of the high, low, and close prices for the day
   - Calculates `vwap_day`, which is a list of the typical price-weighted averages of the volumes for all the entries in `day_df`

3. Returns all the `vwap_day` values appended together as a `pandas.Series` object

We compute VWAP in *step 2* on `historical_data` using the VWAP function and assign it to a new attribute, `vwap`. The `vwap` object is a `pandas.Series` object. We plot `vwap` along with `historical_data` in *step 3* using the `plot_candlesticks_chart` function.

Observe the following points regarding the VWAP indicator values and chart:

- There are no NaN outputs in the table. From the first row itself, we can see all the computed values of VWAP and the corresponding timestamp of the `historical_data` object. One single data point is sufficient to calculate VWAP.
- The values are always positive.
- The rise or fall of the VWAP plot follows the rise and fall in the corresponding prices. Hence, it's a lagging indicator. In other words, it doesn't predict the trend outcome in advance.

6
Placing Regular Orders on the Exchange

This chapter introduces various types of regular orders that can be placed on exchanges via the broker APIs. The recipes include code on placing 16 types of orders, querying their statuses, and exiting completed orders. These recipes will be a fundamental part of your algorithmic trading strategies. Understanding all of the types of orders and knowing which one to place for the given requirement is crucial for building a successful trading strategy.

Every order has multiple attributes, as described in the following list:

- **Order transaction type**: This attribute simply defines whether the order is a BUY transaction or a SELL transaction. Possible values, obviously, can be one of BUY or SELL.
- **Order type**: This attribute defines the type of the order, which would imply the high-level behavior of the order. Commonly used order types are REGULAR order, BRACKET order, COVER order, and so on. Your broker may define many more types of orders. This chapter includes recipes on REGULAR orders.

- **Order code**: This attribute defines whether the order would be squared-off (that is, exited) at the end of the trading hours for the day or be carried to the next trading day. Possible values can be one of INTRADAY or DELIVERY. An INTRADAY order, as the name suggests, has a lifespan of only one day and would be exited at the end of the day by the broker, if it's not exited before. A DELIVERY order, on the other hand, is delivered to the user's Demat account and exists until it is explicitly squared-off by the user. A DELIVERY order may go through multiple states before getting finally delivered to the user's Demat account, as in this example:
  - DELIVERY T+0 (on the day of placing the order)
  - DELIVERY T+1 (on the next trading day of placing the order)
  - DELIVERY T+2 (on and after the second trading day of placing the order)

This depends on the underlying segment. For example, a DELIVERY order for an equity segment instrument would go through these states. A DELIVERY order for a futures and options segment instrument would not go through these states.

- **Order variety**: This attribute is related to the pricing and activation of the order. Possible values can be one of the following:
  - MARKET: The order is placed immediately at the best available market price. The user need not specify the price while placing the order.
  - LIMIT: The order is placed at a specified price, which is either below the **Last Traded Price (LTP)** (for BUY orders) or above the LTP (for SELL orders). The user should specify a *limit price* when placing the order. The *limit price* would be the price at which the user intends to buy/sell the instrument.
  - STOPLOSS_LIMIT: The order is placed at a specified price, which is either above the LTP (for BUY orders) or below the LTP (for SELL orders). The user should specify the *trigger price* and the *limit price*. When the LTP crosses the *trigger price*, the order is activated and places an order at the specified *limit price*.
  - STOPLOSS_MARKET: The order is placed at a specified price, which is either above the LTP (for BUY orders) or below the LTP (for SELL orders). The user should specify the *trigger price*. When the LTP crosses the *trigger price*, the order is activated and places an order at the market price.

All of these attributes together define a complete order. To place an order, all four attributes should be known precisely.

The aforementioned attributes, namely, the order transaction type, order type, order code, and order variety, are defined by the `pyalgotrading` package. The same attribute may be named differently by the broker of your choice. The `pyalgotrading` package handles such translations internally.

Every order placed on the exchange goes through various states during its lifetime. The broker used in this chapter supports the following states for every order:

- `PUT ORDER REQ RECEIVED`
- `VALIDATION PENDING`
- `OPEN PENDING`
- `TRIGGER PENDING`
- `CANCEL PENDING`
- `COMPLETE`
- `CANCELLED`
- `OPEN`
- `REJECTED`

The recipes in this chapter provide detailed state machine diagrams for the state transitions of every variety of a regular order.

If you are using a different broker, the broker might support different order states or name the order states differently. You can consult the broker API documentation to understand the meaning of each of the states.

In this chapter, we will cover the following recipes:

- Placing a regular market order
- Placing a regular limit order
- Placing a regular stoploss-limit order
- Placing a regular stoploss-market order

Please make sure you try all of these recipes during live market hours with sufficient balance in your broking account. If these recipes are tried outside of market hours or with insufficient balance, your orders would be rejected by the broker. This means the orders would never reach the exchange and you would not get the expected response.

Technical requirements

You will need the following to successfully execute the recipes in this chapter:

- Python 3.7+
- Python packages: pyalgotrading ($ pip install pyalgotrading)

The latest Jupyter notebook for this chapter can be found on GitHub at https://github.com/PacktPublishing/Python-Algorithmic-Trading-Cookbook/tree/master/Chapter06.

The first thing needed for setting connectivity with the broker is getting the API keys. The broker would provide each customer with unique keys, typically as an api-key and api-secret key pair. These API keys are chargeable, usually on a monthly subscription basis. You need to get your copy of api-key and api-secret from the broker website before starting this. You can refer to *Appendix I* for more details.

The following steps will help you to set up the broker connection with Zerodha, which will be used by all of the recipes in this chapter. Please make sure you have followed these steps before trying out any recipe:

1. Import the necessary modules:

   ```
   >>> from pyalgotrading.broker.broker_connection_zerodha import
   BrokerConnectionZerodha
   >>> from pyalgotrading.constants import *
   ```

   All pyalgotrading constants are now available in your Python namespace.

2. Get the api_key and api_secret keys from the broker. These are unique to you and will be used by the broker to identify your Demat account:

   ```
   >>> api_key = "<your-api-key>"
   >>> api_secret = "<your-api-secret>"
   >>> broker_connection = BrokerConnectionZerodha(api_key,
                                                    api_secret)
   ```

We get the following output:

```
Installing package kiteconnect via pip. This may take a while...
Please login to this link to generate your request token:
https://kite.trade/connect/login?api_key=<your-api-key>&v=3
```

If you are running this for the first time and `kiteconnect` is not installed, `pyalgotrading` will automatically install it for you. The final output of *step 2* will be a link. Click on the link and log in with your Zerodha credentials. If the authentication is successful, you will see a link in your browser's address bar similar
to `https://127.0.0.1/?request_token=<alphanimeric-toke>&action=login&status=success`.

We have the following example:

```
https://127.0.0.1/?request_token=H06I6Ydv95y23D2Dp7NbigFjKweGwRP7&action=login&status=success
```

3. Copy the alphanumeric-token and paste it in `request_token`:

```
>>> request_token = "<your-request-token>"
>>> broker_connection.set_access_token(request_token)
```

The `broker_connection` instance is now ready for performing API calls.

The `pyalgotrading` package supports multiple brokers and provides a connection object class per broker, with the same methods. It abstracts broker APIs behind a unified interface so users need not worry about the underlying broker API calls and can use all of the recipes in this chapter as is. Only the procedure to set up the broker connection would vary from broker to broker. You can refer to the `pyalgotrading` documentation for setting up the broker connection if you are not using Zerodha as your broker. For Zerodha users, the steps mentioned in the preceding section would suffice.

Placing a regular market order

A regular market order is the simplest type of order. This order type is used for placing a single order immediately at the best available market price. The market price is equivalent to the LTP (as explained in the *Last traded price of a financial instrument* recipe of `Chapter 3`, *Fetching Financial Data*).

On placing a regular market order, it goes through various intermediate states before finally reaching an end state (COMPLETE or REJECTED). A regular market order immediately moves to the end state without waiting on any intermediate states. The following state machine diagram demonstrates the various states of a regular market order during its lifetime:

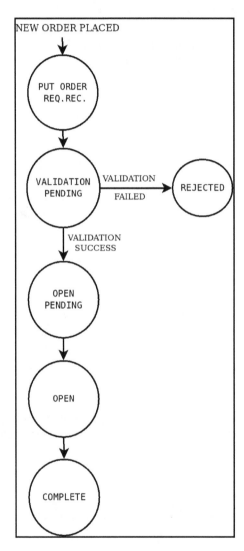

This recipe demonstrates placing of the following regular market orders and querying their status:

- BUY, REGULAR, INTRADAY, MARKET order
- SELL, REGULAR, INTRADAY, MARKET order
- BUY, REGULAR, DELIVERY, MARKET order
- SELL, REGULAR, DELIVERY, MARKET order

Getting ready

Make sure the `broker_connection` object and constants from the `pyalgotrading` package are available in your Python namespace. Refer to the *Technical requirements* section of this chapter to set up this object.

How to do it...

We execute the following steps for this recipe:

1. Fetch a financial instrument and assign it to `instrument`:

```
>>> instrument = broker_connection.get_instrument('NSE',
                                                  'HDFCBANK')
```

2. Place a BUY, REGULAR, INTRADAY, MARKET order and display the order ID:

```
>>> order1_id = broker_connection.place_order(
            instrument=instrument,
            order_transaction_type= \
                BrokerOrderTransactionTypeConstants.BUY,
            order_type=BrokerOrderTypeConstants.REGULAR,
            order_code=BrokerOrderCodeConstants.INTRADAY,
            order_variety=BrokerOrderVarietyConstants.MARKET,
            quantity=1)
>>> order1_id
```

We get the following output (your output may differ):

```
'200304002243710'
```

3. Fetch and display the order status:

```
>>> broker_connection.get_order_status(order1_id)
```

We get the following output:

```
'COMPLETE'
```

If you log in to the broker site with your credentials and go to the orders section, you can find your order details as shown in the following screenshot (some data may differ for you):

4. Place a SELL, REGULAR, INTRADAY, MARKET order and display the order ID:

```
>>> order2_id = broker_connection.place_order(
            instrument=instrument,
            order_transaction_type= \
                BrokerOrderTransactionTypeConstants.SELL,
            order_type=BrokerOrderTypeConstants.REGULAR,
            order_code=BrokerOrderCodeConstants.INTRADAY,
            order_variety=BrokerOrderVarietyConstants.MARKET,
            quantity=1)
>>> order2_id
```

We get the following output (your output would differ):

```
'200304002244044'
```

5. Fetch and display the order status:

```
>>> broker_connection.get_order_status(order2_id)
```

We get the following output:

```
'COMPLETE'
```

If you log in to the broker site with your credentials and go to the orders section, you can find your order details as shown in the following screenshot (some data may differ for you):

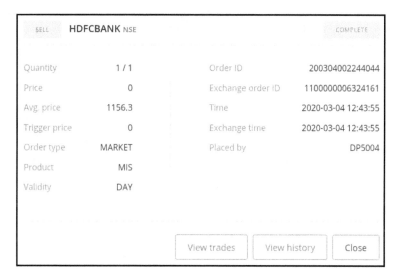

6. Place a BUY, REGULAR, DELIVERY, MARKET order and display the order ID:

```
>>> order3_id = broker_connection.place_order(
            instrument=instrument,
            order_transaction_type= \
                BrokerOrderTransactionTypeConstants.BUY,
            order_type=BrokerOrderTypeConstants.REGULAR,
            order_code=BrokerOrderCodeConstants.DELIVERY,
            order_variety=BrokerOrderVarietyConstants.MARKET,
            quantity=1)
>>> order3_id
```

We get the following output (your output may differ):

```
'200304002244263'
```

7. Fetch and display the order status:

```
>>> broker_connection.get_order_status(order3_id)
```

We get the following output:

```
'COMPLETE'
```

If you log in to the broker site with your credentials and go to the orders section, you can find your order details as shown in the following screenshot (some data may differ for you):

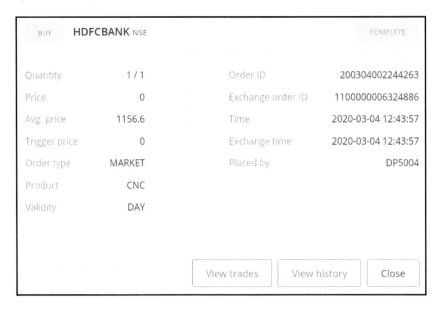

BUY	**HDFCBANK** NSE		COMPLETE
Quantity	1 / 1	Order ID	200304002244263
Price	0	Exchange order ID	1100000006324886
Avg. price	1156.6	Time	2020-03-04 12:43:57
Trigger price	0	Exchange time	2020-03-04 12:43:57
Order type	MARKET	Placed by	DP5004
Product	CNC		
Validity	DAY		

View trades   View history   Close

8. Place a SELL, REGULAR, DELIVERY, MARKET order and display the order ID:

```
>>> order4_id = broker_connection.place_order(
                instrument=instrument,
                order_transaction_type= \
                    BrokerOrderTransactionTypeConstants.SELL,
                order_type=BrokerOrderTypeConstants.REGULAR,
                order_code=BrokerOrderCodeConstants.DELIVERY,
                order_variety=BrokerOrderVarietyConstants.MARKET,
                quantity=1)
>>> order4_id
```

We get the following output (your output may differ):

```
'200304002244333'
```

9. Fetch and display the order status:

```
>>> broker_connection.get_order_status(order4_id)
```

We get the following output:

```
'COMPLETE'
```

If you log in to the broker site with your credentials and go to the orders section, you can find your order details as shown in the following screenshot (some data may differ for you):

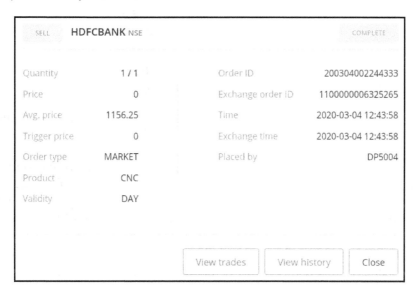

SELL	HDFCBANK NSE			COMPLETE
Quantity	1 / 1	Order ID		200304002244333
Price	0	Exchange order ID		1100000006325265
Avg. price	1156.25	Time		2020-03-04 12:43:58
Trigger price	0	Exchange time		2020-03-04 12:43:58
Order type	MARKET	Placed by		DP5004
Product	CNC			
Validity	DAY			

View trades   View history   Close

How it works...

In *step 1*, you use the `get_instrument()` method of the `BrokerConnectionZerodha` class to fetch an instrument and assign it to a new attribute, `instrument`. This object is an instance of the `Instrument` class. The two parameters needed to call `get_instrument` are the exchange (`'NSE'`) and the trading-symbol (`'HDFCBANK'`).

In *step 2*, you use the `place_order` method of the `broker_connection` object to place a BUY, REGULAR, INTRADAY, MARKET order on the exchange. The `place_order` method is a wrapper on the broker specific place order API. It takes the following attributes:

- `instrument`: This is the financial instrument for which the order must be placed and should be an instance of the `Instrument` class. We pass `instrument` here.
- `order_transaction_type`: This is the order transaction type and should be an enum of the `BrokerOrderTransactionTypeConstants` type. We pass `BrokerOrderTransactionTypeConstants.BUY` here.
- `order_type`: This is the order type and should be an enum of the `BrokerOrderTypeConstants` type. We pass `BrokerOrderTypeConstants.REGULAR` here.

- `order_code`: This is the order code and should be an enum of the `BrokerOrderCodeConstants` type. We pass `BrokerOrderCodeConstants.INTRADAY` here.
- `order_variety`: This is the order variety and should be an enum of the `BrokerOrderVarietyConstants` type. We pass `BrokerOrderVarietyConstants.MARKET` here.
- `quantity`: This is the number of shares to be traded for the given instrument and it should be a positive integer. We pass `1` here.

(The attributes passed to the `place_order` method are broker-agnostic constants, imported earlier from the `pyalgotrading.constants` module.)

On placing the order in *step 2*, you get an order ID from the broker, which you assign to a new attribute, `order1_id`. The `order1_id` object is a `string` type. If the order placement is not successful for some reason, you may not get an order ID. In *step 3*, you fetch the status of the placed order using the `get_order_status()` method of the `broker_connection` object. You pass `order1_id` as the parameter to the `get_order_status()` method. You get the order status as `'COMPLETE'`, a `string` type. You can use `order1_id` to fetch the status of the placed order at any later point of time as well.

You can also verify the successful placement of your order by logging in to the broker website and checking the orders section there. You should see data similar to the screenshot shown in the output of *step 3*.

The other steps in this recipe follow the same pattern of placing an order and getting its status, for a different combination of attributes:

- *Steps 4* and *5*: SELL, REGULAR, INTRADAY, MARKET order
- *Steps 6* and *7*: BUY, REGULAR, DELIVERY, MARKET order
- *Steps 8* and *9*: SELL, REGULAR, DELIVERY, MARKET order

 The order ID returned by the broker for an order is unique across all its clients. You will never get the same order ID again and you will never get an order ID that was assigned to an order placed by someone else.

Placing a regular limit order

A regular limit order is a type of order where a single order is placed at a specific price. Unlike the regular market order, this is not the market price. To place this order, a specific parameter called the *limit price* is needed. This parameter should satisfy the following conditions:

- The *limit price* should be below the market price for a BUY order.
- The *limit price* should be above the market price for a SELL order.

If these conditions are not satisfied, the order may either get placed at the market price, essentially converting it into a regular market order, or it may be rejected by the broker as an invalid order.

On placing a regular limit order, it goes through various intermediate states before finally reaching an end state (COMPLETE, CANCELLED, or REJECTED). A regular limit order could stay in the OPEN state for a while until favorable market conditions are achieved, before moving to the COMPLETE state. The following state machine diagram demonstrates the various states of a regular limit order during its lifetime:

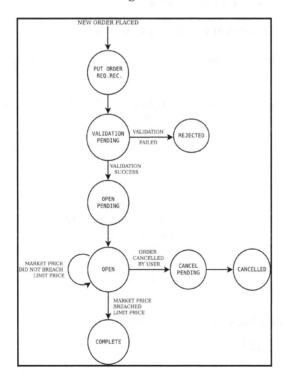

This recipe demonstrates placing the following regular limit orders and querying their statuses:

- BUY, REGULAR, INTRADAY, LIMIT order
- SELL, REGULAR, INTRADAY, LIMIT order
- BUY, REGULAR, DELIVERY, LIMIT order
- SELL, REGULAR, DELIVERY, LIMIT order

Getting ready

Make sure the `broker_connection` object and constants from the `pyalgotrading` package are available in your Python namespace. Refer to the *Technical requirements* section of this chapter to set up this object.

How to do it...

We execute the following steps for this recipe:

1. Fetch a financial instrument and assign it to `instrument`:

```
>>> instrument = broker_connection.get_instrument('NSE',
                                                  'ICICIBANK')
```

2. Fetch the LTP. Place a BUY, REGULAR, INTRADAY, LIMIT order and display the order ID:

```
>>> ltp = broker_connection.get_ltp(instrument)
>>> order1_id = broker_connection.place_order(
            instrument=instrument,
            order_transaction_type= \
                BrokerOrderTransactionTypeConstants.BUY,
            order_type=BrokerOrderTypeConstants.REGULAR,
            order_code=BrokerOrderCodeConstants.INTRADAY,
            order_variety=BrokerOrderVarietyConstants.LIMIT,
            quantity=1,
            price=ltp-1)
>>> order1_id
```

We get the following output (your output may differ):

```
'200303003518407'
```

3. Fetch and display the order status:

```
>>> broker_connection.get_order_status(order1_id)
```

We get the following output (your output may differ):

```
'OPEN'
```

If you log in to the broker site with your credentials and go to the orders section, you can find your order details as shown in the following screenshot (some data may differ for you):

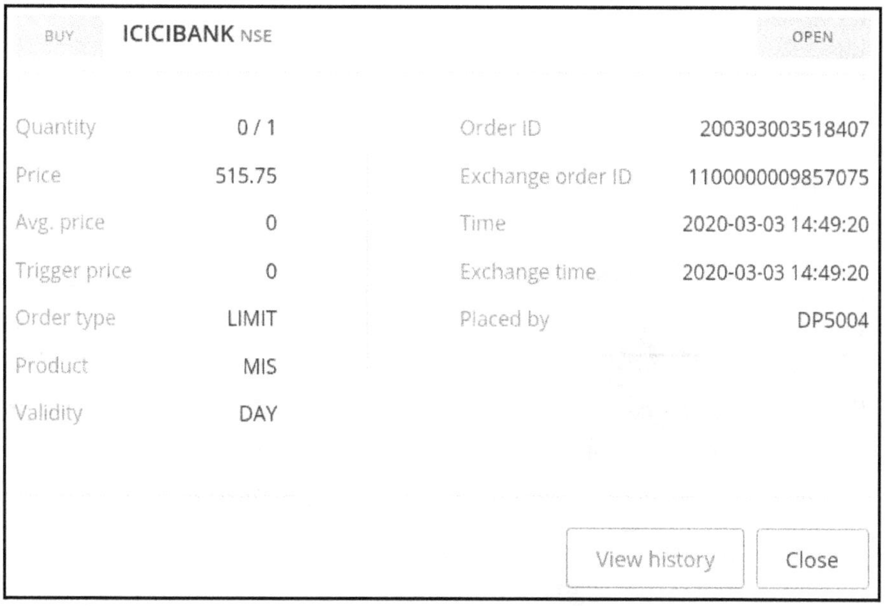

BUY	**ICICIBANK** NSE			OPEN
Quantity	0 / 1	Order ID		200303003518407
Price	515.75	Exchange order ID		1100000009857075
Avg. price	0	Time		2020-03-03 14:49:20
Trigger price	0	Exchange time		2020-03-03 14:49:20
Order type	LIMIT	Placed by		DP5004
Product	MIS			
Validity	DAY			
			View history	Close

4. Fetch and display the order status again after some time:

```
>>> broker_connection.get_order_status(order1_id)
```

We get the following output (your output may differ):

```
'COMPLETE'
```

If you log in to the broker site with your credentials and go to the orders section, you can find your order details as shown in the following screenshot (some data may differ for you):

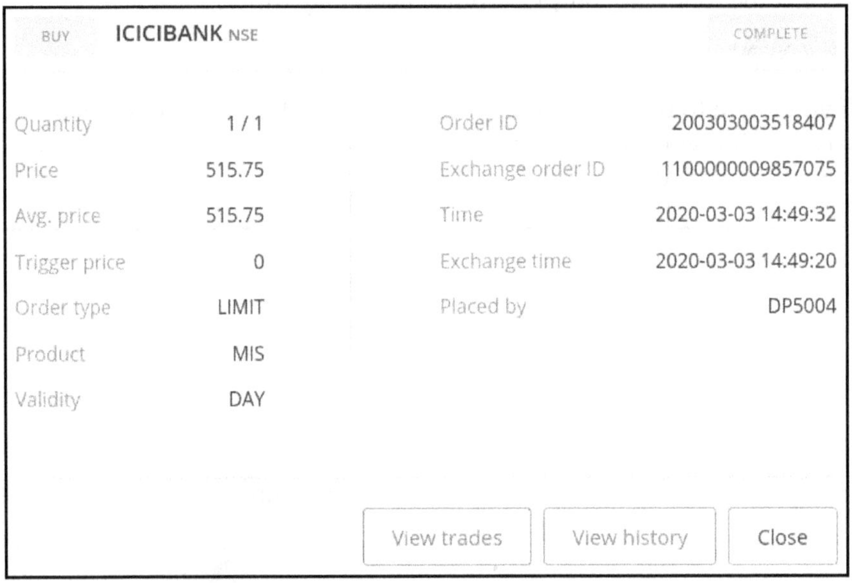

BUY	**ICICIBANK** NSE			COMPLETE
Quantity	1 / 1	Order ID		200303003518407
Price	515.75	Exchange order ID		1100000009857075
Avg. price	515.75	Time		2020-03-03 14:49:32
Trigger price	0	Exchange time		2020-03-03 14:49:20
Order type	LIMIT	Placed by		DP5004
Product	MIS			
Validity	DAY			
		View trades	View history	Close

5. Fetch the LTP. Place a SELL, REGULAR, INTRADAY, LIMIT order and display the order ID:

```
>>> ltp = broker_connection.get_ltp(instrument)
>>> order2_id = broker_connection.place_order(
                instrument=instrument,
                order_transaction_type= \
                    BrokerOrderTransactionTypeConstants.SELL,
                order_type=BrokerOrderTypeConstants.REGULAR,
                order_code=BrokerOrderCodeConstants.INTRADAY,
                order_variety=BrokerOrderVarietyConstants.LIMIT,
                quantity=1,
                price=ltp+1)
>>> order2_id
```

We get the following output (your output may differ):

```
'200303003243352'
```

6. Fetch and display the order status:

```
>>> broker_connection.get_order_status(order2_id)
```

We get the following result:

```
'OPEN'
```

If you log in to the broker site with your credentials and go to the orders section, you can find your order details as shown in the following screenshot (some data may differ for you):

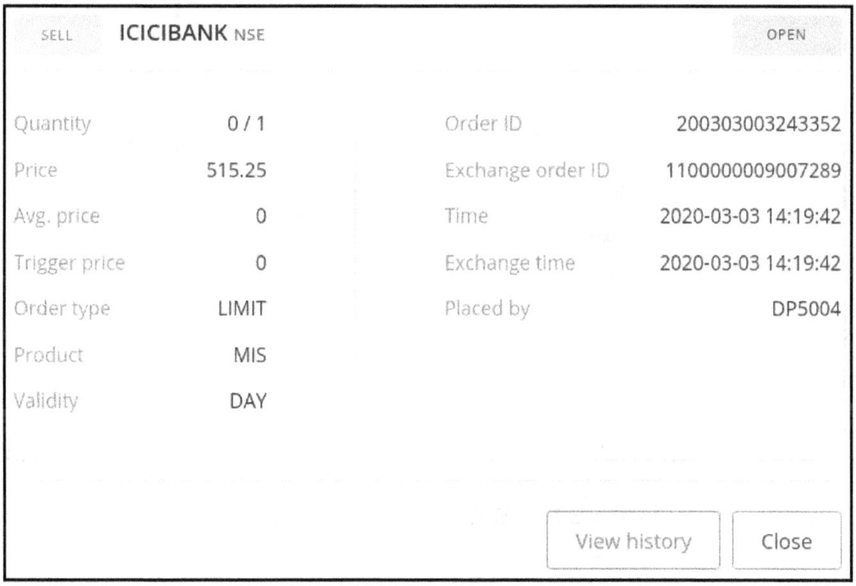

SELL	**ICICIBANK** NSE			OPEN
Quantity	0 / 1	Order ID		200303003243352
Price	515.25	Exchange order ID		1100000009007289
Avg. price	0	Time		2020-03-03 14:19:42
Trigger price	0	Exchange time		2020-03-03 14:19:42
Order type	LIMIT	Placed by		DP5004
Product	MIS			
Validity	DAY			
			View history	Close

7. Fetch and display the order status again after some time:

```
>>> broker_connection.get_order_status(order2_id)
```

We get the following output (your output may differ):

```
'COMPLETE'
```

If you log in to the broker site with your credentials and go to the orders section, you can find your order details as shown in the following screenshot (some data may differ for you):

SELL **ICICIBANK** NSE			COMPLETE
Quantity	1 / 1	Order ID	200303003243352
Price	515.25	Exchange order ID	1100000009007289
Avg. price	515.25	Time	2020-03-03 14:19:45
Trigger price	0	Exchange time	2020-03-03 14:19:42
Order type	LIMIT	Placed by	DP5004
Product	MIS		
Validity	DAY		

View trades   View history   Close

8. Fetch the LTP. Place a BUY, REGULAR, DELIVERY, LIMIT order and display the order ID:

```
>>> ltp = broker_connection.get_ltp(instrument)
>>> order3_id = broker_connection.place_order(
                instrument=instrument,
                order_transaction_type= \
                    BrokerOrderTransactionTypeConstants.BUY,
                order_type=BrokerOrderTypeConstants.REGULAR,
                order_code=BrokerOrderCodeConstants.DELIVERY,
                order_variety=BrokerOrderVarietyConstants.LIMIT,
                quantity=1,
                price=ltp-1)
>>> order3_id
```

We get the following output (your output may differ):

```
'200303003266560'
```

9. Fetch and display the order status:

```
>>> broker_connection.get_order_status(order3_id)
```

We get the following output:

```
'OPEN'
```

If you log in to the broker site with your credentials and go to the orders section, you can find your order details as shown in the following screenshot (some data may differ for you):

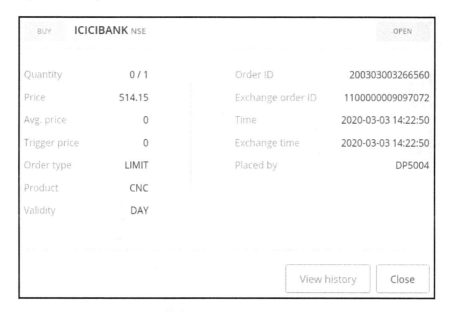

10. Fetch and display the order status again after some time:

```
>>> broker_connection.get_order_status(order3_id)
```

We get the following output:

```
'COMPLETE'
```

If you log in to the broker site with your credentials and go to the orders section, you can find your order details as shown in the following screenshot (some data may differ for you):

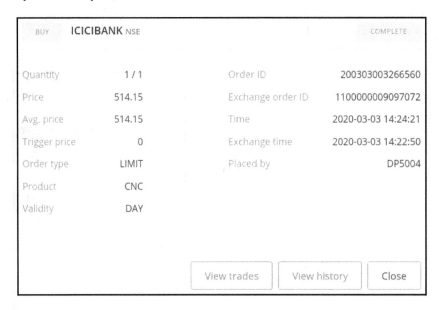

BUY	**ICICIBANK** NSE			COMPLETE
Quantity	1 / 1	Order ID	200303003266560	
Price	514.15	Exchange order ID	1100000009097072	
Avg. price	514.15	Time	2020-03-03 14:24:21	
Trigger price	0	Exchange time	2020-03-03 14:22:50	
Order type	LIMIT	Placed by	DP5004	
Product	CNC			
Validity	DAY			

View trades   View history   Close

11. Fetch the LTP. Place a SELL, REGULAR, DELIVERY, LIMIT order and display the order ID:

```
>>> ltp = broker_connection.get_ltp(instrument)
>>> order4_id = broker_connection.place_order(
            instrument=instrument,
            order_transaction_type= \
                BrokerOrderTransactionTypeConstants.SELL,
            order_type=BrokerOrderTypeConstants.REGULAR,
            order_code=BrokerOrderCodeConstants.DELIVERY,
            order_variety=BrokerOrderVarietyConstants.LIMIT,
            quantity=1,
            price=ltp+1)
>>> order4_id
```

We get the following output (your output may differ):

```
'200303003280699'
```

12. Fetch and display the order status:

```
>>> broker_connection.get_order_status(order4_id)
```

We get the following output:

```
'OPEN'
```

If you log in to the broker site with your credentials and go to the orders section, you can find your order details as shown in the following screenshot (some data may differ for you):

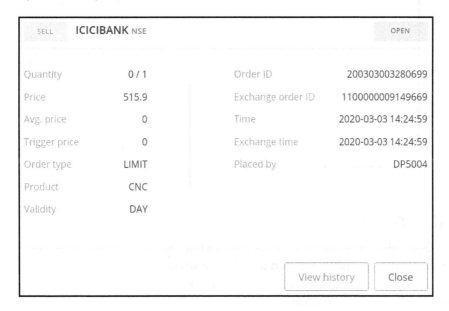

13. Fetch and display the order status again after some time:

```
>>> broker_connection.get_order_status(order4_id)
```

We get the following output:

```
'COMPLETE'
```

If you log in to the broker site with your credentials and go to the orders section, you can find your order details as shown in the following screenshot (some data may differ for you):

SELL	**ICICIBANK** NSE		COMPLETE
Quantity	1 / 1	Order ID	200303003280699
Price	515.9	Exchange order ID	1100000009149669
Avg. price	515.9	Time	2020-03-03 14:25:56
Trigger price	0	Exchange time	2020-03-03 14:24:59
Order type	LIMIT	Placed by	DP5004
Product	CNC		
Validity	DAY		

View trades   View history   Close

How it works...

In *step 1*, you use the get_instrument() method of the BrokerConnectionZerodha class to fetch an instrument and assign it to a new attribute, instrument. This object is an instance of the Instrument class. The two parameters needed to call get_instrument are the exchange ('NSE') and the trading-symbol ('ICICIBANK').

In *step 2*, you fetch the LTP of the instrument using the get_ltp() method of the BrokerConnectionZerodha class and assign it to a new attribute, ltp. The instrument object is passed as the parameter here. Next, you use the place_order method of the broker_connection object to place a BUY, REGULAR, INTRADAY, LIMIT order on the exchange. The place_order method is a wrapper on the broker specific place order API. It takes the following attributes:

- instrument: This is the financial instrument for which the order must be placed and should be an instance of the Instrument class. We pass instrument here.
- order_transaction_type: This is the order transaction type and should be an enum of the BrokerOrderTransactionTypeConstants type. We pass BrokerOrderTransactionTypeConstants.BUY here.

- `order_type`: This is the order type and should be an enum of the `BrokerOrderTypeConstants` type. We pass `BrokerOrderTypeConstants.REGULAR` here.
- `order_code`: This is the order code and should be an enum of the `BrokerOrderCodeConstants` type. We pass `BrokerOrderCodeConstants.INTRADAY` here.
- `order_variety`: This is the order variety and should be an enum of the `BrokerOrderVarietyConstants` type. We pass `BrokerOrderVarietyConstants.LIMIT` here.
- `quantity`: The number of shares to be traded for the given instrument and should be a positive integer. We pass 1 here.
- `price`: This is the limit price at which the order should be placed. We pass `ltp-1` here, which means 1 unit price below `ltp`.

(The attributes passed to the `place_order` method are broker-agnostic constants, imported earlier from the `pyalgotrading.constants` module.)

On placing the order in *step 2*, you get an order ID from the broker, which you assign to a new attribute, `order1_id`. The `order1_id` object is a string. If the order placement is not successful for some reason, you may not get an order ID. Observe that the price parameter is passed a value of `ltp-1`. This means the order is placed below the market price, which is a necessary condition for placing BUY LIMIT orders.

In *step 3*, you fetch the status of the placed order using the `get_order_status()` method of the `broker_connection` object. You pass `order1_id` as the parameter to the `get_order_status()` method. You get the order status as `'OPEN'`, a string. You can use `order1_id` to fetch the status of the placed order at any later point of time as well. In *step 4*, you fetch the order status again, and if the order is completed, you get the order status as `'COMPLETE'`.

You can also verify the successful placement of your order by logging in to the broker website and checking the orders section there. You should see data similar to the screenshot shown in the outputs of *step 3* and *step 4*.

In *step 3*, if you see the status as 'COMPLETE' instead of 'OPEN', this could be due to high volatility. If you want the order to stay in the 'OPEN' state for a while, try placing the order further away from the market price.

The other steps in this recipe follow the same pattern of placing an order and getting its status, for a different combination of attributes:

- *Steps 5, 6*, and *7*: SELL, REGULAR, INTRADAY, LIMIT order
- *Steps 8, 9*, and *10*: BUY, REGULAR, DELIVERY, LIMIT order
- *Steps 11, 12*, and *13*: SELL, REGULAR, DELIVERY, LIMIT order

Placing a regular stoploss-limit order

A regular stoploss-limit order is a type of order where a single order is placed at a specific price. Unlike the regular market order, this is not the market price. To place this order, two specific parameters are needed, the *trigger price* and the *limit price*. These parameters should satisfy the following conditions:

- For a BUY order, we need to observe the following:
    - The *trigger price* and *limit price* should be above the market price.
    - The *limit price* should be greater than the *trigger price.*
- For a SELL order, the following should be observed:
    - The *trigger price* and *limit price* should be below the market price.
    - The *limit price* should be lower than the *trigger price.*

If these conditions are not satisfied, the order may either get placed at the market price, essentially converting it into a regular market order, or may be rejected by the broker as an invalid order.

On placing a regular stoploss-limit order, it goes through various intermediate states before finally reaching an end state (COMPLETE, CANCELLED, or REJECTED). A regular stoploss-limit order could stay in the TRIGGER_PENDING state for a while until favorable market conditions are achieved, before moving to the COMPLETE state. The following state machine diagram demonstrates the various states of a regular stoploss-limit order during its lifetime:

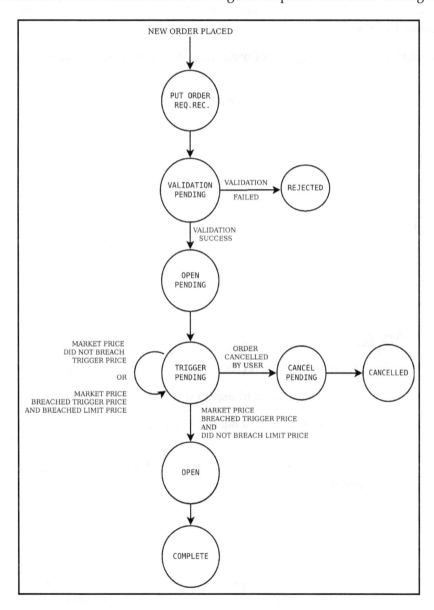

After the order is placed, it stays in the TRIGGER_PENDING state until the market price breaches the *trigger price* but not the *limit price*. That is when this order gets activated and is sent to the exchange. The order then gets executed at the best available market price, which is between the *trigger price* and the *limit price*. The order state transitions from TRIGGER_PENDING to OPEN to the COMPLETE state. If the market is too volatile and the market price breaches both *trigger price* and *limit price,* the order remains in the TRIGGER_PENDING state.

This recipe demonstrates placing the following regular stoploss-limit orders and querying their statuses:

- BUY, REGULAR, INTRADAY, STOPLOSS_LIMIT order
- SELL, REGULAR, INTRADAY, STOPLOSS_LIMIT order
- BUY, REGULAR, DELIVERY, STOPLOSS_LIMIT order
- SELL, REGULAR, DELIVERY, STOPLOSS_LIMIT order

Getting ready...

Make sure the broker_connection object and constants from the pyalgotrading package are available in your Python namespace. Refer to the *Technical requirements* section of this chapter to set up this object.

How to do it...

We execute the following steps for this recipe:

1. Fetch a financial instrument and assign it to instrument:

```
>>> instrument = broker_connection.get_instrument('NSE',
                                                  'AXISBANK')
```

2. Fetch the LTP. Place a BUY, REGULAR, INTRADAY, STOPLOSS_LIMIT order and display the order ID:

```
>>> ltp = broker_connection.get_ltp(instrument)
>>> order1_id = broker_connection.place_order(
        instrument=instrument,
        order_transaction_type= \
            BrokerOrderTransactionTypeConstants.BUY,
        order_type=BrokerOrderTypeConstants.REGULAR,
        order_code=BrokerOrderCodeConstants.INTRADAY,
```

```
        order_variety= \
            BrokerOrderVarietyConstants.STOPLOSS_LIMIT,
        quantity=1,
        price=ltp+1,
        trigger_price=ltp+1)
>>> order1_id
```

We get the following output (your output may differ):

```
'200303003296676'
```

3. Fetch and display the order status:

```
>>> broker_connection.get_order_status(order1_id)
```

We get the following output:

```
'TRIGGER PENDING'
```

If you log in to the broker site with your credentials and go to the orders section, you can find your order details as shown in the following screenshot (some data may differ for you):

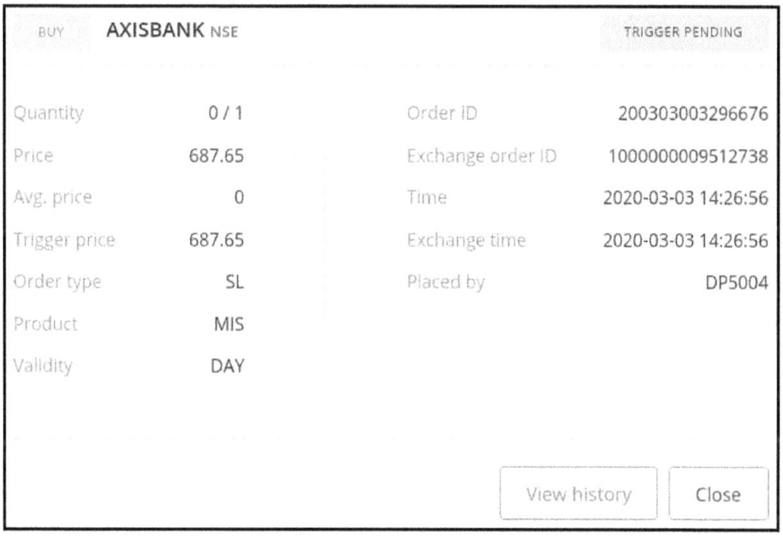

BUY	**AXISBANK** NSE			TRIGGER PENDING
Quantity	0 / 1	Order ID		200303003296676
Price	687.65	Exchange order ID		1000000009512738
Avg. price	0	Time		2020-03-03 14:26:56
Trigger price	687.65	Exchange time		2020-03-03 14:26:56
Order type	SL	Placed by		DP5004
Product	MIS			
Validity	DAY			
			View history	Close

4. Fetch and display the order status again after some time:

```
>>> broker_connection.get_order_status(order1_id)
```

We get the following output:

```
'COMPLETE'
```

If you log in to the broker site with your credentials and go to the orders section, you can find your order details as shown in the following screenshot (some data may differ for you):

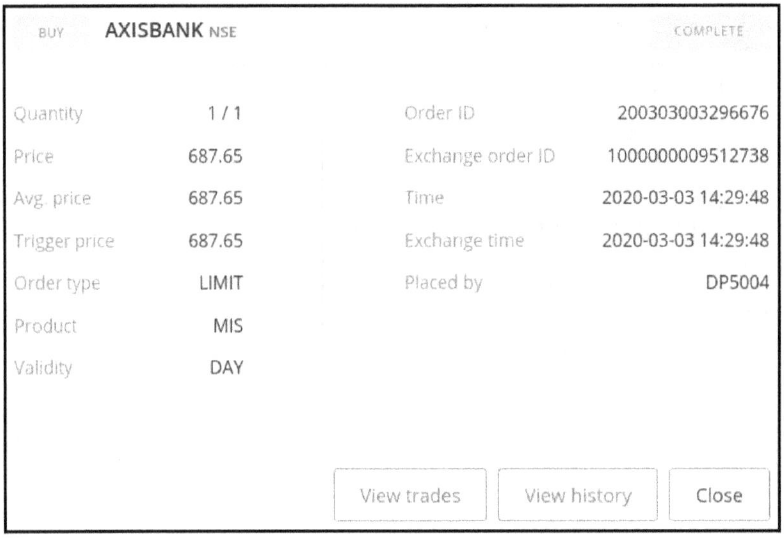

5. Fetch the LTP. Place a SELL, REGULAR, INTRADAY, STOPLOSS_LIMIT order and display the order ID:

```
>>> ltp = broker_connection.get_ltp(instrument)
>>> order2_id = broker_connection.place_order(
                instrument=instrument,
                order_transaction_type= \
                    BrokerOrderTransactionTypeConstants.SELL,
                order_type=BrokerOrderTypeConstants.REGULAR,
                order_code=BrokerOrderCodeConstants.INTRADAY,
                order_variety= \
                    BrokerOrderVarietyConstants.STOPLOSS_LIMIT,
                quantity=1,
                price=ltp-1,
                trigger_price=ltp-1)
>>> order2_id
```

We get the following output (your output may differ):

```
'200303003576828'
```

6. Fetch and display the order status:

```
>>> broker_connection.get_order_status(order2_id)
```

We get the following output:

```
'TRIGGER PENDING'
```

If you log in to the broker site with your credentials and go to the orders section, you can find your order details as shown in the following screenshot (some data may differ for you):

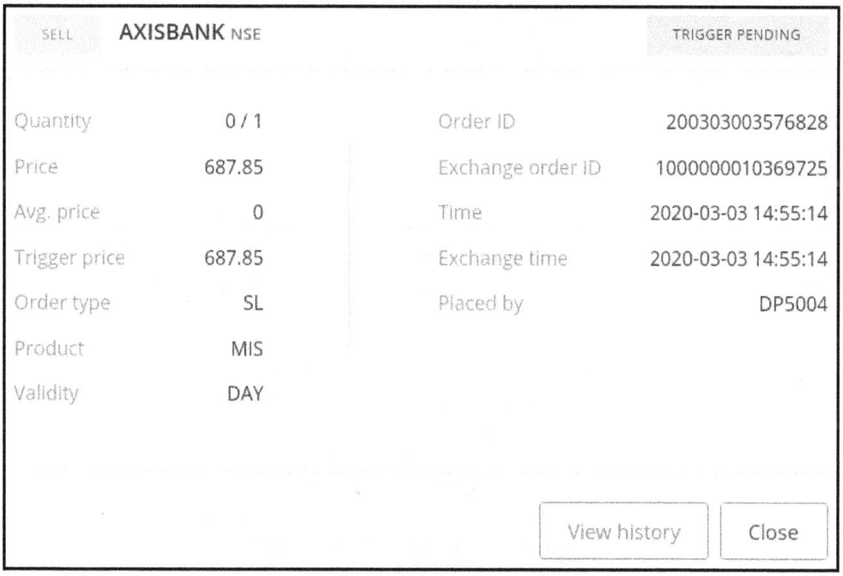

SELL	**AXISBANK** NSE			TRIGGER PENDING
Quantity	0 / 1	Order ID	200303003576828	
Price	687.85	Exchange order ID	1000000010369725	
Avg. price	0	Time	2020-03-03 14:55:14	
Trigger price	687.85	Exchange time	2020-03-03 14:55:14	
Order type	SL	Placed by	DP5004	
Product	MIS			
Validity	DAY			
			View history	Close

7. Fetch and display the order status again after some time:

```
>>> broker_connection.get_order_status(order2_id)
```

We get the following output:

```
'COMPLETE'
```

If you log in to the broker site with your credentials and go to the orders section, you can find your order details as shown in the following screenshot (some data may differ for you):

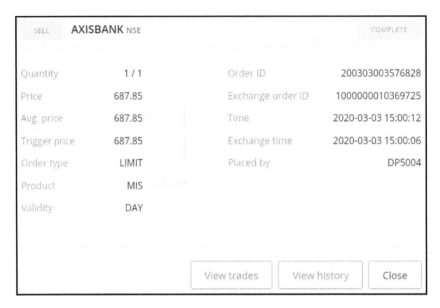

8. Fetch the LTP. Place a BUY, REGULAR, DELIVERY, STOPLOSS_LIMIT order and display the order id:

```
>>> ltp = broker_connection.get_ltp(instrument)
>>> order3_id = broker_connection.place_order(
            instrument=instrument,
            order_transaction_type= \
                BrokerOrderTransactionTypeConstants.BUY,
            order_type=BrokerOrderTypeConstants.REGULAR,
            order_code=BrokerOrderCodeConstants.DELIVERY,
            order_variety= \
                BrokerOrderVarietyConstants.STOPLOSS_LIMIT,
            quantity=1,
            price=ltp+1,
            trigger_price=ltp+1)
>>> order3_id
```

We get the following output (your output may differ):

```
'200303003308116'
```

9. Fetch and display the order status:

```
>>> broker_connection.get_order_status(order3_id)
```

We get the following output:

```
'TRIGGER PENDING'
```

If you log in to the broker site with your credentials and go to the orders section, you can find your order details as shown in the following screenshot (some data may differ for you):

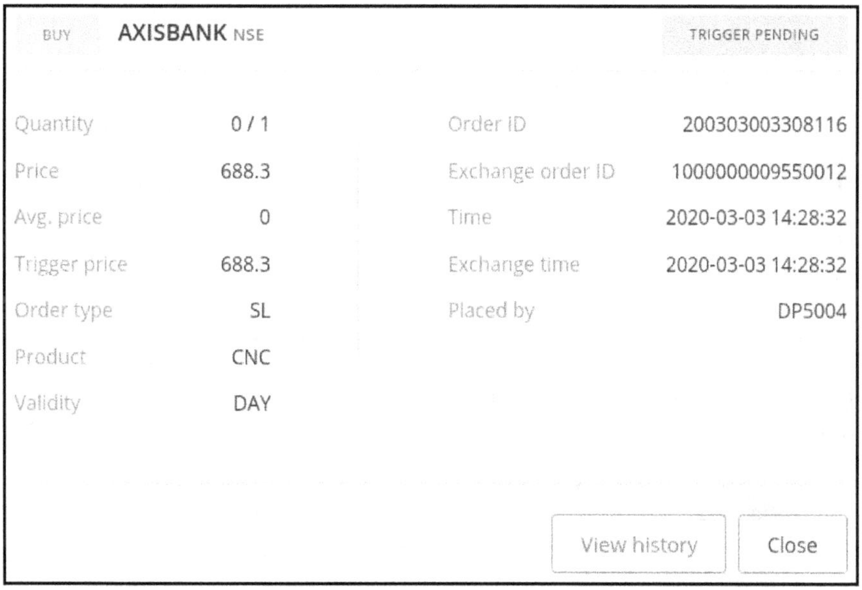

BUY	AXISBANK NSE			TRIGGER PENDING
Quantity	0 / 1	Order ID		200303003308116
Price	688.3	Exchange order ID		1000000009550012
Avg. price	0	Time		2020-03-03 14:28:32
Trigger price	688.3	Exchange time		2020-03-03 14:28:32
Order type	SL	Placed by		DP5004
Product	CNC			
Validity	DAY			

View history   Close

10. Fetch and display the order status again after some time:

```
>>> broker_connection.get_order_status(order3_id)
```

We get the following output:

```
'COMPLETE'
```

If you log in to the broker site with your credentials and go to the orders section, you can find your order details as shown in the following screenshot (some data may differ for you):

11. Fetch the LTP. Place a `SELL`, `REGULAR`, `DELIVERY`, `STOPLOSS_LIMIT` order and display the order ID:

```
>>> ltp = broker_connection.get_ltp(instrument)
>>> order4_id = broker_connection.place_order(
            instrument=instrument,
            order_transaction_type= \
                BrokerOrderTransactionTypeConstants.SELL,
            order_type=BrokerOrderTypeConstants.REGULAR,
            order_code=BrokerOrderCodeConstants.DELIVERY,
            order_variety= \
                BrokerOrderVarietyConstants.STOPLOSS_LIMIT,
            quantity=1,
            price=ltp-1,
            trigger_price=ltp-1)
>>> order4_id
```

We get the following output (your output may differ):

```
'200303003312976'
```

12. Fetch and display the order status:

```
>>> broker_connection.get_order_status(order4_id)
```

We get the following output:

```
'TRIGGER PENDING'
```

If you log in to the broker site with your credentials and go to the orders section, you can find your order details as shown in the following screenshot (some data may differ for you):

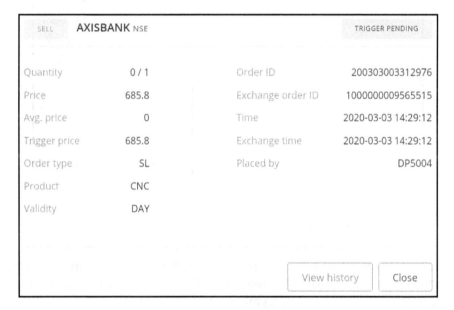

SELL **AXISBANK** NSE			TRIGGER PENDING
Quantity	0 / 1	Order ID	200303003312976
Price	685.8	Exchange order ID	1000000009565515
Avg. price	0	Time	2020-03-03 14:29:12
Trigger price	685.8	Exchange time	2020-03-03 14:29:12
Order type	SL	Placed by	DP5004
Product	CNC		
Validity	DAY		
		View history	Close

13. Fetch and display the order status again after some time:

```
>>> broker_connection.get_order_status(order4_id)
```

We get the following output:

```
'COMPLETE'
```

If you log in to the broker site with your credentials and go to the orders section, you can find your order details as shown in the following screenshot (some data may differ for you):

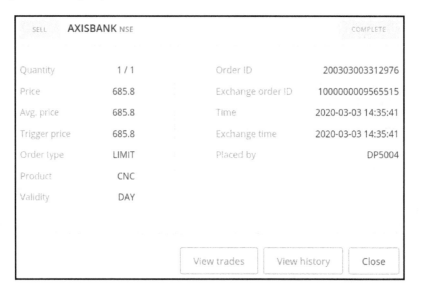

SELL	**AXISBANK** NSE			COMPLETE
Quantity	1 / 1	Order ID	200303003312976	
Price	685.8	Exchange order ID	1000000009565515	
Avg. price	685.8	Time	2020-03-03 14:35:41	
Trigger price	685.8	Exchange time	2020-03-03 14:35:41	
Order type	LIMIT	Placed by	DP5004	
Product	CNC			
Validity	DAY			

View trades   View history   Close

How it works...

In *step 1*, you use the `get_instrument()` method of the `BrokerConnectionZerodha` class to fetch an instrument and assign it to a new attribute, `instrument`. This object is an instance of the `Instrument` class. The two parameters needed to call `get_instrument` are the exchange (`'NSE'`) and the trading-symbol (`'AXISBANK'`).

In *step 2*, you fetch the LTP of the instrument using the `get_ltp()` method of the `BrokerConnectionZerodha` class and assign it to a new attribute, `ltp`. The `instrument` object is passed as the parameter here. Next, you use the `place_order` method of the `broker_connection` object to place a BUY, REGULAR, INTRADAY, STOPLOSS_LIMIT order on the exchange. The `place_order` method is a wrapper on the broker specific place order API. It takes the following attributes:

- `instrument`: This is the financial instrument for which the order must be placed and should be an instance of the `Instrument` class. We pass `instrument` here.
- `order_transaction_type`: This is the order transaction type and should be an enum of the type, `BrokerOrderTransactionTypeConstants`. We pass `BrokerOrderTransactionTypeConstants.BUY` here.

- `order_type`: This is the order type and should be an enum of the type `BrokerOrderTypeConstants`. We pass `BrokerOrderTypeConstants.REGULAR` here.

- `order_code`: This is the order code and should be an enum of the type `BrokerOrderCodeConstants`. We pass `BrokerOrderCodeConstants.INTRADAY` here.

- `order_variety`: This is the order variety and should be an enum of the type `BrokerOrderVarietyConstants`. We pass `BrokerOrderVarietyConstants.STOPLOSS_LIMIT` here.

- `quantity`: This is the number of shares to be traded for the given instrument and should be a positive integer. We pass `1` here.

- `price`: This is the limit price at which the order should be placed. We pass `ltp+1` here, which means 1 unit price above `ltp`.

- `trigger_price`: This is the trigger price at which the order should be placed. We pass `ltp+1` here, which means 1 unit price above `ltp`.

(The attributes passed to the `place_order` method are broker-agnostic constants, imported earlier from the `pyalgotrading.constants` module.)

On placing the order in *step 2*, you get an order ID from the broker, which you assign to a new attribute, `order1_id`. The `order1_id` object is a string. If the order placement is not successful for some reason, you may not get an order ID. Observe that the price and `trigger_price` parameters are passed a value of `ltp+1`. This means the order is placed above the market price, which is a necessary condition for placing BUY `STOPLOSS_LIMIT` orders.

In *step 3*, you fetch the status of the placed order using the `get_order_status()` method of the `broker_connection` object. You pass `order1_id` as the parameter to the `get_order_status()` method. You get the order status as `'TRIGGER PENDING'`, a string. You can use `order1_id` to fetch the status of the placed order at any later point of time as well. In *step 4*, you fetch the order status again, and if the order is completed, you get the order status as `'COMPLETE'`.

You can also verify the successful placement of your order by logging in to the broker website and checking the orders section there. You should see data similar to the screenshots shown in the outputs of *step 3* and *step 4*.

 In *step 3*, if you see the status as 'COMPLETE' instead of 'TRIGGER PENDING', this could be due to high volatility. If you want the order to stay in the 'OPEN' state for a while, try placing the order further away from the market price.

The other steps in this recipe follow the same pattern of placing an order and getting its status, for a different combination of attributes:

- *Steps 5, 6,* and *7*: SELL, REGULAR, INTRADAY, STOPLOSS_LIMIT order
- *Steps 8, 9,* and *10*: BUY, REGULAR, DELIVERY, STOPLOSS_LIMIT order
- *Steps 11, 12,* and *13*: SELL, REGULAR, DELIVERY, STOPLOSS_LIMIT order

Placing a regular stoploss-market order

A regular stoploss-market order is a type of order where a single order is placed at a specific price. Unlike the regular market order, this is not the market price. To place this order, a specific parameter called the *trigger price* is needed. This parameter should satisfy the following conditions:

- The *trigger price* should be above the market price for a BUY order.
- The *trigger price* should be below the market price for a SELL order.

If these conditions are not satisfied, the order may either get placed at the market price, essentially converting it into a regular market order, or may be rejected by the broker as an invalid order.

On placing a regular stoploss-market order, it goes through various intermediate states before finally reaching an end state (COMPLETE, CANCELLED, or REJECTED). A regular stoploss-market order could stay in the TRIGGER_PEDNING state for a while until favorable market conditions are achieved, before moving to the COMPLETE state.

The following state machine diagram demonstrates the various states of a regular stoploss-market order during its lifetime:

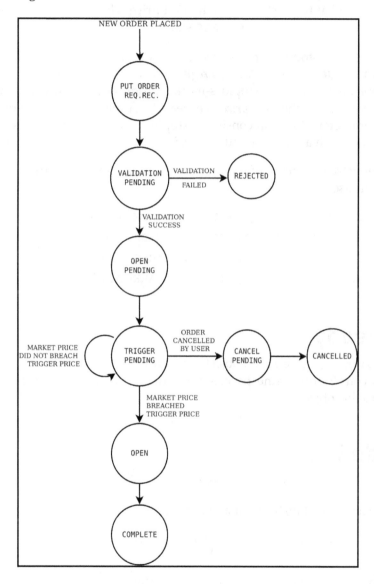

After the order is placed, it stays in the TRIGGER_PENDING state until the market price breaches the *trigger price*. That is when this order is activated and sent to the exchange. The order is then executed at the best available market price. The order state transitions from TRIGGER_PENDING to OPEN to the COMPLETE state.

A regular stoploss-market order behaves similarly to a regular stoploss-limit order (see the *Placing a regular stoploss-Limit Order* recipe), except for one difference—the stoploss-market order requires only the *trigger price* and not the *limit price*, whereas the stoploss-limit order requires both parameters. You can consider a stoploss-market order as a stoploss-limit order with an unbounded *limit price*.

This recipe demonstrates placing of the following regular stoploss-market orders and querying their statuses:

- BUY, REGULAR, INTRADAY, STOPLOSS_MARKET order
- SELL, REGULAR, INTRADAY, STOPLOSS_MARKET order
- BUY, REGULAR, DELIVERY, STOPLOSS_MARKET order
- SELL, REGULAR, DELIVERY, STOPLOSS_MARKET order

Getting ready

Make sure the broker_connection object and constants from pyalgotrading package are available in your Python namespace. Refer to the *Technical requirements* section of this chapter to set up this object.

How to do it...

We execute the following steps for this recipe:

1. Fetch a financial instrument and assign it to instrument:

```
>>> instrument = broker_connection.get_instrument('NSE',
                                                'KOTAKBANK')
```

2. Fetch the LTP. Place a BUY, REGULAR, INTRADAY, STOPLOSS_MARKET order and display the order ID:

```
>>> ltp = broker_connection.get_ltp(instrument)
>>> order1_id = broker_connection.place_order(
            instrument=instrument,
```

```
                    order_transaction_type= \
                        BrokerOrderTransactionTypeConstants.BUY,
                    order_type=BrokerOrderTypeConstants.REGULAR,
                    order_code=BrokerOrderCodeConstants.INTRADAY,
                    order_variety= \
                        BrokerOrderVarietyConstants.STOPLOSS_MARKET,
                    quantity=1,
                    trigger_price=ltp+1)
>>> order1_id
```

We get the following output (your output may differ):

```
'200727003362763'
```

3. Fetch and display the order status:

```
>>> broker_connection.get_order_status(order1_id)
```

We get the following output:

```
'TRIGGER PENDING'
```

If you log in to the broker site with your credentials and go to the orders section, you can find your order details as shown in the following screenshot (some data may differ for you):

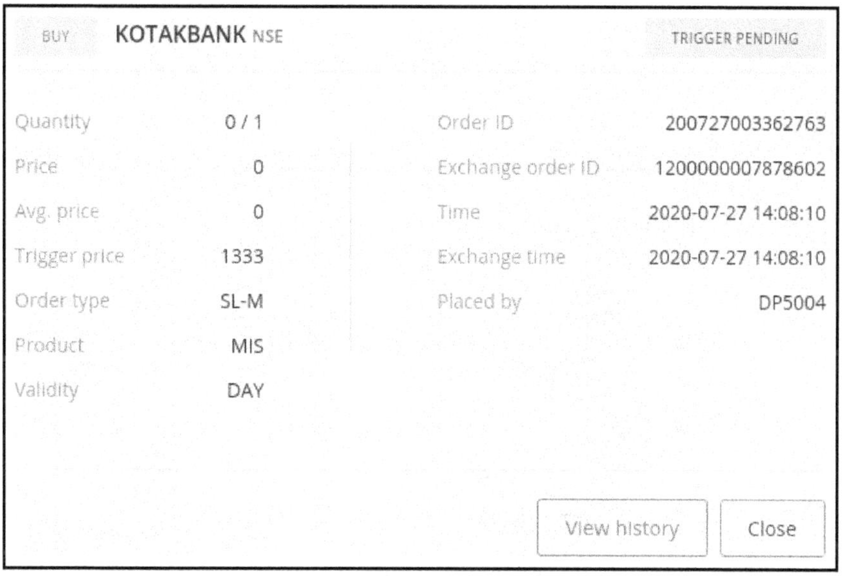

BUY	**KOTAKBANK** NSE			TRIGGER PENDING
Quantity	0 / 1	Order ID		200727003362763
Price	0	Exchange order ID		1200000007878602
Avg. price	0	Time		2020-07-27 14:08:10
Trigger price	1333	Exchange time		2020-07-27 14:08:10
Order type	SL-M	Placed by		DP5004
Product	MIS			
Validity	DAY			

View history   Close

4. Fetch and display the order status again after some time:

```
>>> broker_connection.get_order_status(order1_id)
```

We get the following output:

```
'COMPLETE'
```

If you log in to the broker site with your credentials and go to the orders section, you can find your order details as shown in the following screenshot (some data may differ for you):

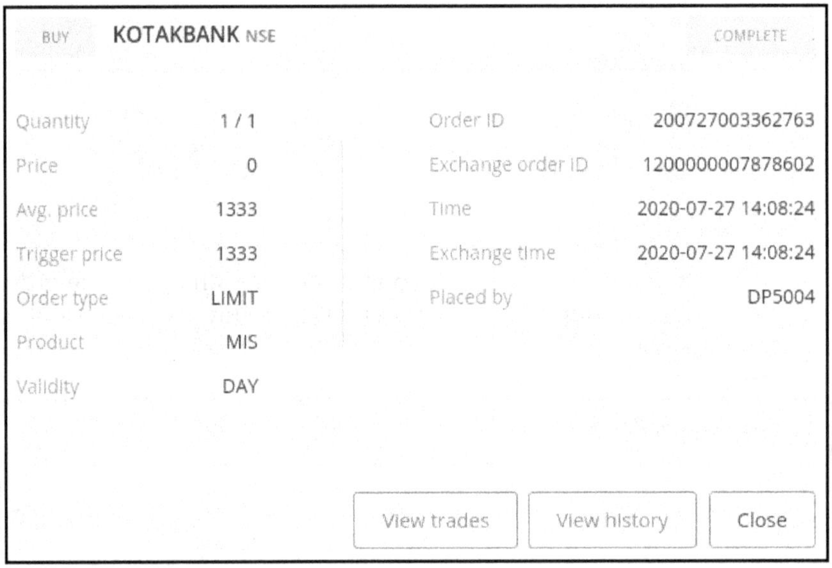

5. Fetch the LTP. Place a SELL, REGULAR, INTRADAY, STOPLOSS_MARKET order and display the order ID:

```
>>> ltp = broker_connection.get_ltp(instrument)
>>> order2_id = broker_connection.place_order(
                instrument=instrument,
                order_transaction_type= \
                    BrokerOrderTransactionTypeConstants.SELL,
                order_type=BrokerOrderTypeConstants.REGULAR,
                order_code=BrokerOrderCodeConstants.INTRADAY,
                order_variety= \
                    BrokerOrderVarietyConstants.STOPLOSS_MARKET,
                quantity=1,
                trigger_price=ltp-1)
>>> order2_id
```

We get the following output (your output may differ):

```
'200303003345436'
```

6. Fetch and display the order status:

```
>>> broker_connection.get_order_status(order2_id)
```

We get the following output:

```
'TRIGGER PENDING'
```

If you log in to the broker site with your credentials and go to the orders section, you can find your order details as shown in the following screenshot (some data may differ for you):

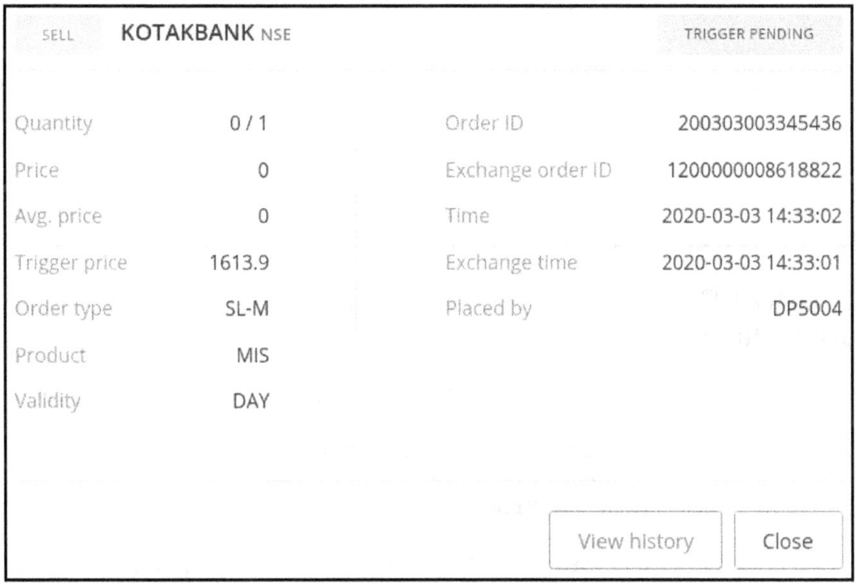

SELL	**KOTAKBANK** NSE		TRIGGER PENDING
Quantity	0 / 1	Order ID	200303003345436
Price	0	Exchange order ID	1200000008618822
Avg. price	0	Time	2020-03-03 14:33:02
Trigger price	1613.9	Exchange time	2020-03-03 14:33:01
Order type	SL-M	Placed by	DP5004
Product	MIS		
Validity	DAY		
		View history	Close

7. Fetch and display the order status again after some time:

```
>>> broker_connection.get_order_status(order2_id)
```

We get the following output:

```
'COMPLETE'
```

If you log in to the broker site with your credentials and go to the orders section, you can find your order details as shown in the following screenshot (some data may differ for you):

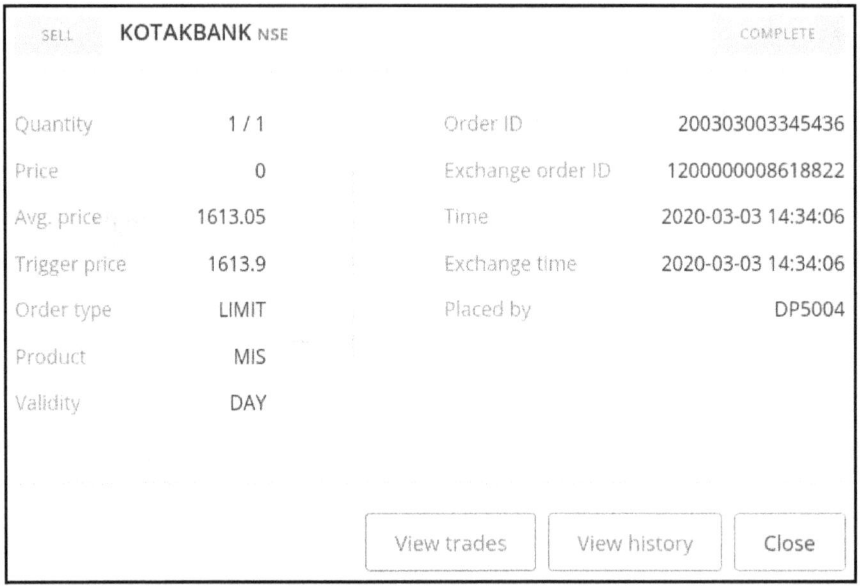

SELL **KOTAKBANK** NSE			COMPLETE
Quantity	1 / 1	Order ID	200303003345436
Price	0	Exchange order ID	1200000008618822
Avg. price	1613.05	Time	2020-03-03 14:34:06
Trigger price	1613.9	Exchange time	2020-03-03 14:34:06
Order type	LIMIT	Placed by	DP5004
Product	MIS		
Validity	DAY		
		View trades	View history	Close

8. Fetch the LTP. Place a BUY, REGULAR, DELIVERY, STOPLOSS_MARKET order and display the order ID:

```
>>> ltp = broker_connection.get_ltp(instrument)
>>> order3_id = broker_connection.place_order(
              instrument=instrument,
              order_transaction_type= \
                  BrokerOrderTransactionTypeConstants.BUY,
              order_type=BrokerOrderTypeConstants.REGULAR,
              order_code=BrokerOrderCodeConstants.DELIVERY,
              order_variety= \
                  BrokerOrderVarietyConstants.STOPLOSS_MARKET,
              quantity=1,
              trigger_price=ltp+1)
>>> order3_id
```

We get the following output (your output may differ):

```
'200727003580657'
```

9. Fetch and display the order status:

```
>>> broker_connection.get_order_status(order3_id)
```

We get the following output:

```
'TRIGGER PENDING'
```

If you log in to the broker site with your credentials and go to the orders section, you can find your order details as shown in the following screenshot (some data may differ for you):

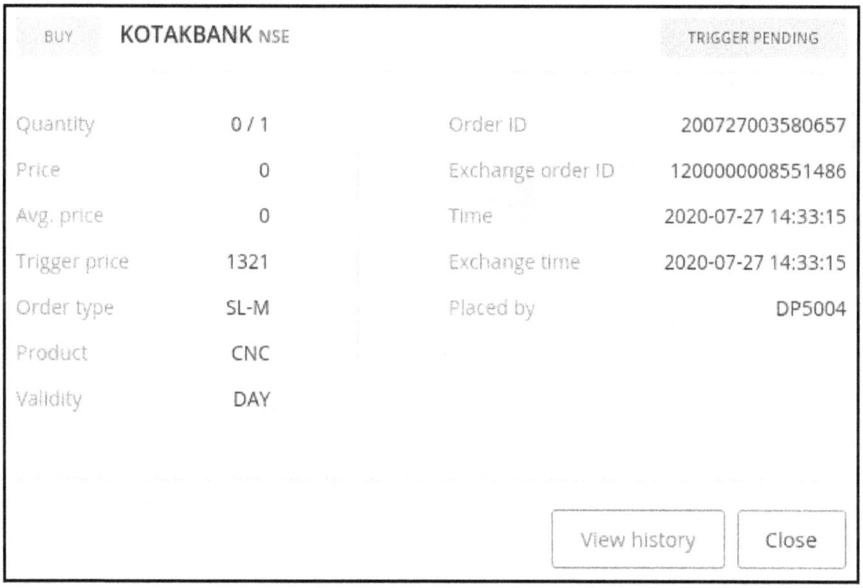

10. Fetch and display the order status again after some time:

```
>>> broker_connection.get_order_status(order3_id)
```

We get the following output:

```
'COMPLETE'
```

If you log in to the broker site with your credentials and go to the orders section, you can find your order details as shown in the following screenshot (some data may differ for you):

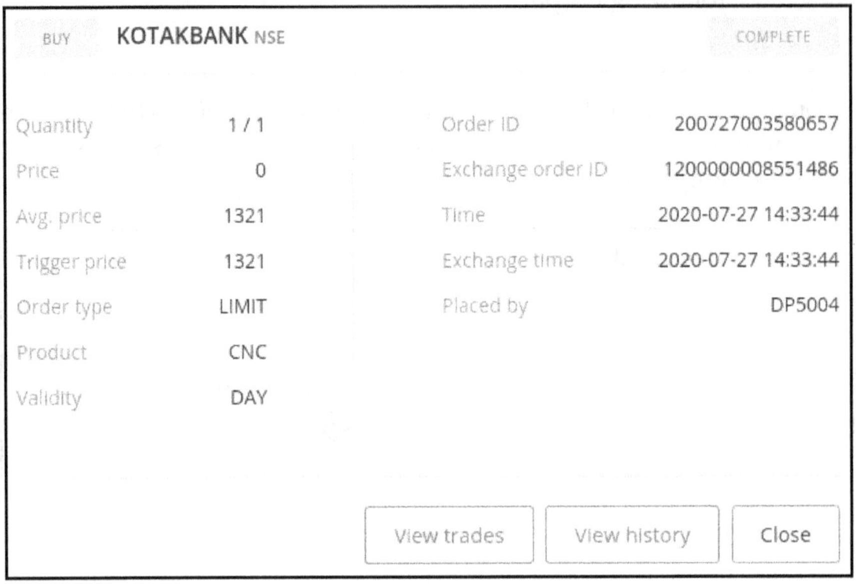

BUY	KOTAKBANK NSE			COMPLETE
Quantity	1 / 1	Order ID		200727003580657
Price	0	Exchange order ID		1200000008551486
Avg. price	1321	Time		2020-07-27 14:33:44
Trigger price	1321	Exchange time		2020-07-27 14:33:44
Order type	LIMIT	Placed by		DP5004
Product	CNC			
Validity	DAY			

View trades   View history   Close

11. Fetch the LTP. Place a SELL, REGULAR, DELIVERY, STOPLOSS_MARKET order and display the order ID:

```
>>> ltp = broker_connection.get_ltp(instrument.segment)
>>> order4_id = broker_connection.place_order(
            instrument=instrument,
            order_transaction_type= \
                BrokerOrderTransactionTypeConstants.SELL,
            order_type=BrokerOrderTypeConstants.REGULAR,
            order_code=BrokerOrderCodeConstants.DELIVERY,
            order_variety= \
                BrokerOrderVarietyConstants.STOPLOSS_MARKET,
            quantity=1,
            trigger_price=ltp-1)
>>> order4_id
```

We get the following output (your output may differ):

```
'200727003635594'
```

12. Fetch and display the order status:

```
>>> broker_connection.get_order_status(order4_id)
```

We get the following output:

```
'TRIGGER PENDING'
```

If you log in to the broker site with your credentials and go to the orders section, you can find your order details as shown in the following screenshot (some data may differ for you):

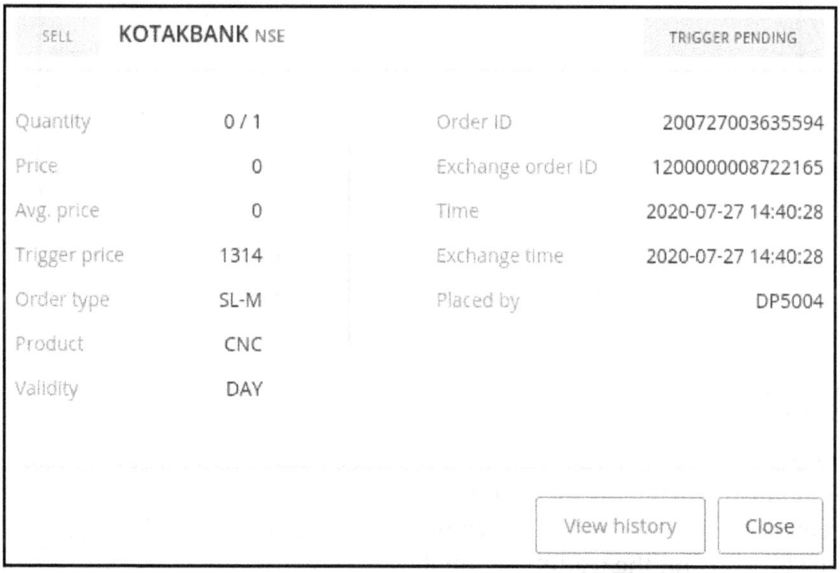

SELL	KOTAKBANK NSE				TRIGGER PENDING
Quantity	0 / 1		Order ID		200727003635594
Price	0		Exchange order ID		1200000008722165
Avg. price	0		Time		2020-07-27 14:40:28
Trigger price	1314		Exchange time		2020-07-27 14:40:28
Order type	SL-M		Placed by		DP5004
Product	CNC				
Validity	DAY				
				View history	Close

13. Fetch and display the order status again after some time:

```
>>> broker_connection.get_order_status(order4_id)
```

We get the following output:

```
'COMPLETE'
```

If you log in to the broker site with your credentials and go to the orders section, you can find your order details as shown in the following screenshot (some data may differ for you):

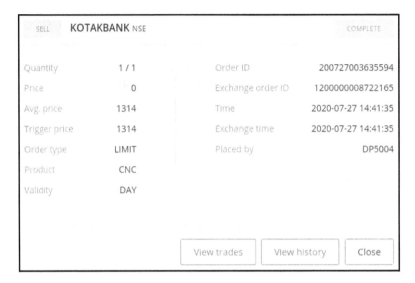

How it works…

In *step 1*, you use the `get_instrument()` method of the `BrokerConnectionZerodha` class to fetch an instrument and assign it to a new attribute, `instrument`. This object is an instance of the `Instrument` class. The two parameters needed to call `get_instrument` are the exchange (`'NSE'`) and the trading-symbol (`'KOTAKBANK'`).

In *step 2*, you fetch the LTP of the instrument using the `get_ltp()` method of the `BrokerConnectionZerodha` class and assign it to a new attribute, `ltp`. The `instrument` object is passed as the parameter here. Next, you use the `place_order` method of the `broker_connection` object to place a BUY, REGULAR, INTRADAY, STOPLOSS_MARKET order on the exchange. The `place_order` method is a wrapper on the broker specific place order API. It takes the following attributes:

- `instrument`: This is the financial instrument for which the order must be placed and should be an instance of the `Instrument` class. We pass `instrument` here.
- `order_transaction_type`: This is the order transaction type and should be an enum of the `BrokerOrderTransactionTypeConstants` type. We pass `BrokerOrderTransactionTypeConstants.BUY` here.

- `order_type`: This is the order type and should be an enum of the `BrokerOrderTypeConstants` type. We pass `BrokerOrderTypeConstants.REGULAR` here.
- `order_code`: This is the order code and should be an enum of the `BrokerOrderCodeConstants` type. We pass `BrokerOrderCodeConstants.INTRADAY` here.
- `order_variety`: This is the order variety and should be an enum of the `BrokerOrderVarietyConstants` type. We pass `BrokerOrderVarietyConstants.STOPLOSS_MARKET` here.
- `quantity`: This is the number of shares to be traded for the given instrument and should be a positive integer. We pass `1` here.
- `trigger_price`: This is the trigger price at which the order should be placed. We pass `ltp+1` here, which means 1 unit price above `ltp`.

(The attributes passed to the `place_order` method are broker-agnostic constants, imported earlier from the `pyalgotrading.constants` module.)

On placing the order in *step 2*, you get an order ID from the broker, which you assign to a new attribute, `order1_id`. The `order1_id` object is a string. If the order placement is not successful for some reason, you may not get an order ID. Observe that the `trigger_price` parameter is passed a value of `ltp+1`. This means the order is placed above the market price, which is a necessary condition for placing BUY `STOPLOSS_MARKET` orders.

In *step 3*, you fetch the status of the placed order using `get_order_status()` method of the `broker_connection` object. You pass `order1_id` as the parameter to the `get_order_status()` method. You get the order status as `'TRIGGER PENDING'`, a string. You can use `order1_id` to fetch the status of the placed order at any later point of time as well. In *step 4*, you fetch the order status again, and if the order is completed, you get the order status as `'COMPLETE'`.

You can also verify the successful placement of your order by logging in to the broker website and checking the orders section there. You should see data similar to the screenshot shown in the outputs of *step 3* and *step 4*.

> In *step 3*, if you see the status as `'COMPLETE'` instead of `'TRIGGER PENDING'`, this could be due to high volatility. If you want the order to stay in the `'OPEN'` state for a while, try placing the order further away from the market price.

The other steps in this recipe follow the same pattern of placing an order and getting its status, for a different combination of attributes:

- *Steps 5, 6, and 7*: SELL, REGULAR, INTRADAY, STOPLOSS_MARKET order
- *Steps 8, 9, and 10*: BUY, REGULAR, DELIVERY, STOPLOSS_MARKET order
- *Steps 11, 12, and 13*: SELL, REGULAR, DELIVERY, STOPLOSS_MARKET order

7
Placing Bracket and Cover Orders on the Exchange

This chapter introduces various types of bracket and cover orders that can be placed on exchanges via the broker APIs. The recipes include code for placing 12 types of orders and querying their statuses, canceling open orders, and exiting completed orders. These recipes will be a fundamental part of your algorithmic trading strategies. Understanding all of the types of orders and knowing which one to place for the given requirement is crucial for building a successful trading strategy.

Each order has four attributes that together define the order completely:

- Order transaction type
- Order type
- Order code
- Order variety

For placing an order, all four attributes should be known precisely. To know more about these attributes, refer to the introduction to `Chapter 6`, *Placing Regular Orders on the Exchange*.

The recipes in this chapter provide detailed flowcharts for each order type. Every order placed on the exchange goes through various states during its lifetime. To know more about the order states supported by the broker used in this chapter, refer to the introduction to Chapter 6, *Placing Regular Orders on the Exchange*.

In this chapter, we will cover the following recipes:

- Placing a bracket limit order
- Placing a bracket stoploss-limit order
- Placing a bracket limit order with a trailing stoploss
- Placing a bracket stoploss-limit order with a trailing stoploss
- Placing a cover market order
- Placing a cover limit order

 Please make sure you try all of these recipes during live market hours with sufficient balance in your broking account. If these recipes are tried outside of market hours or with insufficient balance, your orders will be rejected by the broker. This means the orders would never reach the exchange and you would not get the expected response.

Technical requirements

You will need the following to successfully execute the recipes in this chapter:

- Python 3.7+
- Python packages: pyalgotrading ($ pip install pyalgotrading)

The latest Jupyter notebook for this chapter can be found on GitHub at https://github.com/PacktPublishing/Python-Algorithmic-Trading-Cookbook/tree/master/Chapter07.

The first thing needed for setting connectivity with the broker is getting the API keys. The broker will provide each customer with unique keys, typically as an api-key and api-secret key pair. These API keys are chargeable, usually on a monthly subscription basis. You need to get your copy of api-key and api-secret from the broker website before starting this. You can refer to *Appendix I* for more details.

The following steps will help you to set up the broker connection with Zerodha, which will be used by all of the recipes in this chapter. Please make sure you have followed these steps before trying out any recipe:

1. Import the necessary modules:

    ```
    >>> from pyalgotrading.broker.broker_connection_zerodha import
    BrokerConnectionZerodha
    >>> from pyalgotrading.constants import *
    ```

    All `pyalgotrading` constants are now available in your Python namespace.

2. Get the `api_key` and `api_secret` keys from the broker. These are unique to you and will be used by the broker to identify your Demat account:

    ```
    >>> api_key = "<your-api-key>"
    >>> api_secret = "<your-api-secret>"
    >>> broker_connection = BrokerConnectionZerodha(api_key,
                                                    api_secret)
    ```

    We get the following output:

    ```
    Installing package kiteconnect via pip. This may take a while...
    Please login to this link to generate your request token:
    https://kite.trade/connect/login?api_key=<your-api-key>&v=3
    ```

    If you are running this for the first time and `kiteconnect` is not installed, `pyalgotrading` will automatically install it for you. The final output of *step 2* will be a link. Click on the link and log in with your Zerodha credentials. If the authentication is successful, you will see a link in your browser's address bar similar to `https://127.0.0.1/?request_token=<alphanumeric-token>&action=login&status=success`.

    We have the following example:

    ```
    https://127.0.0.1/?request_token=H06I6Ydv95y23D2Dp7NbigFjKweGwRP7&a
    ction=login&status=success
    ```

3. Copy the alphanumeric-token and paste it in `request_token`:

```
>>> request_token = "<your-request-token>"
>>> broker_connection.set_access_token(request_token)
```

The `broker_connection` instance is now ready for performing API calls.

> The `pyalgotrading` package supports multiple brokers and provides a connection object class per broker, with the same methods. It abstracts broker APIs behind a unified interface so users need not worry about the underlying broker API calls and can use all of the recipes in this chapter as is. Only the procedure to set up the broker connection would vary from broker to broker. You can refer to the `pyalgotrading` documentation for setting up the broker connection if you are not using Zerodha as your broker. For Zerodha users, the steps mentioned in the preceding section would suffice.

Placing a bracket limit order

Bracket orders are complex orders that are meant to help to make a profit when trade becomes favorable, or limit the loss when it becomes unfavorable, with predefined values. A bracket order is essentially a combination of three regular orders together—an initial order, a target order, and a stoploss order—which act together to help to achieve the specified profit or limit the loss. Along with the regular order parameters, a bracket order takes additional parameters—`target`, `stoploss`, and `trailing stoploss` (optional). The three regular orders are described as follows:

- **Initial order**: This order is equivalent to a regular limit order or regular stoploss-limit order. Once placed, it remains in the `'OPEN'` state until the market price reaches its trigger price value. Once the market crosses the trigger price value, this order moves from the `'OPEN'` to `'COMPLETE'` state and the target and stoploss orders are placed, which are described next.
- **Target order**: This order is equivalent to a regular limit order, with its trigger price as the specified target value and transaction type opposite to that of the initial order. For a buy initial order, the target order is placed at a higher price than the initial order. This would be vice versa for a sell initial order. The quantity matches that of the initial order. So, if this order executes, it exits the position created by the initial order.

- **Stoploss order**: This order is equivalent to a regular stoploss-limit order, with the specified `stoploss` value as its trigger price and transaction type opposite to that of the initial order. For a buy initial order, the stoploss order is placed at a lower price than the initial order. This would be vice versa for a sell initial order. The quantity matches that of the initial order. So, if this order executes, it exits the position created by the initial order. If a `trailing stoploss` parameter is specified, every time the initial order price moves in the direction of the target order price, the stoploss order is modified in the direction of the initial order price by as many points as the value of `trailing stoploss`. This helps to further reduce the loss in case the price movement direction of the initial order changes.

Since a target order and a stoploss order are placed on opposite sides of an initial order, they form a *bracket* around the initial order, and hence this order is called a **bracket order**. Also, as the target and stoploss orders are on opposite sides, only one of them would get executed (which means its status would go from `'OPEN'` to `'COMPLETE'`) at a given time, and when it does, the order (either the stoploss order or the target order) is automatically canceled. The target and stoploss orders are also collectively called **child orders** of the initial order, and the latter is called the **parent order** of the former.

A bracket order is usually meant for intraday trading unless otherwise supported by the broker. If the initial order or the child orders are not completed by the end of the trading session, they are automatically canceled or exited by the broker.

The following flowchart explains the workings of a **bracket order**:

```
                          ┌─────────┐
                          │  START  │
                          └────┬────┘
                               ▼
                     ┌──────────────────┐
                     │ Place Bracket Order │
                     └──────────┬─────────┘
                                ▼
                     ┌───────────────────────┐
                     │ Initial Order is placed │
                     │ Order Status goes to 'OPEN' │
                     └───────────┬───────────┘
                                              Check status again
                          ◇ Is Initial            No
                            Order Status   ──────────────►  Wait
                            COMPLETE?
                               │ Yes
                               ▼
                     ┌──────────────────┐
                     │ Place Child Orders │
                     └─────────┬─────────┘
             ┌───────────────┘       └───────────────┐
             ▼                                        ▼
   ┌──────────────────┐                    ┌────────────────────┐
   │ Place Target Order │                   │ Place Stoploss Order │
   └──────────────────┘                    └────────────────────┘

 Check status again                              Check status again
        Is Target                                     Is Stoploss
  Wait ◄── Order Status                            Order Status ──► Wait
       No COMPLETE?                               COMPLETE?   No
           │ Yes                                      │ Yes
           ▼                                          ▼
  ┌─────────────────────┐                  ┌────────────────────┐
  │ Cancel Stoploss Order │                │ Cancel Target Order │
  └─────────────────────┘                  └────────────────────┘
                   └──────────┐    ┌──────────┘
                              ▼    ▼
                          ┌──────────┐
                          │ COMPLETE │
                          └──────────┘
```

The following are references to the state machine diagrams for a bracket limit order:

- **Initial order**: Refer to the state machine diagram from the *Placing a regular limit order* recipe in the previous chapter.
- **Target order**: Refer to the state machine diagram from the *Placing a regular limit order* recipe in the previous chapter.
- **Stoploss order**: Refer to the state machine diagram from the *Placing a regular stoploss-limit order* recipe in the previous chapter.

You can use the bracket limit order when a buy bracket order has to be placed below the market price or a sell bracket order has to be placed above the market price.

This recipe demonstrates the placing of the following bracket limit orders and querying their statuses:

- The `BUY, BRACKET, INTRADAY, LIMIT` order (without trailing stoploss)
- The `SELL, BRACKET, INTRADAY, LIMIT` order (without trailing stoploss)

Getting ready

Make sure the `broker_connection` object and constants from the `pyalgotrading` package are available in your Python namespace. Refer to the *Technical requirements* section of this chapter to set up this object.

How to do it...

We execute the following steps for this recipe:

1. Fetch a financial instrument and assign it to `instrument`:

```
>>> instrument = broker_connection.get_instrument('NSE', 'SBIN')
```

2. Fetch the LTP. Place a `BUY, BRACKET, INTRADAY, LIMIT` order and display the order ID:

```
>>> ltp = broker_connection.get_ltp(instrument)
>>> order1_id = broker_connection.place_order(
                    instrument=instrument,
                    order_transaction_type= \
                        BrokerOrderTransactionTypeConstants.BUY,
                    order_type=BrokerOrderTypeConstants.BRACKET,
                    order_code=BrokerOrderCodeConstants.INTRADAY,
                    order_variety= \
                        BrokerOrderVarietyConstants.LIMIT,
                    quantity=1,
                    price=ltp-1,
                    stoploss=2,
                    target=2)
>>> order1_id
```

We get the following output (your output may differ):

```
'2003030003491923'
```

3. Fetch and display the order status:

```
>>> broker_connection.get_order_status(order1_id)
```

We get the following output:

```
'OPEN'
```

If you log in to the broker site with your credentials and go to the orders section, you can find your order details as shown in the following screenshot (some data may differ for you):

BUY	**SBIN** NSE		OPEN
Quantity	0 / 1	Order ID	200303003491923
Price	291	Exchange order ID	1300000009478195
Avg. price	0	Time	2020-03-03 14:46:44
Trigger price	0	Exchange time	2020-03-03 14:46:44
Order type	LIMIT	Placed by	DP5004
Product	BO		
Validity	DAY		

View history   Close

4. Fetch and display the order status again after some time:

```
>>> broker_connection.get_order_status(order1_id)
```

We get the following output:

```
'COMPLETE'
```

If you log in to the broker site with your credentials and go to the orders section, you can find your order details as shown in the following screenshot (some data may differ for you):

BUY	SBIN NSE			COMPLETE
Quantity	1 / 1	Order ID	200303003491923	
Price	291	Exchange order ID	1300000009478195	
Avg. price	291	Time	2020-03-03 14:49:31	
Trigger price	0	Exchange time	2020-03-03 14:46:44	
Order type	LIMIT	Placed by	DP5004	
Product	BO			
Validity	DAY			

View trades   View history   Close

5. Fetch the LTP. Place a `SELL`, `BRACKET`, `INTRADAY`, `LIMIT` order and display the order ID:

```
>>> ltp = broker_connection.get_ltp(instrument)
>>> order2_id = broker_connection.place_order(
                instrument=instrument,
                order_transaction_type= \
                    BrokerOrderTransactionTypeConstants.SELL,
                order_type=BrokerOrderTypeConstants.BRACKET,
                order_code=BrokerOrderCodeConstants.INTRADAY,
                order_variety= \
                    BrokerOrderVarietyConstants.LIMIT,
                quantity=1,
                price=ltp+1,
                stoploss=2,
                target=2)
>>> order2_id
```

We get the following output (your output may differ):

```
'200303003639902'
```

6. Fetch and display the order status:

```
>>> broker_connection.get_order_status(order2_id)
```

We get the following output:

```
'OPEN'
```

If you log in to the broker site with your credentials and go to the orders section, you can find your order details as shown in the following screenshot (some data may differ for you):

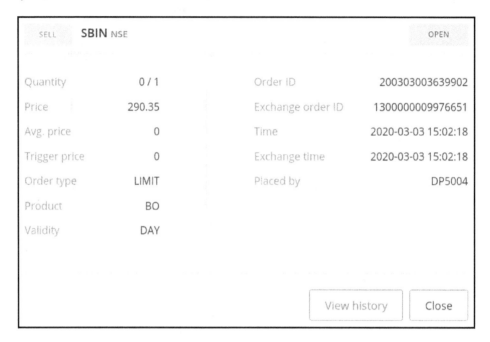

7. Fetch and display the order status again after some time:

```
>>> broker_connection.get_order_status(order2_id)
```

We get the following output:

```
'COMPLETE'
```

If you log in to the broker site with your credentials and go to the orders section, you can find your order details as shown in the following screenshot (some data may differ for you):

SELL	**SBIN** NSE		COMPLETE

Quantity	1 / 1	Order ID	200303003639902
Price	290.35	Exchange order ID	1300000009976651
Avg. price	290.35	Time	2020-03-03 15:16:47
Trigger price	0	Exchange time	2020-03-03 15:02:18
Order type	LIMIT	Placed by	DP5004
Product	BO		
Validity	DAY		

View trades   View history   Close

How it works...

In *step 1*, you use the `get_instrument()` method of
the `BrokerConnectionZerodha` class to fetch an instrument and assign it to a new attribute, `instrument`. This object is an instance of the `Instrument` class. The two parameters needed to call `get_instrument` are the exchange (`'NSE'`) and the trading-symbol (`'SBI'`).

In *step 2*, you fetch the LTP of the instrument using the `get_ltp()` method of the `BrokerConnectionZerodha` class and assign it to a new attribute, `ltp`.
The `instrument` object is passed as the parameter here. Next, you use
the `place_order()` method of the `broker_connection` object to place a BUY, BRACKET, INTRADAY, LIMIT order on the exchange. The `place_order()` method is a wrapper on the broker-specific place order API. It takes the following attributes:

- `instrument`: This is the financial instrument for which the order must be placed and should be an instance of the `Instrument` class. We pass `instrument` here.
- `order_transaction_type`: This is the order transaction type and should be an enum of the type, `BrokerOrderTransactionTypeConstants`. We pass `BrokerOrderTransactionTypeConstants.BUY` here.

- `order_type`: This is the order type and should be an enum of the type, `BrokerOrderTypeConstants`. We pass `BrokerOrderTypeConstants.BRACKET` here.
- `order_code`: This is the order code and should be an enum of the type, `BrokerOrderCodeConstants`. We pass `BrokerOrderCodeConstants.INTRADAY` here.
- `order_variety`: This is the order variety and should be an enum of the type, `BrokerOrderVarietyConstants`. We pass `BrokerOrderVarietyConstants.LIMIT` here.
- `quantity`: This is the number of shares to be traded for the given instrument and should be a positive integer. We pass 1 here.
- `price`: This is the limit price at which the order should be placed. We pass `ltp-1` here, which means 1 unit price below `ltp`.
- `stoploss`: This is the price difference from the initial order price, at which the stoploss order should be placed. It should be a positive `int` or `float` value. We pass 2 here.
- `target`: This is the price difference from the initial order price, at which the target order should be placed. It should be a positive `int` or `float` value. We pass 2 here.

(The attributes passed to the `place_order()` method are broker-agnostic constants, imported earlier from the `pyalgotrading.constants` module.)

On placing the order in *step 2*, you get an order ID from the broker, which you assign to a new attribute, `order1_id`. The `order1_id` object is a string. If the order placement is not successful for some reason, you may not get an order ID. Observe that the price parameter is passed a value of `ltp-1`. This means the order is placed below the market price, which is a necessary condition for placing buy limit orders. The `stoploss` parameter is specified as 2. This means the stoploss order would be placed at the price, which is two price units lower than the execution price of the initial order. Similarly, the `target` parameter is specified as 2. This means the target order would be placed at the price that is two price units higher than the execution price of the initial order.

In *step 3*, you fetch the status of the placed order using the `get_order_status()` method of the `broker_connection` object. You pass `order1_id` as a parameter to the `get_order_status()` method. You get the order status as `'OPEN'`, a string. You can use `order1_id` to fetch the status of the placed order at any later point of time as well.

In *step 4*, you fetch the order status again, and if the order is completed, you get the order status as 'COMPLETE'. Immediately after this, the target and stoploss orders are placed, at the prices mentioned earlier. The target order executes as a regular limit order. The stoploss order executes as a regular stoploss-limit order. When one of them gets executed and reaches the 'COMPLETE' state, the other order is automatically canceled by the broker, so it moves to the 'CANCELLED' state. Recall, both target and stoploss orders are on opposite sides of the initial order, so both target and stoploss orders cannot execute at the same time.

You can also verify the successful placement of your order by logging in to the broking website and checking the orders section there. You should see data similar to the screenshot shown in the outputs of *step 3* and *step 4*.

> In *step 3*, if you see the status as 'COMPLETE' instead of 'OPEN'; this could be due to high volatility. If you want the order to stay in the 'OPEN' state for a while, try placing the order further away from the market price.
>
> The following are references for more details on the execution of the initial order, target order, and stoploss order:
>
> - **Initial order**: Refer to the *Placing a regular limit order* recipe in the previous chapter.
> - **Target order**: Refer to the *Placing a regular limit order* recipe in the previous chapter.
> - **Stoploss order**: Refer to the *Placing a regular stoploss-limit order* recipe in the previous chapter.

The other steps in this recipe follow the same pattern of placing an order and getting its status for different combinations of attributes:

- *Steps 5, 6,* and *7*: The SELL, BRACKET, INTRADAY, LIMIT order

There's more...

You can exit a bracket order by exiting one of its child orders. The child order that you exit is executed at market price and moves to the COMPLETE state. The other child moves to the CANCELLED state.

For example, let's consider the case if you exit the stoploss order. In this case, the target order will be canceled and it will transition to the CANCELLED state. The stoploss order will be executed at market price and it will transition to the COMPLETE state. If you log in to the broker site with your credentials and go to the orders section, you can find the child order details as shown in the following screenshot. Some data may differ for you.

The following is the target order, for the initial order placed in *step 2*, before exiting the bracket order:

The following is the target order after exiting the bracket order:

This screenshot shows the stoploss order, for the initial order placed in *step 2*, before exiting:

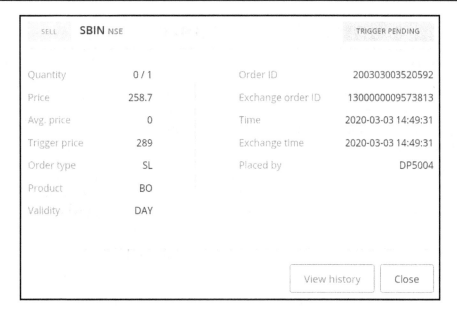

The following screenshot shows the stoploss order after exiting:

Placing a bracket stoploss-limit order

Bracket orders are complex orders that are meant to help to make a profit when trade becomes favorable, or limit the loss when it becomes unfavorable, with predefined values. A bracket order is essentially a combination of three regular orders together —an initial order, a target order, and a stoploss order, which act together to help to achieve the specified profit or limit the loss. Along with the regular order parameters, a bracket order takes additional parameters—`target`, `stoploss`, and `trailing stoploss` (optional).

Please refer to the introduction of the *Placing a bracket limit order* recipe for an in-depth understanding of the working of bracket orders. You can use a bracket stoploss-limit order if you want to place a buy bracket order above the market price or a sell bracket order below the market price.

This recipe demonstrates the placing of the following bracket stoploss-limit orders and querying their statuses:

- The `BUY, BRACKET, INTRADAY, STOPLOSS_LIMIT` order (without trailing stoploss)
- The `SELL, BRACKET, INTRADAY, STOPLOSS_LIMIT` order (without trailing stoploss)

The following are references to the state machine diagrams for a bracket stoploss-limit order:

- **Initial order**: Refer to the state machine diagram from the *Placing a regular stoploss-limit order* recipe in the previous chapter.
- **Target order**: Refer to the state machine diagram from the *Placing a regular limit order* recipe in the previous chapter.
- **Stoploss order**: Refer to the state machine diagram from the *Placing a regular stoploss-limit order* recipe in the previous chapter.

Getting ready

Make sure the `broker_connection` object and constants from the `pyalgotrading` package are available in your Python namespace. Refer to the *Technical requirements* section of this chapter to set up this object.

How to do it...

We execute the following steps for this recipe:

1. Fetch a financial instrument and assign it to `instrument`:

```
>>> instrument = broker_connection.get_instrument('NSE',
                                                  'INDUSINDBK')
```

2. Fetch the LTP. Place a BUY, BRACKET, INTRADAY, STOPLOSS_LIMIT order and display the order ID:

```
>>> ltp = broker_connection.get_ltp(instrument.segment)
>>> order1_id = broker_connection.place_order(
                    instrument=instrument,
                    order_transaction_type=\
                        BrokerOrderTransactionTypeConstants.BUY,
                    order_type=BrokerOrderTypeConstants.BRACKET,
                    order_code=BrokerOrderCodeConstants.INTRADAY,
                    order_variety= \
                        BrokerOrderVarietyConstants.STOPLOSS_LIMIT,
                    quantity=1,
                    price=ltp+1,
                    trigger_price=ltp+1,
                    stoploss=2,
                    target=2)
>>> order1_id
```

We get the following output (your output may differ):

```
'200226003619998'
```

3. Fetch and display the order status:

```
>>> broker_connection.get_order_status(order1_id)
```

We get the following output:

```
'TRIGGER PENDING'
```

4. Fetch and display the order status again after some time:

```
>>> broker_connection.get_order_status(order1_id)
```

We get the following output:

```
'COMPLETE'
```

5. Fetch the LTP. Place a SELL, BRACKET, INTRADAY, STOPLOSS_LIMIT order and display the order ID:

```
>>> ltp = broker_connection.get_ltp(instrument)
>>> order2_id = broker_connection.place_order(
                instrument=instrument,
                order_transaction_type= \
                    BrokerOrderTransactionTypeConstants.SELL,
                order_type=BrokerOrderTypeConstants.BRACKET,
                order_code=BrokerOrderCodeConstants.INTRADAY,
                order_variety= \
                    BrokerOrderVarietyConstants.STOPLOSS_LIMIT,
                quantity=1,
                price=ltp-1,
                trigger_price=ltp-1,
                stoploss=2,
                target=2)
>>> order2_id
```

We get the following output (your output may differ):

```
'200226003620002'
```

6. Fetch and display the order status:

```
>>> broker_connection.get_order_status(order2_id)
```

We get the following output:

```
'TRIGGER PENDING'
```

7. Fetch and display the order status again after some time:

```
>>> broker_connection.get_order_status(order2_id)
```

We get the following output:

```
'COMPLETE'
```

How it works...

In *step 1*, you use the get_instrument() method of the BrokerConnectionZerodha class to fetch an instrument and assign it to a new attribute, instrument. This object is an instance of the Instrument class. The two parameters needed to call get_instrument are the exchange ('NSE') and the trading-symbol ('INDUSINDBK').

In *step 2*, you fetch the LTP of the instrument using the `get_ltp()` method of the `BrokerConnectionZerodha` class and assign it to a new attribute, `ltp`. The `instrument` object is passed as the parameter here. Next, you use the `place_order()` method of the `broker_connection` object to place a BUY, BRACKET, INTRADAY, STOPLOSS_LIMIT order on the exchange. The `place_order()` method is a wrapper on the broker-specific place order API. It takes the following attributes:

- `instrument`: This is the financial instrument for which the order must be placed and should be an instance of the `Instrument` class. We pass `instrument` here.
- `order_transaction_type`: This is the order transaction type and should be an enum of the type, `BrokerOrderTransactionTypeConstants`. We pass `BrokerOrderTransactionTypeConstants.BUY` here.
- `order_type`: This is the order type and should be an enum of the type, `BrokerOrderTypeConstants`. We pass `BrokerOrderTypeConstants.BRACKET` here.
- `order_code`: This is the order code and should be an enum of the type, `BrokerOrderCodeConstants`. We pass `BrokerOrderCodeConstants.INTRADAY` here.
- `order_variety`: This is the order variety and should be an enum of the type, `BrokerOrderVarietyConstants`. We pass `BrokerOrderVarietyConstants.STOPLOSS_LIMIT` here.
- `quantity`: This is the number of shares to be traded for the given instrument and should be a positive integer. We pass 1 here.
- `price`: This is the limit price at which the order should be placed. We pass `ltp+1` here, which means 1 unit price above `ltp`.
- `trigger_price`: This is the trigger price at which the order should be placed. We pass `ltp+1` here, which means 1 unit price above `ltp`.
- `stoploss`: This is the price difference from the Initial Order price, at which the stoploss order should be placed. It should be a positive `int` or `float` value. We pass 2 here.
- `target`: This is the price difference from the Initial Order price, at which the target order should be placed. It should be a positive `int` or `float` value. We pass 2 here.

(The attributes passed to the `place_order()` method are broker-agnostic constants, imported earlier from the `pyalgotrading.constants` module.)

On placing the order in *step 2*, you get an order ID from the broker, which you assign to a new attribute, `order1_id`. The `order1_id` object is a string. If the order placement is not successful for some reason, you may not get an order ID. Observe that the `price` and `trigger_price` parameters are passed a value of `ltp+1`. This means the order is placed above the market price, which is a necessary condition for placing buy stoploss-limit orders. The stoploss parameter is specified as 2. This means the stoploss order would be placed at the price that is 2 price units lower than the execution price of the initial order. Similarly, the target parameter is specified as 2. This means the target order would be placed at the price that is 2 price units higher than the execution price of the Initial Order.

In *step 3*, you fetch the status of the placed order using the `get_order_status()` method of the `broker_connection` object. You pass `order1_id` as a parameter to the `get_order_status()` method. You get the order status as `'TRIGGER PENDING'`, a string. You can use `order1_id` to fetch the status of the placed order at any later point of time as well. In *step 4*, you fetch the order status again, and if the order is completed, you get the order status as `'COMPLETE'`. Immediately after this, the target and stoploss orders are placed, at the prices mentioned earlier. The target order executes as a regular limit order. The stoploss order executes as a regular stoploss-limit order. When one of them gets executed and reaches the `'COMPLETE'` state, the other order is automatically canceled by the broker, so it moves to the `'CANCELLED'` state. Recall, both target and stoploss orders are on opposite sides of the initial order, so both target and stoploss orders cannot execute at the same time.

In *step 3*, if you see the status as `'COMPLETE'` instead of `'TRIGGER PENDING'`, this could be due to high volatility. If you want the order to stay in the `'OPEN'` state for a while, try placing the order further away from the market price.

The following are references to more details on the execution of the initial order, target order, and stoploss order:

- **Initial order**: Refer to the *Placing a regular stoploss-limit order* recipe in the previous chapter.
- **Target order**: Refer to the *Placing a regular limit order* recipe in the previous chapter.
- **Stoploss order**: Refer to the *Placing a regular stoploss-limit order* recipe in the previous chapter.

You can verify the successful placement of your order by logging in to the broking website and checking the orders section there. You should see data similar to the screenshots shown in the *Placing bracket limit orders on the exchange* recipe.

The other steps in this recipe follow the same pattern of placing an order and getting its status for a different combination of attributes:

- *Steps 5, 6,* and *7*: The SELL, BRACKET, INTRADAY, STOPLOSS_LIMIT order

Placing a bracket limit order with trailing stoploss

Bracket orders are complex orders that are meant to help to make a profit when trade becomes favorable, or limit the loss when it becomes unfavorable, with predefined values. A bracket order is essentially a combination of three regular orders together—an initial order, a target order, and a stoploss order, which act together to help to achieve the specified profit or limit the loss. Along with the regular order parameters, a bracket order takes additional parameters—target, stoploss, and trailing stoploss (optional).

Please refer to the introduction of the *Placing a bracket limit order* recipe for an in-depth understanding of the working of bracket orders.

You can use a bracket limit order if you want to place a buy bracket order below the market price or a sell bracket order above the market price. The trailing stoploss feature improvises the positioning of the stoploss order by modifying its price in the direction of the initial order price by as many points as the value of trailing stoploss. This happens every time the initial order price moves in the direction of the target order price. This helps to further reduce the loss in case the price movement direction of the initial order changes.

This recipe demonstrates the placing of the following bracket limit orders with a trailing stoploss and querying their statuses:

- The BUY, BRACKET, INTRADAY, LIMIT order with trailing stoploss
- The SELL, BRACKET, INTRADAY, LIMIT order with trailing stoploss

The following are references to the state machine diagrams for a bracket limit order:

- **Initial order**: Refer to the state machine diagram from the *Placing a regular limit order* recipe in the previous chapter.
- **Target order**: Refer to the state machine diagram from the *Placing a regular limit order* recipe in the previous chapter.
- **Stoploss order**: Refer to the state machine diagram from the *Placing a regular stoploss-limit order* recipe in the previous chapter.

Getting ready

Make sure the `broker_connection` object and constants from the `pyalgotrading` package are available in your Python namespace. Refer to the *Technical requirements* section of this chapter to set up this object.

How to do it...

We execute the following steps for this recipe:

1. Fetch a financial instrument and assign it to `instrument`:

```
>>> instrument = broker_connection.get_instrument('NSE',
'FEDERALBNK')
```

2. Fetch the LTP. Place a BUY, BRACKET, INTRADAY, LIMIT order and display the order ID:

```
>>> ltp = broker_connection.get_ltp(instrument)
>>> order1_id = broker_connection.place_order(
                instrument=instrument,
                order_transaction_type= \
                    BrokerOrderTransactionTypeConstants.BUY,
                order_type=BrokerOrderTypeConstants.BRACKET,
                order_code=BrokerOrderCodeConstants.INTRADAY,
                order_variety= \
                    BrokerOrderVarietyConstants.LIMIT,
                quantity=1,
                price=ltp-1,
                trigger_price=ltp-1,
```

```
                                stoploss=2,
                                target=2,
                                trailing_stoploss=1)
>>> order1_id
```

We get the following output (your output may differ):

```
'200226003620004'
```

3. Fetch and display the order status:

```
>>> broker_connection.get_order_status(order1_id)
```

We get the following output:

```
'OPEN'
```

4. Fetch and display the order status again after some time:

```
>>> broker_connection.get_order_status(order1_id)
```

We get the following output:

```
'COMPLETE'
```

5. Fetch the LTP. Place a SELL, BRACKET, INTRADAY, LIMIT order and display the order ID:

```
>>> ltp = broker_connection.get_ltp(instrument)
>>> order2_id = broker_connection.place_order(
                        instrument=instrument,
                        order_transaction_type= \
                            BrokerOrderTransactionTypeConstants.SELL,
                        order_type=BrokerOrderTypeConstants.BRACKET,
                        order_code=BrokerOrderCodeConstants.INTRADAY,
                        order_variety= \
                            BrokerOrderVarietyConstants.LIMIT,
                        quantity=1,
                        price=ltp+1,
                        trigger_price=ltp+1,
                        stoploss=2,
                        target=2,
                        trailing_stoploss=1)
>>> order1_id
```

We get the following output (your output may differ):

```
'200226003620009'
```

6. Fetch and display the order status:

```
>>> broker_connection.get_order_status(order2_id)
```

We get the following output:

```
'OPEN'
```

7. Fetch and display the order status again after some time:

```
>>> broker_connection.get_order_status(order2_id)
```

We get the following output:

```
'COMPLETE'
```

How it works...

In *step 1*, you use the `get_instrument()` method of the `BrokerConnectionZerodha` class to fetch an instrument and assign it to a new attribute, `instrument`. This object is an instance of the `Instrument` class. The two parameters needed to call `get_instrument` are the exchange (`'NSE'`) and the trading-symbol (`'FEDERALBNK'`).

In *step 2*, you fetch the LTP of the instrument using the `get_ltp()` method of the `BrokerConnectionZerodha` class and assign it to a new attribute, `ltp`. The `instrument` object is passed as the parameter here. Next, you use the `place_order()` method of the `broker_connection` object to place a BUY, BRACKET, INTRADAY, LIMIT order on the exchange. The `place_order()` method is a wrapper on the broker-specific place order API. It takes the following attributes:

- `instrument`: This is the financial instrument for which the order must be placed and should be an instance of the `Instrument` class. We pass `instrument` here.
- `order_transaction_type`: This is the order transaction type and should be an enum of the type, `BrokerOrderTransactionTypeConstants`. We pass `BrokerOrderTransactionTypeConstants.BUY` here.
- `order_type`: This is the order type and should be an enum of the type, `BrokerOrderTypeConstants`. We pass `BrokerOrderTypeConstants.BRACKET` here.
- `order_code`: This is the order code and should be an enum of the type, `BrokerOrderCodeConstants`. We pass `BrokerOrderCodeConstants.INTRADAY` here.

- `order_variety`: This is the order variety and should be an enum of the type, `BrokerOrderVarietyConstants`. We pass `BrokerOrderVarietyConstants.LIMIT` here.
- `quantity`: This is the number of shares to be traded for the given instrument and should be a positive integer. We pass 1 here.
- `price`: This is the limit price at which the order should be placed. We pass `ltp-1` here, which means 1 unit price below `ltp`.
- `stoploss`: This is the price difference from the Initial Order price, at which the Stoploss Order should be placed. It should be a positive `int` or `float` value. We pass 2 here.
- `target`: This is the price difference from the Initial Order price, at which the Target Order should be placed. It should be a positive `int` or `float` value. We pass 2 here.
- `trailing_stoploss`: This is the price difference by which the stoploss order should be modified every time the market price moves in the direction of the target order. We pass 1 here.

(The attributes passed to the `place_order()` method are broker-agnostic constants, imported earlier from the `pyalgotrading.constants` module.)

On placing the order in *step 2*, you get an order ID from the broker, which you assign to a new attribute, `order1_id`. The `order1_id` object is a string. If the order placement is not successful for some reason, you may not get an order ID. Observe that the `price` parameter is passed a value of `ltp-1`. This means the order is placed below the market price, which is a necessary condition for placing buy limit orders. The `stoploss` parameter is specified as 2. This means the stoploss order would be placed at the price that is two price units lower than the execution price of the initial order. Similarly, the target parameter is specified as 2. This means the target order would be placed at the price that is two price units higher than the execution price of the initial order. Finally, the `trailing_stoploss` parameter is specified as 1. This means, after the stoploss order is placed, the stoploss order would be modified and placed at a price higher than the previous price by one unit, every time the market price increases in multiples of one unit from the price of the initial order.

So, for example, let's say the market price for the instrument was 100 at the time of placing this order, and so the target and stoploss orders would be placed at 102 and 98, respectively. Suppose the market price reaches 101, which is one unit higher than 100, then the stoploss order would be modified and placed at 99, which is again one unit higher than its previous price. By doing so, you have reduced your maximum loss from 2 to 1.

In *step 3*, you fetch the status of the placed order using the `get_order_status()` method of the `broker_connection` object. You pass `order1_id` as a parameter to the `get_order_status()` method. You get the order status as `'OPEN'`, a string. You can use `order1_id` to fetch the status of the placed order at any later point in time as well. In *step 4*, you fetch the order status again, and if the order is completed, you get the order status as `'COMPLETE'`. Immediately after this, the target and stoploss orders are placed, at the prices mentioned earlier. The target order executes as a regular limit order. The stoploss order executes as a regular stoploss-limit order. When one of them gets executed and reaches the `COMPLETE` state, the other order is automatically canceled by the broker, so it moves to the `CANCELLED` state. Recall, both target and stoploss orders are on opposite sides of the initial order, so both target and stoploss orders cannot execute at the same time. The stoploss order may be modified by one price unit, as mentioned earlier.

In *step 3*, if you see the status as `COMPLETE` instead of `OPEN`, this could be due to high volatility. If you want the order to stay in the `OPEN` state for a while, try placing the order further away from the market price.

The following are references for more details on the execution of the initial order, target order, and stoploss order:

- **Initial order**: Refer to the *Placing a regular limit order* recipe in the previous chapter.
- **Target order**: Refer to the *Placing a regular limit order* recipe in the previous chapter.
- **Stoploss order**: Refer to the *Placing a regular stoploss-limit order* recipe in the previous chapter.

You can verify the successful placement of your order by logging in to the broking website and checking the orders section there. You should see data similar to the screenshots shown in the *Placing bracket limit orders on the exchange* recipe.

The other steps in this recipe follow the same pattern of placing an order and getting its status for a different combination of attributes:

- *Steps 5, 6,* and *7*: The SELL, BRACKET, INTRADAY, LIMIT order with trailing stoploss

Placing a bracket stoploss-limit order with trailing stoploss

Bracket orders are complex orders that are meant to help to make a profit when trade becomes favorable, or limit the loss when it becomes unfavorable, with predefined values. A bracket order is essentially a combination of three regular orders together—an initial order, a target order, and a stoploss order, which act together to help to achieve the specified profit or limit the loss. Along with the regular order parameters, a bracket order takes additional parameters—`target`, `stoploss`, and `trailing stoploss` (optional).

Please refer to the introduction of the *Placing a bracket limit order* recipe for an in-depth understanding of the working of bracket orders.

You can use a bracket stoploss-limit order if you want to place a buy bracket order above the market price or a sell bracket order below the market price. The trailing stoploss improvises the positioning of the stoploss order by modifying its price in the direction of the initial order price by as many points as the value of `trailing stoploss`, every time the initial order price moves in the direction of the target order price. This helps to further reduce the loss, in case the direction of the price movement of the initial order changes.

This recipe demonstrates the placing of the following bracket stoploss-limit orders with trailing stoploss and querying their statuses:

- The BUY, BRACKET, INTRADAY, STOPLOSS_LIMIT order with trailing stoploss
- The SELL, BRACKET, INTRADAY, STOPLOSS_LIMIT order with trailing stoploss

The following are references to the state machine diagrams for a bracket stoploss-limit order:

- **Initial order**: Refer to the state machine diagram from the *Placing a regular stoploss-limit order* recipe in the previous chapter.
- **Target order**: Refer to the state machine diagram from the *Placing a regular limit order* recipe in the previous chapter.
- **Stoploss order**: Refer to the state machine diagram from the *Placing a regular stoploss-limit order* recipe in the previous chapter.

Getting ready

Make sure the `broker_connection` object and constants from the `pyalgotrading` package are available in your Python namespace. Refer to the *Technical requirements* section of this chapter to set up this object.

How to do it...

We execute the following steps for this recipe:

1. Fetch a financial instrument and assign it to `instrument`:

    ```
    >>> instrument = broker_connection.get_instrument('NSE', 'RBLBANK')
    ```

2. Fetch the LTP. Place a BUY, BRACKET, INTRADAY, STOPLOSS_LIMIT order and display the order ID:

    ```
    >>> ltp = broker_connection.get_ltp(instrument)
    >>> order1_id = broker_connection.place_order(
                      instrument=instrument,
                      order_transaction_type= \
                          BrokerOrderTransactionTypeConstants.BUY,
                      order_type=BrokerOrderTypeConstants.BRACKET,
                      order_code=BrokerOrderCodeConstants.INTRADAY,
                      order_variety= \
                          BrokerOrderVarietyConstants.STOPLOSS_LIMIT,
                      quantity=1,
                      price=ltp+1,
                      trigger_price=ltp+1,
                      stoploss=2,
                      target=2,
                      trailing_stoploss=1)
    >>> order1_id
    ```

    We get the following output (your output may differ):

    ```
    '200226003620011'
    ```

3. Fetch and display the order status:

    ```
    >>> broker_connection.get_order_status(order1_id)
    ```

    We get the following output:

    ```
    'TRIGGER PENDING'
    ```

4. Fetch and display the order status again after some time:

```
>>> broker_connection.get_order_status(order1_id)
```

We get the following output:

```
'COMPLETE'
```

5. Fetch the LTP. Place a SELL, BRACKET, INTRADAY, STOPLOSS_LIMIT order and display the order ID:

```
>>> ltp = broker_connection.get_ltp(instrument)
>>> order2_id = broker_connection.place_order(
                instrument=instrument,
                order_transaction_type= \
                    BrokerOrderTransactionTypeConstants.SELL,
                order_type=BrokerOrderTypeConstants.BRACKET,
                order_code=BrokerOrderCodeConstants.INTRADAY,
                order_variety= \
                    BrokerOrderVarietyConstants.STOPLOSS_LIMIT,
                quantity=1,
                price=ltp-1,
                trigger_price=ltp-1,
                stoploss=2,
                target=2,
                trailing_stoploss=1)
>>> order2_id
```

We get the following output (your output may differ):

```
'200226003620023'
```

6. Fetch and display the order status:

```
>>> broker_connection.get_order_status(order2_id)
```

We get the following output:

```
'TRIGGER PENDING'
```

7. Fetch and display the order status again after some time:

```
>>> broker_connection.get_order_status(order2_id)
```

We get the following output:

```
'COMPLETE'
```

How it works...

In *step 1*, you use the `get_instrument()` method of the `BrokerConnectionZerodha` class to fetch an instrument and assign it to a new attribute, `instrument`. This object is an instance of the `Instrument` class. The two parameters needed to call `get_instrument` are the exchange (`'NSE'`) and the trading-symbol (`'RBLBANK'`).

In *step 2*, you fetch the LTP of the instrument using the `get_ltp()` method of the `BrokerConnectionZerodha` class and assign it to a new attribute, `ltp`.
The `instrument` object is passed as the parameter here. Next, you use the `place_order()` method of the `broker_connection` object to place a BUY, REGULAR, INTRADAY, STOPLOSS_LIMIT order on the exchange. The `place_order()` method is a wrapper on the broker-specific place order API. It takes the following attributes:

- `instrument`: This is the financial instrument for which the order must be placed and should be an instance of the `Instrument` class. We pass `instrument` here.
- `order_transaction_type`: This is the order transaction type and should be an enum of the type, `BrokerOrderTransactionTypeConstants`. We pass `BrokerOrderTransactionTypeConstants.BUY` here.
- `order_type`: This is the order type and should be an enum of the type, `BrokerOrderTypeConstants`. We pass `BrokerOrderTypeConstants.BRACKET` here.
- `order_code`: This is the order code and should be an enum of the type, `BrokerOrderCodeConstants`. We pass `BrokerOrderCodeConstants.INTRADAY` here.
- `order_variety`: This is the order variety and should be an enum of the type, `BrokerOrderVarietyConstants`. We pass `BrokerOrderVarietyConstants.STOPLOSS_LIMIT` here.
- `quantity`: This is the number of shares to be traded for the given instrument and should be a positive integer. We pass 1 here.
- `price`: This is the limit price at which the order should be placed. We pass `ltp+1` here, which means 1 unit price above `ltp`.

- `trigger_price`: This is the trigger price at which the order should be placed. We pass `ltp+1` here, which means 1 unit price above `ltp`.
- `stoploss`: This is the price difference from the initial order price, at which the stoploss order should be placed. It should be a positive `int` or `float` value. We pass 2 here.
- `target`: This is the price difference from the Initial Order price, at which the Target Order should be placed. It should be a positive `int` or `float` value. We pass 2 here.
- `trailing_stoploss`: This is the price difference by which the stoploss order should be modified every time the market price moves in the direction of the target order. We pass 1 here.

(The attributes passed to the `place_order()` method are broker-agnostic constants, imported earlier from the `pyalgotrading.constants` module.)

On placing the order in *step 2*, you get an order ID from the broker, which you assign to a new attribute, `order1_id`. The `order1_id` object is a string. If the order placement is not successful for some reason, you may not get an order ID. Observe that the `price` and `trigger_price` parameters are passed a value of `ltp+1`. This means the order is placed above the market price, which is a necessary condition for placing buy stoploss-limit orders. The `stoploss` parameter is specified as 2. This means the stoploss order would be placed at the price that is two price units lower than the execution price of the initial order. Similarly, the `target` parameter is specified as 2. This means the target order would be placed at the price that is two price units higher than the execution price of the initial order. Finally, the `trailing_stoploss` parameter is specified as 1. This means, after the stoploss order is placed, the stoploss order would be modified and placed at a price higher than the previous price by one unit, every time the market price increases in multiples of one unit from the price of the initial order.

So, for example, let's say the market price for the instrument was 100 at the time of placing this order, and so the target and stoploss orders would be placed at 102 and 98 respectively. Suppose the market price reaches 101, which is one unit higher than 100, then the stoploss order would be modified and placed at 99, which is again one unit higher than its previous price. By doing so, you have reduced your maximum loss from 2 to 1.

In *step 3*, you fetch the status of the placed order using the `get_order_status()` method of the `broker_connection` object. You pass `order1_id` as a parameter to the `get_order_status()` method. You get the order status as `'TRIGGER PENDING'`, a string. You can use `order1_id` to fetch the status of the placed order at any later point of time as well. In *step 4*, you fetch the order status again, and if the order is completed, you get the order status as `'COMPLETE'`. Immediately after this, the target and stoploss orders are placed, at the prices mentioned earlier. The target order executes as a regular limit order. The stoploss order executes as a regular stoploss-limit order. When one of them gets executed and reaches the `'COMPLETE'` state, the other order is automatically canceled by the broker, so it moves to the `'CANCELLED'` state. Recall, both target and stoploss orders are on opposite sides of the initial order, so both target and stoploss orders cannot execute at the same time. The stoploss order may be modified by one price unit, as mentioned earlier.

In *step 3*, if you see the status as `'COMPLETE'` instead of `'TRIGGER PENDING'`, this could be due to high volatility. If you want the order to stay in the `'TRIGGER PENDING'` state for a while, try placing the order further away from the market price.

The following are references to more details on the execution of the target order and stoploss order:

- **Initial order**: Refer to the *Placing a regular stoploss-limit order* recipe in the previous chapter.
- **Target order**: Refer to the *Placing a regular limit order* recipe in the previous chapter.
- **Stoploss order**: Refer to the *Placing a regular stoploss-limit order* recipe chapter in the previous chapter.

You can verify the successful placement of your order by logging in to the broking website and checking the orders section there. You should see data similar to the screenshots shown in the *Placing bracket limit orders on the exchange* recipe.

The other steps in this recipe follow the same pattern of placing an order and getting its status for a different combination of attributes:

- *Steps 5, 6*, and 7: The SELL, BRACKET, INTRADAY, STOPLOSS_LIMIT order

Placing a cover market order

Cover orders are complex orders that are meant to help to limit the loss within predefined values if trade becomes unfavorable. A cover order is essentially a combination of two regular orders together—an initial order and a stoploss order:

- **Initial order**: This order can be equivalent to a regular market order or regular limit order, depending on whether you are placing a cover market order or cover limit order. Once the order moves to the 'COMPLETE' state, the stoploss order is placed, which is described next.
- **Stoploss order**: This order is equivalent to a regular stoploss-market order (the *Placing a regular stoploss-market order* recipe in the previous chapter), with the specified trigger price value as its trigger price and a transaction type opposite to that of the initial order. For a buy initial order, the stoploss order is placed at a lower price than the initial order. This would be vice versa for a sell initial order. The quantity matches that of the initial order. So, if this order executes, it exits the position created by the initial order.

Since the stoploss order is placed to cover the initial order from making unexpected losses, this order is called a **cover order**. Usually, the broker won't allow canceling the stoploss order once it is placed. It can only be exited via completion.

A cover order is usually meant for intraday trading unless otherwise supported by the broker. If the initial order or the stoploss order is not completed by the end of the trading session, they are automatically canceled or exited by the broker.

The following flowchart summarizes the preceding points and explains the working of a cover order:

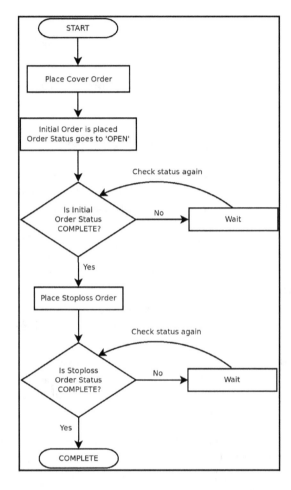

You can use the cover market order when a cover order has to be placed at the market price.

This recipe demonstrates placing the following cover market orders and querying their statuses:

- The BUY, COVER, INTRADAY, MARKET order
- The SELL, COVER, INTRADAY, MARKET order

The following are references to the state machine diagrams for a cover market order:

- **Initial order**: Refer to the state machine diagram from the *Placing a regular market order* recipe in the previous chapter.
- **Stoploss order**: Refer to the state machine diagram from the *Placing a regular stoploss-market order* recipe in the previous chapter.

Getting ready

Make sure the `broker_connection` object and constants from the `pyalgotrading` package are available in your Python namespace. Refer to the *Technical requirements* section of this chapter to set up this object.

How to do it...

We execute the following steps for this recipe:

1. Fetch a financial instrument and assign it to `instrument`:

```
>>> instrument = broker_connection.get_instrument('NSE',
                                                   'BANKBARODA')
```

2. Fetch the LTP. Place a BUY, COVER, INTRADAY, MARKET order and display the order ID:

```
>>> ltp = broker_connection.get_ltp(instrument)
>>> order1_id = broker_connection.place_order(
                    instrument=instrument,
                    order_transaction_type=\
                        BrokerOrderTransactionTypeConstants.BUY,
                    order_type=BrokerOrderTypeConstants.COVER,
                    order_code=BrokerOrderCodeConstants.INTRADAY,
                    order_variety= \
                        BrokerOrderVarietyConstants.MARKET,
                    quantity=1,
                    trigger_price=ltp-1)
>>> order1_id
```

We get the following output (your output may differ):

```
'200303003717532'
```

3. Fetch and display the order status:

```
>>> broker_connection.get_order_status(order1_id)
```

We get the following output:

```
'COMPLETE'
```

If you log in to the broker site with your credentials and go to the orders section, you can find your order details as shown in the following screenshots (some data may differ for you):

- The following screenshot shows the initial order:

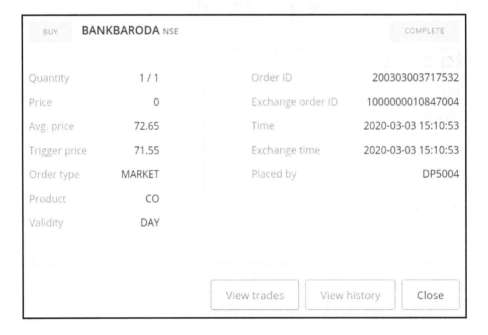

- The following screenshot shows the stoploss order:

SELL	**BANKBARODA** NSE		TRIGGER PENDING
Quantity	0 / 1	Order ID	200303003717536
Price	0	Exchange order ID	1000000010847019
Avg. price	0	Time	2020-03-03 15:10:53
Trigger price	71.55	Exchange time	2020-03-03 15:10:53
Order type	SL-M	Placed by	DP5004
Product	CO		
Validity	DAY		

View history   Close

4. Fetch the LTP. Place a SELL, COVER, INTRADAY, MARKET order and display the order ID:

```
>>> ltp = broker_connection.get_ltp(instrument)
>>> order2_id = broker_connection.place_order(
                 instrument=instrument,
                 order_transaction_type= \
                     BrokerOrderTransactionTypeConstants.SELL,
                 order_type=BrokerOrderTypeConstants.COVER,
                 order_code=BrokerOrderCodeConstants.INTRADAY,
                 order_variety= \
                     BrokerOrderVarietyConstants.MARKET,
                 quantity=1,
                 trigger_price=ltp+1)
>>> order2_id
```

We get the following output (your output may differ):

```
'200303003732941'
```

5. Fetch and display the order status:

```
>>> broker_connection.get_order_status(order2_id)
```

We get the following output:

```
'TRIGGER PENDING'
```

If you log in to the broker site with your credentials and go to the orders section, you can find your order details as shown in the following screenshots (some data may differ for you):

- The following screenshot shows the initial order:

- The following screenshot shows the stoploss order:

How it works...

In *step 1*, you use the `get_instrument()` method of the
`BrokerConnectionZerodha` class to fetch an instrument and assign it to a new
attribute, `instrument`. This object is an instance of the `Instrument` class. The two
parameters needed to call `get_instrument` are the exchange (`'NSE'`) and the trading-
symbol (`'BANKBARODA'`).

In *step 2*, you fetch the LTP of the instrument using the `get_ltp()` method of the
`BrokerConnectionZerodha` class and assign it to a new attribute, `ltp`.
The `instrument` object is passed as the parameter here. Next, you use
the `place_order()` method of the `broker_connection` object to place a BUY, COVER,
INTRADAY, MARKET order on the exchange. The `place_order()` method is a wrapper on
the broker-specific place order API. It takes the following attributes:

- `instrument`: This is the financial instrument for which the order must be placed
  and should be an instance of the `Instrument` class. We pass `instrument` here.
- `order_transaction_type`: This is the order transaction type and should be an
  enum of the type, `BrokerOrderTransactionTypeConstants`. We pass
  `BrokerOrderTransactionTypeConstants.BUY` here.
- `order_type`: This is the order type and should be an enum of the type,
  `BrokerOrderTypeConstants`. We pass
  `BrokerOrderTypeConstants.COVER` here.
- `order_code`: This is the order code and should be an enum of the type,
  `BrokerOrderCodeConstants`. We pass
  `BrokerOrderCodeConstants.INTRADAY` here.
- `order_variety`: This is the order variety and should be an enum of the type,
  `BrokerOrderVarietyConstants`. We pass
  `BrokerOrderVarietyConstants.MARKET` here.
- `quantity`: This is the number of shares to be traded for the given instrument and
  should be a positive integer. We pass 1 here.
- `trigger_price`: This is the trigger price for the Stoploss Order. We pass
  `ltp-1` here, which means one unit price below `ltp`.

(The attributes passed to the `place_order()` method are broker-agnostic constants,
imported earlier from the `pyalgotrading.constants` module.)

On placing the order in *step 2*, you get an order ID from the broker, which you assign to a new attribute, order1_id. The order1_id object is a string. If the order placement is not successful for some reason, you may not get an order ID. Observe that the trigger_price parameter is passed a value of ltp-1. This means the stoploss order is placed below the market price, which is a necessary condition for placing sell stoploss-market orders.

In *step 3*, you fetch the status of the placed order using the get_order_status() method of the broker_connection object. You pass order1_id as a parameter to the get_order_status() method. You get the order status as 'COMPLETE', a string. Immediately after this, the stoploss order is placed, at the price mentioned earlier. This order is then executed as a regular stoploss-market order.

If the stoploss order is executed at any point in time, it would mean your trade has incurred a loss, but has safe-guarded you from making more losses. The stoploss order transitions to the 'COMPLETE' state and the position created by the cover order is exited. You can also verify the successful placement of your order by logging in to the broking website and checking the orders section there. You should see data similar to the screenshot shown in the output of *step 3*.

The following are references to more details on the execution of stoploss orders:

- **Initial order**: Refer to the *Placing a regular market order* recipe in the previous chapter.
- **Stoploss order**: Refer to the *Placing a regular stoploss-market order* recipe in the previous chapter.

The other steps in this recipe follow the same pattern of placing an order and getting its status for a different combination of attributes:

- *Steps 4* and *5*: The SELL, COVER, INTRADAY, MARKET order

Placing a cover limit order

Cover orders are complex orders that are meant to help to limit the loss within predefined values if trade becomes unfavorable. A cover order is essentially a combination of two regular orders—an initial order and a stoploss order, which act together to help to limit the loss in case trade becomes unfavorable.

Please refer to the introduction of the *Placing a cover market order* recipe for an in-depth understanding of the working of cover orders. You can use a cover limit order if you want to place a buy cover order below the market price or a sell cover order above the market price. This recipe demonstrates the placing of the following cover limit orders and querying their statuses:

- The BUY, COVER, INTRADAY, LIMIT order
- The SELL, COVER, INTRADAY, LIMIT order

> The following are references to the state machine diagrams for a cover limit order:
>
> - **Initial order**: Refer to the state machine diagram from the *Placing a regular limit order* recipe in the previous chapter.
> - **Stoploss order**: Refer to the state machine diagram from the *Placing a regular stoploss-market order* recipe in the previous chapter.

Getting ready

Make sure the broker_connection object and constants from the pyalgotrading package are available in your Python namespace. Refer to the *Technical requirements* section of this chapter to set up this object.

How to do it...

We execute the following steps for this recipe:

1. Fetch a financial instrument and assign it to instrument:

```
>>> instrument = broker_connection.get_instrument('NSE', 'YESBANK')
```

2. Fetch the LTP. Place a BUY, COVER, INTRADAY, LIMIT order and display the order ID:

```
>>> ltp = broker_connection.get_ltp(instrument)
>>> order1_id = broker_connection.place_order(
                    instrument=instrument,
                    order_transaction_type= \
                        BrokerOrderTransactionTypeConstants.BUY,
```

```
                         order_type=BrokerOrderTypeConstants.COVER,
                         order_code=BrokerOrderCodeConstants.INTRADAY,
                         order_variety= \
                             BrokerOrderVarietyConstants.LIMIT,
                         quantity=1,
                         price=ltp-0.5,
                         trigger_price=ltp-1)
>>> order1_id
```

We get the following output:

```
'200303003749622'
```

3. Fetch and display the order status:

```
>>> broker_connection.get_order_status(order1_id)
```

We get the following output:

```
'OPEN'
```

If you log in to the broker site with your credentials and go to the orders section, you can find your order details as shown in the following screenshots (some data may differ for you):

- The following screenshot shows the initial order:

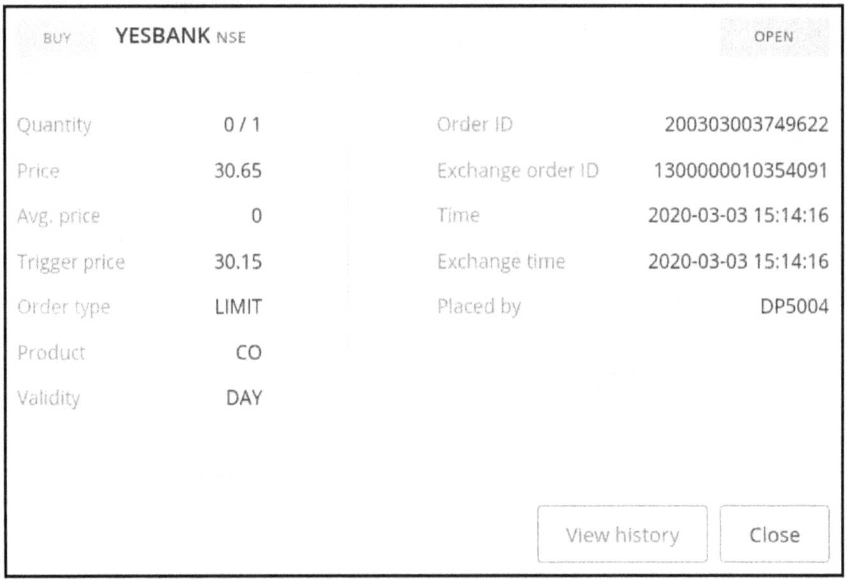

BUY YESBANK NSE			OPEN
Quantity	0 / 1	Order ID	200303003749622
Price	30.65	Exchange order ID	1300000010354091
Avg. price	0	Time	2020-03-03 15:14:16
Trigger price	30.15	Exchange time	2020-03-03 15:14:16
Order type	LIMIT	Placed by	DP5004
Product	CO		
Validity	DAY		
		View history	Close

- The following screenshot shows the stoploss order:

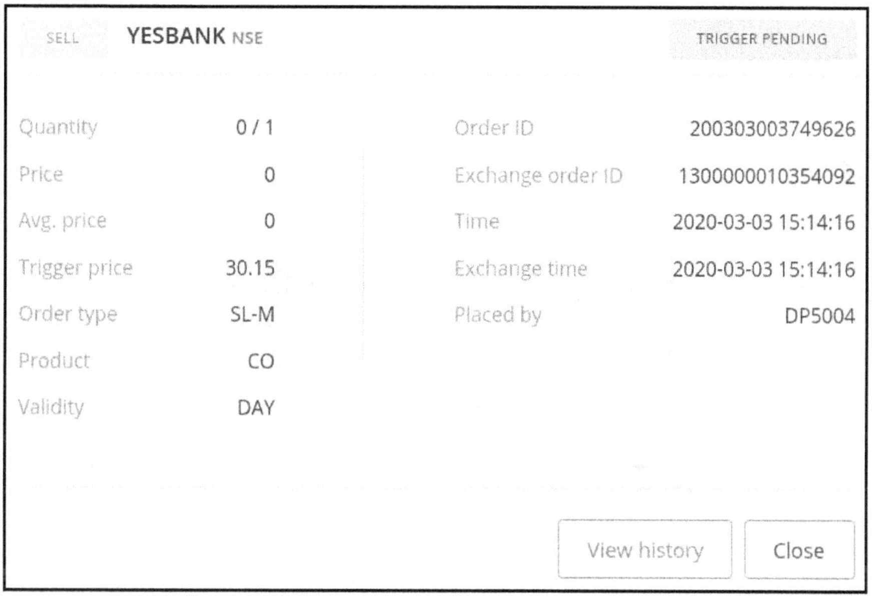

SELL	**YESBANK** NSE			TRIGGER PENDING
Quantity	0 / 1	Order ID		200303003749626
Price	0	Exchange order ID		1300000010354092
Avg. price	0	Time		2020-03-03 15:14:16
Trigger price	30.15	Exchange time		2020-03-03 15:14:16
Order type	SL-M	Placed by		DP5004
Product	CO			
Validity	DAY			

View history   Close

4. Fetch and display the order status again after some time:

```
>>> broker_connection.get_order_status(order1_id)
```

We get the following output:

```
'COMPLETE'
```

5. Fetch the LTP. Place a SELL, COVER, INTRADAY, LIMIT order and display the order ID:

```
>>> ltp = broker_connection.get_ltp(instrument)
>>> order2_id = broker_connection.place_order(
                instrument=instrument,
                order_transaction_type=\
                    BrokerOrderTransactionTypeConstants.SELL,
                order_type=BrokerOrderTypeConstants.COVER,
                order_code=BrokerOrderCodeConstants.INTRADAY,
                order_variety= \
                    BrokerOrderVarietyConstants.LIMIT,
                quantity=1,
                price=ltp+0.5,
                trigger_price=ltp+1)
>>> order2_id
```

We get the following output (your output may differ):

```
'200303003751757'
```

6. Fetch and display the order status:

```
>>> broker_connection.get_order_status(order2_id)
```

We get the following output:

```
'OPEN'
```

If you log in to the broker site with your credentials and go to the orders section, you can find your order details as shown in the following screenshots (some data may differ for you):

- The following screenshot shows the initial order:

SELL	**YESBANK** NSE			OPEN
Quantity	0 / 1	Order ID		200303003751757
Price	31.65	Exchange order ID		1300000010362457
Avg. price	0	Time		2020-03-03 15:14:31
Trigger price	32.15	Exchange time		2020-03-03 15:14:31
Order type	LIMIT	Placed by		DP5004
Product	CO			
Validity	DAY			

View history   Close

- The following screenshot shows the stoploss order:

BUY	**YESBANK** NSE		TRIGGER PENDING
Quantity	0 / 1	Order ID	200303003751758
Price	0	Exchange order ID	1300000010362450
Avg. price	0	Time	2020-03-03 15:14:31
Trigger price	32.15	Exchange time	2020-03-03 15:14:31
Order type	SL-M	Placed by	DP5004
Product	CO		
Validity	DAY		

View history   Close

7. Fetch and display the order status:

```
>>> broker_connection.get_order_status(order2_id)
```

We get the following output:

```
'COMPLETE'
```

How it works...

In *step 1*, you use the `get_instrument()` method of the
`BrokerConnectionZerodha` class to fetch an instrument and assign it to a new
attribute, `instrument`. This object is an instance of the `Instrument` class. The two
parameters needed to call `get_instrument` are the exchange (`'NSE'`) and the trading-
symbol (`'YESBANK'`).

In *step 2*, you fetch the LTP of the instrument using the `get_ltp()` method of the `BrokerConnectionZerodha` class and assign it to a new attribute, `ltp`. The `instrument` object is passed as the parameter here. Next, you use the `place_order()` method of the `broker_connection` object to place a BUY, COVER, INTRADAY, LIMIT order on the exchange. The `place_order()` method is a wrapper on the broker-specific place order API. It takes the following attributes:

- `instrument`: This is the financial instrument for which the order must be placed and should be an instance of the `Instrument` class. We pass `instrument` here.
- `order_transaction_type`: This is the order transaction type and should be an enum of the type, `BrokerOrderTransactionTypeConstants`. We pass `BrokerOrderTransactionTypeConstants.BUY` here.
- `order_type`: This is the order type and should be an enum of the type, `BrokerOrderTypeConstants`. We pass `BrokerOrderTypeConstants.COVER` here.
- `order_code`: This is the order code and should be an enum of the type, `BrokerOrderCodeConstants`. We pass `BrokerOrderCodeConstants.INTRADAY` here.
- `order_variety`: This is the order variety and should be an enum of the type, `BrokerOrderVarietyConstants`. We pass `BrokerOrderVarietyConstants.LIMIT` here.
- `quantity`: This is the number of shares to be traded for the given instrument and should be a positive integer. We pass 1 here.
- `price`: This is the limit price for the Initial Order. We pass `ltp-0.5` here, which means 0.5 unit of a price below `ltp`.
- `trigger_price`: This is the trigger price for the Stoploss Order. We pass `ltp-1` here, which means one unit price below `ltp`.

(The attributes passed to the `place_order()` method are broker-agnostic constants, imported earlier from the `pyalgotrading.constants` module.)

On placing the order in *step 2*, you get an order ID from the broker, which you assign to a new attribute, `order1_id`. The `order1_id` object is a string. If the order placement is not successful for some reason, you may not get an order ID. Observe that the `price` parameter is passed a value of `ltp-0.5`. This means the initial order is placed below the market price, which is a necessary condition for placing buy limit orders. Also, observe that the `trigger_price` parameter is passed a value of `ltp-1`. This means the stoploss order is placed below `price` (which will be the market price at the time of placing the stoploss order), which is a necessary condition for placing sell stoploss-market orders.

In *step 3*, you fetch the status of the placed order using the get_order_status() method of the broker_connection object. You pass order1_id as a parameter to the get_order_status() method. You get the order status as 'OPEN', a string. You can use order1_id to fetch the status of the placed order at any later point of time as well. In *step 4*, you fetch the order status again, and if the order is completed, you get the order status as 'COMPLETE'. Immediately after this, the stoploss order is placed, at the price mentioned earlier. This order is then executed as a regular stoploss-market order.

If the stoploss order is executed at any point in time, it would mean your trade has incurred a loss, but has safe-guarded you from making more losses. The stoploss order transitions to the 'COMPLETE' state and the position created by the cover order is exited. You can also verify the successful placement of your order by logging in to the broking website and checking the orders section there. You should see data similar to the screenshot shown in the output of *step 3*.

The following are references to more details on the execution of the initial order and stoploss order:

- **Initial order**: Refer to the *Placing a regular limit order* recipe in the previous chapter.
- **Stoploss order**: Refer to the *Placing a regular stoploss-market order* recipe in the previous chapter.

The other steps in this recipe follow the same pattern of placing an order and getting its status for a different combination of attributes:

- *Steps 4* and *5*: The SELL, COVER, INTRADAY, LIMIT order

8
Algorithmic Trading Strategies – Coding Step by Step

It is a complex task to build your own algorithmic trading strategies. A trading platform with numerous components is required to test and run your strategy. Some of these components are the compute engine, real-time data feeds, broker connectivity, blotter, fund manager, clocks, a virtual order-management system, and so on.

In this chapter, you will be using the services provided by AlgoBulls, an algorithmic trading platform (https://algobulls.com). This platform provides a Python package called pyalgotrading (https://github.com/algobulls/pyalgotrading). You will code your strategy as a Python class by subclassing the StrategyBase abstract class provided in the package. The abstract class acts as a template for developing and validating new strategies quickly with minimal effort. You can use the AlgoBulls platform to perform backtesting, paper trading, and real trading on your strategy. The pyalgotrading package helps us focus on developing the strategy and takes care of talking to the AlgoBulls platform for execution purposes.

This chapter introduces two strategies:

- **EMA-Regular-Order strategy**: This strategy is based on the technical indicator exponential moving average. It uses regular orders.
- **MACD-Bracket-Order strategy**: This strategy is based on the technical indicator moving average convergence divergence. It uses bracket orders.

Initially, you may find strategy coding a daunting task. Therefore, the coding part is divided into five recipes. Each recipe demonstrates one or more methods enforced by the `StrategyBase` class. The sixth recipe demonstrates how to upload the strategy to the AlgoBulls platform.

The skeleton for a strategy looks as shown:

```
class MyCustomStrategy(StrategyBase):
    def __init__(self, *args, **kwargs): # [Recipes 1, 7]
        ...
    def name(): # [Recipes 1, 7]
        ...
    def versions_supported(): # [Recipes 1, 7]
        ...
    def initialize(self): # [Recipes 1, 7]
        ...
    def strategy_select_instruments_for_entry(self, candle,
                                                instruments_bucket):
        ... # [Recipes 2, 8]
    def strategy_enter_position(self, candle, instrument, sideband_info):
        ... # [Recipes 3, 9]
    def strategy_select_instruments_for_exit(self, candle,
                                                instruments_bucket):
        ... # [Recipes 4, 10]
    def strategy_exit_position(self, candle, instrument, sideband_info):
        ... # [Recipes 5, 11]
```

The AlgoBulls core engine is the trading engine powering the AlgoBulls platform. It is responsible for reading your strategies and executing them for backtesting, paper trading, and real trading. The AlgoBulls core engine uses the following flowchart for executing your strategy successfully:

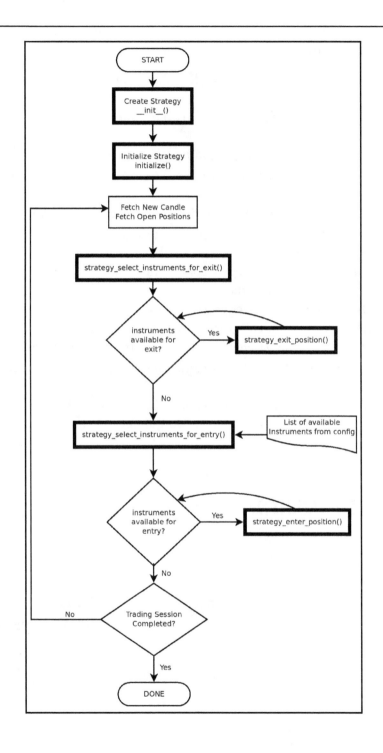

In this chapter, we will cover the following recipes:

- EMA-Regular-Order strategy – coding the __init__, initialize, name, and versions_supported methods
- EMA-Regular-Order strategy – coding the strategy_select_instruments_for_entry method
- EMA-Regular-Order strategy – coding the strategy_enter_position method
- EMA-Regular-Order strategy – coding the strategy_select_instruments_for_exit method
- EMA-Regular-Order strategy – coding the strategy_exit_position method
- EMA-Regular-Order strategy – uploading the strategy onto the AlgoBulls trading platform
- MACD-Bracket-Order strategy – coding the __init__, initialize, name, and versions_supported methods
- MACD-Bracket-Order strategy – coding the strategy_select_instruments_for_entry method
- MACD-Bracket-Order strategy – coding the strategy_enter_position method
- MACD-Bracket-Order strategy – coding the strategy_select_instruments_for_exit method
- MACD-Bracket-Order strategy – coding the strategy_exit_position method
- MACD-Bracket-Order strategy – uploading the strategy onto AlgoBulls trading platform

Technical requirements

You will need the following to execute the recipes in this chapter:

- Python 3.7+
- Python packages:
    - `pyalgotrading` ($ pip install pyalgotrading)
    - `pyalgostrategypool` ($ pip install pyalgostrategypool)
    - `TA-Lib` ($ pip install TA-Lib)

If you face errors while installing `TA-Lib`, it will mostly be due to missing dependencies. You can follow these instructions to fix the issue:

- **For Mac OS X, use the following**:

  ```
  $ brew install ta-lib
  ```

- **For Windows, use the following instructions**:

  You can install the latest `TA-Lib` binary from `https://www.lfd.uci.edu/~gohlke/pythonlibs/#ta-lib` based on your Windows build (32 bit/64 bit) and Python version. So, for example, this link on the site, `TA_Lib-0.4.18-cp38-cp38-win_amd64.whl`, is for TA-Lib version 0.4.18 (`TA_Lib-0.4.18`) and Python version 3.8 (`cp38`), and is Windows 64-bit-compatible (`win_amd64`).

- **For Linux, take the following steps**:

  Download this `gzip` file—`http://prdownloads.sourceforge.net/ta-lib/ta-lib-0.4.0-src.tar.gz`—and run the following commands from your Linux Terminal:

  1. Extract the downloaded `gzip` file containing the source code for `TA-Lib`:

     ```
     $ tar -xzf ta-lib-0.4.0-src.tar.gz
     ```

  2. Change your current working directory to the extracted folder:

     ```
     $ cd ta-lib/
     ```

  3. Run the `configure` command to configure `TA-Lib` for your machine:

     ```
     $ ./configure --prefix=/usr
     ```

  4. Run the `make` command to build `TA-Lib` from the downloaded source code:

     ```
     $ make
     ```

  5. Run the `install` command to install built executables and libraries to specific directories on your machine:

     ```
     $ sudo make install
     ```

If this doesn't help and you still get errors, please refer to the official `TA-Lib` GitHub page at `https://github.com/mrjbq7/ta-lib#dependencies`. The latest Jupyter notebook for this chapter can be found on GitHub at `https://github.com/PacktPublishing/Python-Algorithmic-Trading-Cookbook/tree/master/Chapter08`.

The following code will help you import the necessary modules that are used by all the recipes in this chapter. Please make sure you have followed this step before trying out any of the recipes:

```
>>> from pyalgotrading.strategy.strategy_base import StrategyBase
>>> from pyalgotrading.constants import *
```

In the first five recipes, you will create a complete algorithmic trading strategy based on the EMA technical indicator. This strategy is called the **EMA-Regular-Order** strategy and is described as follows:

- **Technical indicators**:
  - `EMA(timeperiod=4)` or `EMA4`
  - `EMA(timeperiod=9)` or `EMA9`

  While the typical values of the time periods are 4 and 9, both of the time periods are taken as parameters, so they can be changed at runtime without having to recreate the strategy again. This is discussed more in the first recipe of this chapter.

- **Order attributes**:
  - Order transaction type: `BUY` and `SELL`
  - Order type: `Regular`
  - Order code: `INTRADAY`
  - Order variety: `Market`
- **Strategy algorithm**:
  - Whenever `EMA4` crosses `EMA9` upward, note the following:
    - The previous `SHORT` position, if present, should be exited.
    - A `BUY` signal is generated by the strategy and a new `LONG` position should be entered.
  - Whenever `EMA4` crosses `EMA9` downward, note the following:
    - The previous `LONG` position, if present, should be exited.
    - A `SELL` signal is generated by the strategy and a new `SHORT` position should be entered.

You will code the entire logic as a single Python class called `StrategyEMARegularOrder`. This class will be a subclass of `StrategyBase` from the `pyalgotrading` package. After uploading `StrategyEMARegularOrder` on the AlgoBulls platform, you can backtest (refer to the first six recipes of `Chapter 9`, *Backtesting Strategies*), paper trade (refer to the first five recipes of `Chapter 10`, *Paper Trading*), and real trade (refer to the first five recipes of `Chapter 11`, *Real Trading*) on this strategy.

In the seventh to eleventh recipes, you will create a complete algorithmic trading strategy based on the MACD technical indicator. This strategy is called as the **MACD-Bracket-Order** strategy and is described as follows:

- **Technical indicators**:
  - MACD: This technical indicator has three components: the MACD line, MACD signal, and MACD histogram. We are concerned only with the MACD line and MACD signal components for this strategy.
- **Order attributes**:
  - Order transaction type: BUY and SELL
  - Order type: Bracket
  - Order code: INTRADAY
  - Order variety: Limit
- **Strategy algorithm**:
  - Whenever the MACD line crosses the MACD signal upward, note the following:
    - The previous SHORT position, if present, should be exited.
    - A BUY signal is generated by the strategy and a new LONG position should be entered.
  - Whenever the MACD line crosses the MACD signal downward, note the following:
    - The previous LONG position, if present, should be exited.
    - A SELL signal is generated by the strategy and a new SHORT position should be entered.

You will code the entire logic as a single Python class, called `StrategyMACDBracketOrder`. This class will be a subclass of `StrategyBase` from the `pyalgotrading` package. After uploading `StrategyMACDBracketOrder` onto the AlgoBulls platform, you can backtest (refer to the seventh to twelfth recipes of `Chapter 9`, *Algorithmic Trading – Backtesting*), paper trade (refer to the seventh to twelfth recipes of `Chapter 10`, *Algorithmic Trading – Paper Trading*), and real trade (refer to the seventh to eleventh recipes of `Chapter 11`, *Algorithmic Trading – Real Trading*) on this strategy.

For more information on these topics, please refer to the following corresponding chapters:

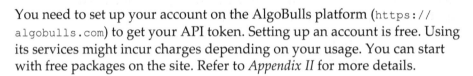

- **Technical indicators**: `Chapter 5`, *Computing and Plotting Technical Indicators*
- **Order attributes**: `Chapter 6`, *Placing Regular Orders on the Exchange* and `Chapter 7`, *Placing Bracket and Cover Orders on the Exchange.*

You need to set up your account on the AlgoBulls platform (`https://algobulls.com`) to get your API token. Setting up an account is free. Using its services might incur charges depending on your usage. You can start with free packages on the site. Refer to *Appendix II* for more details.

EMA-Regular-Order strategy – coding the __init__, initialize, name, and versions_supported methods

This recipe demonstrates the initial coding of the `StrategyEMARegularOrder` class. The complete class will be coded by the end of the *EMA-Regular-Order strategy – coding the strategy_exit_position method* recipe of this chapter. In this recipe, you will code the following methods:

- `__init__()`
- `initialize()`
- `name()`
- `versions_supported()`

To learn more about the EMA technical indicator, please refer to the *Trend indicator – exponential moving average* recipe of `Chapter 5`, *Computing and Plotting Technical Indicators*.

Please refer to the flowchart in the introduction of this chapter to understand how the AlgoBulls core engine calls the `__init__()` and `initialize()` methods during strategy execution.

Getting ready

Make sure you have the `StrategyBase` and `pyalgotrading` constants in your Python namespace. Refer to the *Technical requirements* section of this chapter to set it up.

How to do it...

Create a new class named `StrategyEMARegularOrder`, which will be a subclass from `StrategyBase` and then define the required four methods:

```
class StrategyEMARegularOrder(StrategyBase):
    def __init__(self, *args, **kwargs):
        super().__init__(*args, **kwargs)
        self.timeperiod1 = self.strategy_parameters['timeperiod1']
        self.timeperiod2 = self.strategy_parameters['timeperiod2']
        self.main_order = None
    def initialize(self):
        self.main_order = {}
    @staticmethod
    def name():
        return 'EMA Regular Order Strategy'
    @staticmethod
    def versions_supported():
        return AlgoBullsEngineVersion.VERSION_3_2_0
```

How it works...

In this recipe, we create the `StrategyEMARegularOrder` class, subclassed from `StrategyBase`. We define four methods for this class and describe them as follows:

- The `__init__()` method: This is the first thing to do when you create a new strategy. First, you create this method and call the parent class `__init__()` method using `super()`. This helps the AlgoBulls core engine create the necessary data structures needed for further development of the strategy. Next, you create two new attributes from `self.strategy_parameters`—`self.timeperiod1` and `self.timeperiod2`. `self.strategy_parameters` is a dictionary object available for every strategy subclassed from `StrategyBase`. (The second recipe of `Chapter 8`, *Backtesting Strategies*, discusses how these values are passed at runtime to `self.strategy_parameters`.) You will use these parameters as time periods of both the EMAs in the next recipe.

Lastly, you create a new attribute, `self.main_order`, which is an empty dictionary. We will use this to save the handles to all the open orders placed during the execution of this strategy.

- The `initialize()` method: This method is called at the beginning of every market day to initialize any internal variables to their default state. For real trading and paper trading, this method is called once. For multi-day backtesting, this method is called multiple times, once at the beginning of every new trading day. In this method, you initialize `self.main_order` to an empty dictionary.
- The `name()` method: This is a static method, which returns the name of this strategy. This is used while availing backtesting, paper trading, and real trading services on this strategy. In this method, you simply return a string, `Exponential Moving Average Regular Order`. You can return any string of your choice.
- The `versions_supported()` method: This static method is used for returning the AlgoBulls core engine version for which this strategy has been created. Often, as new upgrades come to the AlgoBulls core engine, some backward-incompatible changes may get introduced. This method helps to ensure this strategy is run on the correct version of the AlgoBulls core engine at all times. In this method, you return the highest available version from the constants module, which at the time of writing this chapter is VERSION_3_2_0.

These four methods are mandatory; they are enforced by the `StrategyBase` base class and cannot be skipped.

EMA-Regular-Order strategy – coding the strategy_select_instruments_for_entry method

In this recipe, you continue coding the `StrategyEMARegularOrder` class. Here, you code the `strategy_select_instruments_for_entry()` method, a mandatory method enforced by the `StrategyBase` base class. This method is called by the AlgoBulls core engine on every new candle for backtesting, paper trading, and real trading services.

Please refer to the flowchart in the introduction of this chapter to understand how the AlgoBulls core engine calls the `strategy_select_instruments_for_entry()` method during strategy execution.

Getting ready

Make sure you have followed the preceding recipe to create the `StrategyEMARegularOrder` class before starting this recipe.

How to do it...

Continue coding the `StrategyEMARegularOrder` class. We need to define two new methods—a method for getting the crossover value between the MACD line and MACD history signals and a method for selecting instruments from `instruments_bucket` for entering a new position based on the computed crossover value:

```
class StrategyEMARegularOrder(StrategyBase):
    # Previous methods not shown
    def get_crossover_value(self, instrument):
        hist_data = self.get_historical_data(instrument)
        ema_x = talib.EMA(hist_data['close'], timeperiod=self.timeperiod1)
        ema_y = talib.EMA(hist_data['close'], timeperiod=self.timeperiod2)
        crossover_value = self.utils.crossover(ema_x, ema_y)
        return crossover_value
    def strategy_select_instruments_for_entry(self, candle,
                                              instruments_bucket):
        selected_instruments_bucket = []
        sideband_info_bucket = []
        for instrument in instruments_bucket:
            crossover_value = self.get_crossover_value(instrument)
            if crossover_value == 1:
                selected_instruments_bucket.append(instrument)
                sideband_info_bucket.append({'action': 'BUY'})
            elif crossover_value == -1:
                if self.strategy_mode is StrategyMode.INTRADAY:
                    selected_instruments_bucket.append(instrument)
                    sideband_info_bucket.append({'action': 'SELL'})
        return selected_instruments_bucket, sideband_info_bucket
```

How it works...

In this recipe, we continue coding the `StrategyEMARegularOrder` class. We define two new methods for this class, described as follows:

- The `get_crossover_value()` method: This method takes `instrument` as an argument (along with `self`). This is the financial instrument for which the crossover value has to be computed. You fetch the latest historical data using the `self.get_historical_data()` method and assign it to a new attribute, `hist_data`. We pass `instrument` as the argument to this method. The `hist_data` attribute is a `pandas.DataFrame` object with `timestamp`, `open`, `high`, `low`, `close`, and `volume` columns. The default duration of the fetched historical data is the last 15 days.

  You compute EMA on the close of `hist_data` using the `talib.EMA` function, for a time period of `self.timeperiod1`, and assign it to `ema_x`. This data is a `pandas.Series` object. (Refer to the second recipe of `Chapter 5`, *Computing and Plotting of Technical Indicators*, for more details on the computation of EMA.) Similarly, you compute EMA on the close of `hist_data` for a time period of `self.timeperiod2` and assign it to `ema_y`. This return data is again a `pandas.Series` object.

  You compute the crossover value between `ema_x` and `ema_y` using `self.utils.crossover(ema_x, ema_y)` and assign it to a new attribute, `crossover_value`. The `crossover()` function call works as follows:

  - It takes two iterables as input. We pass `ema_x` and `ema_y` here.
  - If `ema_x` crosses `ema_y` upward, the crossover function returns `1`.
  - If `ema_x` crosses `ema_y` downward, the crossover function returns `-1`.
  - If there is no crossover between `ema_x` and `ema_y`, then the crossover function returns `0`.

  Finally, you return `crossover_value`.

- The `strategy_select_instruments_for_entry()` method: This method takes two arguments, other than `self`—candle, an object of the `CandleTime` type that contains the timestamp of the current candle, and `instruments_bucket`, an object of the `SetInstruments` type that contains all the financial instruments available for creating a new position. We pass this data at the time of strategy execution. You create two empty lists, `selected_instruments_bucket` and `sideband_info_bucket`. Then you run a `for` loop over `instruments_bucket`, and for each instrument, you call `self.get_crossover_value()` and save its value to a new attribute, `crossover_value`. Based on the value of `crossover_value`, you make a decision, as follows:
  - If `crossover_value` is 1, it means the strategy is giving a BUY signal. You do the following:
    - Append `instrument` to `selected_instruments_bucket`.
    - Append an `{'action': 'BUY'}` dictionary to the `sideband_info_bucket` attribute.
  - If `crossover_value` is −1, it means the strategy is giving a SELL signal. You do the following:
    - Append `instrument` to `selected_instruments_bucket`.
    - Append an `{'action': 'SELL'}` dictionary to the `sideband_info_bucket` attribute.
  - If `crossover_value` is neither 1 nor −1, it means the strategy is not giving any signals. You do nothing here.

Finally, you return both the attributes: `selected_instruments_bucket` and `sideband_info_bucket`. These attributes may have been populated or may remain as empty lists.

Recall that the `strategy_select_instruments_for_entry()` method is called for every candle, so the preceding steps are repeated for every new candle. In the appropriate candle, you would get a BUY or a SELL signal, and in the others, you won't get any signal. Based on the signal, you can place the appropriate order, which is discussed in the next recipe.

 The `strategy_select_instruments_for_entry()` method is enforced by the `StrategyBase` base class and has to be defined for every strategy. The `get_crossover_value()` method is a helper method, meaning it is not enforced by the `StrategyBase` base class. You may choose not to define this or to define multiple of these helper functions.

EMA-Regular-Order strategy – coding the strategy_enter_position method

In this recipe, you continue with the coding of the `StrategyEMARegularOrder` class. Here, you code the `strategy_enter_position()` method, a mandatory method enforced by the `StrategyBase` base class. This method is called by the AlgoBulls core engine every time the `strategy_select_instruments_for_entry` method returns non-empty data. This method may not be called for every new candle for backtesting, paper trading, and real trading services.

 Please refer to the flowchart in the introduction of this chapter to understand how the AlgoBulls core engine calls the `strategy_enter_position()` method during strategy execution.

Getting ready

Make sure you have followed the preceding recipe before starting this recipe.

How to do it...

Continue coding the `StrategyEMARegularOrder` class. We need to define a method to punch new orders for a given instrument and enter a new position:

```
class StrategyEMARegularOrder(StrategyBase):
    # Previous methods not shown
    def strategy_enter_position(self, candle, instrument, sideband_info):
        if sideband_info['action'] == 'BUY':
            qty = self.number_of_lots * instrument.lot_size
            self.main_order[instrument] = \
                self.broker.BuyOrderRegular(instrument=instrument,
                        order_code=BrokerOrderCodeConstants.INTRADAY,
                        order_variety=BrokerOrderVarietyConstants.MARKET,
                        quantity=qty)
        elif sideband_info['action'] == 'SELL':
            qty = self.number_of_lots * instrument.lot_size
            self.main_order[instrument] = \
                self.broker.SellOrderRegular(instrument=instrument,
                        order_code=BrokerOrderCodeConstants.INTRADAY,
                        order_variety=BrokerOrderVarietyConstants.MARKET,
                        quantity=qty)
```

```
else:
    raise SystemExit(f'Got invalid sideband_info value:
                     {sideband_info}')
return self.main_order[instrument]
```

How it works...

In this recipe, we continue coding the `StrategyEMARegularOrder` class. We define a new method for this class, `strategy_enter_position()`, described as follows:

- This method takes three arguments, other than `self`:
  - `candle`: An object of the `CandleTime` type that contains the timestamp of the current candle.
  - `instrument`: An object of the `Instrument` type that represents a financial instrument.
  - `sideband_info`: A dictionary object that holds information on trades to be placed for the `instrument` attribute. This object looks like `{'action':` `[action_value]}`, where `[action_value]` can be either `'BUY'` or `'SELL'`.
- You calculate the quantity for order to be placed by multiplying `self.number_of_lots` with `instrument.lot_size` and assign it to a new attribute `qty`. The `self.number_of_lots` attribute holds information on the number of lots to trade, which you can pass while executing this strategy. The `instrument.lot_size` attribute holds `lot_size` for `instrument`, which is a positive integer. For example, if number of lots is passed as 2 and lot size for instrument is 10, then the quantity for the order would be 2 * 10 = 20.
- If `sideband_info` is `{'action': 'BUY'}`, you place a `Regular` order of the `BUY` transaction type by creating an instance of the `self.broker.BuyOrderRegular` class (the first recipe of `Chapter 6`, *Placing Regular Orders on the Exchange*) and assigning its value to `self.main_order[instrument]`.
- If `sideband_info` is `{'action': 'SELL'}`, you place a `Regular` order of the `SELL` transaction type by creating an instance of the `self.broker.SellOrderRegular` class (the first recipe of `Chapter 6`, *Placing Regular Orders on the Exchange*) and assigning its value to `self.main_order[instrument]`.

In both cases, the `self.main_order dictionary` object holds the `instrument` and `order` instances as a key-value pair. This will be useful later (in the *EMA-Regular-Order strategy – coding the strategy_exit_position method* recipe) for exiting positions created by this method.

The `self.broker` attribute is replaced by the appropriate broker instance at runtime by the AlgoBulls core engine. So, the same code can work across all the brokers supported by the AlgoBulls platform.

EMA-Regular-Order strategy – coding the strategy_select_instruments_for_exit method

In this recipe, you continue with the coding of the `StrategyEMARegularOrder` class. Here, you code the `strategy_select_instruments_for_exit()` method, a mandatory method enforced by the `StrategyBase` base class. This method is called by the AlgoBulls core engine for every new candle for backtesting, paper trading, and real trading services if there are any open positions.

 Please refer to the flowchart in the introduction of this chapter to understand how the AlgoBulls core engine calls the `strategy_select_instruments_for_exit()` method during strategy execution.

Getting ready

Make sure you have followed the preceding recipe before starting this recipe.

How to do it...

Continue coding the `StrategyEMARegularOrder` class. We need to define a new method for selecting instruments from `instruments_bucket` for exiting an existing position based on the computation of the crossover value:

```
class StrategyEMARegularOrder(StrategyBase):
    # Previous methods not shown
    def strategy_select_instruments_for_exit(self, candle,
```

```
                                        instruments_bucket):
    selected_instruments_bucket = []
    sideband_info_bucket = []
    for instrument in instruments_bucket:
        if self.main_order.get(instrument) is not None:
            crossover_value = self.get_crossover_value(instrument)
            if crossover_value in [1, -1]:
                selected_instruments_bucket.append(instrument)
                sideband_info_bucket.append({'action': 'EXIT'})
    return selected_instruments_bucket, sideband_info_bucket
```

How it works...

In this recipe, we continue coding the `StrategyEMARegularOrder` class. We define a new method for this class, `strategy_select_instruments_for_exit()`, described as follows:

- This method takes two arguments, other than `self`:
  - `candle`: An object of the `CandleTime` type that contains the timestamp of the current candle.
  - `instruments_bucket`: An object of the `SetInstruments` type. This object holds financial instruments that have been entered into a position earlier by the `strategy_enter_position()` method.
- You create two empty lists, `selected_instruments_bucket` and `sideband_info_bucket`.
- You run a `for` loop over `instruments_bucket`. For each instrument, you check whether there is a position entered for the given instrument using the `'if self.main_order.get(instrument) is not None:'` line. You proceed only if a position exists already.
- You call `self.get_crossover_value()` and save its value to a new attribute, `crossover_value`. Based on the value of `crossover_value`, you make a decision, as follows:
  - If `crossover_value` is either 1 or -1, it means there has been a crossover. You do the following:
    - Append the `instrument` attribute to `selected_instruments_bucket`.
    - Append an `{'action': 'EXIT'}` dictionary to the `sideband_info_bucket` attribute.

- If `crossover_value` is neither 1 nor -1, it means the strategy is not giving any signal. You do nothing here.
- Finally, you return both the attributes: `selected_instruments_bucket` and `sideband_info_bucket`. These attributes may have gotten populated or may remain as empty lists.

Recall that the `strategy_select_instruments_for_exit()` method is called for every candle, so the preceding steps are repeated for every new candle. In the appropriate candle, if there is a position, you may get an `EXIT` signal, and in the others, you won't get any signal. Based on the signal, you can exit the position by placing an appropriate order, which is discussed in the next recipe.

EMA-Regular-Order strategy – coding the strategy_exit_position method

In this recipe, you will continue with the coding of the `StrategyEMARegularOrder` class. Here, you will code the `strategy_exit_position()` method, the last mandatory method enforced by the `StrategyBase` base class. This method is called by the AlgoBulls core engine every time the `strategy_select_instruments_for_exit` method returns non-empty data. By the end of this recipe, you will have completed coding the `StrategyEMARegularOrder` class.

 Please refer to the flowchart in the introduction of this chapter to understand how AlgoBulls core engine calls the `strategy_select_instruments_for_exit()` method during strategy execution.

Getting ready

Make sure you have followed the previous recipe before starting this recipe.

How to do it...

Continue coding the `StrategyEMARegularOrder` class. Define a method to the exit position for a given instrument based on `sideband_info`:

```
class StrategyEMARegularOrder(StrategyBase):
    # Previous methods not shown
    def strategy_exit_position(self, candle, instrument, sideband_info):
        if sideband_info['action'] == 'EXIT':
            self.main_order[instrument].exit_position()
            self.main_order[instrument] = None
            return True
        return False
```

How it works...

In this recipe, we continue coding the `StrategyEMARegularOrder` class. We define a new method for this class, `strategy_exit_position()`, described as follows:

- This method takes three arguments, other than `self`:
    - `candle`: An object of `CandleTime` type that contains the timestamp of the current candle.
    - `instrument`: An object of `Instrument` type that represents a financial instrument.
    - `sideband_info`: A dictionary object that holds information on trades to be placed for the `instrument` attribute. This object looks like `{'action': 'EXIT'}`.
- If `sideband_info` is `{'action': 'EXIT'}`, do the following:
    - You fetch the order using `self.main_order[instrument]` (recall that `self.main_order` is a dictionary that holds instruments and corresponding order instances as key-value pairs.)
    - You exit the position for this order by calling its `exit_position()` method.
    - You reset the value corresponding to the key `instrument` in `self.main_order` as `None`. This indicates that there is no longer a position open corresponding to `instrument`.
    - You return `True`, signaling to the AlgoBulls core engine that a position has been exited for `instrument` in this call.

- If `sideband_info` is not `{'action': 'EXIT'}`, you return `False`, signaling to the AlgoBulls core engine that no position was not exited for `instrument` in this call.

The `self.broker` attribute is replaced by the appropriate broker instance at runtime by the AlgoBulls core engine. So, the same code can work across all the brokers supported by the AlgoBulls platform.

You have now completed the coding for the `StrategyEMARegularOrder` class.

EMA-Regular-Order strategy – uploading the strategy on the AlgoBulls trading platform

In this recipe, you will upload the strategy class, `StrategyEMARegularOrder`, which you created in the preceding recipes, on the AlgoBulls trading platform. Once it is uploaded, you can perform backtesting, paper trading, and real trading on the same code base.

Getting ready

Make sure you have set up your account on the AlgoBulls platform (`https://algobulls.com`) to get your API token. Setting up an account is free. Using its services might incur charges depending on your usage. You can start with free packages on the site. Refer to *Appendix II* for more details.

How to do it...

We execute the following steps for this recipe:

1. Import the necessary modules:

```
>>> import inspect
>>> from pyalgotrading.algobulls import AlgoBullsConnection
>>> from pyalgostrategypool.strategy_ema_regular_order import
StrategyEMARegularOrder
```

2. Create a new AlgoBulls connection object:

```
>>> algobulls_connection = AlgoBullsConnection()
```

3. Fetch the authorization URL:

```
>>> algobulls_connection.get_authorization_url()
```

We get the following output:

```
Please login to this URL with your AlgoBulls credentials and get
your developer access token: https://app.algobulls.com/user/login
'https://app.algobulls.com/user/login'
```

4. Log in to the preceding link with your AlgoBulls credentials, fetch your token, and set it here (refer to *Appendix II* for more details):

```
>>>
algobulls_connection.set_access_token('80b7a69b168c5b3f15d56688841a
8f2da5e2ab2c')
```

5. Before uploading your strategy, you can inspect your strategy code to ensure you are uploading the right strategy:

```
>>> print(inspect.getsource(StrategyEMARegularOrder))
```

We get the following output:

```
class StrategyEMARegularOrder(StrategyBase):

    def __init__(self, *args, **kwargs):
        super().__init__(*args, **kwargs)

        self.timeperiod1 = self.strategy_parameters['timeperiod1']
        self.timeperiod2 = self.strategy_parameters['timeperiod2']

        self.main_order = None

    def initialize(self):
        self.main_order = {}

    @staticmethod
    def name():
        return 'EMA Regular Order Strategy'
    ...
    def strategy_exit_position(self, candle, instrument,
                               sideband_info):
        if sideband_info['action'] == 'EXIT':
            self.main_order[instrument].exit_position()
            self.main_order[instrument] = None
            return True
        return False
```

The complete output is not shown here. Please visit the following link to read the complete output:

```
https://github.com/algobulls/pyalgostrategypool/blob/master/
pyalgostrategypool/strategy_ema_regular_order.py.
```

6. Upload `StrategyEMARegularOrder` onto the AlgoBulls platform. This creates a new strategy for your AlgoBulls account:

```
>>> algobulls_connection.create_strategy(StrategyEMARegularOrder)
```

We get the following output (your output may differ):

```
Validating Strategy...
{'details': `'strategy_code': '49287246f9704bbcbad76ade9e2091d9'}
```

How it works...

We import the necessary modules in *step 1*. In *step 2*, an instance of the `AlgoBullsConnection` class is created, named `algobulls_connection`. In *step 3*, you get the authorization URL using the `get_authorization_url()` method of the `algobulls_connection` object. You should visit this URL from your web browser to sign in to the AlgoBulls platform and fetch your developer access token. (You can find more details with screenshots in *Appendix II* on fetching the developer access token from the AlgoBulls platform.) You copy the access token and set it in *step 4* using the `set_access_token()` method of `algobulls_connection`. If the token is accepted, a successful connection is set up with the AlgoBulls platform.

The `StrategyEMARegularOrder` strategy class that we coded in *steps 1 to 5* is also available in the `pyalgostrategypool` package. We import this class in *step 1*. Alternatively, you can also save your strategy class in a separate Python module and import it in *step 1* instead of importing it from `pyalgostrategypool`.

You upload the `StrategyEMARegularOrder` strategy class using the `upload_strategy()` method of `algobulls_connection` by passing it as a parameter. If the upload is successful, you will get a success message with `strategy_code`, which is a unique string. `strategy_code` can be used later to do everything related to the strategy—for example, editing the strategy, performing backtesting (Chapter 9, *Algorithmic Trading – Backtesting*), performing paper trading (Chapter 10, *Algorithmic Trading – Paper Trading*), and performing real trading (Chapter 11, *Algorithmic Trading – Real Trading*).

There's more…

If there are changes done to a strategy after uploading, you can update the strategy on the AlgoBulls platform using the `upload_strategy()` method of `algobulls_connection` with the updated class and `overwrite=True` as arguments. If the changes are uploaded successfully, you will get a success message.

Modify an already-uploaded strategy:

```
>>> algobulls_connection.create_strategy(StrategyEMARegularOrder,
                                         overwrite=True)
```

We get the following output:

```
Validating Strategy...
{'details': 'success'}
```

Multiple strategies with the same name (returned by the `name()` method) are not allowed by the AlgoBulls platform. The `overwrite=True` parameter updates an existing strategy with the same name if present. If `overwrite=True` is not passed to the `create_strategy()` method, the default value is `False`, which means it tries to create a new strategy on the AlgoBulls platform.

MACD-Bracket-Order strategy – coding the __init__, initialize, name, and versions_supported methods

This recipe demonstrates the initial coding of the `StrategyMACDBracketOrder` class. The complete class will be coded by the end of the eleventh recipe of this chapter. In this recipe, you will code the following methods:

- `__init__()`
- `initialize()`
- `name()`
- `versions_supported()`

To learn more about the MACD technical indicator, please refer to the *Trend indicator – moving average convergence divergence* recipe of `Chapter 5`, *Computing and Plotting Technical Indicators*.

 Please refer to the flowchart in the introduction of this chapter to understand how the AlgoBulls core engine calls the `__init__()` and `initialize()` methods during strategy execution.

Getting ready

Make sure you have the `StrategyBase` and `pyalgotrading` constants in your Python namespace. Refer to the *Technical requirements* section of this chapter to set it up.

How to do it...

Create a new class named `StrategyMACDBracketOrder`. Subclass it from `StrategyBase`. Define the required four methods:

```
class StrategyMACDBracketOrder(StrategyBase):

    def __init__(self, *args, **kwargs):
        super().__init__(*args, **kwargs)

        self.fastMA_period = self.strategy_parameters['fastma_period']
        self.slowMA_period = self.strategy_parameters['slowma_period']
        self.signal_period = self.strategy_parameters['signal_period']
        self.stoploss = self.strategy_parameters['stoploss_trigger']
        self.target = self.strategy_parameters['target_trigger']
        self.trailing_stoploss = \
                    self.strategy_parameters['trailing_stoploss_trigger']

        self.main_order = None

    def initialize(self):
        self.main_order = {}

    @staticmethod
    def name():
        return 'MACD Bracket Order Strategy'
    @staticmethod
    def versions_supported():
        return VERSION_3_2_0
```

How it works...

In this recipe, we will create the `StrategyEMARegularOrder` class, subclassed from `StrategyBase`. We will define four methods for this class, described as follows:

- The `__init__()` method: This is the first thing you do when you create a new strategy. First, you create this method and call the parent class `__init__()` method using `super()`. This helps the AlgoBulls core engine create the necessary data structures needed for the further development of the strategy. Next, you create six attributes from `self.strategy_parameters`:

  - `self.fastMA_period`
  - `self.slowMA_period`
  - `self.signal_period`
  - `self.stoploss`
  - `self.target`
  - `self.trailing_stoploss`

  `self.strategy_parameters` is a dictionary object available for every strategy subclassed from `StrategyBase`. (The seventh recipe of `Chapter 9`, *Algorithmic Trading – Backtesting*, discusses how these values are passed at runtime to `self.strategy_parameters`.) These parameters will be used in the next recipe of this chapter as parameters to the MACD technical indicator. Lastly, you create a new attribute, `self.main_order`, an empty dictionary. We will use this for saving the handles to all the open orders placed during the execution of this strategy.

- The `initialize()` method: This method is called at the beginning of every market day to initialize any internal variables to their default state. For real trading and paper trading, this method is called once. For multi-day backtesting, this method is called multiple times, once at the beginning of every new trading day. In this method, you initialize `self.main_order` to an empty dictionary.

- The `name()` method: This is a static method that returns the name of this strategy. This is used while utilizing backtesting, paper trading, and real trading services on this strategy. In this method, you simply return a string, `MACD Bracket Order`. You can return any string of your choice in this method.

- The `versions_supported()` method: This static method is used for returning the AlgoBulls core engine version for which this strategy has been created. Often, as new upgrades come to the AlgoBulls core engine, some backward-incompatible changes may get introduced. This method helps to ensure this strategy is run on the correct version of the AlgoBulls core engine at all times. In this method, you return the highest available version from the constants module, which at the time of writing this chapter is VERSION_3_2_0.

These four methods are mandatory; they are enforced by the `StrategyBase` base class and cannot be skipped.

MACD-Bracket-Order strategy – coding the strategy_select_instruments_for_entry method

In this recipe, you will continue coding the `StrategyMACDBracketOrder` class. Here, you will code the `strategy_select_instruments_for_entry()` method, a mandatory method enforced by the `StrategyBase` base class. This method is called by the AlgoBulls core engine on every new candle for backtesting, paper trading, and real trading services.

 Please refer to the flowchart in the introduction of this chapter to understand how the AlgoBulls core engine calls the `strategy_select_instruments_for_entry()` method during strategy execution.

Getting ready

Make sure you have followed the previous recipe to create the `StrategyMACDBracketOrder` class before starting this recipe.

How to do it...

Continue coding the `StrategyMACDBracketOrder` class. Define two new methods—a method for getting the crossover value between the MACD line and MACD history signals and a method for selecting instruments from `instruments_bucket` for entering a new position based on the computed crossover value:

```python
class StrategyMACDBracketOrder(StrategyBase):
    # Note: Some methods are not shown here
    def get_crossover_value(self, instrument):
        hist_data = self.get_historical_data(instrument)
        macdline, macdsignal, _ = talib.MACD(hist_data['close'],
                                    fastperiod=self.fastMA_period,
                                    slowperiod=self.slowMA_period,
                                    signalperiod=self.signal_period)
        crossover_value = self.utils.crossover(macdline, macdsignal)
        return crossover_value
    def strategy_select_instruments_for_entry(self, candle,
                                            instruments_bucket):
        selected_instruments_bucket = []
        sideband_info_bucket = []
        for instrument in instruments_bucket:
            crossover_value = self.get_crossover_value(instrument)
            if crossover_value == 1:
                selected_instruments_bucket.append(instrument)
                sideband_info_bucket.append({'action': 'BUY'})
            elif crossover_value == -1:
                if self.strategy_mode is StrategyMode.INTRADAY:
                    selected_instruments_bucket.append(instrument)
                    sideband_info_bucket.append({'action': 'SELL'})
        return selected_instruments_bucket, sideband_info_bucket
```

How it works...

In this recipe, we continue coding the `StrategyMACDBracketOrder` class. We define two new methods for this class, described as follows:

- The `get_crossover_value()` method: This is a helper method. It takes `instrument` as an argument (along with `self`). This is the financial instrument for which the crossover value has to be computed. You fetch the latest historical data using the `self.get_historical_data()` method and assign it to a new attribute, `hist_data`. We pass `instrument` as the argument to this method. The `hist_data` attribute is a `pandas.DataFrame` object with `timestamp`, `open`, `high`, `low`, `close`, and `volume` columns.

The default duration of the fetched historical data is the last 15 days. You compute MACD on the close of `hist_data` using the `talib.MACD` function. It takes the following additional arguments:

- `fastperiod`: We pass `self.fastMA_period` here.
- `slowperiod`: We pass `self.slowMA_period` here.
- `signalperiod`: We pass `self.signal_period` here.

This computed MACD data is a tuple of the `pandas.Series` object, which you assign to `macdline`, `macdsignal`, and `_` (the last object in the tuple is assigned to `_` because it is not required). (Refer to the third recipe in Chapter 5, *Computing and Plotting Technical Indicators*, for more details on computation of MACD.) You compute the crossover value between `macdline` and `macdsignal` using `self.utils.crossover(macdline, macdsignal)` and assign it to a new attribute, `crossover_value`. The `crossover()` function call works as follows:

- It takes two iterables as input. We pass `macdline` and `macdsignal` here.
- If `macdline` crosses `macdsignal` upward, the crossover function returns 1.

- If `macdline` crosses the `macdsignal` downward, the crossover function returns −1.
- If there is no crossover between `macdline` and `macdsignal`, then the crossover function returns 0.

Finally, you return `crossover_value`.

- `strategy_select_instruments_for_entry()` method: This method takes two arguments, other than `self`:
  - `candle`: An object of the `CandleTime` type that contains the timestamp of the current candle.
  - `instruments_bucket`: An object of the `SetInstruments` type that contains all the financial instruments available for creating a new position. We pass this data at the time of strategy execution (the second recipe of Chapter 8, *Backtesting Strategies*).

You create two empty lists, `selected_instruments_bucket` and `sideband_info_bucket`. You run a `for` loop over `instruments_bucket`. For each instrument, you call `self.get_crossover_value()` and save its value to a new attribute, `crossover_value`. Based on the value of `crossover_value`, you make a decision, as follows:

- If `crossover_value` is 1, it means the strategy is giving a `BUY` signal. You do the following:
    - Append `instrument` to `selected_instruments_bucket`.
    - Append an `{'action': 'BUY'}` dictionary to the `sideband_info_bucket` attribute.
- If `crossover_value` is −1, it means the strategy is giving a `SELL` signal. You do the following:
    - Append `instrument` to `selected_instruments_bucket`.
    - Append an `{'action': 'SELL'}` dictionary to the `sideband_info_bucket` attribute.
- If `crossover_value` is neither 1 nor −1, it means the strategy is not giving a signal. You do nothing here.
- Finally, you return both the attributes: `selected_instruments_bucket` and `sideband_info_bucket`. These attributes may have been populated or may remain as empty lists.

Recall that the `strategy_select_instruments_for_entry()` method is called for every candle, so the preceding steps are repeated for every new candle. In the appropriate candle, you will get a `BUY` or `SELL` signal, and in the others, you won't get any signal. Based on the signal, you can place the appropriate order, which is discussed in the next recipe.

> The `strategy_select_instruments_for_entry()` method is enforced by the `StrategyBase` base class and has to be defined for every strategy. The `get_crossover_value()` method is a helper method, meaning it is not enforced by the `StrategyBase` base class. You may choose not to define this or to define multiple of these helper functions.

MACD-Bracket-Order strategy – coding the strategy_enter_position method

In this recipe, you will continue with the coding of the `StrategyMACDBracketOrder` class. Here, you will code the `strategy_enter_position()` method, a mandatory method enforced by the `StrategyBase` base class. This method is called by the AlgoBulls core engine every time the `strategy_select_instruments_for_entry()` method returns non-empty data. This method may not be called for every new candle for backtesting, paper trading, and real trading services.

 Please refer to the flowchart in the introduction of this chapter to understand how the AlgoBulls core engine calls the `strategy_enter_position()` method during strategy execution.

Getting ready

Make sure you have followed the previous recipe before starting this recipe.

How to do it...

Continue coding the `StrategyMACDBracketOrder` class. Define a method to punch new orders for a given instrument and enter a new position:

```
class StrategyMACDBracketOrder(StrategyBase):
    # Note: Some methods are not shown here
    def strategy_enter_position(self, candle, instrument, sideband_info):
        if sideband_info['action'] == 'BUY':
            qty = self.number_of_lots * instrument.lot_size
            ltp = self.broker.get_ltp(instrument)
            self.main_order[instrument] = \
                self.broker.BuyOrderBracket(
                    instrument=instrument,
                    order_code= BrokerOrderCodeConstants.INTRADAY,
                    order_variety= BrokerOrderVarietyConstants.LIMIT,
                    quantity=qty,
                    price=ltp,
                    stoploss_trigger=ltp - (ltp * self.stoploss),
                    target_trigger=ltp + (ltp * self.target),
                    trailing_stoploss_trigger=ltp * self.trailing_stoploss)
        elif sideband_info['action'] == 'SELL':
```

```
        qty = self.number_of_lots * instrument.lot_size
        ltp = self.broker.get_ltp(instrument)
        self.main_order[instrument] = \
            self.broker.SellOrderBracket(
                instrument=instrument,
                order_code=BrokerOrderCodeConstants.INTRADAY,
                order_variety=BrokerOrderVarietyConstants.LIMIT,
                quantity=qty,
                price=ltp,
                stoploss_trigger=ltp + (ltp * self.stoploss),
                target_trigger=ltp - (ltp * self.target),
                trailing_stoploss_trigger=ltp * self.trailing_stoploss)
    else:
        raise SystemExit(f'Got invalid sideband_info value:
                    {sideband_info}')
    return self.main_order[instrument]
```

How it works...

In this recipe, we continue coding the StrategyMACDBracketOrder class. We define a new method for this class, strategy_enter_position(), described as follows:

- This method takes three arguments, other than self:
  - candle: An object of the CandleTime type that contains the timestamp of the current candle.
  - instrument: An object of the Instrument type that represents a financial instrument.
  - sideband_info: A dictionary object that holds information on trades to be placed for the instrument attribute. This object looks like {'action': [action_value]}, where [action_value] can be either 'BUY' or 'SELL'.
- You calculate the quantity for order to be placed by multiplying self.number_of_lots with instrument.lot_size and assign it to a new attribute qty. The self.number_of_lots attribute holds information on the number of lots to trade, which you can pass while executing this strategy. The instrument.lot_size attribute holds lot_size for instrument, which is a positive integer. For example, if number of lots is passed as 2 and lot size for instrument is 10, then the quantity for the order would be 2 * 10 = 20.

- If `sideband_info` is `{'action': 'BUY'}`, you place a `Bracket` order of the `BUY` transaction type by creating an instance of the `self.broker.BuyOrderBracket` class (refer to the first recipe of Chapter 7, *Placing Bracket and Cover Orders on the Exchange*) and assigning its value to `self.main_order[instrument]`.
- Similarly, if `sideband_info` is `{'action': 'SELL'}`, you place a `Bracket` order of the `BUY` transaction type by creating an instance of the `self.broker.SellOrderBracket` class (refer to the first recipe of Chapter 7, *Placing Bracket and Cover Orders on the Exchange*) and assigning its value to `self.main_order[instrument]`.

In both cases, the `self.main_order` dictionary object holds the `instrument` and `order` instances as a key-value pair. This will be useful later (in the *MACD-Bracket-Order strategy – coding the strategy_exit_position method* recipe) for exiting positions created by this method.

The `self.broker` attribute is replaced by the appropriate broker instance at runtime by the AlgoBulls core engine. So, the same code can work across all the brokers supported by the AlgoBulls platform.

MACD-Bracket-Order strategy – coding the strategy_select_instruments_for_exit method

In this recipe, you will continue with the coding of the `StrategyMACDBracketOrder` class. Here, you will code the `strategy_select_instruments_for_exit()` method, a mandatory method enforced by the `StrategyBase` base class. This method is called by the AlgoBulls core engine for every new candle for backtesting, paper trading, and real trading services.

 Please refer to the flowchart in the introduction of this chapter to understand how the AlgoBulls core engine calls the `strategy_select_instruments_for_exit()` method during strategy execution.

Getting ready

Make sure you have followed the previous recipe before starting this recipe.

How to do it...

Continue coding the StrategyMACDBracketOrder class. Define a new method for selecting instruments from instruments_bucket for exiting an existing position based on the computation of the crossover value:

```
class StrategyMACDBracketOrder(StrategyBase):
    # Note: Some methods are not shown here
    def strategy_select_instruments_for_exit(self, candle,
                                             instruments_bucket):
        selected_instruments_bucket = []
        sideband_info_bucket = []
        for instrument in instruments_bucket:
            if self.main_order.get(instrument) is not None:
                crossover_value = self.get_crossover_value(instrument)
                if crossover_value in [1, -1]:
                    selected_instruments_bucket.append(instrument)
                    sideband_info_bucket.append({'action': 'EXIT'})
        return selected_instruments_bucket, sideband_info_bucket
```

How it works...

In this recipe, we continue coding the StrategyMACDBracketOrder class. We define a new method for this class, strategy_select_instruments_for_exit(), described as follows:

- This method takes two arguments, other than self:
  - candle: An object of CandleTime type that contains the timestamp of the current candle.
  - instruments_bucket: An object of SetInstruments type. This object holds financial instruments that have been entered into a position earlier by the strategy_enter_position() method.
- You create two empty lists, selected_instruments_bucket and sideband_info_bucket.

- You run a `for` loop over `instruments_bucket`. For each instrument, you check whether there is a position entered for the given instrument using the `'if self.main_order.get(instrument) is not None:'` line. You proceed only if a position exists already.
- You call `self.get_crossover_value()` and save its value to a new attribute, `crossover_value`. Based on the value of `crossover_value`, you make a decision, as follows:
  - If `crossover_value` is either 1 or −1, it means there has been a crossover. You do the following:
    - Append the `instrument` attribute to `selected_instruments_bucket`.
    - Append a `{'action': 'EXIT'}` dictionary to the `sideband_info_bucket` attribute.
  - If `crossover_value` is neither 1 nor −1, it means the strategy is not giving a signal. You do nothing here.
- Finally, you return both the attributes, `selected_instruments_bucket` and `sideband_info_bucket`. These attributes may have been populated or may remain as empty lists.

Recall that the `strategy_select_instruments_for_exit()` method is called for every candle, so the preceding steps are repeated for every new candle. In the appropriate candle, if there is a position, you may get an `EXIT` signal, and in the others, you won't get any signal. Based on the signal, you can exit the position by placing an appropriate order, which is discussed in the next recipe.

MACD-Bracket-Order strategy – coding the strategy_exit_position method

In this recipe, you will continue with the coding of the `StrategyMACDBracketOrder` class. Here, you will code the `strategy_exit_position()` method, the last mandatory method enforced by the `StrategyBase` base class. This method is called by the AlgoBulls core engine every time the `strategy_select_instruments_for_exit` method returns non-empty data. By the end of this recipe, you will have completed coding the `StrategyMACDBracketOrder` class.

Please refer to the flowchart in the introduction of this chapter to understand how the AlgoBulls core engine calls the `strategy_select_instruments_for_exit()` method during strategy execution.

Getting ready

Make sure you have followed the previous recipe before starting this recipe.

How to do it...

Continue coding the `StrategyMACDBracketOrder` class. Define a method to the exit position for a given instrument based on `sideband_info`:

```
class StrategyMACDBracketOrder(StrategyBase):
    # Note: Some methods are not shown here
    def strategy_exit_position(self, candle, instrument,
                               sideband_info):
        if sideband_info['action'] == 'EXIT':
            self.main_order[instrument].exit_position()
            self.main_order[instrument] = None
            return True
        return False
```

How it works...

In this recipe, we continue coding the `StrategyMACDBracketOrder` class. We define a new method for this class, `strategy_exit_position()`, described as follows:

- This method takes three arguments, other than `self`:
    - `candle`: An object of the `CandleTime` type that contains the timestamp of the current candle.
    - `instrument`: An object of the `Instrument` type that represents a financial instrument.

- sideband_info: A dictionary object that holds information on trades to be placed for the instrument attribute. This object looks like {'action': `EXIT`}.

- If sideband_info is {'action': 'EXIT'}, do the following:
    - You fetch the order using self.main_order[instrument]. (Recall that self.main_order is a dictionary that holds instruments and corresponding order instances as key-value pairs.)
    - You exit the position for this order by calling its exit_position() method.

      Since it's a Bracket order strategy, there is the possibility for the target or stoploss order to hit and the position to exit without our strategy knowing it. You can still use the exit_position() method to handle these scenarios. The exit_position() method works for both of the following exit scenarios:

        - The position is open and you want to exit it yourself.
        - The position is already exited by the broker due to the completion of either the stoploss order or the target order and there is nothing to be done.

    - You reset the value corresponding to the key instrument in self.main_order as None. This indicates there is no longer a position open corresponding to instrument.
    - You return True, signaling to the AlgoBulls core engine that a position has been exited for instrument in this call.
  - If sideband_info is not {'action': 'EXIT'}, you return False, signaling to the AlgoBulls core engine that no position was exited for instrument in this call.

The self.broker attribute is replaced by the appropriate broker instance at runtime by the AlgoBulls core engine. So, the same code can work across all the brokers supported by the AlgoBulls platform.

You have now completed the coding for the StrategyMACDBracketOrder class.

MACD-Bracket-Order strategy — uploading the strategy on the AlgoBulls trading platform

In this recipe, you will upload the strategy class, `StrategyMACDBracketOrder`, which you created in the preceding five recipes, on the AlgoBulls trading platform. Once it is uploaded, you can perform backtesting, paper trading, and real trading on the same code base.

Getting ready

Make sure you have set up your account on the AlgoBulls platform (`https://algobulls.com`) to get your API token. Setting up an account is free. Using its services might incur charges depending on your usage. You can start with the free packages on the site. Refer to *Appendix II* for more details.

How to do it...

We execute the following steps for this recipe:

1. Import the necessary modules:

   ```
   >>> import inspect
   >>> from pyalgostrategypool.strategy_macd_bracket_order import
   StrategyMACDBracketOrder
   >>> from pyalgotrading.algobulls import AlgoBullsConnection
   ```

2. Create a new AlgoBulls connection object:

   ```
   >>> algobulls_connection = AlgoBullsConnection()
   ```

3. Fetch the authorization URL:

   ```
   >>> algobulls_connection.get_authorization_url()
   ```

   We get the following output:

   ```
   Please login to this URL with your AlgoBulls credentials and get
   your developer access token: https://app.algobulls.com/user/login
   'https://app.algobulls.com/user/login'
   ```

4. Log in to the preceding link with your AlgoBulls credentials, fetch your token, and set it here (refer to *Appendix II* for more details):

```
>>>
algobulls_connection.set_access_token('80b7a69b168c5b3f15d56688841a
8f2da5e2ab2c')
```

5. Before uploading your strategy, you can inspect your strategy code to ensure you are uploading the right strategy:

```
>>> print(inspect.getsource(StrategyMACDBracketOrder))
```

We get the following output:

```
class StrategyMACDBracketOrder(StrategyBase):

    def __init__(self, *args, **kwargs):
        super().__init__(*args, **kwargs)

        self.fastMA_period = \
            self.strategy_parameters['fastma_period']
        self.slowMA_period = \
            self.strategy_parameters['slowma_period']
        self.signal_period = \
            self.strategy_parameters['signal_period']
        self.stoploss =
            self.strategy_parameters['stoploss_trigger']
        self.target =
            self.strategy_parameters['target_trigger']
        self.trailing_stoploss =
            self.strategy_parameters['trailing_stoploss_trigger']

        self.main_order = None

    def initialize(self):
        self.main_order = {}

    @staticmethod
    def name():
        return 'MACD Bracket Order Strategy'
    ...
    def strategy_exit_position(self, candle, instrument,
                               sideband_info):
        if sideband_info['action'] == 'EXIT':
            self.main_order[instrument].exit_position()
            self.main_order[instrument] = None
            return True
        return False
```

The complete output is not shown here. Please visit the following link to read the complete output:

https://github.com/algobulls/pyalgostrategypool/blob/master/
pyalgostrategypool/strategy_macd_bracket_order.py.

6. Upload `StrategyMACDBracketOrder` onto the AlgoBulls platform. This creates a new strategy for your AlgoBulls account:

```
>>> algobulls_connection.create_strategy(StrategyMACDBracketOrder)
```

We get the following output (your output may differ):

```
Validating Strategy...
{'details': 'success', 'strategy_code':
'4faf514fe096432b8e9f80f5951bd2ea'}
```

How it works...

We import the necessary modules in *step 1*. In *step 2*, an instance of the `AlgoBullsConnection` class is created, named `algobulls_connection`. In *step 3*, you get the authorization URL using the `get_authorization_url()` method of the `algobulls_connection` object. You should visit this URL from your web browser to sign in to the AlgoBulls platform and fetch your developer access token. (You can find more details with screenshots in *Appendix II* on fetching the developer access token from the AlgoBulls platform.) You copy the access token and set it in *step 4* using the `set_access_token()` method of `algobulls_connection`. If the token is accepted, a successful connection is set up with the AlgoBulls platform.
The `StrategyMACDBracketOrder` strategy class, which we coded in *step 5*, is also available in the `pyalgostrategypool` package. We import this class in *step 1*. Alternatively, you can also save your strategy class in a separate Python module and import it in *step 1* instead of importing it from `pyalgostrategypool`.

You upload the `StrategyMACDBracketOrder` strategy class using the `upload_strategy()` method of `algobulls_connection` by passing it as a parameter. If the upload is successful, you will get a success message with `strategy_code`, which is a unique string. `strategy_code` can be used in later chapters to do everything related to the strategy—for example, editing the strategy, performing backtesting, performing paper trading, and performing real trading.

There's more...

If there are changes made to a strategy after uploading, you can update the strategy on the AlgoBulls platform using the `upload_strategy()` method of `algobulls_connection` with the updated class and `overwrite=True` as arguments. If the changes are uploaded successfully, you will get a success message.

You can modify an already-uploaded strategy as follows:

```
>>> algobulls_connection.create_strategy(StrategyMACDBracketOrder,
                                         overwrite=True)
```

We get the following output:

```
Validating Strategy...
{'details': 'success'}
```

Multiple strategies with the same name (returned by the `name()` method) are not allowed by the AlgoBulls platform. The `overwrite=True` parameter updates an existing strategy with the same name if present. If `overwrite=True` is not passed to the `create_strategy()` method, the default value is `False`, which means it tries to create a new strategy on the AlgoBulls platform.

9
Algorithmic Trading – Backtesting

After building algorithmic trading strategies, as we did in the previous chapter, the first step is to backtest them over a given duration of time for a given strategy configuration.

Backtesting is a method of evaluating the performance of a trading strategy by virtually executing it over past data and analyzing its risk and return metrics. Real money is not used here. Typical backtesting metrics include **Profit and Loss (P&L)**, maximum drawdown, count of total trades, winning trades, losing trades, long trades and short trades, average profit per winning and losing trade, and more. Until these metrics meet the necessary requirements, the entire process should be repeated with incremental changes being made to strategy parameters and/or strategy implementation.

If a strategy performs well on past data, it is likely to perform well on live data also. Similarly, if a strategy is performing poorly on past data, it is likely to perform poorly on live data. This is the underlying premise of backtesting. You can keep changing the strategy configuration or implementation until the backtesting yields results as intended.

Backtesting also helps validate the strategy behavior before we use the strategy for real money. This means it helps to ensure that the strategy behaves as expected for various marketing scenarios from the past.

For backtesting, a strategy configuration is required. It consists of multiple parameters, some of which are as follows:

- **Start and end timestamps**: The time duration for which backtesting should be run.
- **Financial instrument(s)**: One or more financial instruments for which backtesting should be performed.
- **Candle interval**: One of many possible candle intervals; for example, 1 minute, 15 minutes, 1 hour, or 1 day.

- **Strategy-specific parameters**: Values for custom parameters defined in the strategy.
- **Strategy mode**: One of intraday or delivery. Intraday strategies punch intraday orders, which are squared off at the end of the day. Delivery strategies punch delivery orders. These don't square off at the end of the day and get carried forward to the next trading day.

A backtesting engine is required to perform backtesting on a given strategy. In this chapter, you will use the backtesting engine provided by AlgoBulls (`https://algobulls.com`), an algorithmic trading platform that makes its services available via its developer options. It provides a Python package called `pyalgotrading` (`https://github.com/algobulls/pyalgotrading`) to make these services available.

You coded two algorithmic trading strategies in `Chapter 8`, *Algorithmic Trading Strategies – Coding Step by Step*. Recall that the strategy descriptions are as follows:

- **EMA-Regular-Order strategy**: This strategy is based on the technical indicator EMA and regular orders. (The first six recipes of `Chapter 8`, *Algorithmic Trading Strategies – Coding Step by Step*.)
- **MACD-Bracket-Order strategy**: This strategy is based on the technical indicator MACD and bracket orders. (The remaining six recipes of `Chapter 8`, *Algorithmic Trading Strategies – Coding Step by Step*.)

 These strategies are also available as part of a Python package called `pyalgostrategypool`. You can install it using pip using the `$ pip install pyalgostrategypool` command. You can also check them out on GitHub (`https://github.com/algobulls/pyalgostrategypool`).

In the previous chapter, you uploaded these two strategies to your AlgoBulls account. In this chapter, you will fetch these strategies from your AlgoBulls account and perform backtesting on them. After backtesting, you will gather the strategy execution logs and various reports, namely, the P&L report, the statistics report, and the order history. These logs and reports help validate the strategy's performance and prepare it for the next level, which is paper trading, before we finally go and do real trading. By using `pyalgotrading`, you ensure that you focus on developing and validating the strategy via backtesting, without worrying about the ecosystem needed for the strategy execution.

This chapter includes step-by-step recipes for the aforementioned strategies, from setting up connections with the AlgoBulls platform, fetching the strategy, and running backtesting jobs, to fetching the execution logs and various types of reports.

In this chapter, we will cover the following recipes:

- EMA-Regular-Order strategy – fetching the strategy
- EMA-Regular-Order strategy – backtesting the strategy
- EMA-Regular-Order strategy – fetching backtesting logs in real time
- EMA-Regular-Order strategy – fetching a backtesting report – P&L table
- EMA-Regular-Order strategy – fetching a backtesting report – statistics table
- EMA-Regular-Order strategy – fetching a backtesting report – order history
- MACD-Bracket-Order strategy – fetching the strategy
- MACD-Bracket-Order strategy – backtesting the strategy
- MACD-Bracket-Order strategy – fetching backtesting logs in real time
- MACD-Bracket-Order strategy – fetching a backtesting report – P&L table
- MACD-Bracket-Order strategy – fetching a backtesting report – statistics table
- MACD-Bracket-Order strategy – fetching a backtesting report – order history

Let's get started!

Technical requirements

You will need the following to successfully execute the recipes in this chapter:

- Python 3.7+
- Python packages:
    - pyalgotrading (`$ pip install pyalgotrading`)

The latest Jupyter notebook for this chapter can be found on GitHub at `https://github.com/PacktPublishing/Python-Algorithmic-Trading-Cookbook/tree/master/Chapter09`.

EMA-Regular-Order strategy – fetching the strategy

In this recipe, you will fetch the `StrategyEMARegularOrder` strategy class from your account on the AlgoBulls platform, which you uploaded while going through the *EMA-Regular-Order strategy – uploading the strategy* recipe in `Chapter 8`, *Algorithmic Trading Strategies – Coding Step by Step*, on the AlgoBulls trading platform. This recipe starts with setting up a connection to the AlgoBulls platform, querying all available strategies in your account, and fetching the details of the required strategy class, `StrategyEMARegularOrder`.

 Make sure you have gone through the first six recipes of the previous chapter to get a complete picture of the strategy class we will be using; that is, `StrategyEMARegularOrder`.

How to do it...

We execute the following steps for this recipe:

1. Import the necessary modules:

```
>>> from pyalgotrading.algobulls import AlgoBullsConnection
```

2. Create a new AlgoBulls connection object:

```
>>> algobulls_connection = AlgoBullsConnection()
```

3. Fetch the authorization URL:

```
>>> algobulls_connection.get_authorization_url()
```

We got the following output:

```
Please login to this URL with your AlgoBulls credentials and get
your developer access token: https://app.algobulls.com/user/login
'https://app.algobulls.com/user/login'
```

4. Log into the preceding link with your AlgoBulls credentials, fetch your token, and set it here (refer to *Appendix II* for more details):

```
>>> algobulls_connection.set_access_token('
            80b7a69b168c5b3f15d56688841a8f2da5e2ab2c')
```

5. Fetch and display all the strategies you have created and uploaded so far:

```
>>> all_strategies = algobulls_connection.get_all_strategies()
>>> all_strategies
```

We got the following output. Your output may differ (make sure you have followed the recipes from Chapter 8, *Algorithmic Trading Strategies – Coding Step by Step*, to get a similar output):

	strategyCode	strategyName
0	49287246f9704bbcbad76ade9e2091d9	EMA Regular Order Strategy
1	4faf514fe096432b8e9f80f5951bd2ea	MACD Bracket Order Strategy

6. Fetch and display the strategy code of the first strategy:

```
>>> strategy_code1 = all_strategies.iloc[0]['strategyCode']
>>> strategy_code1
```

We got the following output (your output may differ):

```
'49287246f9704bbcbad76ade9e2091d9'
```

7. Before backtesting your strategy, you can inspect your strategy to ensure you have the right strategy:

```
>>> strategy_details1 = \
        algobulls_connection.get_strategy_details(strategy_code1)
>>> print(strategy_details1)
```

We got the following output:

```
class StrategyEMARegularOrder(StrategyBase):

    def __init__(self, *args, **kwargs):
        super().__init__(*args, **kwargs)

        self.timeperiod1 = self.strategy_parameters['timeperiod1']
        self.timeperiod2 = self.strategy_parameters['timeperiod2']

        self.main_order = None

    def initialize(self):
        self.main_order = {}

    @staticmethod
```

```
def name():
    return 'EMA Regular Order Strategy'
....
def strategy_exit_position(self, candle, instrument,
                           sideband_info):
    if sideband_info['action'] == 'EXIT':
        self.main_order[instrument].exit_position()
        self.main_order[instrument] = None
        return True

    return False
```

The complete output is not shown here. Please visit the following link to read the complete output: `https://github.com/algobulls/pyalgostrategypool/blob/master/pyalgostrategypool/strategy_ema_regular_order.py`.

How it works...

In *step 1*, you import the necessary modules. In *step 2*, an instance of the `AlgoBullsConnection` class is created, named `algobulls_connection`. In *step 3*, you get the authorization URL using the `get_authorization_url()` method of the `algobulls_connection` object. This prints the authorization URL. You should visit this URL from your web browser to sign into the AlgoBulls platform and fetch your developer access token. (You can find more details, along with screenshots, in *Appendix II* in regard to fetching developer access tokens from the AlgoBulls platform.) You copy the access token and set it in *step 4* using the `set_access_token()` method of `algobulls_connection`. If the token is accepted, a successful connection is set up with the AlgoBulls platform.

In *step 5*, you fetch all the strategies you have created and uploaded to the AlgoBulls platform so far. You use the `get_all_strategies()` method for this step and assign it to a new variable, `all_strategies`. This variable is a `pandas.DataFrame` object that has `strategyCode` and `strategyName` columns. This table holds information on the strategy codes and the strategy names you uploaded previously. If you followed the *EMA-Regular-Order strategy – uploading the strategy on AlgoBulls trading platform* recipe from `Chapter 8`, *Algorithmic Trading Strategies – Coding Step by Step*, you will find a strategy called **EMA-Regular-Order strategy**. In *step 6*, you assign the strategy code of the strategy, **EMA-Regular-Order strategy**, to a new variable called `strategy_code1`. The strategy code is shown in the output of this step. This strategy code is unique for every strategy on the AlgoBulls platform.

Finally, in *step 7*, you ensure that the strategy being referred to by `strategy_code1` is indeed the one you uploaded earlier (in the *EMA-Regular-Order strategy – uploading the strategy on AlgoBulls trading platform* recipe of `Chapter 8`, *Algorithmic Trading Strategies – Coding Step by Step*). You use the `get_strategy_details()` method of the `algobulls_connection` object to inspect the strategy. This method takes the strategy code as an argument. You pass `strategy_code1` here. This method returns the entire class code as a string. You assign it to a new variable, `strategy_details1`, and display it.

> If you would like to change the class code being referred to by `strategy_code1`, as shown in *step 7*, please refer to the *There's more...* section of the *EMA-Regular-Order strategy – uploading the strategy on AlgoBulls trading platform* recipe, in `Chapter 8`, *Algorithmic Trading Strategies – Coding Step by Step*.

EMA-Regular-Order strategy – backtesting the strategy

In this recipe, you will perform backtesting on the **EMA-Regular-Order strategy**. You must have fetched this strategy from your account in the AlgoBulls platform in the preceding recipe. You will leverage the backtesting functionality facilitated by `pyalgotrading` for this recipe, which, in turn, submits a backtesting job on the AlgoBulls platform.

Once submitted, backtesting will be run by the AlgoBulls backtesting engine. You can query the status anytime to find the state of the backtesting job. The job goes through the following states, in the given order:

- `STARTING` (intermediate state)
- `STARTED` (stable state)
- `STOPPING` (intermediate state)
- `STOPPED` (stable state)

On submitting a job, it starts with an intermediate state, `STARTING`. In this state, the AlgoBulls backtesting engine fetches the strategy and get the execution environment ready, which may take a couple of minutes. Once done, the job moves to the `STARTED` state. Strategy backtesting happens in this stage. Here, it stays as long as it takes for backtesting to complete. Once done, the job moves to an intermediate state, `STOPPING`. In this state, the AlgoBulls backtesting engine cleans up the resources that have been allocated to this job, which usually takes less than a minute. Finally, the job moves to the `STOPPED` state.

If you have already submitted a strategy backtesting job, you cannot submit another job for the same strategy until the first job completes. This means you have to wait for the first job to move to the STOPPED state. If the first job is long-running and you would like to stop it immediately, you can submit a stop job request via pyalgotrading. You need to ensure the job is in the STARTED state before submitting the request.

The following state machine diagram demonstrates the various states and transitions of a backtesting job during its lifetime on the AlgoBulls platform:

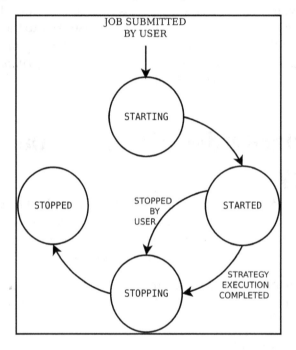

After submitting a backtesting job, you can fetch logs and reports for the strategy execution, in real time. The logs and reports help validate the strategy's performance and debug any potential issues.

 Make sure you have gone through the first six recipes of the previous chapter to get a complete picture of the strategy class we will be using; that is, StrategyEMARegularORder.

Getting ready

Make sure the `algobulls_connection` and `strategy_code1` objects are available in your Python namespace. Refer to the previous recipe to set up the `algobulls_connection` and `strategy_code1` objects.

How to do it...

We execute the following steps for this recipe:

1. Import the necessary modules:

```
>>> from datetime import datetime as dt
>>> from pyalgotrading.constants import *
```

2. Search for an instrument by using its trading symbol as a keyword. Assign the returned object to `instruments`:

```
>>> instruments = algobulls_connection.search_instrument('SBIN')
>>> instruments
```

We get the following output (your output may differ):

```
[{'id': 7, 'value': 'NSE:SBIN'}]
```

3. Get `value` for the instrument of choice from `instruments`:

```
>>> instrument = instruments[0]['value']
>>> instrument
```

We get the following output:

```
'NSE:SBIN'
```

4. Submit a backtesting job for `strategy_code1`:

```
>>> algobulls_connection.backtest(strategy_code=strategy_code1,
        start_timestamp=dt(year=2020, month=7, day=1, hour=9,
                           minute=15),
        end_timestamp=dt(year=2020, month=7, day=7, hour=15,
                         minute=30),
        instrument=instrument,
        lots=1,
        strategy_parameters={
            'timeperiod1': 5,
            'timeperiod2': 12
```

```
},
candle_interval=CandleInterval.MINUTES_15)
```

We get the following output:

```
Setting Strategy Config... Success.
Submitting BACKTESTING job... Success.
```

5. Check the status of the submitted job backtesting job:

    ```
    >>> algobulls_connection.get_backtesting_job_status(strategy_code1)
    ```

    We get the following output:

    ```
    {'data': 'STARTING'}
    ```

6. After some time, check the status of the submitted job once more:

    ```
    >>> algobulls_connection.get_backtesting_job_status(strategy_code1)
    ```

    We get the following output:

    ```
    {'data': 'STARTED'}
    ```

How it works...

In *step 1*, you import the `datetime` class from the `datetime` module and all the constants from the `pyalgotrading.constants` module. In *step 2*, you fetch the instrument that would like to backtest the strategy for, **EMA-Regular-Order strategy**, using the `search_instrument()` method of the `algobulls_connection` object. The `search_instrument()` method accepts a search string as an argument, which should be the trading symbol, in part or complete, of the instrument you are interested in. You pass `'SBIN'` here. This function returns a list with details of instruments that match the search string. There could be multiple instruments that could have the search string in their trading symbols. In *step 3*, you fetch the value of the first matched instrument and assign it to a new variable, `instrument`.

In *step 4*, you submit a backtesting job using the `backtest()` method of the `algobulls_connection()` object. It takes the following arguments:

- `strategy_code`: Strategy code of the strategy for which backtesting has to be performed. This should be a string. You pass `strategy_code1` here.
- `start_timestamp`: Timestamp of the past from which backtesting should be started. This should be a `datetime.datetime` object. Here, you pass an object holding the value 1st July 2020 9:15 hours – `dt(year=2020, month=7, day=1, hour=9, minute=15)`. Refer to the *Creating datetime objects* recipe in `Chapter 1`, *Handling and Manipulating Date, Time, and Time Series Data*, for details on creating a `datetime` object.

- `end_timestamp`: The timestamp of the past when backtesting should be performed. This object should hold a timestamp value ahead of the timestamp value held by `start_timestamp`. This should be a `datetime.datetime` instance. Here, you pass an object holding the value 7th July 2020 15:30 hours – `dt(year=2020, month=7, day=7, hour=15, minute=30)`.
- `instrument`: Financial instrument for which backtesting should be run. Historical data would be fetched for this instrument. This should be a string. You pass `instrument` here.
- `lots`: Number of lots for which backtesting should be performed. This should be an integer. The quantity is calculated by the strategy as *number of lots × lot size of the financial instrument*. (See the *EMA-Regular-Order strategy – coding the strategy_enter_position method* recipe in the previous chapter). You pass 1 here.
- `strategy_parameters`: Parameter names and values expected by the strategy. This should be a dictionary, with `parameter-name` and `parameter-value` as key-value pairs. You pass the following parameters here:
  - `timeperiod1`: 5
  - `timeperiod2`: 12

(Recall that the parameters for the EMA-Regular-Order strategy were defined in its `__init__()` method, as shown in the first recipe of the previous chapter).

- `candle_interval`: The candle interval for the historical data fetched for backtesting. This should be an enum of the `CandleInterval` type. You pass `CandleInterval.MINUTES_15` here. (The `CandleInterval` enum provides various enums for candle intervals, some of which are `MINUTE_1`, `MINUTES_3`, `MINUTES_5`, `MINUTES_10`, `MINUTES_15`, `MINUTES_30`, `HOUR`, and `DAY`.)

If the job submission is successful, you will see `Success` message printed by the `backtest()` function.

Once a job is submitted, it takes a while to start. After starting, it may take some time to finish, depending on the complexity of the strategy and the duration of backtesting specified using the `start_timestamp` and `end_timestamp` arguments. A few days of backtesting may finish in seconds, while a few months of backtesting may take minutes.

In *step 5*, you fetch the job status using the `get_backtesting_job_status()` method of the `algobulls_connection` object. You pass `strategy_code1` as the argument here. This method returns a dictionary with a single key-value pair – the *data* and the *job* status. If you query the status immediately after placing the job, you get `'STARTING'` as the status. In *step 6*, you query the status again after some time, and if the job has started, you get `'STARTED'` as the status.

A successful submission implies that the minimum inputs needed to backtest a strategy have been passed in the required format. However, this does not ensure that the strategy will run without errors. The strategy's execution may still run into errors during backtesting. To debug execution issues, you would need to fetch the output logs, which is explained in the *MACD-Bracket-Order strategy – fetching backtesting logs in real time* recipe. Possible reasons for errors could be either bugs in the strategy class Python code or an incomplete `strategy_parameters` dictionary being passed to the `backtest()` function.

There's more...

If a job is running for a long time and you would like to stop it before its completion, you can use the `stop_backtesting_job()` method of the `algobulls_connection` object. This method accepts strategy code as an argument. You pass `strategy_code1` here. This method submits a stop request to the AlgoBulls backtesting engine. If the request is accepted, you will see a `Success` message here:

```
>>> algobulls_connection.stop_backtesting_job(strategy_code1)
Stopping BACKTESTING job... Success.
```

If you query the status after submitting the stop request, you'll get the status as `'STOPPING`':

```
>>> algobulls_connection.get_backtesting_job_status(strategy_code1)
{'data': 'STOPPING'}
```

If you query the status again after some time, and if the job has stopped, you'll get the status as `'STOPPED'`:

```
>>> algobulls_connection.get_backtesting_job_status(strategy_code1)
{'data': 'STOPPED'}
```

EMA-Regular-Order strategy – fetching backtesting logs in real time

After submitting a backtesting job on the AlgoBulls platform, the AlgoBulls backtesting engine starts executing the strategy. During the execution, every event that occurs and every decision taken by the AlgoBulls backtesting engine are recorded with exact timestamps in the form of textual logs. Examples of recorded activities include the given strategy config, every new candle generated at regular intervals, trades punched by your strategy, the entry and exit of positions created by these trades, waits for new candles, and so on. These logs are quintessential in validating the strategy behavior and debugging behavior or performance issues that are frequently encountered while developing a strategy.

In this recipe, you will fetch the backtesting logs for your strategy. The logs start coming up as soon as your submitted backtesting job reaches the `'STARTED'` state (refer to the previous recipe for more information on the states of a backtesting job). The AlgoBulls platform allows you to fetch logs in real time, even while the backtesting job is still going on. You can get insights into the strategy's execution without having to wait for the backtesting job to complete, which is helpful when jobs are long-running. The pyalgotrading package provides a simple method that can be used to fetch the execution logs for a given strategy.

 Make sure you have gone through the first six recipes of the previous chapter to get a complete picture of the strategy class we will be using; that is, StrategyEMARegularOrder.

Getting ready

Make sure the `algobulls_connection` and `strategy_code1` objects are available in your Python namespace. Refer to the first recipe of this chapter to set up the `algobulls_connection` and `strategy_code1` objects.

How to do it...

We execute the following steps for this recipe:

1. Fetch the backtesting execution logs for `strategy_code1`:

```
>>> logs = algobulls_connection.get_backtesting_logs(
                                            strategy_code1)
>>> print(logs)
```

We get the following output (your output may differ):

```
[2020-07-30 17:25:18] Logs not available yet. Please retry in
sometime.
```

2. Fetch the backtesting execution logs for `strategy_code1` again after some time:

```
>>> logs = algobulls_connection.get_backtesting_logs(
                                            strategy_code1)
>>> print(logs)
```

We get the following output (your output may differ):

```
...
#######################################
 INITIALIZING ALGOBULLS CORE (v3.2.0 SECURE MODE)...
#######################################
[2020-07-30 11:56:29] Welcome ALGOBULLS VIRTUAL USER!
[2020-07-30 11:56:29] Reading strategy...
...
 [BT] [2020-07-01 09:15:00] [INFO] [tls] STARTING ALGOBULLS CORE...
...
[BT] [2020-07-01 09:45:00] [CRITICAL] [order] [PLACING NEW ORDER]
[2020-07-01 09:45:00] [2333198611b744aeb287300d371c8eb5] [BUY]
[NSE:SBIN] [QTY:1] [QTY PENDING: 1] [ENTRY PRICE: 180.25]
[PRICE:None] [TRIGGER PRICE:None] [ORDER_TYPE_REGULAR]
[ORDER_CODE_INTRADAY] [ORDER_VARIETY_MARKET] [ORDER_POSITION_ENTER]
...
 [BT] [2020-07-07 15:30:00] [INFO] [clock] Candle generation has
been stopped...
```

```
[BT] [2020-07-07 15:30:00] [INFO] [tls] Received event END OF
MARKET. Stopping Trading Core Engine...
[BT] [2020-07-07 15:30:00] [INFO] [tls] Exiting all open positions
with order code: ORDER_CODE_INTRADAY (if any)...
[BT] [2020-07-07 15:30:00] [CRITICAL] [tls] [User: ALGOBULLS
VIRTUAL USER] Trading session completed
  ...
```

The complete output is not shown here. Please visit the following link to read the complete output: https://github.com/algobulls/pyalgostrategypool/blob/master/pyalgostrategypool/sample/backtesting/strategy_ema_regular_order/logs.txt.

How it works...

In *step 1*, you use the `get_backtesting_logs()` method of the `algobulls_connection` object to fetch the strategy backtesting logs in real time. This method accepts the strategy code as an argument. You pass `strategy_code1` here. The return data is a string. If you try this step immediately after submitting the job, you get a string, which says the logs are not ready yet (`[2020-07-30 17:27:25] Logs not available yet. Please retry in sometime.`). This happens if the backtesting job is in the `'STARTING'` state.

In *step 2*, you fetch the logs again after some time. If the job is out of the `'STARTING'` state, you start getting your strategy execution logs. You get the entire backtesting logs every time you call the `get_backtesting_logs()` function.

There's more...

Once the backtesting job moves to the `'STOPPED'` state, no new logs are generated. You can fetch the complete logs any time before you submit the next backtesting job for the same strategy. If a new backtesting job is submitted (for the same strategy), these logs will no longer be accessible via the `get_backtesting_logs()` method. You can save the fetched logs to a file if you'd like to refer to it at a later date.

EMA-Regular-Order strategy – fetching a backtesting report – P&L table

After submitting a backtesting job on the AlgoBulls platform, the AlgoBulls backtesting engine starts executing the strategy. During its execution, along with the logs, the AlgoBulls backtesting engine also generates a P&L table in real time. This table holds information on every trade that's been punched by the strategy. It also contains details on the mappings between entry and exit orders, the trade P&L, and the cumulative P&L, sorted chronologically, with the latest order first. This table gives us an insight into the overall strategy's performance with the help of individual and cumulative P&L numbers. The entry-exit order mapping also helps validate the strategy behavior.

In this recipe, you will fetch the P&L table report for your strategy. This report is available as soon as the first trade is punched in by your strategy after you submit a backtesting job. The AlgoBulls platform allows you to fetch the P&L table in real time, even while the backtesting job is still going on. You can get insights into the strategy performance without having to wait for the backtesting job to complete, which is helpful when jobs are long-running. The `pyalgotrading` package provides a simple method that's used to fetch the P&L table for a given strategy.

 Make sure you have gone through the first six recipes of the previous chapter to get a complete picture of the strategy class we will be using; that is, `StrategyEMARegularOrder`.

Getting ready

Make sure the `algobulls_connection` and `strategy_code1` objects are available in your Python namespace. Refer to the first recipe of this chapter to set up the `algobulls_connection` and `strategy_code1` objects.

How to do it…

Fetch the backtesting P&L report for `strategy_code1`:

```
>>> algobulls_connection.get_backtesting_report_pnl_table(strategy_code1)
```

We got the following output. Your output may differ (note that the following output has been split into multiple tables for representation purposes. You will see a single wide table in your Jupyter Notebook):

	instrument	entry_timestamp	entry_transaction_type	entry_quantity	entry_price
0	NSE_EQ:SBIN	2020-07-07 13:15:00	BUY	1	186.55
1	NSE_EQ:SBIN	2020-07-06 14:45:00	SELL	1	187.85
2	NSE_EQ:SBIN	2020-07-06 09:30:00	BUY	1	187.65
3	NSE_EQ:SBIN	2020-07-03 13:15:00	SELL	1	184.6
4	NSE_EQ:SBIN	2020-07-03 12:00:00	BUY	1	185.45
5	NSE_EQ:SBIN	2020-07-02 15:00:00	SELL	1	185.6
6	NSE_EQ:SBIN	2020-07-02 12:00:00	BUY	1	185.55
7	NSE_EQ:SBIN	2020-07-02 11:15:00	SELL	1	184.4
8	NSE_EQ:SBIN	2020-07-01 09:45:00	BUY	1	180.25

	instrument	exit_timestamp	exit_transaction_type	exit_quantity	exit_price
0	NSE_EQ:SBIN	2020-07-07 15:30:00	SELL	1	188
1	NSE_EQ:SBIN	2020-07-06 15:30:00	BUY	1	187.9
2	NSE_EQ:SBIN	2020-07-06 14:45:00	SELL	1	187.85
3	NSE_EQ:SBIN	2020-07-03 15:30:00	BUY	1	184.6
4	NSE_EQ:SBIN	2020-07-03 13:15:00	SELL	1	184.6
5	NSE_EQ:SBIN	2020-07-02 15:30:00	BUY	1	185.7
6	NSE_EQ:SBIN	2020-07-02 15:00:00	SELL	1	185.6
7	NSE_EQ:SBIN	2020-07-02 12:00:00	BUY	1	185.55
8	NSE_EQ:SBIN	2020-07-01 15:30:00	SELL	1	184.45

	pnl_absolute	pnl_percentage	pnl_cumulative_absolute	pnl_cumulative_percentage
0	1.45	0.78	3.75	2.09
1	-0.05	-0.03	2.3	1.31
2	0.2	0.11	2.35	1.34
3	0	0	2.15	1.23
4	-0.85	-0.46	2.15	1.23
5	-0.1	-0.05	3	1.69
6	0.05	0.03	3.1	1.74
7	-1.15	-0.62	3.05	1.71
8	4.2	2.33	4.2	2.33

How it works...

In this recipe, you use the `get_backtesting_report_pnl_table()` method of the `algobulls_connection` object to fetch the backtesting P&L table in real time. This method accepts strategy code as an argument. You pass `strategy_code1` here. The return data is a `pandas.DataFrame` object with multiple columns, described as follows:

- `instrument`: Financial instrument for which the trade was entered.
- `entry_timestamp`: The timestamp at which the entry order was placed. (Note that it may remain in the `'OPEN'` state for a while before it goes to the `'COMPLETE'` state. The time for this state transition can be found using the order history table, as explained in the sixth recipe of this chapter.)
- `entry_transaction_type`: Entry order transaction type (either BUY or SELL).
- `entry_quantity`: Entry order quantity.

- `entry_price`: The price at which the entry order gets executed and goes to the `'COMPLETE'` state.
- `exit_timestamp`: The timestamp at which the exit order was placed. (Note that it may remain in the `'OPEN'` state for a while before it goes to the `'COMPLETE'` state.)
- `exit_transaction_type`: Exit order transaction type (either BUY or SELL).
- `exit_quantity`: Exit order quantity.
- `exit_price`: The price at which the exit order gets executed and goes to the `'COMPLETE'` state.
- `pnl_absolute`: Difference between the exit order execution price and the entry order execution price. Mathematically, this is (*exit_price - entry_price*)*exit_quantity* for a long trade and (*entry_price - exit_price*)*exit_quantity* for a short trade. A positive value would imply that the trade is a profit-making trade. A negative value would imply that the trade is a loss-making trade.
- `pnl_percentage`: The percentage of profit or loss with respect to the entry price. Mathematically, this is *pnl_absolute / entry_price / exit_quantity × 100*.
- `pnl_cumulative_absolute`: Cumulative profit or loss. Mathematically, this is the sum of all the `pnl_absolute` values of the previous trades. This number gives us direct insight into the strategy performance against the simulation time.
- `pnl_cumulative_percentage`: The percentage of cumulative profit or loss with respect to the entry price. Mathematically, this is *pnl_cumulative / entry_price / exit quantity × 100*.

There's more...

Once the backtesting job moves to the 'STOPPED' state, the P&L table report will not update anymore. You can fetch the complete P&L report any time before you submit the next backtesting job for the same strategy. If a new backtesting job is submitted (for the same strategy), this report will no longer be accessible via the `get_backtesting_report_pnl_table()` method. You can save the fetched report as a `.csv` file if you'd like to refer to it at a later date.

EMA-Regular-Order strategy — fetching a backtesting report – statistics table

After submitting a backtesting job on the AlgoBulls platform, the AlgoBulls backtesting engine starts executing the strategy. During its execution, along with the logs and P&L table, the AlgoBulls backtesting engine also generates a summary from the P&L table in real time. This summary is a table of statistics containing various statistical numbers such as `Net P&L` (absolute and percentage), `Max Drawdown` (absolute and percentage), count of total trades, winning trades, losing trades, long trades and short trades, maximum gain and minimum gain (or maximum loss), and average profit per winning and losing trade. This table gives an instant overview of the overall strategy's performance.

In this recipe, you will fetch the statistics table report for your strategy. This report is available as soon as the first trade is punched in by your strategy after you submit a backtesting job. The AlgoBulls platform allows you to fetch the statistics table in real time, even while the backtesting job is still going on. You can get insights into the strategy performance without having to wait for the backtesting job to complete, which is helpful when jobs are long-running. The `pyalgotrading` package provides a simple method that's used to fetch the statistics table for a given strategy.

 Make sure you have gone through the first six recipes of the previous chapter to get a complete picture of the strategy class we will be using; that is, `StrategyEMARegularOrder`.

Getting ready

Make sure the `algobulls_connection` and `strategy_code1` objects are available in your Python namespace. Refer to the first recipe of this chapter to set up the `algobulls_connection` and `strategy_code1` objects.

How to do it...

Fetch the backtesting statistics report for `strategy_code1`:

```
>>> algobulls_connection.get_backtesting_report_statistics(strategy_code1)
```

We got the following output (your output may differ):

	highlight_type	highlight_value
0	Net PnL	3.75
1	Net PnL %	2.09
2	Max Drawdown	2.15
3	Max Drawdown %	1.16
4	Number of Trades	9
5	Number of Wins	5
6	Number of Looses	4
7	Number of Long Trades	5
8	Number of Short Trades	4
9	Max Gain	4.2
10	Min Gain	-1.15
11	Avg. Profit per winning trade	1.48
12	Avg. Profit per losing trade	-0.54

How it works...

In this recipe, you use the `get_backtesting_report_statistics()` method of the `algobulls_connection` object to fetch the backtesting statistics table in real time. This method accepts the strategy code as an argument. You pass `strategy_code1` here. The return data is a `pandas.DataFrame` object with two columns – `highlight_type` and `highlight_value` – and multiple rows. The rows are described as follows:

- `Net PnL`: The cumulative backtesting P&L. This is also the `pnl_cumulative_absolute` value of the first entry in the P&L table.
- `Net PnL %`: The cumulative backtesting P&L percentage. This is also the `pnl_cumulative_percentage` value of the first entry in the P&L table.
- `Max Drawdown`: The lowest value in the `pnl_cumulative` column of the P&L table. This indicates the maximum loss your strategy has encountered during the execution.
- `Max Drawdown %`: Mathematically, this is *(Max Drawdown) / (corresponding entry_price) / exit_quantity × 100*.
- `Number of Trades`: Total trades (entry and exit counted as one) during the session.
- `Number of Wins`: Count of trades where the trade P&L was non-negative.
- `Number of Losses`: Count of trades where the trade P&L was negative.
- `Number of Long Trades`: Count of trades where the entry transaction type was `'BUY'`.
- `Number of Short Trades`: Count of trades where the entry transaction type was `'SELL'`.
- `Max Gain`: P&L of the trade with the maximum P&L value among all trades.
- `Min Gain`: P&L of the trade with the minimum P&L value among all trades.
- `Avg. Profit per winning trade`: Mathematically, this is *(Total P&L of winning trades) / (Count of winning trades)*.
- `Avg. Profit per losing trade`: Mathematically, this is *(Total P&L of losing trades) / (Count of losing trades)*.

There's more...

If the statistics table is fetched while the backtesting job is still running, the aforementioned numbers would be intermediate numbers, based on the trades completed up until that time. The numbers may change as more trades are punched in, until the backtesting job completes.

Once the backtesting job moves to the 'STOPPED' state, the statistics table will not change anymore. You can fetch the complete statistics table any time before you submit the next backtesting job for the same strategy. If a new backtesting job is submitted (for the same strategy), this table will no longer be accessible via the get_backtesting_report_statistics() method. You can save the fetched report table to a .csv file if you'd like to refer to it at a later date.

EMA-Regular-Order strategy – fetching a backtesting report – order history

After submitting a backtesting job on the AlgoBulls platform, the AlgoBulls backtesting engine starts executing the strategy. During its execution, along with the logs, the P&L table and the statistics table of the AlgoBulls backtesting engine generate an order history log in real time. This log contains state transitions of every order, along with the timestamps and additional information (if any) for each order state. The order history log is crucial for understanding how long it has taken for a trade to go from an 'OPEN' state to 'COMPLETE' or 'CANCELLED'. For example, the MARKET orders would immediately go from 'OPEN' to 'COMPLETE' but the LIMIT orders may take a while, based on the market conditions, to go from 'OPEN' to 'COMPLETE' – they may even get to 'CANCELLED'. All this information is available in the order history log. (Refer to the state machine diagrams in Chapter 6, *Placing Regular Orders on the Exchange*, for more information on order state transitions.)

In this recipe, you will fetch the order history log for your strategy. This log is available as soon as the first trade is punched in by your strategy, after you submit a backtesting job. The AlgoBulls platform allows you to fetch the order history log in real time, even while the backtesting job is still going on. This helps us get details for orders in their end states, without having to wait for the backtesting job to complete. The pyalgotrading package provides a simple method we can use to fetch the order history log for a given strategy.

Make sure you have gone through the first six recipes of the previous chapter to get a complete picture of the strategy class we will be using; that is, StrategyEMARegularOrder.

Getting ready

Make sure the algobulls_connection and strategy_code1 objects are available in your Python namespace. Refer to the first recipe of this chapter to set up the algobulls_connection and strategy_code1 objects.

How to do it...

Fetch the backtesting order history report for strategy_code1:

```
>>> order_history = \
        algobulls_connection.get_backtesting_report_order_history(
                                                    strategy_code1)
>>> print(order_history)
```

We got the following output (your output may differ):

```
+--------------+---------------------+---------------------------------------+----
----+
| INST         | TIME                | ID                                    | TT
|
|--------------+---------------------+---------------------------------------+----
---|
| NSE_EQ:SBIN  | 2020-07-01 09:45:00 | 2333198611b744aeb287300d371c8eb5 |
BUY   |
+--------------+---------------------+---------------------------------------+----
----+
+----+---------------------+-----------------------+-------+
|    | TIME                | STATE                 | MSG   |
|----+---------------------+-----------------------+-------|
|  0 | 2020-07-01 09:45:00 | PUT ORDER REQ RECEIVED |       |
|  1 | 2020-07-01 09:45:00 | VALIDATION PENDING     |       |
|  2 | 2020-07-01 09:45:00 | OPEN PENDING           |       |
|  3 | 2020-07-01 09:45:00 | OPEN                   |       |
|  4 | 2020-07-01 09:45:00 | COMPLETE               |       |
+----+---------------------+-----------------------+-------+
+--------------+---------------------+---------------------------------------+----
----+
| INST         | TIME                | ID                                    | TT
```

```
    |
    |-------------+---------------------+------------------------------------+-------|
    | NSE_EQ:SBIN | 2020-07-01 15:30:00 | 67f39f41885b476295e7e959b0470d49 |
    SELL |
    +-------------+---------------------+------------------------------------+-------+

    +----+---------------------+------------------------+-------+
    |    | TIME                | STATE                  | MSG   |
    |----+---------------------+------------------------+-------|
    | 0  | 2020-07-01 15:30:00 | PUT ORDER REQ RECEIVED |       |
    | 1  | 2020-07-01 15:30:00 | VALIDATION PENDING     |       |
    | 2  | 2020-07-01 15:30:00 | OPEN PENDING           |       |
    | 3  | 2020-07-01 15:30:00 | OPEN                   |       |
    | 4  | 2020-07-01 15:30:00 | COMPLETE               |       |
    +----+---------------------+------------------------+-------+
    . . .
```

The complete output is not shown here. Please visit this link to read the complete output:
https://github.com/algobulls/pyalgostrategypool/blob/master/pyalgostrategypool/
sample/backtesting/strategy_ema_regular_order/oms_order_history.log.

How it works...

In this recipe, you use the `get_backtesting_report_order_history()` method of the `algobulls_connection` object to fetch order history logs in real time. This method accepts strategy code as an argument. You pass `strategy_code1` here. The return data is a string, described as follows:

For every order, the log contains the following information:

- A descriptive table of the order, with the following mentioned columns:
  - `INST`: Financial instrument of the order
  - `TIME`: Time at which the order was placed
  - `ID`: The unique ID of the order
  - `TT`: The order transaction type (`BUY` or `SELL`)

  An example of this table is shown here:

```
    +-------------+---------------------+----------------------------
    ----+------+
    | INST        | TIME                | ID
    | TT   |
    |-------------+---------------------+----------------------------
```

```
----+------|
| NSE_EQ:SBIN  |  2020-07-01 09:45:00 |
2333198611b744aeb287300d371c8eb5 | BUY  |
+------------+-------------------+---------------------------
----+------+
```

This information will help you find this exact order in the strategy execution log.

- An order state transition table, with the following columns:
    - TIME: Timestamp at which the order enters the state represented by the 'STATE' column.
    - STATE: The order enters this 'STATE' at the timestamp mentioned in the 'TIME' column.
    - MSG: An additional message from the **Order Management System (OMS)** for any unexpected state transitions. For example, orders that go to the REJECTED state have a message from the OMS stating the reason for their rejection. This column is usually empty.

An example of this table is shown here:

```
+----+-------------------+----------------------+------+
|    | TIME              | STATE                | MSG  |
|----+-------------------+----------------------+------|
|  0 | 2020-07-01 09:45:00 | PUT ORDER REQ RECEIVED |      |
|  1 | 2020-07-01 09:45:00 | VALIDATION PENDING   |      |
|  2 | 2020-07-01 09:45:00 | OPEN PENDING         |      |
|  3 | 2020-07-01 09:45:00 | OPEN                 |      |
|  4 | 2020-07-01 09:45:00 | COMPLETE             |      |
+----+-------------------+----------------------+------+
```

From this table, you can see that, upon placing the order at 9:45 a.m., it transitions to the 'COMPLETE' state immediately. This is expected as the order is a regular market order.

There's more...

Once the backtesting job moves to the 'STOPPED' state, no new order history logs are generated. You can fetch the complete order history logs any time before you submit the next backtesting job for the same strategy. If a new backtesting job is submitted (for the same strategy), these logs will no longer be accessible via the get_backtesting_report_order_history() method. You can save the fetched logs to a file if you'd like to refer to them at a later date.

MACD-Bracket-Order strategy – fetching the strategy

In this recipe, you will fetch the `StrategyMACDBracketOrder` strategy class from your account on the AlgoBulls platform, which you uploaded while going through the last recipe in the previous chapter. This recipe starts with setting up a connection to the AlgoBulls platform, querying all available strategies in your account, and fetching details of the required strategy class, `StrategyMACDBracketOrder`.

 Make sure you have gone through the last six recipes of the previous chapter to get a complete picture of the strategy class we will be using; that is, `StrategyMACDBracketOrder`.

How to do it...

We execute the following steps for this recipe:

1. Import the necessary modules:

   ```
   >>> from pyalgotrading.algobulls import AlgoBullsConnection
   ```

2. Create a new AlgoBulls connection object:

   ```
   >>> algobulls_connection = AlgoBullsConnection()
   ```

3. Fetch the authorization URL:

   ```
   >>> algobulls_connection.get_authorization_url()
   ```

   We get the following output:

   ```
   Please login to this URL with your AlgoBulls credentials and get
   your developer access token: https://app.algobulls.com/user/login
   'https://app.algobulls.com/user/login'
   ```

4. Log into the preceding link with your AlgoBulls credentials, fetch your token, and set it here (refer to *Appendix II* for more details):

   ```
   >>> algobulls_connection.set_access_token('
               80b7a69b168c5b3f15d56688841a8f2da5e2ab2c')
   ```

5. Fetch and display all the strategies you have created and uploaded so far:

```
>>> all_strategies = algobulls_connection.get_all_strategies()
>>> all_strategies
```

We get the following output. Your output may differ (make sure you have followed the recipes in the previous chapter to get a similar output):

	strategyCode	strategyName
0	49287246f9704bbcbad76ade9e2091d9	EMA Regular Order Strategy
1	4faf514fe096432b8e9f80f5951bd2ea	MACD Bracket Order Strategy

6. Fetch and display the strategy code of the second strategy, **MACD-Bracket-Order strategy**:

```
>>> strategy_code2 = all_strategies.iloc[1]['strategyCode']
>>> strategy_code2
```

We get the following output (your output may differ):

```
'49287246f9704bbcbad76ade9e2091d9'
```

7. Before backtesting your strategy, you can inspect your strategy to ensure you have the right strategy:

```
>>> strategy_details2 = \
        algobulls_connection.get_strategy_details(strategy_code2)
>>> print(strategy_details2)
```

We get the following output:

```
class StrategyMACDBracketOrder(StrategyBase):

    def __init__(self, *args, **kwargs):
        super().__init__(*args, **kwargs)

        self.fastMA_period = \
            self.strategy_parameters['fastma_period']
        self.slowMA_period = \
            self.strategy_parameters['slowma_period']
        self.signal_period = \
            self.strategy_parameters['signal_period']
        self.stoploss = \
            self.strategy_parameters['stoploss_trigger']
        self.target = self.strategy_parameters['target_trigger']
        self.trailing_stoploss = \
```

```
                self.strategy_parameters['trailing_stoploss_trigger']

        self.main_order = None

    def initialize(self):
        self.main_order = {}

    @staticmethod
    def name():
        return 'MACD Bracket Order Strategy'
    ....
    def strategy_exit_position(self, candle, instrument,
                                    sideband_info):
        if sideband_info['action'] == 'EXIT':
            self.main_order[instrument].exit_position()
            self.main_order[instrument] = None
            return True

        return False
```

The complete output is not shown here. Please visit the following link to read the complete output: `https://github.com/algobulls/pyalgostrategypool/blob/master/pyalgostrategypool/strategy_macd_bracket_order.py`.

How it works...

You import the necessary modules in *step 1*. In *step 2*, you create an instance of the `AlgoBullsConnection` class, named `algobulls_connection`. In *step 3*, you get the authorization URL using the `get_authorization_url()` method of the `algobulls_connection` object. This prints the authorization URL. You should visit this URL from your web browser to sign into the AlgoBulls platform and fetch your developer access token. (You can find more details, along with screenshots, in *Appendix II* on fetching developer access token from the AlgoBulls platform.) You copy the access token and set it in *step 4* using the `set_access_token()` method of `algobulls_connection`. If the token is accepted, a successful connection is set up with the AlgoBulls platform.

In *step 5*, you fetch all the strategies you have created and uploaded on the AlgoBulls platform so far. You use the `get_all_strategies()` method for this step and assign it to a new variable, `all_strategies`. This variable is a `pandas.DataFrame` object with `strategyCode` and `strategyName` columns. This table holds information about the strategy codes and the strategy names you have uploaded previously. If you followed the *MACD-Bracket-Order strategy – uploading the strategy on AlgoBulls Trading Platform* recipe from `Chapter 8`, *Algorithmic Trading Strategies – Coding Step by Step*, you will find a strategy called **MACD-Regular-Order strategy**. In *step 6*, you assign the strategy code of the strategy, **MACD-Regular-Order strategy**, to a new variable called `strategy_code2`. The strategy code is shown in the output of this step. This strategy code is unique to every strategy on the AlgoBulls platform.

Finally, in *step 7*, you ensure that the strategy being referred to by `strategy_code2` is indeed the one you uploaded earlier (in the last recipe of the previous chapter). You use the `get_strategy_details()` method of the `algobulls_connection` object to inspect the strategy. This method takes strategy code as an argument. You pass `strategy_code2` here. This method returns the entire class code as a string. You assign it to a new variable, `strategy_details2`, and display it.

 If you would like to change the class code being referred to by `strategy_code2`, as shown in *step 7*, please refer to the *There's more...* section of the last recipe in `Chapter 8`, *Algorithmic Trading Strategies – Coding Step by Step*.

MACD-Bracket-Order strategy – backtesting the strategy

In this recipe, you will perform backtesting on the **MACD-Bracket-Order strategy**. You must have fetched this strategy from your account on the AlgoBulls platform in the previous recipe of this chapter. You will leverage the backtesting functionality facilitated by `pyalgotrading` for this recipe, which, in turn, submits a backtesting job on the AlgoBulls platform.

Once submitted, backtesting will be run by the AlgoBulls backtesting engine. You can query the status at any time to find out the state of the backtesting job. The job goes through the following states, in the given order:

- `STARTING` (Intermediate state)
- `STARTED` (Stable state)

- STOPPING (Intermediate state)
- STOPPED (Stable state)

On submitting a job, it starts with an intermediate state, 'STARTING'. In this state, the AlgoBulls backtesting engine fetches the strategy and get the execution environment ready, which may take a couple of minutes. Once done, the job moves to the 'STARTED' state. Strategy backtesting happens at this stage. Here, it stays as long as it takes for backtesting to complete. Once done, the job moves to an intermediate state, 'STOPPING'. In this state, the AlgoBulls backtesting engine cleans up the resources that have been allocated to this job, which usually takes less than a minute. Finally, the job moves to the 'STOPPED' state.

If you have already submitted a backtesting job for a strategy, you cannot submit another job for the same strategy until the first job completes. This means you have to wait for the first job to move to the 'STOPPED' state. If the first job is long-running and you would like to stop it immediately, you can submit a stop job request via pyalgotrading. You need to ensure the job is in the 'STARTED' state before submitting the request.

After submitting a backtesting job, you can fetch logs and reports for the strategy execution in real time. The logs and reports help validate the strategy's performance and debug any potential issues.

You can refer to the second recipe of this chapter to see the state machine diagram of a backtesting job. It demonstrates the various states and transitions of a backtesting job during its lifetime on the AlgoBulls platform.

 Make sure you have gone through the last six recipes of the previous chapter to get a complete picture of the strategy class we will be using; that is, StrategyMACDBracketOrder.

Getting ready

Make sure the algobulls_connection and strategy_code2 objects are available in your Python namespace. Refer to the preceding recipe of this chapter to set up the algobulls_connection and strategy_code2 object.

How to do it...

We execute the following steps for this recipe:

1. Import the necessary modules:

```
>>> from datetime import datetime as dt
>>> from pyalgotrading.constants import *
```

2. Search for an instrument using its trading symbol as a keyword. Assign the returned object to instruments:

```
>>> instrument = algobulls_connection.search_instrument(
                                            'TATASTEEL')
>>> instrument
```

We get the following output (your output may differ):

```
[{'id': 1, 'value': 'NSE:TATASTEEL'}]
```

3. Get value for the instrument of choice from instruments:

```
>>> instrument = instrument[0]['value']
>>> instrument
```

We get the following output:

```
'NSE:TATASTEEL'
```

4. Submit a backtesting job for strategy_code2:

```
>>> algobulls_connection.backtest(
        strategy_code=strategy_code2,
        start_timestamp=dt(year=2020, month=7, day=1, hour=9,
                            minute=15),
        end_timestamp=dt(year=2020, month=7, day=7, hour=15,
                            minute=30),
        instrument=instrument,
        lots=1,
        strategy_parameters={
            'fastma_period': 26,
            'slowma_period': 6,
            'signal_period': 9,
            'target_trigger': 0.01,
            'stoploss_trigger': 0.01,
            'trailing_stoploss_trigger': 1
        },
        candle_interval=CandleInterval.MINUTES_15)
```

We get the following output:

```
Setting Strategy Config... Success.
Submitting BACKTESTING job... Success.
```

5. Check the status of the submitted backtesting job:

```
>>> algobulls_connection.get_backtesting_job_status(strategy_code2)
{'data': 'STARTING'}
```

6. Check the status of the submitted backtesting job again after some time:

```
>>> algobulls_connection.get_backtesting_job_status(strategy_code2)
{'data': 'STARTED'}
```

How it works...

In *step 1*, you import the `datetime` class from the `datetime` module and all the required constants from the `pyalgotrading.constants` module. In *step 2*, you fetch the instrument that you would like to backtest the strategy for, the **MACD-Bracket-Order strategy**, using the `search_instrument()` method of the `algobulls_connection` object. The `search_instrument()` method accepts a search string as an argument, which should be the trading symbol, in part or complete, of the instrument you are interested in. You pass `'TATASTEEL'` here. This function returns a list with details of the instruments that match the search string. There could be multiple instruments that have the search string in their trading symbols. In *step 3*, you fetch the value of the first matched instrument and assign it to a new variable, `instrument`.

In *step 4*, you submit a backtesting job using the `backtest()` method of the `algobulls_connection()` object. It takes the following arguments:

- `strategy_code`: Strategy code of the strategy for which backtesting has to be performed. This should be a string. You pass `strategy_code2` here.
- `start_timestamp`: Timestamp of the past from which backtesting should be started. This should be a `datetime.datetime` object. Here, you pass an object holding the value 1st July 2020 9:15 hours – `dt(year=2020, month=7, day=1, hour=9, minute=15)`. Refer to the first recipe of `Chapter 1`, *Handling and Manipulating Date, Time, and Time Series Data,* for details on creating a `datetime` object.

- `end_timestamp`: Timestamp of the past for when backtesting should be performed. This object should hold a timestamp value ahead of the `timestamp` value held by `start_timestamp`. This should be a `datetime.datetime` instance. Here, you pass an object holding the value 7th July 2020 15:30 hours - `dt(year=2020, month=7, day=7, hour=15, minute=30)`.
- `instrument`: A financial instrument for which backtesting should be run. Historical data will be fetched for this instrument. This should be a string. You pass `instrument` here.
- `lots`: Number of lots for which backtesting should be performed. This should be an integer. The quantity is calculated by the strategy as *number of lots × lot size of the financial instrument*. (See the *MACD-Bracket-Order strategy – coding the strategy_select_instruments_for_entry method* recipe in `Chapter 8`, *Algorithmic Trading Strategies - Coding Step by Step*.) You pass 1 here.
- `strategy_parameters`: Parameter names and values expected by the strategy. This should be a dictionary, with `parameter-name` and `parameter-value` as key-value pairs. You pass the following parameters here:
    - `fastma_period: 26`
    - `slowma_period: 6`
    - `signal_period: 9`
    - `target_trigger: 0.01`
    - `stoploss_trigger: 0.01`
    - `trailing_stoploss_trigger: 1`

    (Recall that the parameters for the MACD-Bracket-Order strategy were defined in its `__init__()` method in the first recipe of the previous chapter).

- `candle_interval`: The candle interval for the historical data fetched for backtesting. This should be an enum of the `CandleInterval` type. You pass `CandleInterval.MINUTES_15` here. (The `CandleInterval` enum provides various enums for candle intervals, some of which are `MINUTE_1`, `MINUTES_3`, `MINUTES_5`, `MINUTES_10`, `MINUTES_15`, `MINUTES_30`, `HOUR`, and `DAY`.)

If the job submission is successful, you will see `Success` messages being printed by the `backtest()` function.

Once a job has been submitted, it takes a while to start. After starting, it may take some time to finish, depending on the complexity of the strategy and duration of backtesting specified using the `start_timestamp` and `end_timestamp` arguments. A few days of backtesting may finish in seconds, while a few months of backtesting may take minutes.

In *step 5*, you fetch the job status using the `get_backtesting_job_status()` method of the `algobulls_connection` object. You pass `strategy_code2` as the argument here. This method returns a dictionary with a single key-value pair – the data and the job status. If you query the status immediately after placing the job, you get `'STARTING'` as the status. In *step 6*, you query the status again after some time, and if the job starts, you get a status of `'STARTED'`.

 A successful submission implies that the minimum inputs needed to backtest a strategy have been passed in the required format. However, this does not ensure that the strategy will run without errors. The strategy's execution may still run into errors during backtesting. To debug execution issues, you will need to fetch the output logs, which will be explained in the next recipe. Possible reasons for errors could be bugs in the strategy class' Python code or an incomplete `strategy_parameters` dictionary being passed to the `backtest()` function.

There's more...

If a job is running for a long time and you would like to stop it before its completion, you can use the `stop_backtesting_job()` method of the `algobulls_connection` object. This method accepts strategy code as an argument. You pass `strategy_code2` here. This method submits a stop request to the AlgoBulls backtesting engine. If the request is accepted, you will see a `Success` message here:

```
>>> algobulls_connection.stop_backtesting_job(strategy_code2)
Stopping BACKTESTING job... Success.
```

If you query the status after submitting the stop request, you will get a status of `'STOPPING`:

```
>>> algobulls_connection.get_backtesting_job_status(strategy_code2)
{'data': 'STOPPING'}
```

If you query the status again after some time, and if the job has stopped, you will get a status of `'STOPPED'`:

```
>>> algobulls_connection.get_backtesting_job_status(strategy_code2)
{'data': 'STOPPED'}
```

MACD-Bracket-Order strategy – fetching backtesting logs in real time

After submitting a backtesting job on the AlgoBulls platform, the AlgoBulls backtesting engine starts executing the strategy. During its execution, every event that occurs and the decisions that have been made by the AlgoBulls backtesting engine are recorded with exact timestamps in the form of textual logs. Examples of recorded activities include the given strategy config, every new candle generated at regular intervals, trades punched in by your strategy, the entry and exit of positions created by these trades, waits for new candles, and so on. These logs are quintessential for validating the strategy's behavior and debugging behavioral or performance issues that are frequently encountered while developing a strategy.

In this recipe, you will fetch backtesting logs for your strategy. The logs start coming up as soon as your submitted backtesting job reaches the 'STARTED' state. The AlgoBulls platform allows you to fetch logs in real time, even while the backtesting job is still going on. You can get insights into the strategy execution without having to wait for the backtesting job to complete, which is helpful when jobs are long-running. The pyalgotrading package provides a simple method for fetching the execution logs for a given strategy.

 Make sure you have gone through the last six recipes of the previous chapter to get a complete picture of the strategy class we will be using; that is, StrategyMACDBracketOrder.

Getting ready

Make sure the algobulls_connection and strategy_code2 objects are available in your Python namespace. Refer to the *MACD-Bracket-Order strategy – fetching the strategy* recipe of this chapter to set up the algobulls_connection and strategy_code2 objects.

How to do it...

We execute the following steps for this recipe:

1. Fetch the backtesting execution logs for `strategy_code2`:

```
>>> logs = algobulls_connection.get_backtesting_logs(
                                            strategy_code2)
>>> print(logs)
```

We get the following output (your output may differ):

```
[2020-07-30 17:27:25] Logs not available yet. Please retry in
sometime.
```

2. Fetch the backtesting execution logs for `strategy_code2` again after some time:

```
>>> logs = algobulls_connection.get_backtesting_logs(
                                            strategy_code2)
>>> print(logs)
```

We get the following output (your output may differ):

```
...
#######################################
 INITIALIZING ALGOBULLS CORE (v3.2.0 SECURE MODE)...
#######################################
...
[BT] [2020-07-01 09:15:00] [INFO] [tls] STARTING ALGOBULLS CORE...
...
[BT] [2020-07-01 12:30:00] [CRITICAL] [order] [PLACING NEW ORDER]
[2020-07-01 12:30:00] [1cbefcf395c344c88a228a1b01c32ef6] [BUY]
[NSE:TATASTEEL] [QTY:1] [QTY PENDING: 1] [ENTRY PRICE: 322.6]
[PRICE:322.6] [TRIGGER PRICE:None] [ORDER_TYPE_BRACKET]
[ORDER_CODE_INTRADAY] [ORDER_VARIETY_LIMIT] [ORDER_POSITION_ENTER]
[STOPLOSS TRIGGER:319.374] [TARGET TRIGGER:325.826] [TRAILING
STOPLOSS TRIGGER:322.6]
...
[BT] [2020-07-07 15:30:00] [INFO] [clock] Candle generation has
been stopped...
[BT] [2020-07-07 15:30:00] [INFO] [tls] Received event END OF
MARKET. Stopping Trading Core Engine...
[BT] [2020-07-07 15:30:00] [CRITICAL] [tls] [User: ALGOBULLS
VIRTUAL USER] Trading session completed
...
```

The complete output is not shown here. Please visit the following link to read the complete output: `https://github.com/algobulls/pyalgostrategypool/blob/master/pyalgostrategypool/sample/backtesting/strategy_macd_bracket_order/logs.txt`.

How it works...

In *step 1*, you use the `get_backtesting_logs()` method of the `algobulls_connection` object to fetch the strategy backtesting logs in real time. This method accepts strategy code as an argument. You pass `strategy_code2` here. The return data is a string. If you try this step immediately after submitting the job, you'll get a string that states that the logs are not ready yet (`[2020-07-30 17:27:25] Logs not available yet. Please retry in sometime.`). This happens if the backtesting job is in the `'STARTING'` state.

In *step 2*, you fetch the logs again after some time. If the job is out of the `'STARTING'` state, you start getting your strategy execution logs. You get the entire backtesting log every time you call the `get_backtesting_logs()` function.

There's more...

Once the backtesting job moves to the `'STOPPED'` state, no new logs are generated. You can fetch the complete logs at any time before you submit the next backtesting job for the same strategy. If a new backtesting job is submitted (for the same strategy), these logs will no longer be accessible via the `get_backtesting_logs()` method. You can save the fetched logs to a file if you'd like to refer to it at a later date.

MACD-Bracket-Order strategy – fetching a backtesting report – P&L table

After submitting a backtesting job on the AlgoBulls platform, the AlgoBulls backtesting engine starts executing the strategy. During its execution, along with the logs, the AlgoBulls backtesting engine also generates a P&L table in real time. This table holds information on every trade that's been punched in by the strategy. It also contains details on the mappings between entry and exit orders, the trade P&L, and the cumulative P&L, sorted chronologically, with the latest order first.

This table gives us insights into the strategy's overall performance with the help of individual and cumulative P&L numbers. The entry-exit order mapping also helps validate the strategy's behavior.

In this recipe, you will fetch the P&L table report for your strategy. This report is available as soon as the first trade is punched in by your strategy after you submit a backtesting job. The AlgoBulls platform allows you to fetch the P&L table in real time, even while the backtesting job is still going on. You can get insights into the strategy's performance without having to wait for the backtesting job to complete, which is helpful when jobs are long-running. The `pyalgotrading` package provides a simple method you can use to fetch the P&L table for a given strategy.

 Make sure you have gone through the last six recipes of the previous chapter to get a complete picture of the strategy class we will be using; that is, `StrategyMACDBracketOrder`.

Getting ready

Make sure the `algobulls_connection` and `strategy_code2` objects are available in your Python namespace. Refer to the *MACD-Bracket-Order strategy – fetching the strategy* recipe of this chapter to set up the `algobulls_connection` and `strategy_code2` objects.

How to do it...

Fetch the backtesting P&L report for `strategy_code2`:

```
>>> algobulls_connection.get_backtesting_report_pnl_table(strategy_code2)
```

We got the following output. Your output may differ (note that the following output has been split into multiple tables for representation purposes. You will see a single wide table in your Jupyter Notebook):

	instrument	entry_timestamp	entry_transaction_type	entry_quantity	entry_price
0	NSE_EQ:TATASTEEL	2020-07-07 14:45:00	SELL	1	329.3
1	NSE_EQ:TATASTEEL	2020-07-07 13:15:00	BUY	1	332.6
2	NSE_EQ:TATASTEEL	2020-07-06 13:30:00	SELL	1	339.65
3	NSE_EQ:TATASTEEL	2020-07-06 09:45:00	BUY	1	332.35
4	NSE_EQ:TATASTEEL	2020-07-03 12:45:00	SELL	1	333.5
5	NSE_EQ:TATASTEEL	2020-07-03 12:30:00	BUY	1	334.45
6	NSE_EQ:TATASTEEL	2020-07-03 09:45:00	SELL	1	330.8
7	NSE_EQ:TATASTEEL	2020-07-01 12:30:00	BUY	1	322.6

	instrument	exit_timestamp	exit_transaction_type	exit_quantity	exit_price
0	NSE_EQ:TATASTEEL	2020-07-07 15:30:00	BUY	1	331
1	NSE_EQ:TATASTEEL	2020-07-07 13:30:00	SELL	1	329.25
2	NSE_EQ:TATASTEEL	2020-07-06 15:30:00	BUY	1	338.85
3	NSE_EQ:TATASTEEL	2020-07-06 10:00:00	SELL	1	335.65
4	NSE_EQ:TATASTEEL	2020-07-03 13:00:00	BUY	1	330.15
5	NSE_EQ:TATASTEEL	2020-07-03 12:45:00	SELL	1	333.5
6	NSE_EQ:TATASTEEL	2020-07-03 10:00:00	BUY	1	334.1
7	NSE_EQ:TATASTEEL	2020-07-01 15:30:00	SELL	1	324.1

	pnl_absolute	pnl_percentage	pnl_cumulative_absolute	pnl_cumulative_percentage
0	-1.7	-0.52	-0.35	-0.12
1	-3.35	-1.01	1.35	0.4
2	0.8	0.24	4.7	1.41
3	3.3	0.99	3.9	1.17
4	3.35	1	0.6	0.18
5	-0.95	-0.28	-2.75	-0.82
6	-3.3	-1	-1.8	-0.54
7	1.5	0.46	1.5	0.46

How it works...

In this recipe, you use the `get_backtesting_report_pnl_table()` method of the `algobulls_connection` object to fetch the backtesting P&L table in real time. This method accepts strategy code as an argument. You pass `strategy_code2` here. The return data is a `pandas.DataFrame` object with multiple columns, described as follows:

- `instrument`: Financial instrument for which the trade was entered.
- `entry_timestamp`: The timestamp at which the entry order was placed. (Note that it may remain in the `'OPEN'` state for a while before it goes to `'COMPLETE'` state. The time for this state transition can be found using the order history table, as explained in the last recipe of this chapter.)

- `entry_transaction_type`: Entry order transaction type (either BUY or SELL).
- `entry_quantity`: Entry order quantity.
- `entry_price`: Price at which the entry order gets executed and goes to the 'COMPLETE' state.
- `exit_timestamp`: The timestamp at which the exit order was placed. (Note that it may remain in the 'OPEN' state for a while before it goes to the 'COMPLETE' state.)
- `exit_transaction_type`: Exit order transaction type (either BUY or SELL).
- `exit_quantity`: Exit order quantity.
- `exit_price`: Price at which the exit order gets executed and goes to the 'COMPLETE' state.
- `pnl_absolute`: Difference between the exit order execution price and the entry order execution price. Mathematically, this can be represented as (*exit_price - entry_price*)*exit_quantity* for a long trade and (*entry_price - exit_price*)*exit_quantity* for a short trade. A positive value would imply that the trade is a profit-making trade. A negative value would imply that the trade is a loss-making trade.
- `pnl_percentage`: Percentage of profit or loss with respect to the entry price. Mathematically, this is *pnl_absolute / entry_price / exit_quantity × 100*.
- `pnl_cumulative_absolute`: Cumulative profit or loss. Mathematically, this is the sum of all the `pnl_absolute` values of the previous trades. This number gives us direct insight into the strategy's performance against the simulation time.
- `pnl_cumulative_percentage`: Percentage of cumulative profit or loss with respect to the entry price. Mathematically, this is *pnl_cumulative / entry_price / exit_quantity × 100*.

There's more...

Once the backtesting job moves to the 'STOPPED' state, the P&L table report won't update anymore. You can fetch the complete P&L report any time before you submit the next backtesting job for the same strategy. If a new backtesting job is submitted (for the same strategy), this report will no longer be accessible via the `get_backtesting_report_pnl_table()` method. You can save the fetched report as a `.csv` file if you'd like to refer to it at a later date.

MACD-Bracket-Order strategy – fetching a backtesting report – statistics table

After submitting a backtesting job on the AlgoBulls platform, the AlgoBulls backtesting engine starts executing the strategy. During its execution, along with the logs and P&L table, the AlgoBulls backtesting engine also generates a summary from the P&L table in real time. This summary is a table of statistics containing various statistical numbers such as Net P&L (absolute and percentage), Max Drawdown (absolute and percentage), count of total trades, winning trades, losing trades, long trades and short trades, maximum gain and minimum gain (or maximum loss), and the average profit per winning and losing trade. This table gives us an instant overview of the strategy's overall performance.

In this recipe, you will fetch the statistics table report for your strategy. This report is available as soon as the first trade is punched in by your strategy after you submit a backtesting job. The AlgoBulls platform allows you to fetch the statistics table in real time, even while the backtesting job is still going on. You can get insights into the strategy performance without having to wait for the backtesting job to complete, which is helpful when jobs are long-running. The pyalgotrading package provides a simple method we can use to fetch the statistics table for a given strategy.

 Make sure you have gone through the last six recipes of the previous chapter to get a complete picture of the strategy class we will be using; that is, StrategyMACDBracketOrder.

Getting ready

Make sure the algobulls_connection and strategy_code2 objects are available in your Python namespace. Refer to the *MACD-Bracket-Order strategy – fetching the strategy* recipe of this chapter to set up the algobulls_connection and strategy_code2 objects.

How to do it...

Fetch the backtesting statistics report for strategy_code2:

```
>>> algobulls_connection.get_backtesting_report_statistics(strategy_code2)
```

We get the following output (your output may differ):

	highlight_type	highlight_value
0	Net PnL	-0.35
1	Net PnL %	-0.12
2	Max Drawdown	-2.75
3	Max Drawdown %	-0.82
4	Number of Trades	8
5	Number of Wins	4
6	Number of Looses	4
7	Number of Long Trades	4
8	Number of Short Trades	4
9	Max Gain	3.35
10	Min Gain	-3.35
11	Avg. Profit per winning trade	2.24
12	Avg. Profit per losing trade	-2.32

How it works...

In this recipe, you use the `get_backtesting_report_statistics()` method of the `algobulls_connection` object to fetch the backtesting statistics table in real time. This method accepts strategy code as an argument. You pass `strategy_code2` here. The return data is a `pandas.DataFrame` object with two columns – `Highlight` and `Value` – and multiple rows. The rows are described as follows:

- `Net PnL`: The cumulative backtesting P&L. This is also the `pnl_cumulative_absolute` value of the first entry in the P&L table.
- `Net PnL %`: The cumulative backtesting P&L percentage. This is also the `pnl_cumulative_percentage` value of the first entry in the P&L table.

- `Max Drawdown`: The lowest value in the `pnl_cumulative` column of the P&L table. This indicates the maximum loss your strategy has encountered during the execution.
- `Max Drawdown %`: Mathematically, this is *(Max Drawdown) / (corresponding entry_price) / exit_quantity × 100*.
- `Number of Trades`: Total trades (entry and exit counted as one) during the session.
- `Number of Wins`: Count of trades where the trade P&L was non-negative.
- `Number of Losses`: Count of trades where the trade P&L was negative.
- `Number of Long Trades`: Count of trades where the entry transaction type was `'BUY'`.
- `Number of Short Trades`: Count of trades where the entry transaction type was `'SELL'`.
- `Max Gain`: P&L of the trade with the maximum P&L value among all trades.
- `Min Gain`: P&L of the trade with the minimum P&L value among all trades.
- `Avg. Profit per winning trade`: Mathematically, this is *(Total P&L of winning trades) / (Count of winning trades)*.
- `Avg. Profit per losing trade`: Mathematically, this is *(Total P&L of losing trades) / (Count of losing trades)*.

There's more...

If the statistics table is fetched while the backtesting job is still running, the aforementioned numbers will be intermediate numbers, based on the trades that had been completed up until that time. The numbers may change as more trades are punched in, until the backtesting job completes.

Once the backtesting job moves to the `'STOPPED'` state, the statistics table will not change anymore. You can fetch the complete statistics table any time before you submit the next backtesting job for the same strategy. If a new backtesting job is submitted (for the same strategy), this table will no longer be accessible via the `get_backtesting_report_statistics()` method. You can save the fetched report as a `.csv` file if you'd like to refer to it at a later date.

MACD-Bracket-Order strategy – fetching a backtesting report – order history

After submitting a backtesting job on the AlgoBulls platform, the AlgoBulls backtesting engine starts executing the strategy. During its execution, along with the logs, the P&L table, and the statistics table, the AlgoBulls backtesting engine also generates an order history log in real time. This log contains the state transitions of every order, along with the timestamps and additional information (if any) for each order state. The order history log is crucial in understanding how long it has taken for a trade to go from an 'OPEN' to 'COMPLETE' or 'CANCELLED' state. For example, MARKET orders would immediately go from 'OPEN' to 'COMPLETE' but LIMIT orders may take a while, based on the market conditions, to go from 'OPEN' to 'COMPLETE' – they may even get 'CANCELLED'. All this information is available in the order history log. (Refer to the state machine diagrams in Chapter 6, *Placing Regular Orders on the Exchange*, for more information on order state transitions.)

In this recipe, you will fetch the order history log for your strategy. This log is available as soon as the first trade is punched in by your strategy after you submit a backtesting job. The AlgoBulls platform allows you to fetch the order history log in real time, even while the backtesting job is still going on. This helps us get details for orders in the end states, without having to wait for the backtesting job to complete. The pyalgotrading package provides a simple method we can use to fetch the order history log for a given strategy.

 Make sure you have gone through the last recipes of the previous chapter to get a complete picture of the strategy class we will be using; that is, StrategyMACDBracketOrder.

Getting ready

Make sure the algobulls_connection and strategy_code2 objects are available in your Python namespace. Refer to the *MACD-Bracket-Order strategy – fetching the strategy* recipe of this chapter to set up the algobulls_connection and strategy_code2 objects.

How to do it...

Fetch the backtesting order history report for `strategy_code2`:

```
>>> order_history =
algobulls_connection.get_backtesting_report_order_history(strategy_code2)
>>> print(order_history)
```

We get the following output (your output may differ):

```
...
+------------------+---------------------+------------------------------
-+------+
| INST             | TIME                | ID
| TT   |
|------------------+---------------------+------------------------------
-+------|
| NSE_EQ:TATASTEEL | 2020-07-03 10:00:00 | 03436b72ad8a47a8b29bb727876b0b95
| BUY  |
+------------------+---------------------+------------------------------
-+------+
+----+---------------------+-----------------------+-------+
|    | TIME                | STATE                 | MSG   |
|----+---------------------+-----------------------+-------|
| 0  | 2020-07-03 10:00:00 | PUT ORDER REQ RECEIVED |      |
| 1  | 2020-07-03 10:00:00 | VALIDATION PENDING    |       |
| 2  | 2020-07-03 10:00:00 | OPEN PENDING          |       |
| 3  | 2020-07-03 10:00:00 | TRIGGER PENDING       |       |
| 4  | 2020-07-03 12:30:00 | OPEN                  |       |
| 5  | 2020-07-03 12:30:00 | COMPLETE              |       |
+----+---------------------+-----------------------+-------+
+------------------+---------------------+------------------------------
-+------+
| INST             | TIME                | ID
| TT   |
|------------------+---------------------+------------------------------
-+------|
| NSE_EQ:TATASTEEL | 2020-07-03 10:00:00 | 62458cf47d5f4a12b6c31c490451fdb0
| BUY  |
+------------------+---------------------+------------------------------
-+-----
+
+----+---------------------+-----------------------+-------+
|    | TIME                | STATE                 | MSG   |
|----+---------------------+-----------------------+-------|
| 0  | 2020-07-03 10:00:00 | PUT ORDER REQ RECEIVED |      |
| 1  | 2020-07-03 10:00:00 | VALIDATION PENDING    |       |
| 2  | 2020-07-03 10:00:00 | OPEN PENDING          |       |
```

```
|   3 | 2020-07-03 10:00:00 | OPEN                   |       |       |
|   4 | 2020-07-03 12:30:00 | CANCEL PENDING         |       |       |
|   5 | 2020-07-03 12:30:00 | CANCELLED              |       |       |
+-----+---------------------+------------------------+-------+
  . . .
```

The complete output is not shown here. Please visit the following link to read the complete output: `https://github.com/algobulls/pyalgostrategypool/blob/master/pyalgostrategypool/sample/backtesting/strategy_macd_bracket_order/oms_order_history.log`.

How it works…

In this recipe, you use the `get_backtesting_report_order_history()` method of the `algobulls_connection` object to fetch order history logs in real time. This method accepts strategy code as an argument. You pass `strategy_code2` here. The return data is a string, described as follows:

For every order, the log contains the following information:

- A descriptive table of the order, with the following mentioned columns:
    - `INST`: Financial instrument of the order
    - `TIME`: Time at which the order was placed
    - `ID`: The unique ID of the order
    - `TT`: The order transaction type (`BUY` or `SELL`)

    An example of the table is shown as follows:

    ```
    +-----------------+---------------------+-----------------------
    ---------+------+
    | INST            | TIME                | ID
    | TT   |
    |-----------------+---------------------+-----------------------
    ---------+------|
    | NSE_EQ:TATASTEEL | 2020-07-03 10:00:00 |
    03436b72ad8a47a8b29bb727876b0b95 | BUY  |
    +-----------------+---------------------+-----------------------
    ---------+------+
    ```

This information will help you find this exact order in the strategy execution log.

- An order state transition table, with the following columns:
  - TIME: Timestamp at which the order enters the state represented by the 'STATE' column.
  - STATE: The order enters this 'STATE' column at the timestamp mentioned in the 'TIME' column.
  - MSG: Additional message from OMS for any unexpected state transitions; for example, orders that go to the REJECTED state have a message from the OMS stating the reason for their rejection. This column is usually empty.

An example of the table is shown as follows:

```
+----+---------------------+------------------------+-------+
|    | TIME                | STATE                  | MSG   |
|----+---------------------+------------------------+-------|
|  0 | 2020-07-03 10:00:00 | PUT ORDER REQ RECEIVED |       |
|  1 | 2020-07-03 10:00:00 | VALIDATION PENDING     |       |
|  2 | 2020-07-03 10:00:00 | OPEN PENDING           |       |
|  3 | 2020-07-03 10:00:00 | TRIGGER PENDING        |       |
|  4 | 2020-07-03 12:30:00 | OPEN                   |       |
|  5 | 2020-07-03 12:30:00 | COMPLETE               |       |
+----+---------------------+------------------------+-------+
```

From this table, you can see that upon placing the order at 10:00 a.m., it transitions to the 'OPEN PENDING' state. It stays there for 2.5 hours before transitioning to the 'COMPLETE' state. This is expected as the order is a bracket limit order.

There's more...

Once the backtesting job moves to the 'STOPPED' state, no new order history logs are generated. You can fetch the complete order history logs any time before you submit the next backtesting job for the same strategy. If a new backtesting job is submitted (for the same strategy), these logs will no longer be accessible via the get_backtesting_report_order_history() method. You can save the fetched logs to a file if you'd like to refer to them at a later date.

Algorithmic Trading – Paper Trading
10

After building algorithmic trading strategies in `Chapter 8`, *Algorithmic Trading Strategies – Coding Step by Step*, and successfully backtesting them with satisfactory results in the previous chapter, the next step is to paper trade the strategies in live markets.

Paper trading is the method of executing a trading strategy in the live market hours by simply recording trades coming from the strategy execution in real time. The trades are not executed with real money via a broker. Earlier, this recording of trades was done on paper, hence the name **paper trading**. These virtual trades can be used for analyzing the risk and return metrics. Typical paper trading metrics include **profit and loss (P&L)**, maximum drawdown, the count of total trades, winning trades, losing trades, long trades and short trades, average profit per winning and losing trade, and more. Paper trading should be performed for at least a few trading days and until these metrics meet the necessary requirements, the entire process should be repeated, which consists of updating the strategy parameters and/or strategy implementation, followed by backtesting and paper trading.

The underlying idea behind paper trading is that the trading strategy can be executed in the live market, in a fashion almost similar to real trading, but without risking real money. Paper trading helps to ensure that the market scenarios from the past, for which backtesting was run, are still valid. If the market scenarios from the past do not prevail currently, even if backtesting results are profitable, paper trading results may turn out to be otherwise. This would suggest that the strategy parameters and/or strategy implementation needs more work before executing the strategy on real money.

For paper trading, a strategy configuration is required. It consists of multiple parameters, some of which are as follows:

- **Start and end times**: The time duration within the current day for which paper trading should be run.
- **Financial instrument(s)**: One or more financial instruments for which paper trading should be performed.
- **Candle interval**: One of the various possible candle intervals – for example, `1 minute`, `15 minutes`, `hour`, or `day`.
- **Strategy specific parameters**: Values for custom parameters defined in the strategy.
- **Strategy mode**: Either intraday or delivery. Intraday strategies punch intraday orders, which are squared-off at the end of the day. Delivery strategies punch delivery orders, which don't square-off at the end of the day and get carried forward to the next trading day.

A paper trading engine is required to perform paper trading on a given strategy. In this chapter, you will use the paper trading engine provided by AlgoBulls (`https://algobulls.com`), an algorithmic trading platform that makes its services available via its **developer options**. It provides a Python package called `pyalgotrading` (`https://github.com/algobulls/pyalgotrading`) to make use of these services.

You have already coded two algorithmic trading strategies in Chapter 8, *Algorithmic Trading Strategies – Coding Step by Step*. Recall that the strategy descriptions are as follows:

- **EMA-Regular-Order strategy**: A strategy based on the technical indicator EMA and regular orders. (The first six recipes of Chapter 8, *Algorithmic Trading Strategies – Coding Step by Step*.)
- **MACD-Bracket-Order strategy**: A strategy based on the technical indicator of MACD and bracket orders. (The latter six recipes of Chapter 8, *Algorithmic Trading Strategies – Coding Step by Step*.)

These strategies are also available as part of a Python package, `pyalgostrategypool`. You can install it using `pip`, as follows: `$ pip install pyalgostrategypool`.

You can also check them out on GitHub (`https://github.com/algobulls/pyalgostrategypool`).

As you have followed `Chapter 8`, *Algorithmic Trading Strategies – Coding Step by Step,* you have uploaded these two strategies to your AlgoBulls account. In this chapter, you will fetch these strategies from your AlgoBulls account and perform paper trading on them. After paper trading, you will get strategy execution logs and various reports – namely, a P&L report, a statistics report, and an order history. These logs and reports help validate the strategy performance and prepare it for real trading. By using `pyalgotrading`, you ensure that you focus on developing and validating the strategy via paper trading without worrying about the ecosystem needed for the strategy execution.

This chapter includes step-by-step recipes for both the previously mentioned strategies, from setting up a connection with the AlgoBulls platform, fetching the strategy, and running paper trading jobs to fetching the execution logs and fetching various types of reports.

In this chapter, you will cover the following recipes:

- EMA-Regular-Order strategy – fetching the strategy
- EMA-Regular-Order strategy – paper trading the strategy
- EMA-Regular-Order strategy – fetching paper trading logs in real time
- EMA-Regular-Order strategy – fetching a paper trading report – P&L table
- EMA-Regular-Order strategy – fetching a paper trading report – statistics table
- EMA-Regular-Order strategy – fetching a paper trading report – order history
- MACD-Bracket-Order strategy – fetching the strategy
- MACD-Bracket-Order strategy – paper trading the strategy
- MACD-Bracket-Order strategy – fetching paper trading logs in real time
- MACD-Bracket-Order strategy – fetching a paper trading report – P&L table
- MACD-Bracket-Order strategy – fetching a paper trading report – statistics table
- MACD-Bracket-Order strategy – fetching a paper trading report - order history

Paper trading is meaningful only if run during the live market hours, unlike backtesting, which can be run at any time. Please make sure you try out the recipes of this chapter during the live market hours.

Technical requirements

You will need the following to successfully execute the recipes in this chapter:

- Python 3.7+
- Python package:
  - pyalgotrading ($ pip install pyalgotrading)

The latest Jupyter notebook for this chapter can be found on GitHub at https://github.com/PacktPublishing/Python-Algorithmic-Trading-Cookbook/tree/master/Chapter10.

EMA-Regular-Order strategy – fetching the strategy

In this recipe, you will fetch the strategy class, StrategyEMARegularOrder, from your account on the AlgoBulls platform, which you will have uploaded while going through the *EMA-Regular-Order strategy – uploading the strategy on the AlgoBulls trading platform* recipe in Chapter 8, *Algorithmic Trading Strategies – Coding Step by Step*. This recipe starts by setting up a connection to the AlgoBulls platform, querying all the available strategies in your account, and fetching details of the required strategy class, StrategyEMARegularOrder.

Make sure you have gone through the first six recipes of Chapter 8, *Algorithmic Trading Strategies – Coding Step by Step,* to get a complete picture of the strategy class used, StrategyEMARegularOrder.

How to do it...

We execute the following steps for this recipe:

1. Import the necessary modules:

   ```
   >>> from pyalgotrading.algobulls import AlgoBullsConnection
   ```

2. Create a new AlgoBulls connection object:

   ```
   >>> algobulls_connection = AlgoBullsConnection()
   ```

3. Fetch the authorization URL:

```
>>> algobulls_connection.get_authorization_url()
```

We get the following output:

```
Please login to this URL with your AlgoBulls credentials and get
your developer access token: https://app.algobulls.com/user/login
'https://app.algobulls.com/user/login'
```

4. Log in to the preceding link with your AlgoBulls credentials, fetch your token, and set it here (refer to *Appendix II* for more details):

```
>>> algobulls_connection.set_access_token(
                '80b7a69b168c5b3f15d56688841a8f2da5e2ab2c')
```

5. Fetch and display all strategies you have created and uploaded so far:

```
>>> all_strategies = algobulls_connection.get_all_strategies()
>>> all_strategies
```

We get the following output. Your output may differ (make sure you have followed the recipes in `Chapter 8`, *Algorithmic Trading Strategies – Coding Step by Step*, to get a similar output):

	strategyCode	strategyName
0	49287246f9704bbcbad76ade9e2091d9	EMA Regular Order Strategy
1	4faf514fe096432b8e9f80f5951bd2ea	MACD Bracket Order Strategy

6. Fetch and display the strategy code for the first strategy:

```
>>> strategy_code1 = all_strategies.iloc[0]['strategyCode']
>>> strategy_code1
```

We get the following output (your output may differ):

```
'49287246f9704bbcbad76ade9e2091d9'
```

7. Before paper trading your strategy, you can inspect it to ensure you have the right strategy:

```
>>> strategy_details1 = \
        algobulls_connection.get_strategy_details(strategy_code1)
>>> print(strategy_details1)
```

We get the following output:

```
class StrategyEMARegularOrder(StrategyBase):

    def __init__(self, *args, **kwargs):
        super().__init__(*args, **kwargs)

        self.timeperiod1 = self.strategy_parameters['timeperiod1']
        self.timeperiod2 = self.strategy_parameters['timeperiod2']

        self.main_order = None

    def initialize(self):
        self.main_order = {}

    @staticmethod
    def name():
        return 'EMA Regular Order Strategy'
    ....
    def strategy_exit_position(self, candle, instrument,
                                    sideband_info):
        if sideband_info['action'] == 'EXIT':
            self.main_order[instrument].exit_position()
            self.main_order[instrument] = None
            return True

        return False
```

The complete output is not shown here. Please visit the following link to read the complete output: `https://github.com/algobulls/pyalgostrategypool/blob/master/pyalgostrategypool/strategy_ema_regular_order.py`

How it works...

You import the necessary modules in *step 1*. In *step 2*, an instance of the `AlgoBullsConnection` class is created, named `algobulls_connection`. In *step 3*, you get the authorization URL using the `get_authorization_url()` method of the `algobulls_connection` object. This prints the authorization URL. You should visit this URL from your web browser to sign in to the AlgoBulls platform and fetch your developer access token. (You can find more details with screenshots in *Appendix II* on fetching developer access tokens from the AlgoBulls platform.) You copy the access token and set it in *step 4* using the `set_access_token()` method of `algobulls_connection`. If the token is accepted, a successful connection is set up with the AlgoBulls platform.

In *step 5*, you fetch all strategies you have created and uploaded on the AlgoBulls platform so far. You use the `get_all_strategies()` method for this step and assign it to a new variable, `all_strategies`. This variable is a `pandas.DataFrame` object with the `strategyCode` and `strategyName` columns. This table holds information on the strategy codes and strategy names you have uploaded previously. If you have followed the *EMA-Regular-Order strategy – uploading the strategy on the AlgoBulls trading platform* recipe from `Chapter 8`, *Algorithmic Trading Strategies – Coding Step by Step*, you will find a strategy with the name `EMA-Regular-Order strategy`. In *step 6*, you assign the strategy code of the `EMA-Regular-Order strategy` strategy to a new variable, `strategy_code1`. The strategy code is shown in the output of this step. This strategy code is unique for every strategy on the AlgoBulls platform.

Finally, in *step 7*, you ensure that the strategy referred by `strategy_code1` is indeed the one you have uploaded earlier (in the *EMA-Regular-Order strategy – uploading the strategy on the AlgoBulls trading platform* recipe in `Chapter 8`, *Algorithmic Trading Strategies – Coding Step by Step*). You use the `get_strategy_details()` method of the `algobulls_connection` object to inspect the strategy. This method takes strategy code as an argument. You pass `strategy_code1` here. This method returns the entire class code as a string. You assign it to a new variable, `strategy_details1`, and display it.

If you would like to change the class code referred to by `strategy_code1`, as shown in *step 7*, please refer to the *There's more...* section of the *EMA-Regular-Order strategy – uploading the strategy on the AlgoBulls trading platform* recipe in `Chapter 8`, *Algorithmic Trading Strategies – Coding Step by Step*.

EMA-Regular-Order strategy – paper trading the strategy

In this recipe, you will perform paper trading on the `EMA-Regular-Order` strategy. You must have fetched this strategy from your account on the AlgoBulls platform in the previous recipe. You will leverage the paper trading functionality facilitated by `pyalgotrading` for this recipe, which in turn submits a paper trading job on the AlgoBulls platform.

Once submitted, paper trading will be run by the AlgoBulls paper trading engine. You can query the status any time to know the state of the paper trading job. The job goes through the following states, in the following given order:

- 'STARTING' (intermediate state)
- 'STARTED' (stable state)
- 'STOPPING' (intermediate state)
- 'STOPPED' (stable state)

On submitting a job, it starts with an intermediate state, 'STARTING'. In this state, the AlgoBulls paper trading engine will fetch the strategy and get the execution environment ready, which may take a couple of minutes. Once done, the job moves to the 'STARTED' state. The paper trading strategy happens in this stage. Here, it stays as long as it takes for paper trading to complete. Once done, the job moves to an intermediate state, 'STOPPING'. In this state, the AlgoBulls paper trading engine cleans up the resources allocated for this job, which usually takes less than a minute. Finally, the job moves to the 'STOPPED' state.

If you have already submitted a strategy paper trading job, you cannot submit another job for the same strategy until the first job completes. This means you have to wait for the first job to move to the 'STOPPED' state. If the first job is long-running and you would like to stop it immediately, you can submit a stop job request via pyalgotrading. You need to ensure the job is in the 'STARTED' state before submitting the request.

The following state machine diagram demonstrates the various states and transitions of a paper trading job during its lifetime on the AlgoBulls platform:

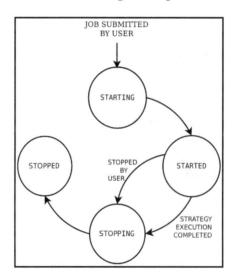

After submitting a paper trading job, you can fetch logs and reports for the strategy execution in real time. The logs and reports help validate the strategy performance and debug any potential issues.

 Make sure you have gone through the first six recipes of Chapter 8, *Algorithmic Trading Strategies – Coding Step by Step* to get a complete picture of the strategy class used, StrategyEMARegularORder.

Getting ready

Make sure the algobulls_connection and strategy_code1 objects are available in your Python namespace. Refer to the first recipe of this chapter to set up the algobulls_connection and strategy_code1 objects.

How to do it...

We execute the following steps for this recipe:

1. Import the necessary modules:

```
>>> from datetime import time
>>> from pyalgotrading.constants import *
```

2. Search for an instrument using its trading symbol as a keyword. Assign the returned object to instruments:

```
>>> instruments = algobulls_connection.search_instrument('SBIN')
>>> instruments
```

We get the following output (your output may differ):

```
[{'id': 7, 'value': 'NSE:SBIN'}]
```

3. Get value for the instrument of choice from instruments:

```
>>> instrument = instruments[0]['value']
>>> instrument
```

We get the following output:

```
'NSE:SBIN'
```

4. Submit a paper trading job for `strategy_code1`:

```
>>> algobulls_connection.papertrade(strategy_code=strategy_code1,
        start_time=time(hour=9, minute=15),
        end_time=time(hour=15, minute=30),
        instrument=instrument,
        lots=1,
        strategy_parameters={
            'timeperiod1': 5,
            'timeperiod2': 12
        },
        candle_interval=CandleInterval.MINUTES_15)
```

We get the following output:

```
Setting Strategy Config... Success.
Submitting PAPERTRADING job... Success.
```

5. Check the status of the submitted paper trading job:

```
>>> algobulls_connection.get_papertrading_job_status(
                                        strategy_code1)
```

We get the following output:

```
{'data': 'STARTING'}
```

6. Check the status of the submitted job again after some time:

```
>>> algobulls_connection.get_papertrading_job_status(
                                        strategy_code1)
```

We get the following output:

```
{'data': 'STARTED'}
```

How it works...

In *step 1*, you import the `time` class from the `datetime` module and all the constants from the `pyalgotrading.constants` module. In *step 2*, you fetch the instrument for which you would like to paper trade the strategy, `EMA-Regular-Order` strategy, using the `search_instrument()` method of the `algobulls_connection` object. The `search_instrument()` method accepts a search string as an argument, which should be the trading symbol, in part or complete, of the instrument you are interested in. You pass `'SBIN'` here. This function returns a list with details of instruments that match the search string. There could be multiple instruments that could have the search string in their trading symbols. In *step 3*, you fetch the value of the first matched instrument and assign it to a new variable, `instrument`.

In *step 4*, you submit a paper trading job using the `papertrade()` method of the `algobulls_connection()` object. It takes the following arguments:

- `strategy_code`: The strategy code of the strategy for which paper trading has to be performed. This should be a string. You pass `strategy_code1` here.
- `start_time`: Today's time from when paper trading should be started. Should be a `datetime.time` object. Here, you pass an object holding the value 9 hours 15 – `time(hour=9, minute=15)`. Refer to the first recipe of this book for details on creating a `time` object.
- `end_time`: Today's time until when paper trading should be performed. This object should hold a time value ahead of the value held by `start_time`. Should be a `datetime.time` instance. Here, you pass an object holding the value 15 hours 30 – `time(hour=15, minute=30)`.
- `instrument`: The financial instrument for which paper trading should be run. Historical data will be fetched for this instrument. Should be a string. You pass `instrument` here.
- `lots`: The number of lots for which paper trading should be performed. This should be an integer. The quantity is calculated by the strategy as *number of lots × lot size of the financial instrument*. You pass 1 here.
- `strategy_parameters`: The parameter names and values expected by the strategy. This should be a dictionary, with `parameter-name` and `parameter-value` as key-value pairs. You pass the following parameters here:
  - `timeperiod1: 5`
  - `timeperiod2: 12`

(Recall that parameters for EMA-Regular-Order strategy have been defined in its `__init__()` method, as shown in the first recipe of `Chapter 8`, *Algorithmic Trading Strategies – Coding Step by Step*).

- `candle_interval`: The candle interval for the historical data fetched for paper trading. This should be an enum of the type `CandleInterval`. You pass `CandleInterval.MINUTES_15` here. (The `CandleInterval` enum provides various enums for candle intervals, some of which are `MINUTE_1`, `MINUTES_3`, `MINUTES_5`, `MINUTES_10`, `MINUTES_15`, `MINUTES_30`, `HOUR`, and `DAY`.)

If the job submission is successful, you will see `Success` messages printed by the `papertrade()` function.

Once a job is submitted, it takes a while to start. After starting, it may take some time to finish depending on the duration of paper trading specified using the `start_time` and `end_time` arguments. Usually, paper trading is run for the entire trading day, which means the job would be running for 6–8 hours.

In *step 5*, you fetch the job status using the `get_papertrading_job_status()` method of the `algobulls_connection` object. You pass `strategy_code1` as the argument here. This method returns a dictionary with a single key-value pair, the *data* and the *job* status. If you query the status immediately after placing the job, you get `'STARTING'` as the status. In *step 6*, you query the status again after some time, and if the job has started, you get the status as `'STARTED'`.

A successful submission implies that the minimum inputs needed to paper trade a strategy have been passed in the required format. It, however, does not ensure that the strategy will run without errors. The strategy execution may still run into errors during paper trading. To debug execution issues, you would need to fetch the output logs, which is explained in the next recipe. Possible reasons for errors could be either bugs in the strategy class Python code or an incomplete `strategy_parameters` dictionary passed to the `papertrade()` function.

There's more...

If a job is running for a long time and you would like to stop it before its completion, you can use the `stop_papertrading_job()` method of the `algobulls_connection` object. This method accepts strategy code as an argument. You pass `strategy_code1` here. This method submits a stop request to the AlgoBulls paper trading engine. If the request is accepted, you see a `Success` message here:

```
>>> algobulls_connection.stop_papertrading_job(strategy_code1)
    Stopping PAPERTRADING job... Success.
```

If you query the status after submitting the stop request, you get the status as `'STOPPING'`:

```
>>> algobulls_connection.get_papertrading_job_status(strategy_code1)
{'data': 'STOPPING'}
```

If you query the status again after some time, and if the job has stopped, you get the status as `'STOPPED'`:

```
>>> algobulls_connection.get_papertrading_job_status(strategy_code1)
{'data': 'STOPPED'}
```

EMA-Regular-Order strategy – fetching paper trading logs in real time

After submitting a paper trading job on the AlgoBulls platform, the AlgoBulls paper trading engine starts executing the strategy. During the execution, every event that occurs and decisions taken by the AlgoBulls paper trading engine are recorded with exact timestamps in the form of textual logs. Some examples of recorded activities include the given strategy config, every new candle generated at regular intervals, trades punched by your strategy, the entry and exit of the positions created by these trades, waits for new candles, and so on. These logs are quintessential in validating the strategy behavior and debugging behavioral or performance issues that are frequently encountered while developing a strategy.

In this recipe, you will fetch paper trading logs for your strategy. The logs start coming up as soon as your submitted paper trading job reaches the `'STARTED'` state (refer to the preceding recipe for more information on the states of a paper trading job). The AlgoBulls platform allows you to fetch logs in real time, even while the paper trading job is still going on. You can get insights into the strategy execution without having to wait for the paper trading job to complete. This is helpful as paper trading jobs are usually long-running. The `pyalgotrading` package provides a simple method to fetch the execution logs for a given strategy.

 Make sure you have gone through the first six recipes of Chapter 8, *Algorithmic Trading Strategies – Coding Step by Step*, to get a complete picture of the strategy class used, `StrategyEMARegularOrder`.

Getting ready

Make sure the `algobulls_connection` and `strategy_code1` objects are available in your Python namespace. Refer to the first recipe of this chapter to set up the `algobulls_connection` and `strategy_code1` objects.

How to do it...

We execute the following steps for this recipe:

1. Fetch the paper trading execution logs for `strategy_code1`:

```
>>> logs = algobulls_connection.get_papertrading_logs(
                                            strategy_code1)
>>> print(logs)
```

We get the following output (your output may differ):

```
[2020-07-09 09:12:18] Logs not available yet. Please retry in
sometime.
```

2. Fetch the paper trading execution logs for `strategy_code1` again after some time:

```
>>> logs = algobulls_connection.get_papertrading_logs(
                                            strategy_code1)
>>> print(logs)
```

We get the following output (your output may differ):

```
...
#########################################
 INITIALIZING ALGOBULLS CORE (v3.2.0 SECURE MODE)...
#########################################
[2020-07-09 09:12:31] Welcome ALGOBULLS VIRTUAL USER!
[2020-07-09 09:12:31] Reading strategy...
...
[PT] [2020-07-09 09:15:00] [INFO] [tls] STARTING ALGOBULLS CORE...
...
[PT] [2020-07-09 10:30:00] [CRITICAL] [order] [PLACING NEW ORDER]
[2020-07-09 10:30:00] [96c24ca4b3e448f381fc5c2bc52f7a29] [BUY]
[NSE:SBIN] [QTY:1] [QTY PENDING: 1] [ENTRY PRICE: 194.7]
[PRICE:None] [TRIGGER PRICE:None] [ORDER_TYPE_REGULAR]
[ORDER_CODE_INTRADAY] [ORDER_VARIETY_MARKET] [ORDER_POSITION_ENTER]
...
[PT] [2020-07-09 15:30:00] [INFO] [clock] Candle generation has
been stopped...
[PT] [2020-07-09 15:30:00] [INFO] [tls] Received event END OF
MARKET. Stopping Trading Core Engine...
[PT] [2020-07-09 15:30:00] [INFO] [tls] Exiting all open positions
with order code: ORDER_CODE_INTRADAY (if any)...
[PT] [2020-07-09 15:30:00] [CRITICAL] [tls] [User: ALGOBULLS
VIRTUAL USER] Trading session completed
...
```

The complete output is not shown here. Please visit the following link to read the complete output: `https://github.com/algobulls/pyalgostrategypool/blob/master/pyalgostrategypool/sample/papertrading/strategy_ema_regular_order/logs.txt`

How it works...

In *step 1*, you use the `get_papertrading_logs()` method of the `algobulls_connection` object to fetch the strategy paper trading logs in real time. This method accepts strategy code as an argument. You pass `strategy_code1` here. The return data is a string. If you try this step immediately after submitting the job, you get a string that says the logs are not ready yet (`[2020-07-09 09:14:18] Logs not available yet. Please retry in sometime.`). This happens if the paper trading job is in the `'STARTING'` state.

In *step 2*, you fetch the logs again after some time. If the job is out of the `'STARTING'` state, you start getting your strategy execution logs. You get the entire paper trading logs every time you call the `get_papertrading_logs()` function.

There's more...

Once the paper trading job moves to the `'STOPPED'` state, no new logs are generated. You can fetch the complete logs any time before you submit the next paper trading job for the same strategy. If a new paper trading job is submitted (for the same strategy), these logs will no longer be accessible via the `get_papertrading_logs()` method. You can save the fetched logs to a file if you'd like to refer to it at a later point in time.

EMA-Regular-Order strategy – fetching a paper trading report – P&L table

After submitting a paper trading job on the AlgoBulls platform, the AlgoBulls paper trading engine starts executing the strategy. During the execution, along with the logs, the AlgoBulls paper trading engine also generates a P&L table in real time. This table holds information on every trade punched by the strategy. It also has details on the mapping between entry and exit orders and the trade P&L and cumulative P&L, sorted chronologically, with the latest order first. This table gives an insight into the overall strategy performance with the help of individual and cumulative P&L numbers. The entry-exit order mapping also helps validate the strategy behavior.

In this recipe, you will fetch the P&L table report for your strategy. This report is available as soon as the first trade is punched by your strategy after you submit a paper trading job. The AlgoBulls platform allows you to fetch the P&L table in real time, even while the paper trading job is still going on. You can get insights into the strategy performance without having to wait for the paper trading job to complete. This is helpful as paper trading jobs are usually long-running. The `pyalgotrading` package provides a simple method to fetch the P&L table for a given strategy.

 Make sure you have gone through the first six recipes of `Chapter 8`, *Algorithmic Trading Strategies – Coding Step by Step*, to get a complete picture of the strategy class used, `StrategyEMARegularOrder`.

Getting ready

Make sure the `algobulls_connection` and `strategy_code1` objects are available in your Python namespace. Refer to the first recipe of this chapter to set up the `algobulls_connection` and `strategy_code1` objects.

How to do it...

Fetch the paper trading P&L report for `strategy_code1`:

```
>>> algobulls_connection.get_papertrading_report_pnl_table(strategy_code1)
```

We get the following output. Your output may differ (note that the following output has been split into multiple tables for representation purposes. You will see a single wide table in your Jupyter notebook):

	instrument	entry_timestamp	entry_transaction_type	entry_quantity	entry_price
0	NSE_EQ:SBIN	2020-07-09 12:45:00	BUY	1	194.45
1	NSE_EQ:SBIN	2020-07-09 11:30:00	SELL	1	194.05
2	NSE_EQ:SBIN	2020-07-09 11:15:00	BUY	1	194.75
3	NSE_EQ:SBIN	2020-07-09 10:45:00	SELL	1	194
4	NSE_EQ:SBIN	2020-07-09 10:30:00	BUY	1	194.7

	instrument	exit_timestamp	exit_transaction_type	exit_quantity	exit_price
0	NSE_EQ:SBIN	2020-07-09 15:30:00	SELL	1	200
1	NSE_EQ:SBIN	2020-07-09 12:45:00	BUY	1	194.45
2	NSE_EQ:SBIN	2020-07-09 11:30:00	SELL	1	194.05
3	NSE_EQ:SBIN	2020-07-09 11:15:00	BUY	1	194.75
4	NSE_EQ:SBIN	2020-07-09 10:45:00	SELL	1	194

	pnl_absolute	pnl_percentage	pnl_cumulative_absolute	pnl_cumulative_percentage
0	5.55	2.85	3	1.53
1	-0.4	-0.21	-2.55	-1.32
2	-0.7	-0.36	-2.15	-1.11
3	-0.75	-0.39	-1.45	-0.75
4	-0.7	-0.36	-0.7	-0.36

How it works...

In this recipe, you use the `get_papertrading_report_pnl_table()` method of the `algobulls_connection` object to fetch the paper trading P&L table in real time. This method accepts strategy code as an argument. You pass `strategy_code1` here. The return data is a `pandas.DataFrame` object with multiple columns, described as follows:

- `instrument`: Financial instrument for which trade was entered.
- `entry_timestamp`: The timestamp at which the entry order was placed. (Note that it may remain in the `'OPEN'` state for a while before it goes to the `'COMPLETE'` state. The time for this state transition can be found using the order history table, explained in the sixth recipe of this chapter.)

- `entry_transaction_type`: The entry order transaction type (either BUY or SELL).
- `entry_quantity`: The entry order quantity.
- `entry_price`: The price at which the entry order gets executed and goes to the 'COMPLETE' state.
- `exit_timestamp`: The timestamp at which the exit order was placed. (Note that it may remain in the 'OPEN' state for a while before it goes to 'COMPLETE' state.)
- `exit_transaction_type`: The exit order transaction type (either BUY or SELL).
- `exit_quantity`: The exit order quantity.
- `exit_price`: The price at which the exit order gets executed and goes to the 'COMPLETE' state.
- `pnl_absolute`: The difference between the exit order execution price and entry order execution price. Mathematically, this is (*exit_price - entry_price*)**exit_quantity* for a long trade and (*entry_price - exit_price*)**exit_quantity* for a short trade. A positive value would imply that the trade is a profit-making trade. A negative value would imply that the trade is a loss-making trade.
- `pnl_percentage`: The percentage of profit or loss with respect to the entry price. Mathematically, this is *pnl_absolute / entry_price / exit_quantity* x 100.
- `pnl_cumulative_absolute`: Cumulative profit or loss. Mathematically, this is the sum of all the `pnl_absolute` values of the previous trades. This number gives a direct insight into the strategy performance against the simulation time.
- `pnl_cumulative_percentage`: The percentage of cumulative profit or loss with respect to the entry price. Mathematically, this is *pnl_cumulative / entry_price / exit_quantity* x 100.

There's more...

Once the paper trading job moves to the 'STOPPED' state, the P&L table report will not update anymore. You can fetch the complete P&L report any time before you submit the next paper trading job for the same strategy. If a new paper trading job is submitted (for the same strategy), this report will no longer be accessible via the `get_papertrading_report_pnl_table()` method. You can save the fetched report to a `.csv` file if you'd like to refer to it at a later point in time.

EMA-Regular-Order strategy – fetching a paper trading report – statistics table

After submitting a paper trading job on the AlgoBulls platform, the AlgoBulls paper trading engine starts executing the strategy. During the execution, along with the logs and the P&L table, the AlgoBulls paper trading engine also generates a summary from the P&L table in real time. This summary is a table of statistics containing various statistical numbers, such as Net P&L (absolute and percentage), Max Drawdown (absolute and percentage), the count of total trades, winning trades, losing trades, long trades, and short trades, maximum gain and minimum gain (or maximum loss), and the average profit per winning and losing trade. This table gives an instant overview of the overall strategy performance.

In this recipe, you will fetch the statistics table report for your strategy. This report is available as soon as the first trade is punched by your strategy after you submit a paper trading job. The AlgoBulls platform allows you to fetch the statistics table in real time, even while the paper trading job is still going on. You can get insights into the strategy performance without having to wait for the paper trading job to complete. This is helpful as paper trading jobs are usually long-running. The pyalgotrading package provides a simple method to fetch the statistics table for a given strategy.

 Make sure you have gone through the first six recipes of Chapter 8, *Algorithmic Trading Strategies – Coding Step by Step*, to get a complete picture of the strategy class used, StrategyEMARegularOrder.

Getting ready

Make sure the algobulls_connection and strategy_code1 objects are available in your Python namespace. Refer to the first recipe of this chapter to set up the algobulls_connection and strategy_code1 objects.

How to do it...

Fetch the paper trading statistics report for strategy_code1:

```
>>> algobulls_connection.get_papertrading_report_statistics(strategy_code1)
```

We get the following output (your output may differ):

	highlight_type	highlight_value
0	Net PnL	3.00
1	Net PnL %	1.53
2	Max Drawdown	-2.55
3	Max Drawdown %	-1.31
4	Number of Trades	5.00
5	Number of Wins	1.00
6	Number of Looses	4.00
7	Number of Long Trades	3.00
8	Number of Short Trades	2.00
9	Max Gain	5.55
10	Min Gain	-0.75
11	Avg. Profit per winning trade	5.55
12	Avg. Profit per losing trade	-0.64

How it works...

In this recipe, you use the `get_papertrading_report_statistics()` method of the `algobulls_connection` object to fetch the paper trading statistics table in real time. This method accepts strategy code as an argument. You pass `strategy_code1` here. The return data is a `pandas.DataFrame` object with two columns—`highlight_type` and `highlight_value`—and multiple rows. The rows are described as follows:

- `Net PnL`: The cumulative paper trading P&L. This is also the `pnl_cumulative_absolute` value of the first entry in the P&L table.
- `Net PnL %`: The cumulative paper trading P&L percentage. This is also the `pnl_cumulative_percentage` value of the first entry in the P&L table.
- `Max Drawdown`: The lowest value in the `pnl_cumulative` column of the P&L table. This indicates the maximum loss your strategy has encountered during the execution.

- Max Drawdown %: Mathematically, this is *(Max Drawdown) / (corresponding entry_price/exit_quantity x 100)*.
- Number of Trades: Total trades (entry and exit counted as one) during the session.
- Number of Wins: The count of trades where the trade P&L was non-negative.
- Number of Losses: The count of trades where the trade P&L was negative.
- Number of Long Trades: The count of trades where the entry transaction type was 'BUY'.
- Number of Short Trades: The count of trades where the entry transaction type was 'SELL'.
- Max Gain: The P&L of the trade with the maximum P&L value among all trades.
- Min Gain: The P&L of the trade with the minimum P&L value among all trades.
- Avg. Profit per winning trade: Mathematically, this is *(Total P&L of winning trades) / (Count of winning trades)*.
- Avg. Profit per losing trade: Mathematically, this is *(Total P&L of losing trades) / (Count of losing trades)*.

There's more...

If the statistics table is fetched while the paper trading job is still running, the previously mentioned numbers will be intermediate numbers, based on the trades completed until that time. The numbers may change as more trades are punched until the paper trading job completes.

Once the paper trading job moves to the 'STOPPED' state, the statistics table will not change anymore. You can fetch the complete statistics table any time before you submit the next paper trading job for the same strategy. If a new paper trading job is submitted (for the same strategy), this table will no longer be accessible via the get_papertrading_report_statistics() method. You can save the fetched report table to a .csv file if you'd like to refer to it at a later point in time.

EMA-Regular-Order strategy – fetching a paper trading report – order history

After submitting a paper trading job on the AlgoBulls platform, the AlgoBulls paper trading engine starts executing the strategy. During the execution, along with the logs, the P&L table, and statistics table, the AlgoBulls paper trading engine also generates an order history log in real time. This log contains state transitions of every order, along with the timestamps and additional information (if any) for each order state. The order history log is crucial in understanding how long it has taken for a trade to go from 'OPEN' to 'COMPLETE' or to the 'CANCELLED' state. For example, the MARKET orders would immediately go from an 'OPEN' to 'COMPLETE' state but the LIMIT orders may take a while, based on the market conditions, to go from an 'OPEN' to 'COMPLETE' state, or they may even get to 'CANCELLED'. All this information is available in the order history log. (Refer to the state machine diagrams in Chapter 6, *Placing Orders on the Exchange*, for more information on order state transitions.)

In this recipe, you will fetch the order history log for your strategy. This log is available as soon as the first trade is punched by your strategy after you submit a paper trading job. The AlgoBulls platform allows you to fetch the order history log in real time, even while the paper trading job is still going on. This helps us get details for orders in the end states without having to wait for the paper trading job to complete. The pyalgotrading package provides a simple method to fetch the order history log for a given strategy.

Make sure you have gone through the first six recipes of Chapter 8, *Algorithmic Trading Strategies – Coding Step by Step*, to get a complete picture of the strategy class used, StrategyEMARegularOrder.

Getting ready

Make sure the `algobulls_connection` and `strategy_code1` objects are available in your Python namespace. Refer to the first recipe of this chapter to set up the `algobulls_connection` and `strategy_code1` objects.

How to do it...

Fetch the paper trading order history report for `strategy_code1`:

```
>>> order_history = \
        algobulls_connection.get_papertrading_report_order_history(
                                                    strategy_code1)
```

We get the following output. Your output may differ:

```
+-------------+---------------------+----------------------------------+---
---+
| INST        | TIME                | ID                               | TT
|
|-------------+---------------------+----------------------------------+---
---|
| NSE_EQ:SBIN | 2020-07-09 10:30:00 | 96c24ca4b3e448f381fc5c2bc52f7a29 |
BUY  |
+-------------+---------------------+----------------------------------+---
---+
+----+---------------------+------------------------+-------+
|    | TIME                | STATE                  | MSG   |
|----+---------------------+------------------------+-------|
|  0 | 2020-07-09 10:30:00 | PUT ORDER REQ RECEIVED |       |
|  1 | 2020-07-09 10:30:00 | VALIDATION PENDING     |       |
|  2 | 2020-07-09 10:30:00 | OPEN PENDING           |       |
|  3 | 2020-07-09 10:30:00 | OPEN                   |       |
|  4 | 2020-07-09 10:30:00 | COMPLETE               |       |
+----+---------------------+------------------------+-------+
+-------------+---------------------+----------------------------------+---
---+
| INST        | TIME                | ID                               | TT
|
|-------------+---------------------+----------------------------------+---
---|
| NSE_EQ:SBIN | 2020-07-09 10:45:00 | 3bbd433edd004630b122de07873864d7 |
SELL |
+-------------+---------------------+----------------------------------+---
---+
+----+---------------------+------------------------+-------+
```

```
|    | TIME                | STATE                 | MSG   |
|----+---------------------+-----------------------+-------|
| 0  | 2020-07-09 10:45:00 | PUT ORDER REQ RECEIVED |      |
| 1  | 2020-07-09 10:45:00 | VALIDATION PENDING    |       |
| 2  | 2020-07-09 10:45:00 | OPEN PENDING          |       |
| 3  | 2020-07-09 10:45:00 | OPEN                  |       |
| 4  | 2020-07-09 10:45:00 | COMPLETE              |       |
+----+---------------------+-----------------------+-------+
 . . .
```

The complete output is not shown here. Please visit the following link to read the complete output: `https://github.com/algobulls/pyalgostrategypool/blob/master/pyalgostrategypool/sample/papertrading/strategy_ema_regular_order/oms_order_history.log`

How it works...

In this recipe, you use the `get_papertrading_report_order_history()` method of the `algobulls_connection` object to fetch order history logs in real time. This method accepts strategy code as an argument. You pass `strategy_code1` here. The return data is a string, described as follows:

For every order, the log has the following information:

- A descriptive table on the order, with the following columns:
  - `INST`: The financial instrument of the order
  - `TIME`: The time at which the order was placed
  - `ID`: The unique ID of the order
  - `TT`: The order transaction type (`BUY` or `SELL`)

  A sample of the table is shown as follows:

```
+-------------+---------------------+----------------------------
----+------+
| INST        | TIME                | ID
| TT   |
|-------------+---------------------+----------------------------
----+------|
| NSE_EQ:SBIN | 2020-07-09 10:30:00 |
96c24ca4b3e448f381fc5c2bc52f7a29 | BUY  |
+-------------+---------------------+----------------------------
----+------+
```

This information will help you find this exact order in the strategy execution log.

- An order state transition table, with the following columns:
  - TIME: The time at which the order is present in the state represented by the 'STATE' column.

  - STATE: The order enters into this state at the time mentioned in the 'TIME' column.

  - MSG: Additional message from the OMS for any unexpected state transitions. For example, orders that go to the REJECTED state have a message from the OMS stating the reason for their rejection. This column is usually empty.

A sample of the table is shown as follows:

```
+----+--------------------+------------------------+-------+
|    | TIME               | STATE                  | MSG   |
|----+--------------------+------------------------+-------|
|  0 | 2020-07-09 10:30:00 | PUT ORDER REQ RECEIVED |       |
|  1 | 2020-07-09 10:30:00 | VALIDATION PENDING     |       |
|  2 | 2020-07-09 10:30:00 | OPEN PENDING           |       |
|  3 | 2020-07-09 10:30:00 | OPEN                   |       |
|  4 | 2020-07-09 10:30:00 | COMPLETE               |       |
+----+--------------------+------------------------+-------+
```

From this table, you can see that upon placing the order at 10:30 AM, it transitions to the 'COMPLETE' state immediately. This is expected as the order is a regular market order. (Refer to the first recipe of Chapter 6, *Placing Regular Orders on the Exchange*, for more details on regular market orders.)

There's more...

Once the paper trading job moves to the 'STOPPED' state, no new order history logs are generated. You can fetch the complete order history logs any time before you submit the next paper trading job for the same strategy. If a new paper trading job is submitted (for the same strategy), these logs will no longer be accessible via the get_papertrading_report_order_history() method. You can save the fetched logs to a file if you'd like to refer to it at a later point in time.

MACD-Bracket-Order strategy – fetching the strategy

In this recipe, you will fetch the strategy class, `StrategyMACDBracketOrder`, from your account on the AlgoBulls platform, which you must have uploaded while going through the last recipe of `Chapter 8`, *Algorithmic Trading Strategies – Coding Step by Step*. This recipe starts with setting up a connection to the AlgoBulls platform, querying all available strategies in your account and fetching details of the required strategy class, `StrategyMACDBracketOrder`.

 Make sure you have gone through the last six recipes of `Chapter 8`, *Algorithmic Trading Strategies – Coding Step by Step*, to get a complete picture of the strategy class used, `StrategyMACDBracketOrder`.

How to do it...

We execute the following steps for this recipe:

1. Import the necessary modules:

   ```
   >>> from pyalgotrading.algobulls import AlgoBullsConnection
   ```

2. Create a new AlgoBulls connection object:

   ```
   >>> algobulls_connection = AlgoBullsConnection()
   ```

3. Fetch the authorization URL:

   ```
   >>> algobulls_connection.get_authorization_url()
   ```

   We get the following output:

   ```
   Please login to this URL with your AlgoBulls credentials and get
   your developer access token: https://app.algobulls.com/user/login
   'https://app.algobulls.com/user/login'
   ```

4. Log in to the preceding link with your AlgoBulls credentials, fetch your token, and set it here (refer to *Appendix II* for more details):

   ```
   >>> algobulls_connection.set_access_token(
               '80b7a69b168c5b3f15d56688841a8f2da5e2ab2c')
   ```

5. Fetch and display all strategies you have created and uploaded so far:

```
>>> all_strategies = algobulls_connection.get_all_strategies()
>>> all_strategies
```

We get the following output. Your output may differ (make sure you have followed the recipes in `Chapter 8`, *Algorithmic Trading Strategies – Coding Step by Step*, to get a similar output):

	strategyCode	strategyName
0	49287246f9704bbcbad76ade9e2091d9	EMA Regular Order Strategy
1	4faf514fe096432b8e9f80f5951bd2ea	MACD Bracket Order Strategy

6. Fetch and display the strategy code of the second strategy, the MACD-Bracket-Order strategy:

```
>>> strategy_code2 = all_strategies.iloc[1]['strategyCode']
>>> strategy_code2
```

We get the following output (your output may differ):

```
'49287246f9704bbcbad76ade9e2091d9'
```

7. Before paper trading your strategy, you can inspect your strategy to ensure you have the right strategy:

```
>>> strategy_details2 = \
        algobulls_connection.get_strategy_details(strategy_code2)
>>> print(strategy_details2)
```

We get the following output:

```
class StrategyMACDBracketOrder(StrategyBase):

    def __init__(self, *args, **kwargs):
        super().__init__(*args, **kwargs)

        self.fastMA_period = \
            self.strategy_parameters['fastma_period']
        self.slowMA_period = \
            self.strategy_parameters['slowma_period']
        self.signal_period = \
            self.strategy_parameters['signal_period']
        self.stoploss = \
            self.strategy_parameters['stoploss_trigger']
```

```
                self.target = self.strategy_parameters['target_trigger']
                self.trailing_stoploss = \
                    self.strategy_parameters['trailing_stoploss_trigger']

                self.main_order = None

        def initialize(self):
            self.main_order = {}

        @staticmethod
        def name():
            return 'MACD Bracket Order Strategy'
        ....
        def strategy_exit_position(self, candle, instrument,
                                        sideband_info):
            if sideband_info['action'] == 'EXIT':
                self.main_order[instrument].exit_position()
                self.main_order[instrument] = None
                return True

            return False
```

The complete output is not shown here. Please visit the following link to read the complete output: `https://github.com/algobulls/pyalgostrategypool/blob/master/pyalgostrategypool/strategy_macd_bracket_order.py`

How it works...

You import the necessary modules in *step 1*. In *step 2*, you create an instance of the `AlgoBullsConnection` class, named `algobulls_connection`. In *step 3*, you get the authorization URL using the `get_authorization_url()` method of the `algobulls_connection` object. This prints the authorization URL. You should visit this URL from your web browser to sign in to the AlgoBulls platform and fetch your developer access token. (You can find more details with screenshots in *Appendix II* on fetching developer access token from the AlgoBulls platform.) You copy the access token and set it in *step 4* using the `set_access_token()` method of `algobulls_connection`. If the token is accepted, a successful connection is set up with the AlgoBulls platform.

In *step 5,* you fetch all strategies you have created and uploaded on the AlgoBulls platform so far. You use the `get_all_strategies()` method for this step and assign it to a new variable, `all_strategies`. This variable is a `pandas.DataFrame` object with the `strategyCode` and `strategyName` columns. This table holds information on the strategy codes and strategy names you have uploaded previously. If you have followed the *MACD-Bracket-Order strategy – uploading the strategy on the AlgoBulls trading platform* recipe from `Chapter 8`, *Algorithmic Trading Strategies – Coding Step by Step,* you will find a strategy with the name `MACD-Regular-Order strategy`. In *step 6,* you assign the strategy code of the `MACD-Regular-Order strategy` strategy, to a new variable, `strategy_code2`. The strategy code is shown in the output of this step. This strategy code is unique for every strategy on the AlgoBulls platform.

Finally, in *step 7,* you ensure that the strategy referred by `strategy_code2` is indeed the one you uploaded earlier (in the last recipe of `Chapter 8`, *Algorithmic Trading Strategies – Coding Step by Step*). You use the `get_strategy_details()` method of the `algobulls_connection` object to inspect the strategy. This method takes strategy code as an argument. You pass `strategy_code2` here. This method returns the entire class code as a string. You assign it to a new variable, `strategy_details2`, and display it.

 If you would like to change the class code referred by `strategy_code2`, as shown in *step 7,* please refer to *There's more...* section of the last recipe in `Chapter 8`, *Algorithmic Trading Strategies – Coding Step by Step.*

MACD-Bracket-Order strategy – paper trading the strategy

In this recipe, you will perform paper trading on the `MACD-Bracket-Order strategy` strategy. You must have fetched this strategy from your account on the AlgoBulls platform in the preceding recipe of this chapter. You will leverage the paper trading functionality facilitated by `pyalgotrading` for this recipe, which in turn submits a paper trading job on the AlgoBulls platform.

Once submitted, paper trading will be run by the AlgoBulls paper trading engine. You can query the status any time to know the state of the paper trading job. The job goes through the following states, in the following given order:

- `'STARTING'` (intermediate state)
- `'STARTED'` (stable state)

- 'STOPPING' (intermediate state)
- 'STOPPED' (stable state)

On submitting a job, it starts with an intermediate state, 'STARTING'. In this state, the AlgoBulls paper trading engine will fetch the strategy and get the execution environment ready, which may take a couple of minutes. Once done, the job moves to the 'STARTED' state. The paper trading strategy happens in this stage. Here, it stays as long as it takes for paper trading to complete. Once done, the job moves to an intermediate state, 'STOPPING'. In this state, the AlgoBulls paper trading engine cleans up the resources allocated for this job, which usually takes less than a minute. Finally, the job moves to the 'STOPPED' state.

If you have already submitted a paper trading job for a strategy, you cannot submit another job for the same strategy until the first job completes. This means you have to wait for the first job to move to the 'STOPPED' state. If the first job is long-running and you would like to stop it immediately, you can submit a stop job request via pyalgotrading. You need to ensure the job is in the 'STARTED' state before submitting the request.

After submitting a paper trading job, you can fetch logs and reports for the strategy execution in real time. The logs and reports help validate the strategy performance and debug any potential issues.

You can refer to the second recipe of this chapter for the state machine diagram of a paper trading job. It demonstrates the various states and transitions of a paper trading job during its lifetime on the AlgoBulls platform.

 Make sure you have gone through the last six recipes of Chapter 8, *Algorithmic Trading Strategies – Coding Step by Step*, to get a complete picture of the strategy class used, StrategyMACDBracketOrder.

Getting ready

Make sure the algobulls_connection and strategy_code2 objects are available in your Python namespace. Refer to the *MACD-Bracket-Order strategy – fetching the strategy* recipe of this chapter to set up the algobulls_connection and strategy_code2 objects.

How to do it...

We execute the following steps for this recipe:

1. Import the necessary modules:

```
>>> from datetime import time
>>> from pyalgotrading.constants import *
```

2. Search for an instrument using its trading symbol as a keyword. Assign the returned object to `instruments`:

```
>>> instrument = algobulls_connection.search_instrument(
                                                'TATASTEEL')
>>> instrument
```

We get the following output (your output may differ):

```
[{'id': 1, 'value': 'NSE:TATASTEEL'}]
```

3. Get `value` for the instrument of choice from `instruments`:

```
>>> instrument = instrument[0]['value']
>>> instrument
```

We get the following output:

```
'NSE:TATASTEEL'
```

4. Submit a paper trading job for `strategy_code2`:

```
>>> algobulls_connection.papertrade(
        strategy_code=strategy_code2,
        start_time=time(hour=9, minute=15),
        end_time=time(hour=15, minute=30),
        instrument=instrument,
        lots=1,
        strategy_parameters={
            'fastma_period': 26,
            'slowma_period': 6,
            'signal_period': 9,
            'target_trigger': 0.01,
            'stoploss_trigger': 0.01,
            'trailing_stoploss_trigger': 1
        },
        candle_interval=CandleInterval.MINUTES_15)
```

We get the following output:

```
Setting Strategy Config... Success.
Submitting PAPERTRADING job... Success.
```

5. Check the status of the submitted paper trading job:

```
>>> algobulls_connection.get_papertrading_job_status(
                                           strategy_code2)
```

{'data': 'STARTING'}

6. Check the status of the submitted paper trading job again after some time:

```
>>> algobulls_connection.get_papertrading_job_status(
                                           strategy_code2)
```

{'data': 'STARTED'}

How it works...

In *step 1*, you import the `time` class from the `datetime` module and all constants from the `pyalgotrading.constants` module. In *step 2*, you fetch the instrument for which you would like to paper trade the strategy, `MACD-Bracket-Order strategy`, using the `search_instrument()` method of the `algobulls_connection` object. The `search_instrument()` method accepts a search string as an argument, which should be the trading symbol, in part or complete, of the instrument you are interested in. You pass `'TATASTEEL'` here. This function returns a list with details of instruments that match the search string. There could be multiple instruments that could have the search string in their trading symbols. In *step 3*, you fetch the value of the first matched instrument and assign it to a new variable, `instrument`.

In *step 4*, you submit a paper trading job using the `papertrade()` method of the `algobulls_connection()` object. It takes the following arguments:

-   `strategy_code`: The strategy code of the strategy for which paper trading has to be performed. Should be a string. You pass `strategy_code2` here.
-   `start_time`: Today's time from when paper trading should be started. Should be a `datetime.time` object. Here, you pass an object holding the value 9 hours 15 – `time(hour=9, minute=15)`. Refer to the first recipe of this book for details on creating a `time` object.

- `end_time`: Today's time until when paper trading should be performed. This object should hold a time value ahead of the value held by `start_time`. Should be a `datetime.time` instance. Here, you pass an object holding the value 15:30 hours – `time(hour=15, minute=30)`.

- `instrument`: The financial instrument for which paper trading should be run. Historical data will be fetched for this instrument. Should be a string. You pass `instrument` here.

- `lots`: The number of lots for which paper trading should be performed. Should be an integer. The quantity is calculated by the strategy as *number of lots × lot size of the financial instrument*. You pass 1 here.

- `strategy_parameters`: The parameter names and values expected by the strategy. Should be a dictionary, with `parameter-name` and `parameter-value` as key-value pairs. You pass the following parameters here:
    - `fastma_period`: 26
    - `slowma_period`: 6
    - `signal_period`: 9

    - `target_trigger`: 0.01
    - `stoploss_trigger`: 0.01
    - `trailing_stoploss_trigger`: 1

    (Recall that the parameters for MACD-Bracket-Order strategy have been defined in its `__init__()` method, as shown in the first recipe of `Chapter 8`, *Algorithmic Trading Strategies – Coding Step by Step*).

- `candle_interval`: The candle interval for the historical data fetched for paper trading. Should be an enum of the type `CandleInterval`. You pass `CandleInterval.MINUTES_15` here. (The `CandleInterval` enum provides various enums for candle intervals, some of which are `MINUTE_1`, `MINUTES_3`, `MINUTES_5`, `MINUTES_10`, `MINUTES_15`, `MINUTES_30`, HOUR, and DAY.)

If the job submission is successful, you will see `Success` messages printed by the `papertrade()` function.

Once a job is submitted, it takes a while to start. After starting, it may take some time to finish depending on the duration of paper trading specified using the `start_time` and `end_time` arguments. Usually, paper trading is run for the entire trading day, which means the job would be running for 6–8 hours.

In *step 5*, you fetch the job status using the `get_papertrading_job_status()` method of the `algobulls_connection` object. You pass `strategy_code2` as the argument here. This method returns a dictionary with a single key-value pair, the *data* and the *job* status. If you query the status immediately after placing the job, you get `'STARTING'` as the status. In *step 6*, you query the status again after some time, and if the job has started, you get the status as `'STARTED'`.

 A successful submission implies that the minimum inputs needed to paper trade a strategy have been passed in the required format. It, however, does not ensure that the strategy will run without errors. The strategy execution may still run into errors during paper trading. To debug execution issues, you would need to fetch the output logs, which is explained in the next recipe. Possible reasons for errors could be either bugs in the strategy class Python code or an incomplete `strategy_parameters` dictionary passed to the `papertrade()` function.

There's more...

If a job is running for a long time and you would like to stop it before its completion, you can use the `stop_papertrading_job()` method of the `algobulls_connection` object. This method accepts strategy code as an argument. You pass `strategy_code2` here. This method submits a stop request to the AlgoBulls paper trading engine. If the request is accepted, you see a `Success` message here:

```
>>> algobulls_connection.stop_papertrading_job(strategy_code2)
Stopping PAPERTRADING job... Success.
```

If you query the status after submitting the stop request, you get the status as `'STOPPING'`:

```
>>> algobulls_connection.get_papertrading_job_status(strategy_code2)
{'data': 'STOPPING'}
```

If you query the status again after some time, and if the job has stopped, you get the status as `'STOPPED'`:

```
>>> algobulls_connection.get_papertrading_job_status(strategy_code2)
{'data': 'STOPPED'}
```

MACD-Bracket-Order strategy – fetching paper trading logs in real time

After submitting a paper trading job on the AlgoBulls platform, the AlgoBulls paper trading engine starts executing the strategy. During the execution, every event that occurs and decisions taken by the AlgoBulls paper trading engine are recorded with exact timestamps in the form of textual logs. Examples of recorded activities include the given strategy config, every new candle generated at regular intervals, trades punched by your strategy, the entry and exit of positions created by these trades, waits for new candles, and so on. These logs are quintessential in validating the strategy behavior and debugging behavioral or performance issues that are frequently encountered while developing a strategy.

In this recipe, you will fetch paper trading logs for your strategy. The logs start coming up as soon as your submitted paper trading job reaches the 'STARTED' state (refer to the preceding recipe for more information on states of a paper trading job). The AlgoBulls platform allows you to fetch logs in real time, even while the paper trading job is still going on. You can get insights into the strategy execution without having to wait for the paper trading job to complete, which is helpful when jobs are long-running. The pyalgotrading package provides a simple method to fetch the execution logs for a given strategy.

 Make sure you have gone through the last six recipes of Chapter 8, *Algorithmic Trading Strategies – Coding Step by Step*, to get a complete picture of the strategy class used, StrategyMACDBracketOrder.

Getting ready

Make sure the algobulls_connection and strategy_code2 objects are available in your Python namespace. Refer to the *MACD-Bracket-Order strategy – fetching the strategy* recipe of this chapter to set up the algobulls_connection and strategy_code2 objects.

How to do it...

We execute the following steps for this recipe:

1. Fetch the paper trading execution logs for strategy_code2:

```
>>> logs = algobulls_connection.get_papertrading_logs(
                                        strategy_code2)
>>> print(logs)
```

We get the following output (your output may differ):

```
[2020-07-09 09:14:12] Logs not available yet. Please retry in
sometime.
```

2. Fetch the paper trading execution logs for strategy_code2 again after some time:

```
>>> logs = algobulls_connection.get_papertrading_logs(
                                        strategy_code2)
>>> print(logs)
```

We get the following output (your output may differ):

```
...
#######################################
 INITIALIZING ALGOBULLS CORE (v3.2.0)...
#######################################
...
[PT] [2020-07-09 09:15:00] [INFO] [tls] STARTING ALGOBULLS CORE...
...
[PT] [2020-07-09 09:45:00] [CRITICAL] [order] [PLACING NEW ORDER]
[2020-07-09 09:45:00] [a310755e3d8b4a1ab4667882bf25751d] [BUY]
[NSE:TATASTEEL] [QTY:1] [QTY PENDING: 1] [ENTRY PRICE: 345.0]
[PRICE:345.0] [TRIGGER PRICE:None] [ORDER_TYPE_BRACKET]
[ORDER_CODE_INTRADAY] [ORDER_VARIETY_LIMIT] [ORDER_POSITION_ENTER]
[STOPLOSS TRIGGER:341.55] [TARGET TRIGGER:348.45] [TRAILING
STOPLOSS TRIGGER:345.0]
...
[PT] [2020-07-09 15:30:00] [INFO] [clock] Candle generation has
been stopped...
[PT] [2020-07-09 15:30:00] [INFO] [tls] Received event END OF
MARKET. Stopping Trading Core Engine...
[PT] [2020-07-09 15:30:00] [INFO] [tls] Exiting all open positions
with order code: ORDER_CODE_INTRADAY (if any)...
[PT] [2020-07-09 15:30:00] [CRITICAL] [tls] [User: ALGOBULLS
VIRTUAL USER] Trading session completed
...
```

The complete output is not shown here. Please visit the following link to read the complete output: `https://github.com/algobulls/pyalgostrategypool/blob/master/pyalgostrategypool/sample/papertrading/strategy_macd_bracket_order/logs.txt`

How it works...

In *step 1*, you use the `get_papertrading_logs()` method of the `algobulls_connection` object to fetch the strategy paper trading logs in real time. This method accepts strategy code as an argument. You pass `strategy_code2` here. The return data is a string. If you try this step immediately after submitting the job, you get a string that says the logs are not ready yet (`[2020-07-09 09:14:12] Logs not available yet. Please retry in sometime.`). This happens if the paper trading job is in the `'STARTING'` state.

In *step 2*, you fetch the logs again after some time. If the job is out of the `'STARTING'` state, you start getting your strategy execution logs. You get the entire paper trading logs every time you call the `get_papertrading_logs()` function.

There's more...

Once the paper trading job moves to the `'STOPPED'` state, no new logs are generated. You can fetch the complete logs any time before you submit the next paper trading job for the same strategy. If a new paper trading job is submitted (for the same strategy), these logs will no longer be accessible via the `get_papertrading_logs()` method. You can save the fetched logs to a file if you'd like to refer to it at a later point in time.

MACD-Bracket-Order strategy – fetching a paper trading report – P&L table

After submitting a paper trading job on the AlgoBulls platform, the AlgoBulls paper trading engine starts executing the strategy. During the execution, along with the logs, the AlgoBulls paper trading engine also generates a P&L table in real time. This table holds information on every trade punched by the strategy. It also has details on the mapping between entry and exit orders and the trade P&L and cumulative P&L, sorted chronologically, with the latest order first. This table gives an insight into the overall strategy performance with the help of individual and cumulative P&L numbers. The entry-exit order mapping also helps validate the strategy behavior.

In this recipe, you will fetch the P&L table report for your strategy. This report is available as soon as the first trade is punched by your strategy after you submit a paper trading job. The AlgoBulls platform allows you to fetch the P&L table in real time, even while the paper trading job is still going on. You can get insights into the strategy performance without having to wait for the paper trading job to complete. This is helpful as paper trading jobs are usually long-running. The `pyalgotrading` package provides a simple method to fetch the P&L table for a given strategy.

 Make sure you have gone through the last six recipes of `Chapter 8`, *Algorithmic Trading Strategies – Coding Step by Step*, to get a complete picture of the strategy class used, `StrategyMACDBracketOrder`.

Getting ready

Make sure the `algobulls_connection` and `strategy_code2` objects are available in your Python namespace. Refer to the *MACD-Bracket-Order strategy – fetching the strategy* recipe of this chapter to set up the `algobulls_connection` and `strategy_code2` objects.

How to do it...

Fetch the paper trading P&L report for `strategy_code2`:

```
>>> algobulls_connection.get_papertrading_report_pnl_table(strategy_code2)
```

We get the following output. Your output may differ (note that the following output has been split into multiple tables for representation purposes. You will see a single wide table in your Jupyter notebook):

	instrument	entry_timestamp	entry_transaction_type	entry_quantity	entry_price
0	NSE_EQ:TATASTEEL	2020-07-09 12:00:00	SELL	1	345.2
1	NSE_EQ:TATASTEEL	2020-07-09 09:45:00	BUY	1	345

	instrument	exit_timestamp	exit_transaction_type	exit_quantity	exit_price
0	NSE_EQ:TATASTEEL	2020-07-09 15:30:00	BUY	1	345
1	NSE_EQ:TATASTEEL	2020-07-09 10:00:00	SELL	1	348.45

	pnl_absolute	pnl_percentage	pnl_cumulative_absolute	pnl_cumulative_percentage
0	0.2	0.06	3.65	1.06
1	3.45	1	3.45	1

How it works...

In this recipe, you use the `get_papertrading_report_pnl_table()` method of the `algobulls_connection` object to fetch the paper trading P&L table in real time. This method accepts strategy code as an argument. You pass `strategy_code2` here. The return data is a `pandas.DataFrame` object with multiple columns, described as follows:

- `instrument`: The financial instrument for which trade was entered.
- `entry_timestamp`: The timestamp at which the entry order was placed. (Note that it may remain in the `'OPEN'` state for a while before it goes to the `'COMPLETE'` state. The time for this state transition can be found using the order history table, explained in the *EMA-Regular-Order strategy – fetching the paper trading report – order history* recipe of this chapter.)
- `entry_transaction_type`: The entry order transaction type (either BUY or SELL).
- `entry_quantity`: The entry order quantity.
- `entry_price`: The price at which the entry order gets executed and goes to the `'COMPLETE'` state.
- `exit_timestamp`: The timestamp at which the exit order was placed. (Note that it may remain in the `'OPEN'` state for a while before it goes to the `'COMPLETE'` state.)
- `exit_transaction_type`: The exit order transaction type (either BUY or SELL).
- `exit_quantity`: The exit order quantity.
- `exit_price`: The price at which the exit order gets executed and goes to the `'COMPLETE'` state.
- `pnl_absolute`: The difference between the exit order execution price and entry order execution price. Mathematically, this is (*exit_price - entry_price*)**exit_quantity* for a long trade and (*entry_price - exit_price*)**exit_quantity* for a short trade. A positive value would imply that the trade is a profit-making trade. A negative value would imply that the trade is a loss-making trade.
- `pnl_percentage`: The percentage of profit or loss with respect to the entry price. Mathematically, this is *pnl_absolute / entry_price / exit_quantity* x 100.

- `pnl_cumulative_absolute`: The cumulative profit or loss. Mathematically, this is the sum of all the `pnl_absolute` values of the previous trades. This number gives a direct insight into the strategy performance against the simulation time.
- `pnl_cumulative_percentage`: The percentage of cumulative profit or loss with respect to the entry price. Mathematically, this is *pnl_cumulative / entry_price / exit_quantity* x 100.

There's more...

Once the paper trading job moves to the `'STOPPED'` state, the P&L table report will not update anymore. You can fetch the complete P&L report any time before you submit the next paper trading job for the same strategy. If a new paper trading job is submitted (for the same strategy), this report will no longer be accessible via the `get_papertrading_report_pnl_table()` method. You can save the fetched report to a `.csv` file if you'd like to refer to it at a later point in time.

MACD-Bracket-Order strategy – fetching a paper trading report – statistics table

After submitting a paper trading job on the AlgoBulls platform, the AlgoBulls paper trading engine starts executing the strategy. During the execution, along with the logs and P&L table, the AlgoBulls paper trading engine also generates a summary from the P&L table in real time. This summary is a table of statistics containing various statistical numbers, such as `Net P&L` (absolute and percentage), `Max Drawdown` (absolute and percentage), the count of total trades, winning trades, losing trades, long trades, and short trades, maximum gain and minimum gain (or maximum loss), and the average profit per winning and losing trade. This table gives an instant overview of the overall strategy performance.

In this recipe, you will fetch the statistics table report for your strategy. This report is available as soon as the first trade is punched by your strategy after you submit a paper trading job. The AlgoBulls platform allows you to fetch the statistics table in real time, even while the paper trading job is still going on. You can get insights into the strategy performance without having to wait for the paper trading job to complete. This is helpful as paper trading jobs are usually long-running. The `pyalgotrading` package provides a simple method to fetch the statistics table for a given strategy.

Make sure you have gone through the last six recipes of `Chapter 8,` *Algorithmic Trading Strategies – Coding Step by Step,* to get a complete picture of the strategy class used, `StrategyMACDBracketOrder`.

Getting ready

Make sure the `algobulls_connection` and `strategy_code2` objects are available in your Python namespace. Refer to the *MACD-Bracket-Order strategy – fetching the strategy* recipe of this chapter to set up the `algobulls_connection` and `strategy_code2` objects.

How to do it...

Fetch the paper trading statistics report for `strategy_code2`:

```
>>> algobulls_connection.get_papertrading_report_statistics(strategy_code2)
```

We get the following output (your output may differ):

	highlight_type	highlight_value
0	Net PnL	3.65
1	Net PnL %	1.06
2	Max Drawdown	3.45
3	Max Drawdown %	1.0
4	Number of Trades	2
5	Number of Wins	2
6	Number of Looses	0
7	Number of Long Trades	1
8	Number of Short Trades	1
9	Max Gain	3.45
10	Min Gain	0.2
11	Avg. Profit per winning trade	1.83
12	Avg. Profit per losing trade	-

How it works...

In this recipe, you use the `get_papertradig_report_statistics()` method of the `algobulls_connection` object to fetch the paper trading statistics table in real time. This method accepts strategy code as an argument. You pass `strategy_code2` here. The return data is a `pandas.DataFrame` object with two columns—`highlight_type` and `highlight_value`—and multiple rows. The rows are described as follows:

- `Net PnL`: The cumulative paper trading P&L. This is also the `pnl_cumulative_absolute` value of the first entry in the P&L table.
- `Net PnL %`: The cumulative paper trading P&L percentage. This is also the `pnl_cumulative_percentage` value of the first entry in the P&L table.
- `Max Drawdown`: The lowest value in the `pnl_cumulative` column of the P&L table. This indicates the maximum loss your strategy has encountered during the execution.
- `Max Drawdown %`: Mathematically, this is *(Max Drawdown) / (corresponding entry_price)/ exit_quantity × 100.*

- `Number of Trades`: Total trades (entry and exit counted as one) during the session.
- `Number of Wins`: The count of trades where the trade P&L was non-negative.
- `Number of Losses`: The count of trades where the trade P&L was negative.
- `Number of Long Trades`: The count of trades where the entry transaction type was `'BUY'`.
- `Number of Short Trades`: The count of trades where the entry transaction type was `'SELL'`.
- `Max Gain`: The P&L of the trade with maximum P&L value among all trades.
- `Min Gain`: The P&L of the trade with the minimum P&L value among all trades.
- `Avg. Profit per winning trade`: Mathematically, this is *(Total P&L of winning trades) / (Count of winning trades).*
- `Avg. Profit per losing trade`: Mathematically, this is *(Total P&L of losing trades) / (Count of losing trades).*

There's more...

If the statistics table is fetched while the paper trading job is still running, the previously mentioned numbers would be intermediate numbers, based on the trades completed until that time. The numbers may change as more trades are punched until the paper trading job completes.

Once the paper trading job moves to the 'STOPPED' state, the statistics table will not change anymore. You can fetch the complete statistics table any time before you submit the next paper trading job for the same strategy. If a new paper trading job is submitted (for the same strategy), this table will no longer be accessible via the `get_papertrading_report_statistics()` method. You can save the fetched report to a `.csv` file if you'd like to refer to it at a later point in time.

MACD-Bracket-Order strategy – fetching a paper trading report – order history

After submitting a paper trading job on the AlgoBulls platform, the AlgoBulls paper trading engine starts executing the strategy. During the execution, along with the logs, P&L table, and statistics table, the AlgoBulls paper trading engine also generates an order history log in real time. This log contains state transitions of every order, along with the timestamps and additional information (if any) for each order state. The order history log is crucial in understanding how long it has taken for a trade to go from 'OPEN' to 'COMPLETE' or to the 'CANCELLED' state. For example, the MARKET orders would immediately go from an 'OPEN' to 'COMPLETE' state but the LIMIT orders may take a while, based on the market conditions, to go from an 'OPEN' to 'COMPLETE' state, or they may even get to the 'CANCELLED' state. All this information is available in the order history log. (Refer to the state machine diagrams in Chapter 6, *Placing Regular Orders on the Exchange*, for more information on order state transitions.)

In this recipe, you will fetch the order history log for your strategy. This log is available as soon as the first trade is punched by your strategy after you submit a paper trading job. The AlgoBulls platform allows you to fetch the order history log in real time, even while the paper trading job is still going on. This helps us get details for orders in the end states without having to wait for the paper trading job to complete. The pyalgotrading package provides a simple method to fetch the order history log for a given strategy.

Make sure you have gone through the last six recipes of `Chapter 8`, *Algorithmic Trading Strategies – Coding Step by Step*, to get a complete picture of the strategy class used, `StrategyMACDBracketOrder`.

Getting ready

Make sure the `algobulls_connection` and `strategy_code2` objects are available in your Python namespace. Refer to the *MACD-Bracket-Order strategy – fetching the strategy* recipe of this chapter to set up the `algobulls_connection` and `strategy_code2` objects.

How to do it...

Fetch the paper trading order history report for `strategy_code2`:

```
>>> order_history = \
        algobulls_connection.get_papertrading_report_order_history(
                                                    strategy_code2)
>>> print(order_history)
```

We get the following output (your output may differ):

```
...
+------------------+---------------------+----------------------------------
-+------+
| INST             | TIME                | ID
| TT   |
|------------------+---------------------+----------------------------------
-+------|
| NSE_EQ:TATASTEEL | 2020-07-09 10:00:00 | 56970bffe8be4650a71857bc4472e6c8
| SELL |
+------------------+---------------------+----------------------------------
-+------+
+----+---------------------+-----------------------+-------+
|    | TIME                | STATE                 | MSG   |
|----+---------------------+-----------------------+-------|
|  0 | 2020-07-09 10:00:00 | PUT ORDER REQ RECEIVED |      |
|  1 | 2020-07-09 10:00:00 | VALIDATION PENDING     |      |
|  2 | 2020-07-09 10:00:00 | OPEN PENDING           |      |
|  3 | 2020-07-09 10:00:00 | OPEN                   |      |
|  4 | 2020-07-09 10:15:00 | COMPLETE               |      |
+----+---------------------+-----------------------+-------+
+------------------+---------------------+----------------------------------
-+------+
```

```
| INST           | TIME                | ID
| TT   |
|----------------+---------------------+---------------------------------
-+------|
| NSE_EQ:TATASTEEL | 2020-07-09 10:00:00 | 0a06e41aac0744adb45bb4d3d2e19728
| SELL |
+----------------+---------------------+---------------------------------
-+------+
+----+--------------------+-----------------------+-------+
|    | TIME               | STATE                 | MSG   |
|----+--------------------+-----------------------+-------|
| 0  | 2020-07-09 10:00:00 | PUT ORDER REQ RECEIVED |       |
| 1  | 2020-07-09 10:00:00 | VALIDATION PENDING     |       |
| 2  | 2020-07-09 10:00:00 | OPEN PENDING           |       |
| 3  | 2020-07-09 10:00:00 | TRIGGER PENDING        |       |
| 4  | 2020-07-09 10:15:00 | CANCEL PENDING         |       |
| 5  | 2020-07-09 10:15:00 | CANCELLED              |       |
+----+--------------------+-----------------------+-------+
 . . .
```

The complete output is not shown here. Please visit the following link to read the complete output: https://github.com/algobulls/pyalgostrategypool/blob/master/ pyalgostrategypool/sample/papertrading/strategy_macd_bracket_order/oms_order_ history.log

How it works...

In this recipe, you use the `get_papertrading_report_order_history()` method of the `algobulls_connection` object to fetch order history logs in real time. This method accepts strategy code as an argument. You pass `strategy_code2` here. The return data is a string, described as follows:

For every order, the log has the following information:

- A descriptive table on the order, with the following mentioned columns:
  - `INST`: The financial instrument of the order
  - `TIME`: The time at which the order was placed
  - `ID`: The unique ID of the order
  - `TT`: The order transaction type (`BUY` or `SELL`)

A sample of the table is shown as follows:

```
+-------------------+--------------------+------------------------
---------+------+
| INST              | TIME               | ID
| TT   |
|-------------------+--------------------+------------------------
---------+------|
| NSE_EQ:TATASTEEL  | 2020-07-09 10:00:00 |
0a06e41aac0744adb45bb4d3d2e19728 | SELL |
+-------------------+--------------------+------------------------
---------+------+
```

This information will help you find this exact order in the strategy execution log.

- An order state transition table, with the following mentioned columns:
  - TIME: The timestamp at which the order enters into the state represented by the STATE column.
  - STATE: The order enters into this state at the timestamp mentioned in the TIME column.
  - MSG: Additional message from OMS for any unexpected state transitions. For example, orders that go to the REJECTED state have a message from the OMS stating the reason for their rejection. This column is usually empty.

A sample of the table is shown as follows:

```
+----+--------------------+----------------------+-------+
|    | TIME               | STATE                | MSG   |
|----+--------------------+----------------------+-------|
|  0 | 2020-07-09 10:00:00 | PUT ORDER REQ RECEIVED |      |
|  1 | 2020-07-09 10:00:00 | VALIDATION PENDING   |       |
|  2 | 2020-07-09 10:00:00 | OPEN PENDING         |       |
|  3 | 2020-07-09 10:00:00 | TRIGGER PENDING      |       |
|  4 | 2020-07-09 10:15:00 | CANCEL PENDING       |       |
|  5 | 2020-07-09 10:15:00 | CANCELLED            |       |
+----+--------------------+----------------------+-------+
```

From this table, you can see that upon placing the order at 10:00 AM, it transitions to the TRIGGER PENDING state. It stays there for 15 minutes before transitioning to the CANCELLED state. This is expected as the order is a bracket limit order.

There's more...

Once the paper trading job moves to the STOPPED state, no new order history logs are generated. You can fetch the complete order history logs any time before you submit the next paper trading job for the same strategy. If a new paper trading job is submitted (for the same strategy), these logs will no longer be accessible via the get_papertrading_report_order_history() method. You can save the fetched logs to a file if you'd like to refer to it at a later point in time.

Algorithmic Trading – Real Trading

11

Now that we've built various algorithmic trading strategies and successfully backtested them with satisfactory results and paper traded them in live markets, it is finally time for real trading.

Real trading is where we execute a trading strategy in the live market hours with real money. If your strategy has performed well in backtesting and paper trading, you can expect similar results with real money. Please note that your strategy may not perform as expected in the real market, despite giving good backtesting and paper trading results. Profitable backtesting and paper trading results are prerequisites for a profitable real trading experience but are not sufficient to guarantee a profit for every session.

For real trading, a strategy configuration is required. It consists of multiple parameters, some of which are as follows:

- **Start and end times**: The time duration within the current day for which paper trading should be run.
- **Financial instrument(s)**: One or more financial instruments for which paper trading should be performed.
- **Candle interval**: One of various possible candle intervals; for example, `1 minute`, `15 minutes`, `hour`, or `day`.
- **Strategy specific parameters**: Values for custom parameters defined in the strategy.
- **Strategy mode**: One of intraday or delivery. Intraday strategies punch intraday orders, which are squared-off at the end of the day. Delivery strategies punch delivery orders, which don't square-off at the end of the day and get carried forward to the next trading day.

A real trading engine is required to perform real trading on a given strategy. In this chapter, you will use the real trading engine provided by AlgoBulls (`https://algobulls.com`), an algorithmic trading platform that makes its services available via its developer options. It provides a Python package called `pyalgotrading` (`https://github.com/algobulls/pyalgotrading`) to make these services available.

You coded two algorithmic trading strategies in `Chapter 8`, *Algorithmic Trading Strategies – Coding Step by Step*. Recall that the strategy descriptions are as follows:

- **EMA-Regular-Order strategy**: A strategy based on the technical indicator EMA and regular orders. (The first six recipes of `Chapter 7`, *Placing Bracket and Cover Orders on the Exchange*)
- **MACD-Bracket-Order strategy**: A strategy based on the technical indicator MACD and bracket orders. (The remaining six recipes of `Chapter 7`, *Placing Bracket and Cover Orders on the Exchange*)

These strategies are also available as part of a Python package, `pyalgostrategypool`. You can install it using pip with the `$ pip install pyalgostrategypool` command. You can also check them out on GitHub (`https://github.com/algobulls/pyalgostrategypool`).

When following `Chapter 8`, *Algorithmic Trading Strategies – Coding Step by Step*, you uploaded these two strategies to your AlgoBulls account. In this chapter, you will fetch these strategies from your AlgoBulls account and perform real trading on them. Real trading is fully automated and requires no involvement from your end while the trading session is going on. Upon real trading, you would gather strategy execution logs and various reports – namely, the profit and loss report and the statistics report. By using `pyalgotrading`, you ensure that you're focusing on developing and executing real trading strategies without worrying about the ecosystem needed for the strategy's execution.

This chapter includes step-by-step recipes for the previously mentioned strategies, from setting up a connection to the AlgoBulls platform, fetching the strategy, and running real trading jobs to fetching the execution logs and fetching various types of reports.

In this chapter, you will cover the following recipes:

- EMA-Regular-Order strategy – fetching the strategy
- EMA-Regular-Order strategy – real trading the strategy
- EMA-Regular-Order strategy – fetching real trading logs in real time
- EMA-Regular-Order strategy – fetching a real trading report – P&L table
- EMA-Regular-Order strategy – fetching a real trading report – statistics table

- MACD-Bracket-Order strategy – fetching the strategy
- MACD-Bracket-Order strategy – real trading the strategy
- MACD-Bracket-Order strategy – fetching real trading logs in real time
- MACD-Bracket-Order strategy – fetching a real trading report – P&L table
- MACD-Bracket-Order strategy – fetching a real trading report – statistics table

Real trading is only meaningful if run during the live market hours, unlike backtesting, which can be run at any time. Please make sure you try out the recipes of this chapter in live market hours.

Technical requirements

You will need the following to successfully execute the recipes in this chapter:

- Python 3.7+
- Python package:
  - pyalgotrading (`$ pip install pyalgotrading`)

Ensure you have added and bound your broking details on `https://algobulls.com`. Refer to *Appendix II* for more details. You can use any broker supported by the AlgoBulls platform for this chapter.

The latest Jupyter notebook for this chapter can be found on GitHub at `https://github.com/PacktPublishing/Python-Algorithmic-Trading-Cookbook/tree/master/Chapter11`.

EMA–Regular–Order strategy – fetching the strategy

In this recipe, you will fetch the `StrategyEMARegularOrder` strategy class from your account on the AlgoBulls platform. This recipe starts with setting up a connection to the AlgoBulls platform, querying all available strategies in your account, and fetching details of the required strategy class; that is, `StrategyEMARegularOrder`.

> Make sure you have gone through the first six recipes of `Chapter 8`, *Algorithmic Trading Strategies – Coding Step by Step*, to get a complete picture of the strategy class we will be using; that is, `StrategyEMARegularOrder`.

How to do it...

We execute the following steps for this recipe:

1. Import the necessary modules:

```
>>> from pyalgotrading.algobulls import AlgoBullsConnection
```

2. Create a new AlgoBulls connection object:

```
>>> algobulls_connection = AlgoBullsConnection()
```

3. Fetch the authorization URL:

```
>>> algobulls_connection.get_authorization_url()
```

We get the following output:

```
Please login to this URL with your AlgoBulls credentials and get
your developer access token: https://app.algobulls.com/user/login
'https://app.algobulls.com/user/login'
```

4. Log into the preceding link with your AlgoBulls credentials, fetch your token, and set it here (refer to *Appendix II* for more details):

```
>>> algobulls_connection.set_access_token(
            '80b7a69b168c5b3f15d56688841a8f2da5e2ab2c')
```

5. Fetch and display all the strategies you have created and uploaded so far:

```
>>> all_strategies = algobulls_connection.get_all_strategies()
>>> all_strategies
```

We get the following output. Your output may differ (make sure you have followed the recipes in `Chapter 8`, *Algorithmic Trading Strategies – Coding Step by Step*, to get a similar output):

	strategyCode	strategyName
0	49287246f9704bbcbad76ade9e2091d9	EMA Regular Order Strategy
1	4faf514fe096432b8e9f80f5951bd2ea	MACD Bracket Order Strategy

6. Fetch and display the strategy code of the first strategy:

```
>>> strategy_code1 = all_strategies.iloc[0]['strategyCode']
>>> strategy_code1
```

We get the following output (your output may differ):

```
'49287246f9704bbcbad76ade9e2091d9'
```

7. Before real trading your strategy, you can inspect your strategy to ensure you have the right strategy:

```
>>> strategy_details1 = \
        algobulls_connection.get_strategy_details(strategy_code1)
>>> print(strategy_details1)
```

We got the following output:

```
class StrategyEMARegularOrder(StrategyBase):

    def __init__(self, *args, **kwargs):
        super().__init__(*args, **kwargs)

        self.timeperiod1 = self.strategy_parameters['timeperiod1']
        self.timeperiod2 = self.strategy_parameters['timeperiod2']

        self.main_order = None

    def initialize(self):
        self.main_order = {}

    @staticmethod
    def name():
        return 'EMA Regular Order Strategy'
    ....
    def strategy_exit_position(self, candle, instrument,
                                    sideband_info):
        if sideband_info['action'] == 'EXIT':
            self.main_order[instrument].exit_position()
            self.main_order[instrument] = None
            return True

        return False
```

The complete output is not shown here. Please visit the following link to read the complete output, at https://github.com/algobulls/pyalgostrategypool/blob/master/ pyalgostrategypool/strategy_ema_regular_order.py.

How it works...

You import the necessary modules in *step 1*. In *step 2*, an instance of the `AlgoBullsConnection` class is created, named `algobulls_connection`. In *step 3*, you get the authorization URL using the `get_authorization_url()` method of the `algobulls_connection` object. This prints the authorization URL. You should visit this URL from your web browser to sign into the AlgoBulls platform and fetch your developer access token. (You can find more details, along with screenshots, in *Appendix II* on fetching developer access tokens from the AlgoBulls platform.) You copy the access token and set it in *step 4* using the `set_access_token()` method of `algobulls_connection`. If the token is accepted, a successful connection is set up with the AlgoBulls platform.

In *step 5*, you fetch all the strategies you have created and uploaded on the AlgoBulls platform so far. You use the `get_all_strategies()` method for this step and assign it to a new variable, `all_strategies`. This variable is a `pandas.DataFrame` object with `strategyCode` and `strategyName` columns. This table holds information on the strategy code and strategy names you have uploaded previously. If you followed the *EMA-Regular-Order strategy – uploading the strategy on the AlgoBulls trading platform* recipe from `Chapter 8`, *Algorithmic Trading Strategies – Coding Step by Step*, you will find a strategy called **EMA regular order strategy**. In *step 6*, you assign the strategy code of the strategy, **EMA regular order strategy**, to a new variable called `strategy_code1`. The strategy code is shown in the output of this step. This strategy code is unique for every strategy on the AlgoBulls platform.

Finally, in *step 7*, you ensure that the strategy being referred to by `strategy_code1` is indeed the one you uploaded earlier (in the *EMA-Regular-Order strategy – uploading the strategy on the AlgoBulls trading platform* recipe in `Chapter 8`, *Algorithmic Trading Strategies – Coding Step by Step*). You use the `get_strategy_details()` method of the `algobulls_connection` object to inspect the strategy. This method takes strategy code as an argument. You pass `strategy_code1` here. This method returns the entire class code as a string. You assign it to a new variable, `strategy_details1`, and display it.

 If, you would like to change the class code being referred to by `strategy_code1`, as shown in *step 7*, please refer to *There's more...* section of the *EMA-Regular-Order strategy – uploading the strategy on the AlgoBulls trading platform* recipe in `Chapter 8`, *Algorithmic Trading Strategies – Coding Step by Step*.

EMA–Regular–Order strategy – real trading the strategy

In this recipe, you will perform real trading on the **EMA-Regular-Order strategy**. You must have fetched this strategy from your account on the AlgoBulls platform in the preceding recipe of this chapter. You will leverage the real trading functionality facilitated by pyalgotrading for this recipe, which, in turn, submits a real trading job on the AlgoBulls platform.

Once submitted, real trading will be run by the AlgoBulls real trading engine. You can query its status any time to find out about the state of the real trading job. The job goes through the following states, in the given order:

- STARTING (intermediate state)
- STARTED (stable state)
- STOPPING (intermediate state)
- STOPPED (stable state)

On submitting a job, it starts with an intermediate state, STARTING. In this state, the AlgoBulls real trading engine fetches the strategy and gets the execution environment ready, which may take a couple of minutes. Once done, the job moves to the STARTED state. The real trading strategy is implemented in this stage. Here, it stays as long as it takes for real trading to complete. Once done, the job moves to an intermediate state, STOPPING. In this state, the AlgoBulls real trading engine cleans up the resources that have been allocated for this job, which usually takes less than a minute. Finally, the job moves to the STOPPED state.

If you have already submitted a strategy real trading job, you cannot submit another job for the same strategy until the first job completes. This means you have to wait for the first job to move to the STOPPED state. If the first job is long-running and you would like to stop it immediately, you can submit a stop job request via pyalgotrading. You need to ensure the job is in the STARTED state before submitting the request.

The following state machine diagram demonstrates the various states and transitions of a real trading job during its lifetime on the AlgoBulls platform:

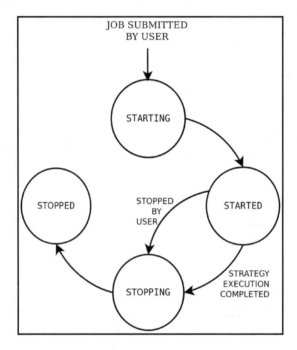

After submitting a real trading job, you can fetch logs and reports for the strategy's execution in real time. The logs and reports help validate the strategy's performance and debug any potential issues.

Make sure you have gone through the first six recipes of `Chapter 8`, *Algorithmic Trading Strategies – Coding Step by Step*, to get a complete picture of the strategy class we will be using; that is, `StrategyEMARegularORder`.

Getting ready

Make sure the `algobulls_connection` and `strategy_code1` objects are available in your Python namespace. Refer to the preceding recipe to set up the `algobulls_connection` and `strategy_code1` objects.

How to do it...

We execute the following steps for this recipe:

1. Import the necessary modules:

```
>>> from datetime import time
>>> from pyalgotrading.constants import *
```

2. Search for an instrument by using its trading symbol as a keyword. Assign the returned object to `instruments`:

```
>>> instruments = algobulls_connection.search_instrument('SBIN')
>>> instruments
```

We got the following output (your output may differ):

```
[{'id': 7, 'value': 'NSE:SBIN'}]
```

3. Get `value` for the instrument of choice from `instruments`:

```
>>> instrument = instruments[0]['value']
>>> instrument
```

We got the following output:

```
'NSE:SBIN'
```

4. Submit a real trading job for `strategy_code1`:

```
>>> algobulls_connection.realtrade(
        strategy_code=strategy_code1,
        start_time=time(hour=9, minute=15),
        end_time=time(hour=15, minute=30),
        instrument=instrument,
        lots=1,
        strategy_parameters={
            'timeperiod1': 5,
            'timeperiod2': 12
        },
        candle_interval=CandleInterval.MINUTES_15)
```

We got the following output:

```
Setting Strategy Config... Success.
Submitting REALTRADING job... Success.
```

5. Check the status of the submitted real trading job:

```
>>> algobulls_connection.get_realtrading_job_status(strategy_code1)
```

We got the following output:

```
{'data': 'STARTING'}
```

6. Check the status of the submitted job again after some time:

```
>>> algobulls_connection.get_realtrading_job_status(strategy_code1)
```

We got the following output:

```
{'data': 'STARTED'}
```

How it works...

In *step 1*, you import the time class from the datetime module and all the constants from the pyalgotrading.constants module. In *step 2*, you fetch the instrument that you would like to real trade the strategy for, **EMA-Regular-Order strategy**, using the search_instrument() method of the algobulls_connection object. The search_instrument() method accepts a search string as an argument, which should be the trading symbol, in part or complete, of the instrument you are interested in. You pass 'SBIN' here. This function returns a list containing details of the instruments that match the search string. There could be multiple instruments that have the search string in their trading symbols. In *step 3*, you fetch the value of the first matched instrument and assign it to a new variable, instrument.

In *step 4*, you submit a real trading job using the realtrade() method of the algobulls_connection() object. It takes the following arguments:

- strategy_code: Strategy code of the strategy for which real trading has to be performed. This should be a string. You pass strategy_code1 here.
- start_time: Today's time when real trading should be started. This should be a datetime.time object. Here, you pass an object holding the value for 9:15 hours – time(hour=9, minute=15). Refer to the first recipe of this book for details on creating a time object.
- end_time: Today's time when real trading should be performed. This object should hold a time value ahead of the value held by start_time. This should be a datetime.time instance. Here, you pass an object holding the value 15:30 hours – time(hour=15, minute=30).

- `instrument`: A financial instrument for which real trading should be run. Historical data will be fetched for this instrument. This should be a string. You pass `instrument` here.
- `lots`: Number of lots for which real trading should be performed. This should be an integer. The quantity is calculated by the strategy as *number of lots × lot size of the financial instrument*. You pass 1 here.
- `strategy_parameters`: Parameter names and values expected by the strategy. This should be a dictionary, with `parameter-name` and `parameter-value` as key-value pairs. You pass the following parameters here:
  - `timeperiod1: 5`
  - `timeperiod2: 12`

  (Recall that the parameters for the EMA-Regular-Order strategy have been defined in its `__init__()` method, as shown in the first recipe of `Chapter` 8, *Algorithmic Trading Strategies – Coding Step by Step*).

- `candle_interval`: The candle interval for the historical data being fetched for real trading. This should be an enum of the `CandleInterval` type. You pass `CandleInterval.MINUTES_15` here. (The `CandleInterval` enum provides various enums for candle intervals, some of which are `MINUTE_1`, `MINUTES_3`, `MINUTES_5`, `MINUTES_10`, `MINUTES_15`, `MINUTES_30`, `HOUR`, and `DAY`.)

If the job submission is successful, you will see `Success` messages printed by the `realtrade()` function.

Once a job has been submitted, it takes a while to start. After starting, it may take some time to finish, depending on the duration of real trading, as specified using the `start_time` and `end_time` arguments. Usually, real trading is run for the entire trading day, which means the job would be running for 6-8 hours.

In *step 5*, you fetch the job's status using the `get_realtrading_job_status()` method of the `algobulls_connection` object. You pass `strategy_code1` as the argument here. This method returns a dictionary with a single key-value pair – the *data* and the *job* status. If you query the status immediately after placing the job, you get `'STARTING'` as the status. In *step 6*, you query the status again after some time, and if the job starts, you get a status of `'STARTED'`.

A successful submission implies that the minimum inputs needed to real trade a strategy have been passed in the required format. However, this does not ensure that the strategy will run without errors. The strategy's execution may still run into errors during real trading. To debug execution issues, you would need to fetch the output logs, which will be explained in the next recipe. Possible reasons for errors could be either bugs in the strategy class' Python code or that an incomplete `strategy_parameters` dictionary has been passed to the `realtrade()` function.

There's more...

If a job is running for a long time and you would like to stop it before its completion, you can use the `stop_realtrading_job()` method of the `algobulls_connection` object. This method accepts strategy code as an argument. You pass `strategy_code1` here. This method submits a stop request to the AlgoBulls real trading engine. If the request is accepted, you will see a `Success` message here:

```
>>> algobulls_connection.stop_realtrading_job(strategy_code1)
Stopping REALTRADING job... Success.
```

If you query the status after submitting the stop request, you'll get `'STOPPING'` as the status:

```
>>> algobulls_connection.get_realtrading_job_status(strategy_code1)
{'data': 'STOPPING'}
```

If you query the status again after some time, and if the job has stopped, you'll get `'STOPPED'` as the status:

```
>>> algobulls_connection.get_realtrading_job_status(strategy_code1)
{'data': 'STOPPED'}
```

EMA–Regular–Order strategy – fetching real trading logs in real time

After submitting a real trading job on the AlgoBulls platform, the AlgoBulls real trading engine starts executing the strategy. During its execution, every event that occurs and the decisions that are made by the AlgoBulls real trading engine are recorded with exact timestamps in the form of textual logs.

Examples of recorded activities include the given strategy config, every new candle generated at regular intervals, trades punched by your strategy, the entry and exit of positions created by these trades, waits for new candles, and so on. These logs are quintessential when validating the strategy and debugging behavior or performance issues that are frequently encountered while developing a strategy.

In this recipe, you will fetch real trading logs for your strategy. The logs start coming up as soon as your submitted real trading job reaches the 'STARTED' state (refer to the preceding recipe for more information on the states of a real trading job). The AlgoBulls platform allows you to fetch logs in real time, even while the real trading job is still going on. You can get insights into the strategy's execution without having to wait for the real trading job to complete. This is helpful as real trading jobs are usually long-running. The pyalgotrading package provides a simple method we can use to fetch the execution logs for a given strategy.

Make sure you have gone through the first six recipes of Chapter 8, *Algorithmic Trading Strategies – Coding Step by Step*, to get a complete picture of the strategy class we will be using; that is, StrategyEMARegularOrder.

Getting ready

Make sure the algobulls_connection and strategy_code1 objects are available in your Python namespace. Refer to the first recipe of this chapter to set up the algobulls_connection and strategy_code1 objects.

How to do it...

Execute the following steps to complete this recipe:

1. Fetch the real trading execution logs for `strategy_code1`:

```
>>> logs = algobulls_connection.get_realtrading_logs(
                                        strategy_code1)
>>> print(logs)
```

We got the following output (your output may differ):

```
[2020-07-09 09:12:25] Logs not available yet. Please retry in
sometime.
```

2. Fetch the real trading execution logs for `strategy_code1` again after some time:

```
>>> logs = algobulls_connection.get_realtrading_logs(
                                        strategy_code1)
>>> print(logs)
```

We got the following output (your output may differ):

```
...
########################################
 INITIALIZING ALGOBULLS CORE (v3.2.0)...
########################################
[2020-07-09 09:13:05] Welcome PUSHPAK MAHAVIR DAGADE!
[2020-07-09 09:13:05] Reading strategy...
[2020-07-09 09:13:05] STARTING ALGOBULLS CORE...
...
[2020-07-09 10:30:00] [CRITICAL] [order] [PLACING NEW ORDER]
[2020-07-09 10:30:00] [2b079bc873f64f53a33f91b6ceec707b] [BUY]
[NSE:SBIN] [QTY:1] [QTY PENDING: 1] [ENTRY PRICE: 194.7]
[PRICE:None] [TRIGGER PRICE:None] [ORDER_TYPE_REGULAR]
[ORDER_CODE_INTRADAY] [ORDER_VARIETY_MARKET] [ORDER_POSITION_ENTER]
...
[2020-07-09 15:30:00] [INFO] [clock] Candle generation has been
stopped...
[2020-07-09 15:30:00] [INFO] [tls] Received event END OF MARKET.
Stopping Trading Core Engine...
[2020-07-09 15:30:00] [INFO] [tls] Exiting all open positions with
order code: ORDER_CODE_INTRADAY (if any)...
[2020-07-09 15:30:00] [CRITICAL] [tls] [User: PUSHPAK MAHAVIR
DAGADE] Trading session completed
...
```

The complete output is not shown here. Please visit the following link to read the complete output: `https://github.com/algobulls/pyalgostrategypool/blob/master/pyalgostrategypool/sample/realtrading/strategy_ema_regular_order/logs.txt`.

How it works...

In *step 1*, you use the `get_realtrading_logs()` method of the `algobulls_connection` object to fetch the strategy real trading logs in real time. This method accepts strategy code as an argument. You pass `strategy_code1` here. The return data is a string. If you try this step immediately after submitting the job, you get a string, which says the logs are not ready yet (`[2020-07-09 09:12:25] Logs not available yet. Please retry in sometime.`). This happens if the real trading job is in the `'STARTING'` state.

In *step 2*, you fetch the logs again after some time. If the job is out of the `'STARTING'` state, you start getting your strategy execution logs. You get all the real trading logs every time you call the `get_realtrading_logs()` function.

There's more...

Once the real trading job moves to the `'STOPPED'` state, no new logs are generated. You can fetch the complete logs any time before you submit the next real trading job for the same strategy. If a new real trading job is submitted (for the same strategy), these logs will no longer be accessible via the `get_realtrading_logs()` method. You can save the fetched logs to a file if you'd like to refer to them at a later date.

EMA–Regular–Order strategy – fetching a real trading report – P&L table

After submitting a real trading job on the AlgoBulls Platform, the AlgoBulls real trading engine starts executing the strategy. During its execution, along with the logs, the AlgoBulls real trading engine also generates a P&L table in real time. This table holds information on every trade punched in by the strategy. It also contains details on the mappings between entry and exit orders, the trade P&L, and the cumulative P&L, sorted chronologically, with the latest order first. This table gives us insight into the strategy's overall performance with the help of individual and cumulative P&L numbers. The entry-exit order mapping also helps validate the strategy's behavior.

In this recipe, you will fetch the P&L table report for your strategy. This report is available as soon as the first trade is punched in by your strategy after you submit a real trading job. The AlgoBulls platform allows you to fetch the P&L table in real time, even while the real trading job is still going on. You can get insights into the strategy's performance without having to wait for the real trading job to complete. This is helpful as real trading jobs are usually long-running. The `pyalgotrading` package provides a simple method we can use to fetch the P&L table for a given strategy.

 Make sure you have gone through the first six recipes of `Chapter 8`, *Algorithmic Trading Strategies – Coding Step by Step*, to get a complete picture of the strategy class we will be using; that is, `StrategyEMARegularOrder`.

Getting ready

Make sure the `algobulls_connection` and `strategy_code1` objects are available in your Python namespace. Refer to the first recipe of this chapter to set up the `algobulls_connection` and `strategy_code1` objects.

How to do it...

Fetch the real trading P&L report for `strategy_code1`:

```
>>> algobulls_connection.get_realtrading_report_pnl_table(strategy_code1)
```

We get the following output. Your output may differ (note that the following output has been split into multiple tables for representation purposes. You will see a single wide table in your Jupyter Notebook):

	instrument	entry_timestamp	entry_transaction_type	entry_quantity	entry_price
0	NSE_EQ:SBIN	2020-07-09 12:45:00	BUY	1	194.45
1	NSE_EQ:SBIN	2020-07-09 11:30:00	SELL	1	194.05
2	NSE_EQ:SBIN	2020-07-09 11:15:00	BUY	1	194.75
3	NSE_EQ:SBIN	2020-07-09 10:45:00	SELL	1	194
4	NSE_EQ:SBIN	2020-07-09 10:30:00	BUY	1	194.7

	instrument	exit_timestamp	exit_transaction_type	exit_quantity	exit_price
0	NSE_EQ:SBIN	2020-07-09 15:30:00	SELL	1	200
1	NSE_EQ:SBIN	2020-07-09 12:45:00	BUY	1	194.45
2	NSE_EQ:SBIN	2020-07-09 11:30:00	SELL	1	194.05
3	NSE_EQ:SBIN	2020-07-09 11:15:00	BUY	1	194.75
4	NSE_EQ:SBIN	2020-07-09 10:45:00	SELL	1	194

	pnl_absolute	pnl_percentage	pnl_cumulative_absolute	pnl_cumulative_percentage
0	5.55	2.85	3	1.53
1	-0.4	-0.21	-2.55	-1.32
2	-0.7	-0.36	-2.15	-1.11
3	-0.75	-0.39	-1.45	-0.75
4	-0.7	-0.36	-0.7	-0.36

How it works...

In this recipe, you use the `get_realtrading_report_pnl_table()` method of the `algobulls_connection` object to fetch the real trading P&L table in real time. This method accepts strategy code as an argument. You pass `strategy_code1` here. The return data is a `pandas.DataFrame` object with multiple columns, described as follows:

- `instrument`: Financial instrument for which the trade was entered.
- `entry_timestamp`: The timestamp at which the entry order was placed. (Note that it may remain in the `'OPEN'` state for a while before it goes to the `'COMPLETE'` state.)
- `entry_transaction_type`: Entry order transaction type (either BUY or SELL).
- `entry_quantity`: Entry order quantity.
- `entry_price`: Price at which the entry order gets executed and goes to the `'COMPLETE'` state.

- `exit_timestamp`: The timestamp at which the exit order was placed. (Note that it may remain in the `'OPEN'` state for a while before it goes to the `'COMPLETE'` state.)
- `exit_transaction_type`: Exit order transaction type (either BUY or SELL).
- `exit_quantity`: Exit order quantity.
- `exit_price`: Price at which the exit order gets executed and goes to the `'COMPLETE'` state.

- `pnl_absolute`: Difference between the exit order execution price and the entry order execution price. Mathematically, this is (*exit_price - entry_price*)*exit_quantity* for a long trade and (*entry_price - exit_price*)*exit_quantity* for a short trade. A positive value would imply that the trade is a profit-making trade. A negative value would imply that the trade is a loss-making trade.
- `pnl_percentage`: Percentage of profit or loss with respect to the entry price. Mathematically, this is *pnl_absolute / entry_price / exit_quantity* x 100.
- `pnl_cumulative_absolute`: Cumulative profit or loss. Mathematically, this is the sum of all the `pnl_absolute` values of the previous trades. This number gives us direct insight into the strategy's performance against the simulation time.
- `pnl_cumulative_percentage`: Percentage of cumulative profit or loss with respect to the entry price. Mathematically, this is *pnl_cumulative / entry_price / exit_quantity* × 100.

There's more...

Once the real trading job moves to the `'STOPPED'` state, the P&L table report will not update anymore. You can fetch the complete P&L report any time before you submit the next real trading job for the same strategy. If a new real trading job is submitted (for the same strategy), this report will no longer be accessible via the `get_realtrading_report_pnl_table()` method. You can save the fetched report to a `.csv` file if you'd like to refer to it at a later date.

EMA–Regular–Order strategy – fetching a real trading report – statistics table

After submitting a real trading job on the AlgoBulls platform, the AlgoBulls real trading engine starts executing the strategy. During its execution, along with the logs and P&L table, the AlgoBulls real trading engine also generates a summary from the P&L table in real time. This summary is a table of statistics containing various statistical numbers, such as `Net P&L` (absolute and percentage), `Max Drawdown` (absolute and percentage), count of total trades, winning trades, losing trades, long trades and short trades, the maximum gain and minimum gain (or maximum loss), and the average profit per winning and losing trade. This table gives an instant overview of the strategy's overall performance.

In this recipe, you will fetch the statistics table report for your strategy. This report is available as soon as the first trade is punched in by your strategy after you submit a real trading job. The AlgoBulls platform allows you to fetch the statistics table in real time, even while the real trading job is still going on. You can get insights into the strategy's performance without having to wait for the real trading job to complete. This is helpful as real trading jobs are usually long-running. The `pyalgotrading` package provides a simple method we can use to fetch the statistics table for a given strategy.

 Make sure you have gone through the first six recipes of `Chapter 8`, *Algorithmic Trading Strategies – Coding Step by Step*, to get a complete picture of the strategy class we will be using; that is, `StrategyEMARegularOrder`.

Getting ready

Make sure the `algobulls_connection` and `strategy_code1` objects are available in your Python namespace. Refer to the first recipe of this chapter to set up the `algobulls_connection` and `strategy_code1` objects.

How to do it...

Fetch the real trading statistics report for `strategy_code1`:

```
>>> algobulls_connection.get_realtrading_report_statistics(strategy_code1)
```

We got the following output (your output may differ):

	highlight_type	highlight_value
0	Net PnL	3.00
1	Net PnL %	1.53
2	Max Drawdown	-2.55
3	Max Drawdown %	-1.31
4	Number of Trades	5.00
5	Number of Wins	1.00
6	Number of Looses	4.00
7	Number of Long Trades	3.00
8	Number of Short Trades	2.00
9	Max Gain	5.55
10	Min Gain	-0.75
11	Avg. Profit per winning trade	5.55
12	Avg. Profit per losing trade	-0.64

How it works...

In this recipe, you use the `get_realtrading_report_statistics()` method of the `algobulls_connection` object to fetch the real trading statistics table in real time. This method accepts strategy code as an argument. You pass `strategy_code1` here. The return data is a `pandas.DataFrame` object with two columns – `highlight_type` and `highlight_value` – and multiple rows. The rows are described as follows:

- `Net PnL`: The cumulative real trading P&L. This is also the `pnl_cumulative_absolute` value of the first entry in the P&L table.
- `Net PnL %`: The cumulative real trading P&L percentage. This is also the `pnl_cumulative_percentage` value of the first entry in the P&L table.
- `Max Drawdown`: The lowest value in the `pnl_cumulative` column of the P&L table. This indicates the maximum loss your strategy has encountered during the execution.

- Max Drawdown %: Mathematically, this is *(Max Drawdown) / (corresponding entry_price) / exit_quantity × 100.*
- Number of Trades: Total trades (entry and exit counted as one) during the session.
- Number of Wins: Count of trades where the trade P&L was non-negative.
- Number of Losses: Count of trades where the trade P&L was negative.
- Number of Long Trades: Count of trades where the entry transaction type was 'BUY'.
- Number of Short Trades: Count of trades where the entry transaction type was 'SELL'.
- Max Gain: P&L of the trade with the maximum P&L value among all trades.
- Min Gain: P&L of the trade with the minimum P&L value among all trades.
- Avg. Profit per winning trade: Mathematically, this is *(Total P&L of winning trades) / (Count of winning trades).*
- Avg. Profit per losing trade: Mathematically, this is *(Total P&L of losing trades) / (Count of losing trades).*

There's more...

If the statistics table is fetched while the real trading job is still running, the aforementioned numbers will be intermediate numbers, based on the trades completed until that time. The numbers may change as more trades are punched in, until the real trading job completes.

Once the real trading job moves to the 'STOPPED' state, the statistics table will not change anymore. You can fetch the complete statistics table any time before you submit the next real trading job for the same strategy. If a new real trading job is submitted (for the same strategy), this table will no longer be accessible via the get_realtrading_report_statistics() method. You can save the fetched report table to a .csv file if you'd like to refer to it at a later date.

MACD–Bracket–Order strategy – fetching the strategy

In this recipe, you will fetch the `StrategyMACDBracketOrder` strategy class from your account on the AlgoBulls platform, which you must have uploaded while going through the last recipe in `Chapter 8`, *Algorithmic Trading Strategies – Coding Step by Step*. This recipe starts with setting up a connection to the AlgoBulls platform, querying all available strategies in your account, and fetching details about the required strategy class; that is, `StrategyMACDBracketOrder`.

 Make sure you have gone through the last six recipes of `Chapter 8`, *Algorithmic Trading Strategies – Coding Step by Step*, to get a complete picture of the strategy class we will be using; that is, `StrategyMACDBracketOrder`.

How to do it...

Execute the following steps to complete this recipe:

1. Import the necessary modules:

```
>>> from pyalgotrading.algobulls import AlgoBullsConnection
```

2. Create a new AlgoBulls connection object:

```
>>> algobulls_connection = AlgoBullsConnection()
```

3. Fetch the authorization URL:

```
>>> algobulls_connection.get_authorization_url()
```

We got the following output:

```
Please login to this URL with your AlgoBulls credentials and get
your developer access token: https://app.algobulls.com/user/login
'https://app.algobulls.com/user/login'
```

4. Log into the preceding link with your AlgoBulls credentials, fetch your token, and set it here (refer to *Appendix II* for more details):

```
>>> algobulls_connection.set_access_token('
            80b7a69b168c5b3f15d56688841a8f2da5e2ab2c')
```

5. Fetch and display all the strategies you have created and uploaded so far:

```
>>> all_strategies = algobulls_connection.get_all_strategies()
>>> all_strategies
```

We got the following output. Your output may differ (make sure you've followed the recipes in `Chapter 8`, *Algorithmic Trading Strategies – Coding Step by Step*, to get a similar output):

	strategyCode	strategyName
0	49287246f9704bbcbad76ade9e2091d9	EMA Regular Order Strategy
1	4faf514fe096432b8e9f80f5951bd2ea	MACD Bracket Order Strategy

6. Fetch and display the strategy code of the second strategy; that is, the MACD-Bracket-Order strategy:

```
>>> strategy_code2 = all_strategies.iloc[1]['strategyCode']
>>> strategy_code2
```

We got the following output (your output may differ):

```
'49287246f9704bbcbad76ade9e2091d9'
```

7. Before real trading your strategy, you can inspect your strategy to ensure you have the right strategy:

```
>>> strategy_details2 = \
        algobulls_connection.get_strategy_details(strategy_code2)
>>> print(strategy_details2)
```

We got the following output:

```
class StrategyMACDBracketOrder(StrategyBase):

    def __init__(self, *args, **kwargs):
        super().__init__(*args, **kwargs)

        self.fastMA_period = \
            self.strategy_parameters['fastma_period']
        self.slowMA_period = \
            self.strategy_parameters['slowma_period']
        self.signal_period = \
            self.strategy_parameters['signal_period']
        self.stoploss = \
            self.strategy_parameters['stoploss_trigger']
```

```
            self.target = self.strategy_parameters['target_trigger']
            self.trailing_stoploss = \
                self.strategy_parameters['trailing_stoploss_trigger']

            self.main_order = None

        def initialize(self):
            self.main_order = {}

        @staticmethod
        def name():
            return 'MACD Bracket Order Strategy'
        ....
        def strategy_exit_position(self, candle, instrument, \
                                   sideband_info):
            if sideband_info['action'] == 'EXIT':
                self.main_order[instrument].exit_position()
                self.main_order[instrument] = None
                return True

            return False
```

The complete output is not shown here. Please visit the following link to read the complete output: `https://github.com/algobulls/pyalgostrategypool/blob/master/pyalgostrategypool/strategy_macd_bracket_order.py`.

How it works...

You import the necessary modules in *step 1*. In *step 2*, you create an instance of the `AlgoBullsConnection` class, named `algobulls_connection`. In *step 3*, you get the authorization URL using the `get_authorization_url()` method of the `algobulls_connection` object. This prints the authorization URL. You should visit this URL from your web browser to sign into the AlgoBulls platform and fetch your developer access token. (You can find more details, along with screenshots, in *Appendix II* on fetching a developer access token from the AlgoBulls platform.) You copy the access token and set it in *step 4* using the `set_access_token()` method of `algobulls_connection`. If the token is accepted, a successful connection is set up with the AlgoBulls platform.

In *step 5*, you fetch all the strategies you have created and uploaded on the AlgoBulls platform so far. You use the `get_all_strategies()` method for this step and assign it to a new variable, `all_strategies`. This variable is a `pandas.DataFrame` object with `strategyCode` and `strategyName` columns. This table holds information on the strategy codes and the strategy names you have uploaded previously.

If you followed the *MACD-Bracket-Order Strategy – uploading the strategy on the AlgoBulls trading platform* recipe from `Chapter 8`, *Algorithmic Trading Strategies – Coding Step by Step*, you will find a strategy called **MACD-Regular-Order strategy**. In *step 6*, you assign the strategy code of the MACD-Regular-Order strategy to a new variable called `strategy_code2`. The strategy code is shown in the output of this step. This strategy code is unique for every strategy on the AlgoBulls platform.

Finally, in *step 7*, you ensure that the strategy being referred to by `strategy_code2` is indeed the one you uploaded earlier (in the last recipe of `Chapter 8`, *Algorithmic Trading Strategies – Coding Step by Step*). You use the `get_strategy_details()` method of the `algobulls_connection` object to inspect the strategy. This method takes strategy code as an argument. You pass `strategy_code2` here. This method returns the entire class code as a string. You assign it to a new variable, `strategy_details2`, and display it.

 If, you'd like to change the class code being referred to by `strategy_code2`, as shown in *step 7*, please refer to the *There's more...* section of the last recipe in `Chapter 8`, *Algorithmic Trading Strategies – Coding Step by Step*.

MACD–Bracket–Order strategy – real trading the strategy

In this recipe, you will perform real trading on the MACD-Bracket-Order strategy. You must have fetched this strategy from your account on the AlgoBulls platform in the preceding recipe of this chapter. You will leverage the real trading functionality facilitated by `pyalgotrading` for this recipe, which, in turn, submits a real trading job on the AlgoBulls platform.

Once submitted, real trading will be run by the AlgoBulls real trading engine. You can query the status anytime to find out the state of the real trading job. The job goes through the following states, in the given order:

- `STARTING` (intermediate state)
- `STARTED` (stable state)
- `STOPPING` (intermediate state)
- `STOPPED` (stable state)

On submitting a job, it starts with an intermediate state, 'STARTING'. In this state, the AlgoBulls real trading engine fetches the strategy and get the execution environment ready, which may take a couple of minutes. Once done, the job moves to the 'STARTED' state. Strategy real trading happens in this stage. Here, it stays as long as it takes for real trading to complete. Once done, the job moves to an intermediate state, 'STOPPING'. In this state, the AlgoBulls real trading engine cleans up the resources allocated for this job, which usually takes less than a minute. Finally, the job moves to the 'STOPPED' state.

If you have already submitted a real trading job for a strategy, you cannot submit another job for the same strategy until the first job completes. This means you have to wait for the first job to move to the 'STOPPED' state. If the first job is long-running and you would like to stop it immediately, you can submit a stop job request via pyalgotrading. You need to ensure the job is in the 'STARTED' state before submitting the request.

After submitting a real trading job, you can fetch logs and reports for the strategy execution in real time. These logs and reports help validate the strategy's performance and debug any potential issues.

You can refer to the second recipe of this chapter for the state machine diagram of a real trading job. It demonstrates the various states and transitions of a real trading job during its lifetime on the AlgoBulls platform.

 Make sure you have gone through the last six recipes of Chapter 8, *Algorithmic Trading Strategies – Coding Step by Step*, to get a complete picture of the strategy class we will be using; that is, StrategyMACDBracketOrder.

Getting ready

Make sure the algobulls_connection and strategy_code2 objects are available in your Python namespace. Refer to the preceding recipe of this chapter to set up the algobulls_connection and strategy_code2 objects.

How to do it...

Execute the following steps to complete this recipe:

1. Import the necessary modules:

```
>>> from datetime import time
>>> from pyalgotrading.constants import *
```

2. Search for an instrument and use its trading symbol as a keyword. Assign the returned object to `instruments`:

```
>>> instrument = algobulls_connection.search_instrument('
                                                    TATASTEEL')
>>> instrument
```

We got the following output (your output may differ):

```
[{'id': 1, 'value': 'NSE:TATASTEEL'}]
```

3. Get `value` for the instrument of choice from `instruments`:

```
>>> instrument = instrument[0]['value']
>>> instrument
```

We got the following output:

```
'NSE:TATASTEEL'
```

4. Submit a real trading job for `strategy_code2`:

```
>>> algobulls_connection.realtrade(
        strategy_code=strategy_code2,
        start_time=time(hour=9, minute=15),
        end_time=time(hour=15, minute=30),
        instrument=instrument,
        lots=1,
        strategy_parameters={
            'fastma_period': 26,
            'slowma_period': 6,
            'signal_period': 9,
            'target_trigger': 0.01,
            'stoploss_trigger': 0.01,
            'trailing_stoploss_trigger': 1
        },
        candle_interval=CandleInterval.MINUTES_15)
```

We got the following output:

```
Setting Strategy Config... Success.
Submitting REALTRADING job... Success.
```

5. Check the status of the submitted real trading job:

```
>>> algobulls_connection.get_realtrading_job_status(strategy_code2)
{'data': 'STARTING'}
```

6. Check the status of the submitted real trading job again after some time:

```
>>> algobulls_connection.get_realtrading_job_status(strategy_code2)
{'data': 'STARTED'}
```

How it works...

In *step 1*, you import the time class from the datetime module and all the constants from the pyalgotrading.constants module. In *step 2*, you fetch the instrument that you would like to real trade the strategy for, the **MACD-Bracket-Order strategy**, using the search_instrument() method of the algobulls_connection object. The search_instrument() method accepts a search string as an argument, which should be the trading symbol, in part or complete, of the instrument you are interested in. You pass 'TATASTEEL' here. This function returns a list with details of instruments that match the search string. There could be multiple instruments that could have the search string in their trading symbols. In *step 3*, you fetch the value of the first matched instrument and assign it to a new variable, instrument.

In *step 4*, you submit a real trading job using the realtrade() method of the algobulls_connection() object. It takes the following arguments:

- strategy_code: Strategy code of the strategy for which real trading has to be performed. This should be a string. You pass strategy_code2 here.
- start_time: Today's time when real trading should be started. This should be a datetime.time object. Here, you pass an object holding the value 9:15 hours – time(hour=9, minute=15). Refer to the first recipe of this book for details on creating a datetime object.
- end_time: Today's time when real trading should be performed. This object should hold a time value ahead of the value held by start_time. This should be a datetime.time instance. Here, you pass an object holding the value 15:30 hours – time(hour=15, minute=30).
- instrument: Financial instrument for which real trading should be run. Historical data will be fetched for this instrument. This should be a string. You pass instrument here.
- lots: Number of lots for which real trading should be performed. This should be an integer. The quantity is calculated by the strategy as *number of lots × lot size of the financial instrument*. You pass 1 here.

- `strategy_parameters`: Parameter names and values expected by the strategy. This should be a dictionary, with `parameter-name` and `parameter-value` as key-value pairs. You pass the following parameters here:
  - `fastma_period`: 26
  - `slowma_period`: 6
  - `signal_period`: 9
  - `target_trigger`: 0.01
  - `stoploss_trigger`: 0.01
  - `trailing_stoploss_trigger`: 1

  (Recall that the parameters for the MACD-Bracket-Order strategy have been defined in its `__init__()` method, as shown in the first recipe of `Chapter 8`, *Algorithmic Trading Strategies – Coding Step by Step*).

- `candle_interval`: The candle interval for the historical data fetched for real trading. This should be an enum of the `CandleInterval` type. You pass `CandleInterval.MINUTES_15` here. (The `CandleInterval` enum provides various enums for candle intervals, some of which are `MINUTE_1`, `MINUTES_3`, `MINUTES_5`, `MINUTES_10`, `MINUTES_15`, `MINUTES_30`, `HOUR`, and `DAY`.)

If the job submission is successful, you will see `Success` messages being printed by the `realtrade()` function.

Once a job has been submitted, it takes a while to start. After starting, it may take some time to finish, depending on the duration of real trading specified using the `start_time` and `end_time` arguments. Usually, real trading is run for the entire trading day, which means the job would be running for 6-8 hours.

In *step 5*, you fetch the job's status using the `get_realtrading_job_status()` method of the `algobulls_connection` object. You pass `strategy_code2` as the argument here. This method returns a dictionary with a single key-value pair – the *data* and the *job* status. If you query the status immediately after placing the job, you get `'STARTING'` as the status. In *step 6*, you query the status again after some time, and if the job has started, you get a status of `'STARTED'`.

A successful submission implies that the minimum inputs needed to real trade a strategy have been passed in the required format. However, this does not ensure that the strategy will run without errors. The strategy's execution may still run into errors during real trading. To debug execution issues, you will need to fetch the output logs, which will be explained in the next recipe. Possible reasons for errors could be either bugs in the strategy class' Python code or that an incomplete `strategy_parameters` dictionary has been passed to the `realtrade()` function.

There's more...

If a job is running for a long time and you would like to stop it before its completion, you can use the `stop_realtrading_job()` method of the `algobulls_connection` object. This method accepts strategy code as an argument. You pass `strategy_code2` here. This method submits a stop request to the AlgoBulls real trading engine. If the request is accepted, you will see a `Success` message here:

```
>>> algobulls_connection.stop_realtrading_job(strategy_code2)
   Stopping REALTRADING job... Success.
```

If you query the status after submitting the stop request, you'll get `'STOPPING'` as the status:

```
>>> algobulls_connection.get_realtrading_job_status(strategy_code2)
{'data': 'STOPPING'}
```

If you query the status again after some time, and if the job has stopped, you'll get `'STOPPED'` as the status:

```
>>> algobulls_connection.get_realtrading_job_status(strategy_code2)
{'data': 'STOPPED'}
```

MACD–Bracket–Order strategy – fetching real trading logs in real time

After submitting a real trading job on the AlgoBulls platform, the AlgoBulls real trading engine starts executing the strategy. During its execution, every event that occurs and every decision that's been made by the AlgoBulls real trading engine is recorded with exact timestamps in the form of textual logs.

Examples of recorded activities include the given strategy config, every new candle generated at regular intervals, trades punched in by your strategy, the entry and exit of positions created by these trades, waits for new candles, and so on. These logs are quintessential for validating the strategy and debugging behavior or performance issues that are frequently encountered while developing a strategy.

In this recipe, you will fetch real trading logs for your strategy. The logs start coming up as soon as your submitted real trading job reaches the 'STARTED' state (refer to the preceding recipe for more information on the states of a real trading job). The AlgoBulls platform allows you to fetch logs in real time, even while the real trading job is still going on. You can get insights into the strategy's execution without having to wait for the real trading job to complete. This is helpful as real trading jobs are usually long-running. The pyalgotrading package provides a simple method we can use to fetch the execution logs for a given strategy.

 Make sure you have gone through the last six recipes of Chapter 8, *Algorithmic Trading Strategies – Coding Step by Step*, to get a complete picture of the strategy class we will be using; that is, StrategyMACDBracketOrder.

Getting ready

Make sure the algobulls_connection and strategy_code2 objects are available in your Python namespace. Refer to the *MACD-Bracket-Order strategy – fetching the strategy* recipe of this chapter to set up the algobulls_connection and strategy_code2 objects.

How to do it...

Execute the following steps to complete this recipe:

1. Fetch the real trading execution logs for strategy_code2:

```
>>> logs = algobulls_connection.get_realtrading_logs(
                                        strategy_code2)
>>> print(logs)
```

We got the following output (your output may differ):

```
[2020-07-09 09:13:45] Logs not available yet. Please retry in
sometime.
```

2. Fetch the real trading execution logs for `strategy_code2` again after some time:

```
>>> logs = algobulls_connection.get_realtrading_logs(
                                         strategy_code2)
>>> print(logs)
```

We got the following output (your output may differ):

```
...
#########################################
 INITIALIZING ALGOBULLS CORE (v3.2.0)...
#########################################
[2020-07-09 09:14:09] Welcome PUSHPAK MAHAVIR DAGADE!
[2020-07-09 09:14:09] Reading strategy...
[2020-07-09 09:14:09] STARTING ALGOBULLS CORE...
...
[2020-07-09 09:45:00] [CRITICAL] [order] [PLACING NEW ORDER]
[2020-07-09 09:45:00][577e6b4cb646463282ae98ec1c0e6c25] [BUY]
[NSE:TATASTEEL] [QTY:1] [QTY PENDING: 1] [ENTRY PRICE: 345.0]
[PRICE:345.0] [TRIGGER PRICE:None] [ORDER_TYPE_BRACKET]
[ORDER_CODE_INTRADAY] [ORDER_VARIETY_LIMIT] [ORDER_POSITION_ENTER]
[STOPLOSS TRIGGER:341.55] [TARGET TRIGGER:348.45] [TRAILING
STOPLOSS TRIGGER:345.0]
...
[2020-07-09 15:30:00] [INFO] [clock] Candle generation has been
stopped...
[2020-07-09 15:30:00] [INFO] [tls] Received event END OF MARKET.
Stopping Trading Core Engine...
[2020-07-09 15:30:00] [INFO] [tls] Exiting all open positions with
order code: ORDER_CODE_INTRADAY (if any)...
[2020-07-09 15:30:00] [CRITICAL] [tls] [User: PUSHPAK MAHAVIR
DAGADE] Trading session completed
...
```

The complete output is not shown here. Please visit the following link to read the complete output: https://github.com/algobulls/pyalgostrategypool/blob/master/ pyalgostrategypool/sample/realtrading/strategy_macd_bracket_order/logs.txt.

How it works...

In *step 1*, you use the `get_realtrading_logs()` method of the `algobulls_connection` object to fetch the strategy real trading logs in real time. This method accepts strategy code as an argument. You pass `strategy_code2` here. The return data is a string. If you try this step immediately after submitting the job, you get a string, which says the logs are not ready yet (`[2020-07-09 09:13:45] Logs not available yet. Please retry in sometime..`) This happens if the real trading job is in the `'STARTING'` state.

In *step 2*, you fetch the logs again after some time. If the job is out of the `'STARTING'` state, you start getting your strategy execution logs. You get all the real trading logs every time you call the `get_realtrading_logs()` function.

There's more...

Once the real trading job moves to the `'STOPPED'` state, no new logs are generated. You can fetch the complete logs any time before you submit the next real trading job for the same strategy. If a new real trading job is submitted (for the same strategy), these logs will no longer be accessible via the `get_realtrading_logs()` method. You can save the fetched logs to a file if you'd like to refer to them at a later date.

MACD–Bracket–Order strategy – fetching a real trading report – P&L table

After submitting a real trading job on the AlgoBulls platform, the AlgoBulls real trading engine starts executing the strategy. During its execution, along with the logs, the AlgoBulls real trading engine also generates a P&L table in real time. This table holds information on every trade punched in by the strategy. It also contains details on the mappings between entry and exit orders, the trade P&L, and the cumulative P&L, sorted chronologically, with the latest order first. This table gives us insight into the strategy's overall performance with the help of individual and cumulative P&L numbers. The entry-exit order mapping also helps validate the strategy's behavior.

In this recipe, you will fetch the P&L table report for your strategy. This report is available as soon as the first trade is punched in by your strategy after you submit a real trading job. The AlgoBulls platform allows you to fetch the P&L table in real time, even while the real trading job is still going on. You can get insights into the strategy's performance without having to wait for the real trading job to complete. This is helpful as real trading jobs are usually long-running. The `pyalgotrading` package provides a simple method we can use to fetch the P&L table for a given strategy.

 Make sure you have gone through the last six recipes of `Chapter 8`, *Algorithmic Trading Strategies – Coding Step by Step*, to get a complete picture of the strategy class we will be using; that is, `StrategyMACDBracketOrder`.

Getting ready

Make sure the `algobulls_connection` and `strategy_code2` objects are available in your Python namespace. Refer to the *MACD-Bracket-Order strategy – fetching the strategy* recipe of this chapter to set up the `algobulls_connection` and `strategy_code2` objects.

How to do it...

Fetch the real trading P&L report for `strategy_code2`:

```
>>> algobulls_connection.get_realtrading_report_pnl_table(strategy_code2)
```

We got the following output. Your output may differ (note that the following output has been split into multiple tables for representation purposes. You will see a single wide table in your Jupyter Notebook):

	instrument	entry_timestamp	entry_transaction_type	entry_quantity	entry_price
0	NSE_EQ:TATASTEEL	2020-07-09 12:00:00	SELL	1	345.2
1	NSE_EQ:TATASTEEL	2020-07-09 09:45:00	BUY	1	345

	instrument	exit_timestamp	exit_transaction_type	exit_quantity	exit_price
0	NSE_EQ:TATASTEEL	2020-07-09 15:30:00	BUY	1	345
1	NSE_EQ:TATASTEEL	2020-07-09 10:00:00	SELL	1	348.45

	pnl_absolute	pnl_percentage	pnl_cumulative_absolute	pnl_cumulative_percentage
0	0.2	0.06	3.65	1.06
1	3.45	1	3.45	1

How it works...

In this recipe, you use the `get_realtrading_report_pnl_table()` method of the `algobulls_connection` object to fetch the real trading P&L table in real time. This method accepts strategy code as an argument. You pass `strategy_code2` here. The return data is a `pandas.DataFrame` object with multiple columns, described as follows:

- `instrument`: Financial instrument for which trade was entered.
- `entry_timestamp`: The timestamp at which the entry order was placed. (Note that it may remain in the `'OPEN'` state for a while before it goes to the `'COMPLETE'` state.)
- `entry_transaction_type`: Entry order transaction type (either BUY or SELL).
- `entry_quantity`: Entry order quantity.
- `entry_price`: Price at which the entry order gets executed and goes to the `'COMPLETE'` state.
- `exit_timestamp`: The timestamp at which the exit order was placed. (Note that it may remain in the `'OPEN'` state for a while before it goes to the `'COMPLETE'` state.)
- `exit_transaction_type`: Exit order transaction type (either BUY or SELL).
- `exit_quantity`: Exit order quantity.
- `exit_price`: Price at which the exit order gets executed and goes to the `'COMPLETE'` state.
- `pnl_absolute`: Difference between the exit order execution price and the entry order execution price. Mathematically, this is (*exit_price - entry_price*)**exit_quantity* for a long trade and (*entry_price - exit_price*)**exit_quantity* for a short trade. A positive value would imply that the trade is a profit-making trade. A negative value would imply that the trade is a loss-making trade.
- `pnl_percentage`: Percentage of profit or loss with respect to the entry price. Mathematically, this is *pnl_absolute / entry_price / exit_quantity* x 100.
- `pnl_cumulative_absolute`: Cumulative profit or loss. Mathematically, this is the sum of all the `pnl_absolute` values of the previous trades. This number gives us direct insight into the strategy's performance against the simulation time.
- `pnl_cumulative_percentage`: Percentage of cumulative profit or loss with respect to the entry price. Mathematically, this is *pnl_cumulative / entry_price / exit_quantity* x 100.

There's more...

Once the real trading job moves to the 'STOPPED' state, the P&L table report will not update anymore. You can fetch the complete P&L report any time before you submit the next real trading job for the same strategy. If a new real trading job is submitted (for the same strategy), this report will no longer be accessible via the `get_realtrading_report_pnl_table()` method. You can save the fetched report to a `.csv` file if you'd like to refer to it at a later date.

MACD–Bracket–Order strategy – fetching a real trading report – statistics table

After submitting a real trading job on the AlgoBulls platform, the AlgoBulls real trading engine starts executing the strategy. During its execution, along with the logs and P&L table, the AlgoBulls real trading engine also generates a summary from the P&L table in real time. This summary is a table of statistics containing various statistical numbers, such as Net P&L (absolute and percentage), Max Drawdown (absolute and percentage), count of total trades, winning trades, losing trades, long trades and short trades, the maximum gain and minimum gain (or maximum loss), and average profit per winning and losing trade. This table gives us an instant overview of the strategy's overall performance.

In this recipe, you will fetch the statistics table report for your strategy. This report is available as soon as the first trade is punched in by your strategy after you submit a real trading job. The AlgoBulls platform allows you to fetch the statistics table in real time, even while the real trading job is still going on. You can get insights into the strategy's performance without having to wait for the real trading job to complete. This is helpful as real trading jobs are usually long-running. The `pyalgotrading` package provides a simple method we can use to fetch the statistics table for a given strategy.

 Make sure you have gone through the last six recipes of Chapter 8, *Algorithmic Trading Strategies – Coding Step by Step*, to get a complete picture of the strategy class we will be using; that is, `StrategyMACDBracketOrder`.

Getting ready

Make sure the `algobulls_connection` and `strategy_code2` objects are available in your Python namespace. Refer to the *MACD-Bracket-Order strategy – fetching the strategy* recipe of this chapter to set up the `algobulls_connection` and `strategy_code2` objects.

How to do it...

Fetch the real trading statistics report for `strategy_code2`:

```
>>> algobulls_connection.get_realtrading_report_statistics(strategy_code2)
```

We got the following output (your output may differ):

	highlight_type	highlight_value
0	Net PnL	3.65
1	Net PnL %	1.06
2	Max Drawdown	3.45
3	Max Drawdown %	1.0
4	Number of Trades	2
5	Number of Wins	2
6	Number of Looses	0
7	Number of Long Trades	1
8	Number of Short Trades	1
9	Max Gain	3.45
10	Min Gain	0.2
11	Avg. Profit per winning trade	1.83
12	Avg. Profit per losing trade	-

How it works...

In this recipe, you use the `get_realtrading_report_statistics()` method of the `algobulls_connection` object to fetch the real trading statistics table in real time. This method accepts strategy code as an argument. You pass `strategy_code2` here. The return data is a `pandas.DataFrame` object with two columns – `highlight_type` and `highlight_value` – and multiple rows. The rows are described as follows:

- `Net PnL`: The cumulative real trading P&L. This is also the `pnl_cumulative_absolute` value of the first entry in the P&L table.
- `Net PnL %`: The cumulative real trading P&L percentage. This is also the `pnl_cumulative_percentage` value of the first entry in the P&L table.
- `Max Drawdown`: The lowest value in the `pnl_cumulative` column of the P&L table. This indicates the maximum loss your strategy has encountered during its execution.
- `Max Drawdown %`: Mathematically, this is *(Max Drawdown) / (corresponding entry_price) / exit_quantity* x 100.
- `Number of Trades`: Total trades (entry and exit are counted as one) during the session.
- `Number of Wins`: Count of trades where the trade P&L was non-negative.
- `Number of Losses`: Count of trades where the trade P&L was negative.
- `Number of Long Trades`: Count of trades where the entry transaction type was `'BUY'`.
- `Number of Short Trades`: Count of trades where the entry transaction type was `'SELL'`.
- `Max Gain`: P&L of the trade with the maximum P&L value among all trades.
- `Min Gain`: P&L of the trade with the minimum P&L value among all trades.
- `Avg. Profit per winning trade`: Mathematically, this is *(Total P&L of winning trades) / (Count of winning trades)*.
- `Avg. Profit per losing trade`: Mathematically, this is *(Total P&L of losing trades) / (Count of losing trades)*.

There's more...

If the statistics table is fetched while the real trading job is still running, the aforementioned numbers will be intermediate numbers, based on the trades completed until that time. The numbers may change as more trades are punched in, until the real trading job completes.

Once the real trading job moves to the `'STOPPED'` state, the statistics table will not change anymore. You can fetch the complete statistics table any time before you submit the next real trading job for the same strategy. If a new real trading job is submitted (for the same strategy), this table will no longer be accessible via the `get_realtrading_report_statistics()` method. You can save the fetched report to a `.csv` file if you'd like to refer to it at a later date.

Appendix I

Setting up your Zerodha account

This appendix will help you set up your broking account with Zerodha (`https://zerodha.com`).

The following sections are explained in this appendix:

- Opening a Zerodha account online
- Logging in to the Zerodha trading platform website
- Setting up your Zerodha Developer Options account
- Logging in to the Zerodha Developer Options website
- Purchasing and enabling the Zerodha Developer Options API
- Testing API keys and authorizing the app by firing your first API call

Opening a Zerodha account online

You can open your Zerodha account online by following the procedure explained in this YouTube video: `https://www.youtube.com/watch?v=dcOIc8YZ9pc`.

If you have the necessary documents handy, as mentioned in the video, account setup can be completed in under 30 minutes. Once it's done, your account opening process is initiated and you have to wait for a response from Zerodha's account opening team. It usually takes up to a week for Zerodha to get back to you with your account credentials.

You can also visit the Zerodha Support link if you need any help in opening your account (`https://support.zerodha.com/category/account-opening/online-account-opening/articles/how-do-i-open-an-account-online`).

Logging in to the Zerodha trading platform website

After successfully opening your account with Zerodha, you can log in to their trading platform, called **Kite**, with the credentials you have received. Visit `https://kite.zerodha.com`.

Upon visiting the website, you can log in to the website in five steps:

1. Enter your user ID.
2. Enter your password.
3. Click the **Login** button:

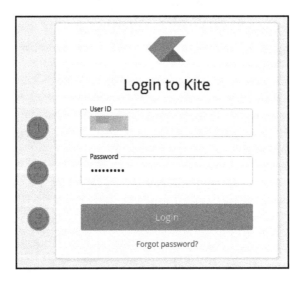

4. Enter your PIN:

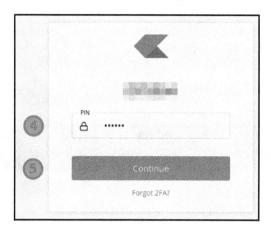

5. Click the **Continue** button.

Once you have logged in successfully, you should see the dashboard as shown in the following screenshot:

Setting up your Zerodha Developer Options account

Once you have got your Zerodha broking account credentials, we can now move on to setting up a Developer Options account with Zerodha.

Please proceed to `https://kite.trade` and click on **Signup**:

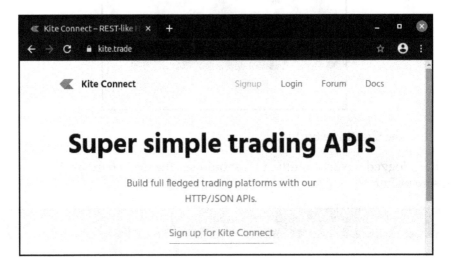

You can register a new account in eight steps:

1. Enter your E-mail ID.
2. Enter your name.
3. Enter your password.
4. Verify your password.
5. Enter your phone number.
6. Select your state of residence.
7. Read and check the **I AGREE TO THE ABOVE TERMS** checkbox.

8. Click the **Signup** button:

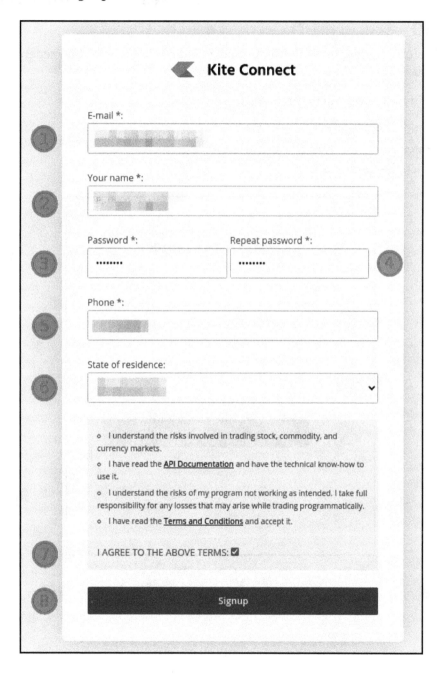

Logging in to the Zerodha Developer Options website

After successfully signing up with Kite Connect, you can log in with the credentials you have set. Visit `https://kite.trade`.

You can log in to the website in three steps:

1. Enter your registered E-mail ID.
2. Enter your password (the one used for signing up).
3. Click the **Login** button:

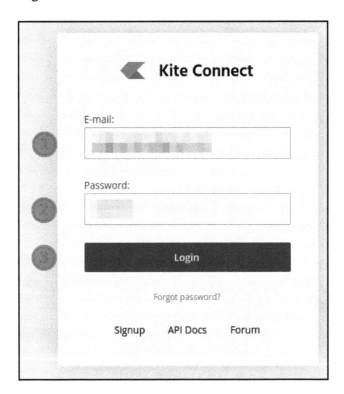

After logging in for the first time, you should land on a page like this:

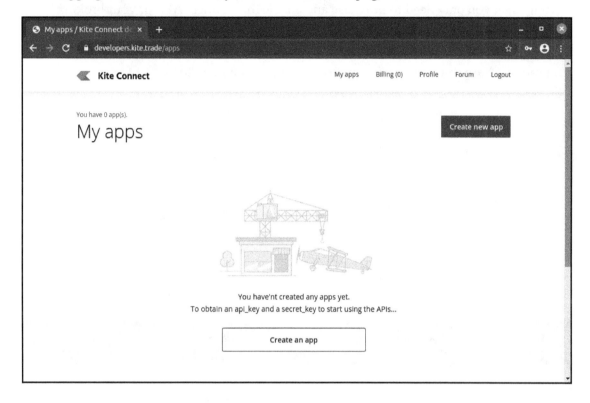

Purchasing and enabling the Zerodha Developer Options API

There are two types of API available:

- **Connect API**: This API allows orders to be placed over APIs, positions/holdings/orders to be fetched, profiles to be fetched, and so on. This API is required for real trading, but is not necessary for backtesting or paper trading.
- **Historical Data API**: This API allows the fetching of historical data. This API may be needed if you are implementing your own algo-trading systems. You can also take historical data from a separate vendor.

The documentation for both these APIs can be found here: `https://kite.trade/docs/connect`.

If you are going to use the AlgoBulls trading platform (`https://algobulls.com`) for real trading, then you only need to purchase and enable the Connect API for your broking account. You don't need to purchase any APIs for backtesting or paper trading. The AlgoBulls platform provides historical data for all services.

You can purchase credits for the required APIs after logging in to `https://kite.trade` in two steps:

1. Click on **Billing** in the top menu. This will load a new page:

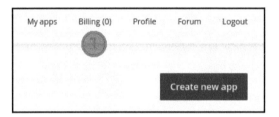

2. Enter the required amount and click the **Add credits** button. Complete the payment through the payment gateway window that pops up:

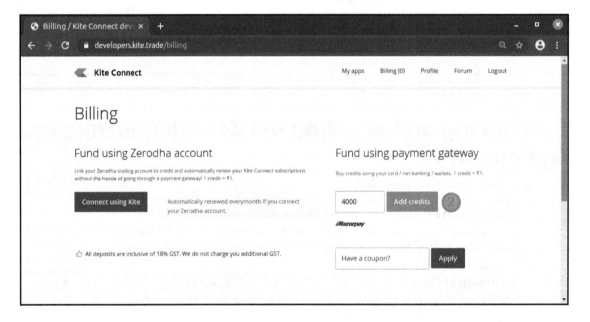

If you want to enable both the APIs, the required amount should be **4000**. If you want to enable just the Connect API, the required amount should be **2000.** Log in to `https://developers.kite.trade/create` to know more about the exact amounts required to purchase the APIs.

Next, to enable the required APIs, the following steps should be executed from the landing page:

1. Click on **Create new app**. This will load a new page:

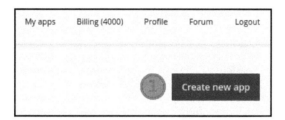

2. Ensure **Type: Connect** is selected.
3. Enter your app name.
4. Enter your Zerodha client ID.
5. Enter `http://127.0.0.1` as your **Redirect URL**. (If you are hosting a server locally on port 80, you can enter a URL with a different port that is not in use, say, `http://127.0.0.1:8000`).
6. Enter a description for your app.

7. Click the **Create** button:

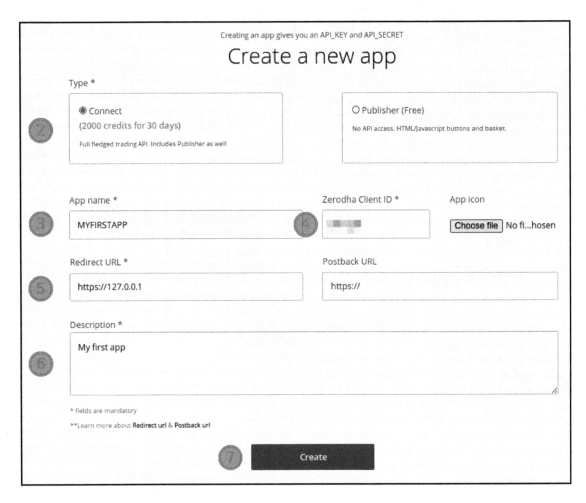

8. Read the confirmation message and type I UNDERSTAND.

9. Click the **OK** button:

This completes the creation of your first app. You should now see your app on the landing page:

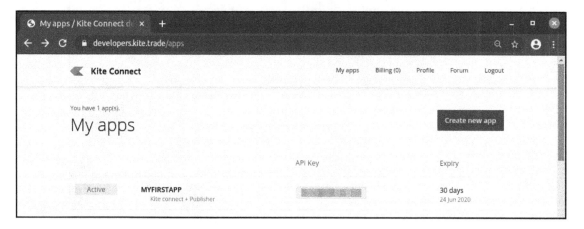

Click the app to check your details and also get the API key and API secret. Optionally, if you like to activate the Historical Data API, please click on **Subscribe** in the **Addons** section and confirm the subscription. This will cost 2,000 credits:

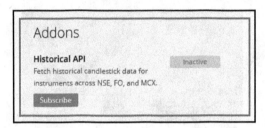

The keys can be obtained as shown in the following screenshot (**API key** and **API secret**). Click the **Show API secret** button to reveal it:

Testing API keys and authorizing the app by firing your first API call

You can test your API keys using a simple Python program. Perform the following steps:

1. Import the Zerodha broker connection class from `pyalgotrading`:

```
>>> from pyalgotrading.broker.broker_connection_zerodha import
BrokerConnectionZerodha
```

2. Create the broker connection using your API key and API secret:

```
>>> api_key = "<your-api-key>"
>>> api_secret = "<your-api-secret>"
>>> broker_connection = BrokerConnectionZerodha(api_key,
api_secret)
```

You will get the following result:

```
https://kite.trade/connect/login?api_key=
```

You need to log in to Zerodha by clicking on the link generated and following these steps:

1. Enter your user ID.
2. Enter your password (for the trading platform).
3. Click the **Login** button:

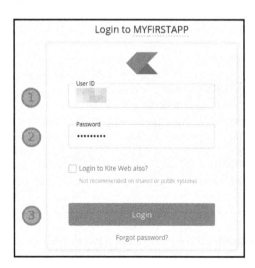

4. Enter your PIN.
5. Click the **Continue** button:

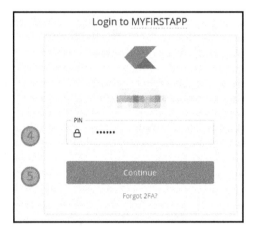

6. Click the **Authorize** button:

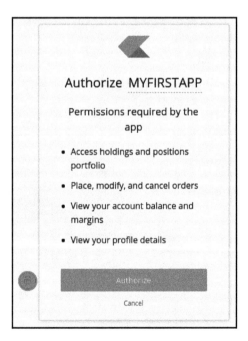

This step happens only once for a new Zerodha Developer Options app.

7. If your credentials are correct, you will be redirected to `127.0.0.1`. Ignore any error messages that may be displayed. Just copy the token from the address bar of your tab. The token is the string between the `request_token=` and `&` characters, both excluded. A new random token is generated each time you follow these steps. For example, if the redirect URL is `https://127.0.0.1/?request_token=iHCKrv8oAM9X2oPRURMNRdZdG4uxhfJq&action=login&status=success`, then the token is `iHCKrv8oAM9X2oPRURMNRdZdG4uxhfJq`:

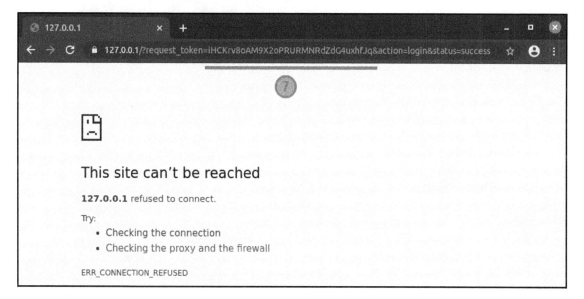

8. Set the token received by the URL given in the previous output:

```
>>> request_token = "<your-request-token>"
>>> broker_connection.set_access_token(request_token)
```

9. You can check whether the connection was successful by fetching your profile detail:

```
>>> broker_connection.get_profile()
```

This produces the following output:

```
{'user_id': <your-user-id>,
 'user_type': 'individual',
 'email': '<your-email-id>',
 'user_name': <your-user-name>',
 'user_shortname': <your-user-shortname>',
 'broker': 'ZERODHA',
 'exchanges': ['CDS', 'MF', 'NFO', 'NSE', 'BSE'],
 'products': ['CNC', 'NRML', 'MIS', 'BO', 'CO'],
 'order_types': ['MARKET', 'LIMIT', 'SL', 'SL-M'],
 'avatar_url': '',
 'meta': {'demat_consent': 'physical'}}
```

This successfully verifies that the API keys are working.

Appendix II

Setting up your AlgoBulls account

This appendix will help you set up your account with AlgoBulls (`https://algobulls.com`).

The following sections are explained in this appendix:

- Registering on the AlgoBulls platform
- Logging in to the AlgoBulls website
- Fetching your AlgoBulls Developer Options token
- Setting up your broking account for real trading

Registering on the AlgoBulls platform

You can register on the AlgoBulls platform by proceeding to the official website, `https://algobulls.com`, and clicking on **SIGNUP**, as illustrated in the following screenshot:

You can register on the site in nine steps, as follows:

1. Enter your name.
2. Enter your email ID.
3. Enter your phone number. Make sure this phone number is accessible for receiving a **one-time password** (**OTP**).
4. Click on the **I'm not a robot** checkbox.
5. Click the **Get OTP** button, as illustrated in the following screenshot:

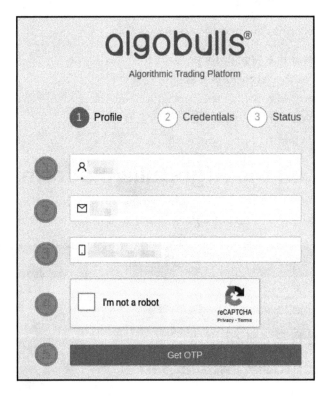

6. Wait until you receive the OTP on your phone. Enter the OTP once you receive it.
7. Enter your password.
8. Confirm your password.

7. Click the **Register** button, as illustrated in the following screenshot:

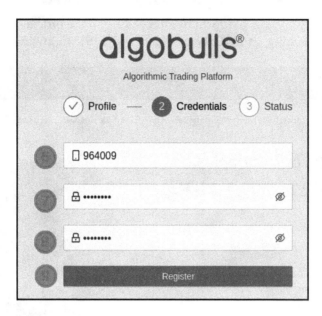

You are now registered on the site. Click the **Go to Login** button to log in to the site, as illustrated in the following screenshot:

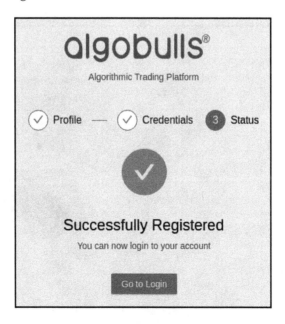

Logging in to the AlgoBulls website

You can log in to the AlgoBulls platform by proceeding to the official website, `https://algobulls.com`, and clicking on **LOGIN**, as illustrated in the following screenshot:

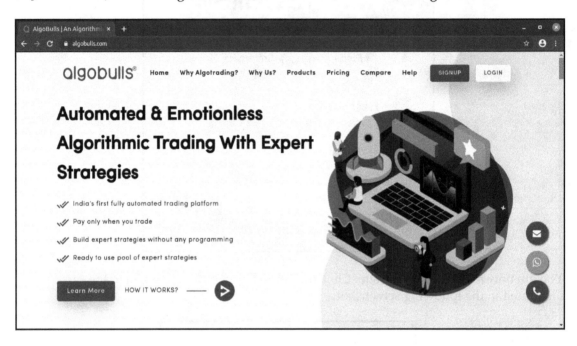

You can log in to the website in three steps, as follows:

1. Enter your registered phone number.
2. Enter your password.
3. Click the **Login** button, as illustrated in the following screenshot:

Fetching your AlgoBulls Developer Options token

After you have logged in, you can fetch your **Developer Options** token by navigating to the **Developer Options** page from the sidebar—**Settings** | **General** | **Developer Options** | **API Token**. You can click on the view button (the eye icon on the right) to view and copy the **application programming interface** (**API**) token, as illustrated in the following screenshot:

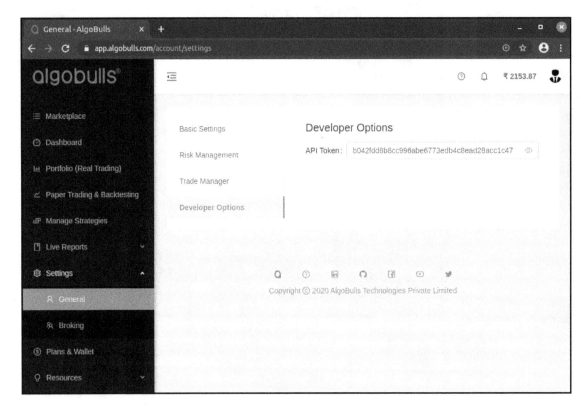

For example, the API token shown in the preceding screenshot is b042fdd8b8cc996abe6773edb4c8ead28acc1c47.

Setting up your AlgoBulls account

You need to do the following to avail algorithmic trading services from the AlgoBulls platform:

- **Subscribe to a Plan**: The services – backtesting, paper trading and real trading – are chargeable. You need to subscribe to a plan before you can avail these services. There are free plans available to use these services for a limited duration. You can subscribe to these plans to test all the recipes in this chapter. Later, you can subscribe to paid plans to avail the services on a monthly basis.
- For real trading (`Chapter 11`, *Algorithmic Trading – Real Trading*), you need to additionally setup the following:
  - Risk Management Settings: These settings help you limit your losses when dealing with real money.
  - **Add a Broker**: You need to connect your broking account with AlgoBulls. You can choose any broker supported by AlgoBulls.

You can find step-by-step information with screenshots for setting up these details at `https://help.algobulls.com/developers/`. Any additional setup instructions, which may come up with time, would be available on that link. You can also contact `developers@algobulls.com` for any additional requirement.

Appendix III

Developing and improving strategies

In this appendix, we will cover a number of key points regarding algorithmic trading strategies that ought to be considered while executing them.

Strategy profitability is subject to seasons

Strategies may not return good results all year round. They can be seasonal, meaning they may perform well at certain times of the year and not so well at other times. So, it is essential to identify the right time or the right season for a strategy and to use it only at those times.

Strategy profitability is subject to its parameter values

A strategy depends on various parameters. The same strategy may perform differently for different instruments and for different values of the technical indicators. For example, an **exponential moving average (EMA)** strategy with parameters (time periods) 4 and 9 may perform well for STOCK X, but the same strategy with different parameter values, say 5 and 13, may not perform well for STOCK X, or even the same strategy with the same parameter values may not perform well for STOCK Y. Hence, finding the right instrument and parameters can make your strategies successful.

You can use optimization algorithms to find the right combination of parameters that make your strategy profitable. The cost function can be your backtesting profit and loss (to be maximized) and drawdown (to be minimized). The variables can be instruments and strategy parameter values.

Backtesting alone does not ensure strategy profitability

A profitable backtesting report is one of the prerequisites for profitable trading, but not the only prerequisite. This increases the chances of a strategy performing well during actual trading, but does not guarantee it. There are many other factors that can affect the actual strategy performance besides historical results. Risk management conditions should be well placed in your strategy to minimize the adverse effects in case of any such unforeseen circumstances. One of the ways of ensuring this is through the use of **bracket** or **cover orders**, where a compulsory stop loss is placed at all times.

Broker limitations

Not all brokers provide APIs for algorithmic trading. Also, if APIs are provided, the broker may not provide support for all types of orders, such as bracket or cover orders that have in-built risk management. Check and verify all support and services offered by a particular broker before availing yourself of their services. Choosing the right broker may minimize strategy coding at your end.

Staying connected with the community

You can get support for coding your own strategy by posing your questions to the community on the forum. You can also get insights and pointers in relation to proven and well-tested strategy coding guidelines. Moreover, you can learn more from books on technical analysis and other forums for algorithmic trading. Keep an eye on GitHub repositories providing free strategies along with their Python code (for example, `https://github.com/algobulls/pyalgostrategypool`).

Be prepared for technology failures during actual trading

No matter how robust your strategy is, strategy execution may not happen as planned during actual trading. This could happen for a variety of reasons:

- Broker APIs may experience a timeout failure due to the overloading of their servers. This frequently happens during market opening hours, where a large number of traders place orders at nearly the same time to grab market opening opportunities.
- A broker technology stack may depend on multiple vendors, besides its own proprietary technology, which means that even if just one of them fails, you can fall victim to it as your order placements might not go through.
- If you are using an algorithmic trading platform, it may fail for the same reasons as mentioned in the first point above.
- Your strategy might fail as it may have encountered a new condition that was not covered in testing. For example, if you place an order involving a very large quantity during actual trading, the order may split into multiple smaller orders that are executed individually. If your strategy hasn't accounted for this, it may fail. Moreover, such scenarios cannot be caught during backtesting as this is virtual trading and orders never split there, so providing a solution for this may be tricky.
- Historical data feeds may go out the window. There can either be stale data or no data, both of which can result in incorrect decisions being taken in relation to your strategy.

Other Books You May Enjoy

If you enjoyed this book, you may be interested in these other books by Packt:

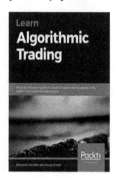

Learn Algorithmic Trading
Sebastien Donadio, Sourav Ghosh

ISBN: 978-1-78934-834-7

- Understand the components of modern algorithmic trading systems and strategies
- Apply machine learning in algorithmic trading signals and strategies using Python
- Build, visualize and analyze trading strategies based on mean reversion, trend, economic releases and more
- Quantify and build a risk management system for Python trading strategies
- Build a backtester to run simulated trading strategies for improving the performance of your trading bot
- Deploy and incorporate trading strategies in the live market to maintain and improve profitability

Mastering Python for Finance - Second Edition
James Ma Weiming

ISBN: 978-1-78934-646-6

- Solve linear and nonlinear models representing various financial problems
- Perform principal component analysis on the DOW index and its components
- Analyze, predict, and forecast stationary and non-stationary time series processes
- Create an event-driven backtesting tool and measure your strategies
- Build a high-frequency algorithmic trading platform with Python
- Replicate the CBOT VIX index with SPX options for studying VIX-based strategies
- Perform regression-based and classification-based machine learning tasks for prediction
- Use TensorFlow and Keras in deep learning neural network architecture

Leave a review - let other readers know what you think

Please share your thoughts on this book with others by leaving a review on the site that you bought it from. If you purchased the book from Amazon, please leave us an honest review on this book's Amazon page. This is vital so that other potential readers can see and use your unbiased opinion to make purchasing decisions, we can understand what our customers think about our products, and our authors can see your feedback on the title that they have worked with Packt to create. It will only take a few minutes of your time, but is valuable to other potential customers, our authors, and Packt. Thank you!

Index

P

pandas.concat() function
  using 42, 43, 44
pandas.DataFrame object
  creating 30, 31, 32, 33
paper trading 397
parabolic stop and reverse (SAR) 186
  trend indicators, plotting 184, 185, 187
parent order 265
product types 58
profit and loss (P&L) 397
pyalgotrading package
  reference link 143
pyalgotrading
  reference link 309
Python connectivity
  setting up, with broker 52, 53, 54

Q

Quandl
  reference link 157
  used, for fetching historical data 157, 158, 159,
    160, 161, 162, 163

R

regular limit order
  placing 225, 226, 227, 228, 229, 230, 231,
    232, 233, 234, 235, 236
regular market order
  placing 217, 218, 219, 220, 221, 222, 223, 224
REGULAR order
  placing 60, 61
regular stoploss-limit order
  placing 236, 238, 239, 240, 241, 242, 243,
    244, 245, 246, 247, 248
regular stoploss-market order
  placing 248, 250, 251, 252, 253, 254, 255,
    256, 257, 258, 259, 260
relative strength index (RSI)
  about 166
  momentum indicators, plotting 188, 190, 191
  reference link 188
Renko candlesticks pattern

used, for fetching historical data 129, 130, 131,
  133, 134, 135, 136, 137, 138, 139, 140, 141,
  142, 143

S

securities 55, 77
segments
  lists, querying 57, 58
simple moving average (SMA)
  about 166, 176
  trend indicators, plotting 173, 174, 175, 176
smoothing 177
stochastic oscillator (STOCH)
  momentum indicators, plotting 191, 192, 193,
    194, 195
stop and reverse (SAR) 184
stoploss order 265, 293

T

target order 264
technical indicator
  about 165
  categories 166
time period 173
time zones 27, 28, 29, 30
timedelta objects
  attributes, modifying 15
  converting, to string 24
  creating 14, 16
trend indicator 173
typical price (TP) 196

U

upper circuit limit 82

V

variety type 58, 59, 60
volume weighted average price (VWAP)
  volume indicators, plotting 207, 208, 209, 210,
    211

W

weighting factor 177

www.ingramcontent.com/pod-product-compliance
Lightning Source LLC
Chambersburg PA
CBHW060638060326
40690CB00020B/4445